GO TO WAR

GO TO WAR

FOOTBALL ON THE BRINK IN THE '80s

JON SPURLING

\B^b\

Biteback Publishing

First published in Great Britain in 2024 by
Biteback Publishing Ltd, London
Copyright © Jon Spurling 2024

Jon Spurling has asserted his right under the Copyright, Designs and Patents Act 1988
to be identified as the author of this work.

ISBN 978-1-78590-749-4

10 9 8 7 6 5 4 3 2 1

A CIP catalogue record for this book is available from the British Library.

Set in Minion Pro

Printed and bound in Great Britain by
CPI Group (UK) Ltd, Croydon CR0 4YY

FSC
www.fsc.org
MIX
Paper | Supporting
responsible forestry
FSC® C171272

Mel Smith (as a sociologist): Well, my team and I have really concerned ourselves fundamentally with a statistical analysis of soccer violence as a whole, in tandem with and related to a psycho-chemical and, broadly speaking, a behavioural analysis of over a thousand individual soccer hooligans. And we've come to the inevitable conclusion that the one course of action that the authorities must take is to cut off their goolies.
Griff Rhys Jones (as the interviewer): (laughs awkwardly) I'm sorry?
Smith: Cut their goolies off.
Not the Nine O'clock News sketch, 1981

'I was on tour with West Ham in the Far East and switched on the television to see footage of the Heysel disaster. We didn't need subtitles to tell us that things couldn't carry on like this anymore.'
Tony Cottee

'Much of what happened in the Premier League era – the TV exposure, the commercialisation – had its roots in the '80s. But few if any could have foreseen that, because football was at war with itself.'
Jimmy Hill

To my dad – the most splendid of fellows.
19/03/1931 – 18/06/2024
X

CONTENTS

FOREWORD *BY MIKE INGHAM*

History in the making can only truly be judged retrospectively. When you are living through turbulent times, it can be hard to stand back and imagine what impact these events will have on the future. When you read this book, it helps you recognise how many seeds were being sown four decades ago for the modern-day game. Just as the new technology of the 1980s went on to pave the way and shape today's popular music, so it was in football.

It was a decade of two halves. The first dominated by English clubs in Europe, the second spent in self-inflicted isolation.

Our national sport will always be a mirror image of society and after the glam rock 'Get It On' era, the '80s, by way of contrast, heralded more anger and disenchantment. There was no greater symbol of that than the Beastie Boys on the terraces. The ticking time-bomb finally exploded, and in this book you are shudderingly transported back to the carnage of Luton v. Millwall and Birmingham v. Leeds, both matches leading to the watershed horror of Heysel.

That fateful night in Brussels was my first European Cup final as a commentator. I ended up becoming a war correspondent, and even today the flashbacks to the game remain painful. I commend Jon for revisiting a story that I believe continues to be an 'elephant in the room' for English football.

The hugely different tragedies of Bradford and Hillsborough defined a decade of misery for the game when arguably the most significant personalities turned out to be Justice Oliver Popplewell and Lord Chief Justice Peter Taylor, whose recommendations brought about so much long-overdue change.

Away from the despair, there were still authentic footballing icons who entertained not only on the pitch but also on these pages. What sets this book apart is the author's foresight in securing interviews many years ago, with several national treasures sadly no longer with us, like Howard Kendall, Ray Wilkins and Trevor Francis.

This was an age when the cult of personality was also being extended to the boardroom and there are hilarious anecdotes and memories of shrinking violets like Doug Ellis, Peter Swales and Robert Maxwell. It is also so heartwarming to read and remember how coveted, still, were the two major cup competitions, which are nowadays in danger of being devalued. Wembley 1987 is still the greatest day in Coventry City's history.

So, there is light and shade in this book, something that my colleague and mentor the late Peter Jones always impressed on me as a commentator. Peter and my predecessor as a correspondent Bryon Butler were the two most mellifluous voices in radio sport and the '80s would be their last decade on the airwaves. Paradoxically, this tormented time represented the last hurrah for football on the wireless before video did it's best to kill the radio star. It was a time when to find out a cup draw you listened to your transistor and sports reports still always led with the classified results. It's amazing to reflect now that when Martin Hayes scored his celebrated Saturday afternoon winner for Arsenal at Middlesbrough on the way to their 'Fever Pitch' title in 1989, you could only listen live and not view.

Go To War steers you to the crossroads when a threatened breakaway by the so called 'Big Five' turned out to be a precursor of Sky TV and the Premier League. This book leads you to the brink of *Super Sunday*, breaking news and the Brit Pop generation. It looks back with a deep, caring sense of historical perspective.

Mike Ingham
August 2024

INTRODUCTION

Go *To War* is a book about 1980s football and its prime movers and shakers, including some of the leading players and managers. But to show what kind of an era it was, it also encompasses heavy hitting Conservative Party politicians like Prime Minister Margaret Thatcher, a new breed of club executives like media mogul Robert Maxwell, whose media profile was on an upward trajectory, and Lord Justice Taylor, whose findings in 1989 and subsequent report in 1990 would irrevocably change the face of English football. It also focuses on some cult heroes and hitherto hidden figures, including inflatable banana-wielding supporters, FA Cup giant killers and those fans and journalists who were present and correct at the decade's most defining matches. Like it's prequel, *Get It On: How the '70s Rocked Football*, it doesn't focus specifically on results and seasons and who went up and down. It's about the game itself, and also the politics, the popular culture and the events of the era. The different strands are interconnected, because not only was football shaped by what swirled around it, the national game in the '80s defined the timbre of the era. Some of the tales, including Malcolm Allison's ill-fated second spell at Manchester City and British players' experiences in the North American Soccer League (NASL), straddle both decades. The far-reaching effects of the Taylor report wouldn't be felt until the '90s. Decades don't adhere to definitive beginnings and ends.

A word or two about the title – *Go To War*. As well as being a phrase from the Frankie Goes to Hollywood song 'Two Tribes', which describes the conflict between the Soviets and the Americans during the Cold War in the '80s, the title neatly sums up the prevailing mood surrounding the sport during this era. Viewing football as a serious law and order problem, the government declared war on the game. Tribes of football supporters declared war on one another, both at home and abroad, inside dilapidated and decaying stadia, and England played at the '82 and '86 World Cups with the Falklands War all too prevalent in the players' minds. Mirroring the combative atmosphere on the terraces, teams also played in a far more direct and abrasive style then too. 'We were skilled, but we were also tough, because you had to be. It was our bread and butter,' Terry Butcher told me.

It was a decade over which the Bradford fire, the Heysel Stadium disaster and the Hillsborough tragedy still loom large. Football fans died watching the sport they loved, and at times football seemed to be stuck in a doom loop. Famously in 1985, a *Times* article described football as 'a slum sport played in slum stadiums, and increasingly watched by slum people, who deter decent folk from turning up.' But English football somehow survived and then morphed into the behemoth it has now become.

Many moons ago, I visited England World Cup winner Jack Charlton at his home in the north-east to interview him and outlined my plans to write a series of books on English football history. Big Jack nodded, told me to 'bloody well get on with it' – which

I didn't actually do for a long time – and asked me if I planned to write a book on '80s football. When I told him that I did, Jack shook his head disapprovingly and opined: 'You should call the book *The Fookin' Basket* Case then, son.' Jack's wife Pat was none too impressed with his idea, and whilst I have ultimately rejected Jack's literary advice, he wasn't exactly wrong in his assessment of what is often regarded as English football's *decadus horribilis*.

Growing up in the '80s in a 'football neutral' house in Hertfordshire, my dad, who sadly faded away as I put the finishing touches to this book, voiced his concern as he watched his son's obsession with the sport grow. He took me to my first few matches but didn't much care for the swearing, the toxic chanting, Duran Duran blasting his ear drums when their songs were played over the tinny stadium Tannoy, and 'those bloody awful leaking toilets' – which he still remembered with a shudder forty years later. In many ways, Dad's opinion on '80s football chimed perfectly with that of many in Middle England. It wasn't that he didn't like football per se, more that he was saddened by what it had become. He'd not been to games since he went to wartime matches at Carrow Road in the early '40s. Much had changed since then. Dad despaired at the awful behaviour on the trains and the aggressive tribalism of match goers, which so often descended into violence, although he did quite like the wagon wheels at half-time with, as he put it, his 'gnat's-pee' tea, and Southampton defender Mark Dennis's amazing mullet. When he saw the *Sportsnight* footage of the riot at Kenilworth Road in 1985, he looked solemnly at me and said: 'Football won't be around too much longer the way things are going.' After the Heysel disaster a few months later, he suggested that the sport be suspended for a season so that it could get its house in order. His face, and that of my mum's, when I told him that I was going to watch a match a few days after the Hillsborough disaster in 1989 spoke a thousand words. With hindsight, it's hard to blame them for their viewpoint. It wasn't big or clever to be a football fan in those days. Most of my parents' friends tutted and changed the subject immediately whenever I started talking 'shop'.

It often surprises me when fans of my age look back wistfully to an era when going to football could sometimes be such a dangerous, life-threatening experience. Grounds weren't welcoming places for women or children. Football was anything but inclusive. Facilities were almost non-existent. The atmosphere was often menacing. But '80s nostalgia exists nonetheless. 'It was proper football back then,' some suggest. 'Men were men. They got on with the game in those days,' others say. The terms 'sportswashing' and 'Video Action Replay' (VAR) didn't exist. Players earned more realistic wages, and football could still broadly be described as the working man's game. Ticket prices were within reach for most fans. There was a raw and unvarnished feel to football then. At times, it felt like a form of 'dark tourism'. That edgy allure is almost entirely lacking in the gleaming, all-seater stadia of the Sky TV era, where the match-day experience is packaged and choreographed to within an inch of its life. Football in the '80s was undoubtedly viscerally 'real', and its very lack of ubiquity was – to some – part of its appeal. After all, anyone can claim to be a fan these days.

I believe that '80s football is long overdue a degree of revisionism. There is a danger that, as the pre-1992 era fades to grey, it is reduced to a selection of YouTube clips and oft-repeated tales handed down via the after-dinner speaking circuit. It's far more nuanced than those increasingly grainy clips and cliched *bon mots* suggest. The mullets, ludicrously tight shorts, artificial pitches, yawning gaps on the terraces and often rudimentary style of football lend it a distinctly 'otherworldly' feel, but beneath the surface, the '80s teemed with compelling stories of triumph and despair, creation and invention, and political manoeuvrings, both in boardrooms and Parliament. Before 1985, English teams enjoyed a golden era in European competitions, a period of dominance that abruptly ended with the European ban after the Heysel disaster. Plummeting attendances then acted as a catalyst for executives like Martin Edwards at Manchester United, David Dein at Arsenal and Irving Scholar at Tottenham to shape and sculpt English football's future. If the '80s were the decade the '70s could have been (stadium disasters could easily have happened in the previous decade, either at home or abroad), then it was also the period that sowed the seeds for the Sky revolution in the '90s. Like a magnet, it attracted many of the iron filings of broader cultural changes at that time; multiculturalism, declinism, deindustrialisation, urban decay, postcolonialism, Thatcherism and the Boy George-coined expression 'playboyeurism'.

Although the game in that era has (often rightly) been given a good kicking during the ensuing decades, football was ultimately a sport worth saving, and there are nuggets of joy to be mined from the '80s seam. The FA Cup retained its kitschy likeability, continuing to produce heroes, whether they were giant killers, Wembley winners or small-town boys from the shires making their mark. Poring over old *Shoot!* profiles is always fun, even though they often confirm what we already knew: that most players were obsessed with watching *Dallas*, eating steak and drinking lager top. England's kit for the '82 World Cup – with its red and blue epaulettes on a white shirt – remains an all-time classic. Several fans from the era, including erudite fanzine writers and anti-racist campaigners, prove that the image of '80s supporters being a bunch of warring knuckle-scrapers is patently wrong. Many footballers and managers from the era possess a wonderful sledgehammer wit and a bleak sense of humour. They're harder to pin down than their '70s counterparts were. Some have homes in Spain or regularly pop over to Dubai for golfing holidays. Others have become spokesmen for worthy causes like cardiac health, racial equality, and fighting dementia. Once they open up, though, their tales and experiences are fascinating.

Enjoy the book.

Jon Spurling
August 2024

1

THE MIGHTY MOUSE
AND THE MALVINAS

*'The nation that gave football to the world can
now only give it the football hooligan.'*
DAILY MIRROR, MAY 1981

Stadio Comunale, Turin – June 1980. There's a rumpus behind him, but England goalkeeper Ray Clemence is doing his best to concentrate on the game, his country's first in a tournament finals since 1970. Jan Ceulemans has just equalised for Belgium against Ron Greenwood's men in a Group A European Championships clash. Following several loud bangs, Clemence's eyes begin to stream. In medical vernacular, a lachrymatory agent has stimulated the nerves of the lacrimal glands in his eyes. In layman's speak, Clemence is standing downwind of tear gas, which is now billowing across the terraces and the pitch. Turin's zealous riot police have fired grenades at the mass of England supporters hurling beer bottles and warring with locals, who are celebrating Ceulemans' goal.

A yellow fog envelops the terrace and referee Heinz Aldinger blows his whistle to bring the match to a temporary halt. England players gather in the centre circle and watch the fighting behind Clemence's goal with weary resignation. The fact that a strain of the 'English disease' – hooliganism – has now taken root in Italy is hardly surprising. England's top brass are furious. Normally reasoned and measured, Greenwood fumes: 'These bastards let you down. I wish they could all be put in a boat and dropped in the ocean.' Prime Minister Margaret Thatcher, in Venice for a Common Market summit, adds: 'The behaviour of some supporters in Turin was disgraceful. This is a dark day for Britain.'

The tournament – notable for poor attendances and forgettable matches – will be all but airbrushed from football history, but it sets a troubling blueprint for English football in the '80s.

• • •

Six days before England's footballers took on the Belgians in Turin, they were guests of honour at a Downing Street cocktail party. As she mingled with the squad, sipping champagne and nibbling on canapes, Margaret Thatcher was charm personified. Taking an unlikely shine to Southampton's long-haired, Status-Quo-loving central defender Dave Watson, whose state-of-the-art stereo, with its microscopic black and white TV, was a source of endless fascination for his teammates, Thatcher grabbed Watson's hand and took him on a magical-mystery tour of the portraits of former Prime Ministers. 'I really enjoyed it,' Watson said. So, it seemed, did the Prime Minister, who'd been in the job for just over a year. Channelling her inner Boudicca inside No. 10, the Iron Lady, clad in a floral dress and pearl necklace, stood on a chair and informed the players: 'We'll love you whether you win or lose.' Beaming at the cameras outside No. 10, she radiated national pride whilst fielding questions about the England team and the recent hostage crisis at the Iranian Embassy in London, during which the SAS stormed the embassy and killed the terrorists. 'The SAS are the finest and the bravest this country has,' she beamed. Segueing smoothly towards the suited and booted players around her, she expressed hope that 'in Italy, the England football team and their supporters will also show the best of Britain'. A successful showing by the team would also enable her to bask in the reflective glory.

In her memoirs *The Downing Street Years*, Thatcher makes one single fleeting reference to football (on the Heysel disaster) in around 900 pages of dense text. Charles Moore's three-part, 3,000-page exploration of her life and times doesn't mention football once. It's remarkable, given the extent to which Thatcher and Thatcherism became completely entwined with the national sport in the '80s; by the end of the decade, they even began to reshape it. Back in 1970, Chancellor Roy Jenkins wrote that Prime Minister Harold Wilson believed 'a mystical symbiosis' existed between football and politics. Yet Thatcher's relationship with football, and footballers, was never as symbiotic as it was on that slightly surreal June afternoon at Downing Street. As usual, she was well briefed. 'You'll be heading it soon,' Ron Greenwood told her when a football, signed by the squad, was held in front of her for the photoshoot. 'Oh no,' she corrected him. 'That's Trevor Brooking's job.' Brooking's stooping header had just won Second Division West Ham the FA Cup final. She'd met Emlyn Hughes before, telling him that she always watched the FA Cup final and the England v. Scotland home international. 'A follower, perhaps, but not exactly a football fan,' Hughes reckoned. 'When she went to games, she always looked out of place.' Before the squad departed, there was just time for the most experienced members of the squad, Hughes and Kevin Keegan, to simultaneously plant a kiss on Thatcher's cheeks. With the Prime Minister's good wishes ringing in their ears (she also sent Ron Greenwood a handwritten letter personally thanking him for 'restoring the pride to English football'), the team returned to their training camp.

Greenwood – previously general manager at West Ham – had taken charge in the summer of 1977. He had arrived too late to steer England to the 1978 World Cup finals in Argentina but had built an impressive-looking team by focusing on the basics. 'Ron wasn't swayed by the press, like Don Revie was,' said midfielder Ray Wilkins. 'He was loyal to those who served him well.' Greenwood had a reputation for being a football purist, with clear ideas of how his teams should play. His emphasis on the passing game and an insistence that his teams avoided foul play had earned him the nickname 'Reverend Ron' with former Hammers players. Behind his back, England players sometimes sniggered about the manager they nicknamed 'the Pope'. 'He could be a bit preachy, a bit holier than thou,' smiled forward Trevor Francis. As a young coach, Greenwood watched England being dismantled by Hungary at Wembley in 1953 and marvelled at the Mighty Magyars' ability to exploit and anticipate the space on the pitch. As a young coach at Arsenal, he baffled the players with his fascination of space, walked into training one day with a copy of *Time* magazine, which had Soviet cosmonaut Yuri Gagarin on the front cover, and extolled the possibility of life on other planets, telling the players how they must, as he put it, 'embrace space' – in every sense.

He was a visionary. At West Ham in the '60s, he converted left-half Bobby Moore into a central defender and Geoff Hurst from a winger into a centre forward. His West Ham sides played fluid football and won the FA Cup in 1964 and the European Cup Winners' Cup in 1965. But a decade or so on, Greenwood wrote of the 'depression' he felt after he was moved 'upstairs' and John Lyall took over the day-to-day running of the team. Approaching sixty, he seemed set to retire, but then Don Revie walked out on England in 1977 to take the job as manager of the United Arab Emirates, and Greenwood was invited by the Football Association to become manager on a temporary basis. His subsequent permanent appointment may not have captured the imagination, but with the players still in shock from Revie's departure, Greenwood was just what was needed. 'Ron was a consensus man, a committee man and a bridge builder,' explained Ray Wilkins. Unlike Ramsey, Revie or Clough, he didn't appear to have any enemies amongst the press, or in the Football Association.

The irony of Greenwood wearing his favourite vanilla overcoat wasn't lost on Nottingham Forest boss Brian Clough, who described Greenwood as being 'as neutral as a human being can possibly be'. Revie's departure in '77 was English football's version of the Watergate Scandal, which saw Richard Nixon resign in 1974 before he was impeached. But that didn't necessarily make Greenwood English football's Gerald Ford, Nixon's hapless successor, who, after officially pardoning Nixon, lost the 1976 presidential election and was largely lampooned during his two-year presidency.

Greenwood remained in post for five years and, to a degree, imposed his own philosophy of leadership. But the respective scandals cast giant shadows over Ford and Greenwood. 'There's a feeling that after what's happened with him [Revie], the role of England manager has been sullied. My job is to restore some pride,' Greenwood argued. And that he did. With qualification sealed from a group featuring Denmark, the two Irelands and Bulgaria, plus Keegan leading the way with seven goals, England were amongst the favourites to lift the trophy. This was the first European Championships to resemble a proper tournament, with the quarter-finals no longer played over two legs. Instead, there would now be two groups of four, with the winners of each section progressing to the final. England were in the easier-looking of the two groups, having avoided a section that included holders Czechoslovakia, World Cup runners-up Netherlands and 1974 world champions West Germany. Instead, England's main concern looked to be the hosts Italy, whom they would face along with Belgium and Spain.

Although the qualifying campaign had raised expectations for England, the build-up to the tournament was low-key. There was no team song, no Esso coin collection as there had been for the 1970 World Cup, no palpable frisson of excitement in the media, no funky Euro '80 moniker. *Match Weekly*'s slightly underwhelming free gift – the Dial-a-Star, fashioned in the style of a cardboard England rosette, which enabled readers to 'dial' the international records of the 22-man England squad – encapsulated the less-than-enthusiastic mood. The sports papers appeared far more interested in events elsewhere. Eric 'the Crafty Cockney' Bristow beat Bobby 'Dazzler' George in the 1980 World Darts final. TV audiences, which topped 10 million, were glued to the drama and the close-ups, as the two showmen, with their embossed collars, glistening brows and flashy jewellery, went toe to toe. There was also the headline-capturing rivalry of middle-distance runners Steve Ovett and Sebastian Coe, who smashed one another's world records in the 800 and 1500 metres and were about to go toe to toe at the 1980 Moscow Olympics. The Romford-based Matchroom sports management company, owned by promoter Barry Hearn, was on the cusp of glamorising snooker, with branded Matchroom products, including cues, aftershave and duvet covers. 'Players like Steve Davis and Jimmy White – they became nationally recognised figures thanks to good branding, and television,' Hearn said. Football was in desperate need of a reboot and a makeover, but that wouldn't happen for more than a decade. 'For now, it had to fight for its right to be seen,' football commentator Barry Davies remarked.

At least England's new Admiral kit, unveiled for the friendly match with Argentina at Wembley in June, garnered attention. Replacing the red and blue tramline number, which the team had worn since Don Revie's appointment in 1974, the latest design had red and blue epaulettes on the shoulders. 'It eventually became our biggest seller,' said Admiral chief executive Bert Patrick, 'but of course it wouldn't have been an Admiral launch without the usual degree of controversy.' Much of the Fleet Street media immediately showed disdain for the kit, which was the result of a £1 million deal signed in 1979 between the Football Association and the Leicester-based firm. When news of its impending launch broke in the *Daily Mirror* in January 1980, the pun-loving paper screamed 'Strip off' and accused the company of 'taking commercialism too far'. Forty years on, Patrick reiterated the view he'd held throughout Admiral's dramatic rise to prominence: 'All publicity was good publicity. The new, shinier strip was designed to impress under floodlights and on TV. Within three years, every team in England had a shiny kit. We blazed the trail.' In a column for *Match* magazine, Brian Clough blasted: 'The wraps are off England's new kit – and I'm saying now I don't like it. It has the looks of one of my mother's old pinnies!' After the Argentina match, though, which saw England win 3–1, Ron Greenwood was buoyant and, alluding to England's new Admiral design, insisted: 'Everything about us tonight was luminous, I thought.'

The squad arrived in Italy three days before the Belgium match. Greenwood, the first England manager since Walter Winterbottom in 1962 to lead England to a tournament after qualifying from the group stages, had good reason to feel confident. He had a group of players that, in terms of honours at least, was far superior to Alf Ramsey's 1966 vintage. With Liverpool and Nottingham Forest providing nine of Greenwood's 22-man squad, which also included Forest old-boy Tony Woodcock and ex-Anfield stars Emlyn Hughes and Kevin Keegan (the double European Footballer of the Year at Hamburg), the group boasted a staggering nineteen European Cup winners. The key issue for England was that – Emlyn Hughes aside – there was no international tournament experience in the squad whatsoever. With Greenwood's first-choice forward Trevor Francis ruled out after rupturing his Achilles tendon, thereby depriving the team of pace, England's hopes appeared to rest largely upon Keegan.

Famously, his Hamburg striking partner Horst Hrubesch said: 'Kevin is as comfortable in a business suit as a football kit.' In 1978–79, Keegan had been instrumental during his team's run-in, scoring eleven goals in the last twelve games of the season, and Hamburg were crowned Bundesliga champions. Fans christened him *der Mächtig Maus* (the Mighty Mouse). At the end of the title-winning season, his first single, 'Head Over Heels in Love', was released, which reached No. 31 in the UK charts. Prior to the 1979–80 season, with Keegan again making noises about moving on, Hamburg insisted that he make up his mind one way or another, in order that their proposed sponsorship deal with British Petroleum wasn't jeopardised. Keegan stayed. By 1980, his annual wage at Hamburg was £150,000, and extras netted him an estimated £500,000 a year. BP paid him £125,000, he advertised milk on German television and he earned around £3,500 pounds an hour for autograph sessions.

'Kevin operated in a different universe financially from the rest of us,' explained Ray Clemence. 'The players thought "Good luck to you", but there was sniping towards Kevin from some quarters. I think the fact he'd gone to Germany was a reminder that English football wasn't perhaps in the best of health.' Ironically, in the week that Margaret Thatcher welcomed the England team to 10 Downing Street, she'd vowed to 'stem the "brain drain", which was how sections of the press dubbed the 'stampede' of British scientists and businessmen to the United States and fellow EEC countries. 'There was a certain feeling that Kevin, who was so sure of what he wanted and keen to fulfil himself commercially, wasn't acting in a proper English way,' Trevor Francis argued.

A level of disquiet surrounded Keegan. His right knee had troubled him for several months, and due to Hamburg's appearance in the 1980 European Cup final, Keegan took no part in the May–June home internationals, but he insisted: 'I'm ready for Italy. There are no excuses now if we don't do well.' Keegan's former Liverpool teammate Ray Kennedy – whom Bob Paisley labelled 'the most underrated English player of his generation' – expressed concern about the clout that former Liverpool teammate Keegan and midfielder Trevor Brooking – who'd played under Greenwood at West Ham – held within the England camp. Kennedy was convinced that the two roommates had Greenwood's ear when it came to tactics and team selection. In the mid '70s, Kennedy alleged that Keegan 'wanted to run the entire show at Liverpool. Kevin's determination to be involved all the time disrupted the team's flow. It was the same with England.' Football writer Brian Glanville later claimed that Keegan was 'neither fish nor fowl' and suggested that Greenwood struggled to successfully deploy Keegan – neither an orthodox centre forward, nor a conventional midfielder – in his teams.

The normally taciturn Bob Paisley had also criticised Greenwood's tactics. After taking the reins in 1977, Greenwood announced his keenness to tap into Paisley's knowledge at newly crowned European champions Liverpool in order to 'recreate the magic of the Anfield Boot Room at international level'. To that end, when England played Switzerland in a Wembley friendly later that year, Greenwood selected no less than six Liverpool players – Clemence, Neal, Hughes, Callaghan, McDermott and Kennedy – for the team. The game ended in a dour 0–0 draw, with Paisley criticising Greenwood for omitting the crucial fourth man – Jimmy Case – in the midfield quartet completed by Callaghan, McDermott and Kennedy.

With Case not playing, the unit was fatally disrupted by the absence of the 'runner'. Paisley believed that Greenwood should have 'made them [the Liverpool midfield] the fulcrum of the England team going into the 1980 European Championships'. Instead, when Ray Kennedy played, he was pushed forward to stop the opposite full-back attacking, thereby denying him the freedom of space he enjoyed at Liverpool. Greenwood then abandoned his fixation with Liverpool's finest and deployed a raft of other formations that became a feature of his five-year tenure.

• • •

'Today England will begin to learn the true currency of the recovery that has been achieved under the direction of Ron Greenwood over the last three years,' wrote David Lacey in his preview of the Belgium match for *The Guardian*. Kicking off at 4.45 p.m., the match was shown live on BBC One. Tournament wise, it was the first 'communal' TV experience England supporters had enjoyed in a decade. The game was broadcast on BBC1, with Barry Davies and Bobby Charlton as commentator and co-commentator. In the days before the match, the Belgians – managed by Guy Thys – were quoted as saying they did not expect to beat England, but Greenwood wasn't having it. 'We don't in any way underestimate them. They are a strong side, a side with experience, even if they are unpredictable.' Just 15,186 were in the Stadio Comunale to see Ray Wilkins put England ahead after twenty-five minutes. Not a renowned goal scorer, Wilkins expertly lobbed the ball over the Belgian defence and ran through to chip goalkeeper Jean-Marie Pfaff and score. 'It was a masterpiece of a goal,' Wilkins smiled when I spoke to him. 'Albeit a forgotten one.'

The night before, police arrested thirty-six English supporters in Turin, mainly for drunkenness. This was the first time that England fans, who, according to their banners, hailed from places as diverse as Grimsby, Gravesend and Grantham, had travelled *en masse* to an international tournament. Amongst them was Peter Myers: 'Before the Belgium match, fans were puking up in the city centre in front of Italian families, beer glasses were smashed, chairs thrown about.' At the match, there was a blend of jingoist and sick chanting. 'Two world wars and one World Cup' was a favourite. So was 'No surrender to the IRA.' 'Some fans from Bradford chanted: "There's only one Peter Sutcliffe,"' Myers recalls. The mob's de facto national anthem: 'You're gonna get your fuckin' 'ead kicked in' was audible. Belgium's equaliser at the Stadio Comunale sparked more violence. England fans threw some of the tear gas cannisters, fired by the Turin police, back towards the pitch. 'That's the irony of what happened,' Ray Clemence told me. 'The gas that affected me actually came from cannisters that were lobbed by England fans.' Clemence likened the effect of tear gas to 'someone sticking pins in the back of your eyes. My chest tightened. It tasted like pepper in my mouth.' The stinging sensation disappeared after a few minutes, by which point Clemence was clear-eyed enough to see the mayhem for what it was. 'I'd seen football hooliganism in England before. We all had. But tear gas? That was on a whole different level.' Up in the commentary box, Bobby Charlton, one of the heroes from '66, told Barry Davies he was 'ashamed to be British'.

The match was always going to struggle to get going again after the trouble. Kenny Sansom described it as 'feeling like a testimonial'. It ended 1–1, representing a point dropped for England but with them still in with a shout of reaching the final. The tournament consisted of eight teams playing in two groups of four, with the winners of each group contesting the final. UEFA convened an emergency meeting to discuss the violent scenes, with a points deduction or even expulsion from the tournament mooted as possible punishments. The resulting £8,000 fine was seen as lenient, with FA chairman Harold Thompson admitting: 'It could have been a lot more serious. But it is a pity we have to pay for the actions of those sewer rats.' It was a token gesture amidst fears of possible expulsion. Under the headline of 'Softies', Frank McGhee angrily wrote in the *Daily Mirror*: 'That is roughly the equivalent of a slap on the wrist with a wet lettuce leaf ... Punishment should hurt – and this one doesn't.'

Travelling England fans were urged to hide their colours en route to their next match – a Sunday-night showdown with Italy in Turin. The Mayor of Turin, Signor Diego Novelli, threatened to cancel the match in the event of any more trouble from English fans and banned the sale of alcohol in the Stadio Comunale. On the pitch, whoever lost was staring elimination in the face. Italy had drawn 0–0 with Spain in their opening game, with the Spaniards then losing to Belgium. The match between Italy and England was the blue riband fixture of the group, and a crowd of 59,649 was the highest of the tournament. Greenwood handed a start to young

Nottingham Forest forward Garry Birtles, and to Ray Kennedy, who replaced Trevor Brooking. Kennedy, who'd publicly criticised Brooking's unwillingness to 'track back', had England's best chance, crashing a superb volley off a post. Eleven minutes from time, Italy's Fiorentina playmaker Antognoni fed Graziani near the left flank. Right-back Phil Neal was brushed aside by the Italian wide man, whose low cross was headed into the back of the net by Marco Tardelli. Late on, Dino Zoff brilliantly pushed out the subdued Keegan's last-gasp overhead kick.

Keegan later admitted that the effects of a stomach bug had laid him low, but the day after the match, Italian newspaper *Tuttosport* reported that Keegan had accused Romanian referee Rainea of taking a bribe. 'Nobody can take it out of my mind that he has accepted money,' England's skipper was alleged to have said. England's Asti training camp was besieged by paparazzi desperate to talk to Keegan. Greenwood seemed powerless to prevent a media circus from gathering around his star man. A pair of photographers approached Keegan and asked if the England man could oblige with a photograph with an Italian model they had in tow. After England press officer Glen Kirton agreed, the photographers snapped away and quickly sold their images to Italian publications. 'It created a lot of ridiculous gossip,' Greenwood later recalled, 'with journalists asking if the players were entertaining other women at the training camp.'

England's route to the final was now blocked, and even though a much-changed side defeated Spain 2–1 in their final match, with goals from Brooking and Woodcock, it was too little too late. Peter Shilton replaced Clemence in goal, continuing Greenwood's unusual practice of alternating his goalkeepers. 'It became an annoyance,' admitted Ray Clemence, 'and I think that it made Ron look like he was a prevaricator.' England were out, failing even to make it to the third place play-off match because Italy couldn't break through against Belgium, who reached the final to face West Germany. Jupp Derwall's team beat Belgium in the final, with Keegan's Hamburg strike partner Horst Hrubesch scoring the winner. Once it was confirmed that England would not be playing in the playoff, the BBC ditched live coverage of the Italy v. Czechoslovakia third-place play-off match and replaced it with the Tommy Steele film *Half a Sixpence*. If one decision summed up the lack of enthusiasm for Euro '80, then this was it.

The mood was one of disappointment, rather than abject failure. Nonetheless, the knives quickly came out from the gentlemen of the press. 'He used nineteen players in three games,' wrote Norman Fox in *The Times*. 'His argument that all twenty-two players in the squad were equals was wrong and told of a nice guy who didn't like to hurt feelings.'

The spectre of the 1980 European Championships loomed large for a long time. Greenwood lamented: 'We travelled to Italy in high hope and returned with empty hearts.' Margaret Thatcher insisted that English football had been 'shamed abroad'. Throughout the '80s, studies into the causes of hooliganism came thick and fast, with urban decay, rising unemployment and the increasing divorce rate once again blamed. But as Colin Ward's *Steaming In: Journal of a Football Fan* and Bill Buford's *Among the Thugs* illustrated, many wreaked havoc purely for the craic and because they knew they'd likely get away with it.

Pilloried from all sides as England embarked on qualifying for the 1982 World Cup, Greenwood continued to chop and change his side and his tactics in order to get the right blend. Ray Kennedy continued to flit in and out of the side, until he decided, in

September 1981, to quit international football. *The Sun*'s headline read: 'GREENWOOD CAN STICK IT.' 'I am resigning here and now as Greenwood's bridesmaid,' announced the outspoken Liverpool forward, adding: 'I never felt like I was playing in a team for England. There was no unit.' Perhaps most controversially of all, Greenwood stuck with his favoured – but ageing – duo of Brooking and Keegan.

• • •

With the England team failing to fire on all cylinders, hooliganism rampant and post-imperial Britain plunged into a recession, the issue of declinism, first applied to football in 1970 when England lost their world champions crown at the Mexico World Cup, was back on the menu. Throughout England's tortuous qualification route to the 1982 World Cup finals in Spain, there was much hand-wringing about how the team's fortunes appeared to mirror the waning state of decay in the country. On the face of it, England's qualifying group – consisting of Norway, Switzerland, Romania and Hungary – shouldn't have posed too many problems, especially with two qualifying slots available, since the World Cup had now been expanded from eighteen to twenty-four countries. But instead, Greenwood's men slipped and stumbled on their way to Spain.

All looked straightforward after Norway were crushed 4–0 at Wembley, but warning signs were in place after England fell to a 2–1 defeat in Bucharest against Romania. 'We were like rabbits in the headlights,' recalled Dave Watson, 'and struggled to get the ball off them. They were excellent passers of the ball.' England drew against Romania in the return match and narrowly defeated Switzerland at Wembley, before an infamous return match in Basel.

The Swiss were not, as *The Sun* described them, 'a bunch of cuckoo clock makers and waiters', and in Claudio Sulser, Switzerland had the type of singular playmaker who always caused England trouble. If the hosts' 2–1 win laid bare the deficiencies of England's muddled tactics, it was the behaviour of visiting fans off it that attracted most media headlines. A jewellers was looted and bars smashed up as England fans rampaged through the city. 'It was an unpleasant type of Englishness,' Ray Wilkins commented. '"We are England. We'll get pissed in your city and smash it up." They were like drunken Crusades.' Officially, 2,000 England supporters travelled to the game, but with tickets available at the stadium on the day, many more made the journey. It was little wonder that in such a depressing atmosphere, Ron Greenwood informed his players he was resigning on the plane on the way home. 'The players rallied around Ron,' Dave Watson recalled. 'We told him we'd see it through together. Ron relented and carried on.' But it was a clear illustration that even the manager doubted whether England would actually make it to Spain.

The 2–1 defeat in Norway was at least hooliganism-free. But, typically of this era, it had clear socio-political ramifications. England's chaotic, panic-stricken play was punished by the determined and energised hosts, who'd ultimately finish bottom of the qualifying group. The final whistle not only provoked a joyous pitch invasion but one of the most legendary pieces of football commentary. 'We have beaten England 2–1 in football! It is completely unbelievable! We have beaten England! England, birthplace of giants. Lord Nelson, Lord Beaverbrook, Sir Winston Churchill, Sir Anthony Eden, Clement Attlee, Henry Cooper, Lady Diana – we have beaten them all. We have beaten them all. Maggie Thatcher … your boys took a hell of a beating,' ranted radio commentator Bjørge Lillelien.

Lillelien's stream of consciousness was so impassioned that the Norwegian Arts Council later selected it to represent their country's contribution to mankind's cultural heritage, along with a written part of Grieg's concerto and Antarctic explorer Roald Amundsen's letter to the Norwegian Prime Minister. But it was the lesser-known preamble to Lillelien's outburst, where he described England as a 'giant', which really crystallised England's plight.

The 'giant' that gave the game to the world had taken its eye off the ball. Whilst lesser lights like Norway and Switzerland invested in science-driven coaching programmes from youth football upwards, England still relied on its brand of muscularity and physicality and, as Trevor Francis put it, had a 'suspicion of players who dwelt on the ball for any length of time'. *The Guardian*'s Robert Armstrong believed that English football was suffering from the same affliction that blighted British industry; a lack of capital investment. As stadia at home crumbled and the living and playing styles of English footballers remained rooted in the past, other countries caught up. Remarkably, though, thanks to Romania failing to win either of their two final matches and England defeating Hungary at Wembley in their last match, Ron Greenwood's men somehow made it to Spain.

Delighted skipper Kevin Keegan said: 'We did all the things English football is renowned for.' Keegan elected not to develop his point, but, with England showing a real togetherness that night, it's likely he was alluding to effort, work rate and defensive organisation. In the nick of time, Greenwood's men had found their distinctly English collective mojo, and that was in no small part due to the influence of new first-team coach Don Howe.

When I interviewed the bespectacled Howe about the adventures of Ron's XXII in Spain, I was delighted to see that his faintly menacing and unnerving stare had lost none of its potency. Was he ever tempted – I asked him – to join the lines and bark out England's official World Cup song 'This Time (We'll Get It Right)', which reached No. 2 in the charts? 'Certainly not,' he snapped in his broad Wolverhampton brogue. 'A rather different sound came out of my mouth when it came to football.' I didn't bother asking Howe if he'd ever heard the (almost) forgotten long-playing version, which featured Justin Fashanu's disco-cum-breakdancing hit 'Do It 'Cos You Like It'. In the recording studio, with England's finest clad in Partridgesque sports casual England jumpers, Kevin Keegan sings 'This Time' with typical gusto, and defender Steve Foster deliberately garbles the words. 'I actually thought it all sounded a bit Germanic,' Howe said, 'with the oompah band in the background.' Also present and correct was Aston Villa winger Tony Morley. The debate around whether he deserved a place in the final XXII crystallised Howe's and Greenwood's differing philosophies:

> Ron was more idealistic and a purist. I was more concerned with the unit, the defensive shape of the team. We were yin and yang in many ways. He wanted Tony in, whereas I thought that, explosive player though he was on his day, he was perhaps a luxury. In the end, Tony didn't make the cut. We opted to play Steve Coppell out wide on the right and Graham Rix, a midfielder, on the left.

There was also the ongoing question of how – or if at all – Glenn Hoddle should be incorporated. 'The finest talent of his generation. Breathtaking ability,' Howe reckoned, before the inevitable 'but' was deployed. 'But a team couldn't be built around Glenn. For long periods, Glenn wouldn't impose himself on matches. A Bryan Robson or a Kevin Keegan were more rounded players.' So, with no out-and-out wingers and Hoddle on the periphery, the England side was resolute, defensively strong, solid but perhaps lacking genuine inspiration. And with Greenwood's loyal lieutenants Brooking and Keegan injured ('We were damned in some quarters for taking them, but their injuries were expected to clear up more quickly than actually transpired,' Howe explained), some believed it lacked a touch of gravitas too.

· · ·

In late spring, there was strong speculation in the tabloids that, due to the crisis in the Falkland Islands, the home nations might withdraw from the tournament. Ron's (and Don's) XXII might not have made the trip at all. World Cup hosts Spain had abstained in a United Nations vote that saw all members – bar Panama – deem Argentina the aggressors in the conflict. The tabloids printed stories of British expats in Spain being shunned by their neighbours, and, outside several English bars in Spain, crosses of St George were torn down and burnt by hostile Spaniards. According to (then) Sports Minister Sir Neil McFarlane, *The Sun*, with its headline 'WORLD CUP CRISIS', put unnecessary fears into British fans that a World Cup withdrawal was imminent.

Via letter (the method of correspondence favoured by politicians of a certain vintage), McFarlane outlined to me the Prime Minister's thinking during that fraught period:

Margaret Thatcher had an emergency meeting with the Queen shortly before the tournament. Both were of the opinion that the home nations should go to Spain. Rumours were rife. The world and his mother seemed to have an opinion on what would happen if any of the three home nations met Argentina at the second group stage. The FA and the Foreign Office discussed the situation fully, and frankly, there was no solution. If 'Domesday scenario' had arisen, the game would probably have been played behind closed doors, or scrapped. We just hoped and prayed that the situation never arose.

McFarlane went on to say: 'There was more concern about the hooligan element in England's travelling support ... if rival Argentinians met English or Scottish fans in the streets.' Events over the next fortnight hinted that a home nation boycott may have been closer to reality than McFarlane cares to admit. On 12 May, eight days after ARA *General Belgrano* was torpedoed, the *Daily Mirror* predicted: 'World Cup pull out looming.' Around 20,000 copies of a government advice booklet for travelling English fans were pulped. In his column for *The Sun*, Jimmy Greaves advocated a four-way tournament between the home nations (including non-qualifiers Wales), the proceeds of which would be donated to families of the British victims of the Falklands crisis. The doom-laden forecast contrasted with Margaret Thatcher's public assertion: 'A good showing from our teams is just what our boys need.' Ultimately, that's how it played out. England travelled to Spain, along with Scotland and Northern Ireland. At the opening ceremony on 1 June, the Spanish crowd booed the English flag relentlessly, and Dick Wragg and Sir Bert Millichipp walked out in protest. But Greenwood's men were present and correct.

By and large, the England camp was a happy one. Paul Mariner explained: 'Most of us were just pleased to be at the party.' There was none of the melodrama that ensued at rival camps. Italian players refused to speak with their own journalists after fake stories circulated in the Italian press about Paolo Rossi's and Antonio Cabrini's rumoured 'affair'. From inside their luxury hotel rooms, West German players lobbed water filled balloons at their protesting fans who gathered to demand answers following the notorious Disgrace of Gijón match, during which the West Germans and Austrians time-wasted after Horst Hrubesch gave the Germans the lead. The result saw both teams progress to the next stage at the expense of Algeria, who'd beaten Jupp Derwall's men in the opening game.

The England players entertained themselves with 'Pac-Man' and ping-pong competitions, played cards and read English tabloids. Try as they might, though, the Ipswich duo of Mariner and Terry Butcher, with cassette player going full blast, couldn't convince teammates that Saxon and Iron Maiden were the best bands on the planet. 'Neil Diamond, ABBA, ELO and Wings were more to everyone else's taste,' Mariner said. Greenwood's men steered clear of the room occupied by the injured duo of Trevor Brooking and Kevin Keegan. 'There was a bit of an atmosphere,' Trevor Francis recalled. 'I don't blame either of them, but we could sense their frustration.' England supporters, clad in their 'World Cup Task Force '82' T-shirts, travelled in vast numbers. Reports abound of unpaid bar and restaurant bills, looted tills, broken glass around the city, fighting and urinating in public. The favoured chant was: 'Argentina, Argentina, what's it like to lose a war?'

There was concern within the management team about the growing number of English flags on the terraces. When the team performed the B-side to 'This Time (We'll Get It Right)' on *Top of the Pops*, the England players (with British Airways stewardesses joining in) flew Union Jack flags as they belted out 'England We'll Fly the Flag'. 'We had a tie-in with British Airways,' Don Howe explained, 'and Ron and the FA thought the Union Jack was more inclusive.' Photographs from the era suggest, however, that there were as many Union Jacks as English flags at matches. Given the caution about using the Cross of St George, it's perhaps surprising that 'Bulldog Bobby' – with his protruding beer gut – was chosen as the official team mascot, given that 'Bulldog' was also the title of a National Front publication.

• • •

The heat in Bilbao before England's first match against France was every bit as searing as it had been in Leon twelve years earlier, the last time England had contested a World Cup finals match. 'Even as we inspected the pitch in our flip flops,' Paul Mariner recalled, 'I was sweating from every orifice. The grass was hot. Wearing those bloody nylon Admiral tracksuits didn't help, and I saw the thermometer shoot through 100 degrees as we ran out.' The Basque capital's notoriously poor air quality also affected the players (Ray Wilkins recalled 'a clogging in the lungs'), but England made the fastest of starts, scoring after twenty-seven seconds from a well-constructed set piece, with Terry Butcher flicking on Steve Coppell's long throw to Bryan Robson, who spectacularly hammered the ball home. Butcher, who was the youngest member of the squad at twenty-two – told me: 'We'd rehearsed that move from the left, as Kenny Sansom's throw was judged the more potent, but not from the right. It was fantastic improvisation.' The French equalised before half-time, but England's midfield proved more than a match for France's dazzling talents Michel Platini, Jean Tigana and Alain Giresse. During the interval, at the behest of Don Howe, the England players removed their shirts and placed iced towels over their heads 'to avoid passing out', Butcher said.

In the second half, England's doughty defending and pressing of the French midfield continued to work well, and Robson and Paul Mariner added two more. Mariner, who'd lost around twelve pounds of fluid during the match, put his arms up to the jubilant England fans, then dropped them and ambled back to the halfway line. 'We were all totally spent,' he told me. It had been a remarkably positive start, against a lavishly gifted side that would ultimately reach the semi-finals. Perhaps the team's 'we'll get it right' chorus from 'This Time' wasn't misplaced. But the truth is that was the high point of England's Spanish adventure. They beat Czechoslovakia 2–0, thus qualifying for the second group stage, after which Ron Greenwood instructed his men to 'go and get drunk'.

His charges did as they were instructed. Many uncorked the bottles of Rioja they'd been presented with upon arrival at their hideaway on the coast near Bilbao (the deceased canine which saw the tabloids label the stretch of sand 'Dead Dog Beach' after the draw had been made in the winter was now removed) and then got stuck into crates of Sangria. 'It was a monumental piss up,' explained Paul Mariner. Many got sunburnt, and Ray Wilkins was so much the worse for wear that he slept on a hotel couch as the media conducted a press conference with Ron Greenwood. 'The press didn't muck rake,' Wilkins recalled. 'They could have made our lives awkward.' The 1–0 victory over Kuwait was more than a little subdued.

As England entered the second phase and shifted bases from Bilbao to Madrid, the concerns surrounding Trevor Brooking's calf injury and Kevin Keegan's back problem were openly discussed by the squad. 'The obsession amongst the press over whether the two fellas would be fit became an annoyance,' Ray Wilkins explained. 'It was a bit disrespectful to the rest of us.' The two roommates, still unable to join full training, largely kept themselves to themselves, and their room became known as the VIP room thanks to Brooking's MBE and Keegan's OBE. 'Kevin saw the funny side and stuck a Red Cross on the door like he and Trevor had the plague,' Trevor Francis said. The fact that Keegan's moonlight flit in a car borrowed from a member of staff at the hotel to his German specialist in a desperate bid to get fit wasn't widely known about until after the tournament showed that the press weren't all knowing.

The side that faced West Germany was the same as the one that opened against France. But with the reigning European champions the masters of the pressing game, England were never going to be afforded as much space as they were given against Michel Hidalgo's side. In a tight match, England looked solid but one-paced and short of inspiration, both in midfield or up front. West Germany often outmuscled England. 'Out of my way, little fly,' barked the oak-tree-thighed midfielder Hans-Peter Briegel at the diminutive Steve Coppell as he barged him out of the way. In a 0–0 draw, Karl-Heinz Rummenigge crashed a shot off England's crossbar, with Greenwood's men creating precious little. Following the West Germans' 2–1 win over Spain, England needed to better the score against the hosts to progress to the semi-final. By then, Keegan, whose epidural had cured his back injury, and Brooking were fit to play and were amongst the substitutes.

Generally not one for counterfactuals, Don Howe recalled that he and Greenwood, in the aftermath of the tournament, spent time discussing how England's World Cup may have panned out differently. 'We did say that winning our first group did us no favours, because we ended up playing West Germany, who were formidable, and Spain, who I always felt couldn't dare to lose to us for fear of a huge backlash at home.'

Had England finished runners-up in Group A, they would have progressed to a second stage group containing Northern Ireland and Austria. 'It might have given us time to get Keegan and Brooking fully match fit,' explained Don Howe, 'and then they would have been fit for a semi-final, but those weren't the cards we were dealt.' In the event, the duo entered the fray in the sixty-sixth minute against Spain, and although they carved out England's two best chances – Brooking's shot was well smothered by Luis Arconada, and Keegan's header flew agonisingly wide – the 0–0 draw meant that England were eliminated. They'd conceded a single goal in five matches ('I was originally brought in to shore up the defence, and that aspect clearly improved,' Howe said) but huffed and puffed ineffectually in the latter stages of the tournament. 'We really missed Steve Coppell through injury during the Spain game. He'd have given us some dynamism down the right-hand side.' Could the unused Hoddle – I asked Howe – have made a difference in either of the two second group stage matches? 'Perhaps,' Howe said,

> but my gut feeling was that both sides would have double-marked him. My mind did flit to Tony Morley. He'd turned the Bayern Munich defence inside out for Villa's winner in the European Cup final a month before. He was off the cuff but inconsistent.

Ron's solid and stoic XXII didn't get it quite right, but made a decent fist of it at the World Cup, and the major hooligan incidents that the government feared were mercifully avoided. Ultimately, they exited España '82 not because, as Paul Mariner suggested (jokingly), the lighter Aertex Admiral shirts that the players asked for weren't actually delivered until the day England headed for home, or because of a boozy bonding session or two, but because they lacked a dash of panache in midfield and up front.

England and their supporters stumbled through the rest of the decade, amidst fevered debates about hooliganism, tactical vacillation and misfiring star players.

2

THE BREAK-UP

*'Both of us, though, are aware that it cannot last for ever and
that we must part again one day. I hope we part on
a high note and on the friendliest of terms...'*
Peter Taylor, quoted in *With Clough, By Taylor*

Bernabéu Stadium, Madrid – May 1980. With twenty-one minutes gone, John Robertson darts in from the left and feints past Hamburg's Manny Kaltz. After nudging the ball to the prostrate Garry Birtles, the Forest wide man latches onto Birtles' toe-poked return pass, evades England captain Kevin Keegan's lunge and drills the ball past goalkeeper Rudi Kargus. It's the only goal of a tight European Cup final. Forest retain their trophy. After the final whistle, there are no choreographed celebrations on a podium, no gold confetti storms, no classical anthems, firework displays, selfies or dignitaries trying to steal the limelight. Forest players form an orderly queue behind their captain John McGovern, with his short, neat hair, as he prepares to lift the trophy. It is placed on a plain wooden desk, which looks like it has been commandeered from a local school. McGovern holds it aloft for the second time in twelve months. 'Win something once, there's always someone who can say it was down to luck. Win summat twice, and it shuts the buggers up,' says manager Brian Clough. Assistant Peter Taylor reckons there's no limit to what the club can achieve. But rather than heralding an era of continued success, within months, Forest will become also-rans.

•   •   •

A unique blend of unorthodoxy and inspiration had been at the root of Forest's second European Cup victory. Following a lacklustre 1–0 defeat at home to Dynamo Berlin in the first leg of the quarter-final, the game seemed to be up. Two weeks later on a freezing night behind the Iron Curtain, with grey-coated soldiers ringing the pitch, Peter Taylor took one look at the home side warming up, strode into the Forest dressing room, and talked animatedly about their 'zombified' appearance. 'They're beaten before they start,' he said. 'Their chins are on the floor.' Kidology it may have been, but Forest, with two goals from Trevor Francis and a John Robertson penalty, were out of sight by half-time, eventually winning 3–2 on aggregate. John McGovern enjoyed the Cold War joke he'd heard prior to the match. Dynamo's Friedrich-Ludwig-Jahn-Sportpark stadium was positioned very close to the Berlin Wall, and those East Berliners brave enough to laugh about such things said that when a ball got hoofed out of the compact ground, and thus over the wall, 20,000 East Berliners immediately offered to go and fetch it. Peter Taylor relaxed the players on the evening before Forest's away leg against Ajax by marching them around the city's red-light district after dinner (to the bewilderment of travelling Forest fans in the vicinity) and trying unsuccessfully to negotiate a group discount in a bar. Taylor's comedic range of facial ticks and furtive glances had the players in hysterics as usual.

Their place in the final secured, Forest decamped to the Majorcan resort of Cala Millor; Clough and Taylor's favourite bolt hole. The beer flowed, and training was hardly taxing. The threat posed by Kevin Keegan – who'd joined Hamburg three years earlier from Liverpool – was airily dismissed by Taylor, who told the Forest players that the England captain had 'shot it. He's over the hill.' Clough never even mentioned Keegan in his team talks – although he did tell his players not to look at him, believing it would put him on edge. An exception was made in Kenny Burns' case. Instructed to intimidate Keegan by whatever means necessary, Burns sidled up alongside him in the tunnel before the game, removed his false teeth and gave him a manic smile. Apparently. It's a story that Keegan has always disputed, although he was subdued during the match, thanks in no small measure to Forest's pressing game, which afforded him precious little space in which to operate.

Hamburg had twenty-five shots compared with Forest's one from Robertson. 'But mine was the only one that counted, wasn't it?' laughed the smoky-voiced Scot during our 2010 conversation, which coincided with the release of his autobiography *Supertramp*. 'We played superbly to outmanoeuvre Hamburg. Tactically, we were spot on,' Robertson said. Clough had reckoned Hamburg were clear favourites, although he never shared his doubts with his players. The core of Hamburg's team formed the West German squad that won the 1980 European Championships that summer, including striker Horst Hrubesch and midfielder Manny Kaltz. Awash with money from Hitachi, they were light years ahead of Forest financially. Clough's men received a taxable £5,000 each for winning the game.

Some of them received £500 each for wearing Adidas boots. Hamburg's stars pocketed 13,000 marks just for reaching the final, had lucrative long-term boot deals and drove sponsored Mercedes cars. Their multi-functional Volksparkstadion could hold up to 75,000 supporters, in contrast to the far more compact City Ground. Yet not for the first time, Forest prevailed against the odds.

Unlike the other 'corner shop' clubs who'd fallen at the final hurdle in the European Cup in the late '70s – Saint-Étienne, Bruges and Borussia Mönchengladbach – Clough's side had delivered when it really counted. Twice. Their unlikely rise to the top couldn't have been more speedy, perfect or absolute: promotion from Division 2 in 1977; league champions in 1978; European champions in 1979 and 1980; European Super Cup winners in 1979. John Robertson was the ultimate manifestation of the potency of the Clough–Taylor alchemy. Shuffling down the left flank, the heavy-looking Scot, who'd struggled to give up smoking and fried food despite Clough's encouragement, looked anything but a tricky winger. 'Whenever Pete [Taylor] rang up, he'd always ask: "Is that the sound of bacon I hear sizzling in the background?"' Robertson told me. A Forest banner headline in Madrid read: 'ROBBO EATS HAMBURGERS.' It was as much a reference to his prowess on the pitch as his calorific intake. There was no finer winger or deliverer of the ball in Europe during that era. 'Between them, Clough and Taylor called me every name under the sun to get me playing and living properly. God knows where I would have ended up without them. I owe them everything,' Robertson said.

Clough himself appeared to have messianic powers that stretched beyond football. In January 1980, following a call from a hospice manager in the city, he convinced a 47-year-old Nottingham widow, Barbara Taylor, to start eating again after her weight fell to around five stone. She did so, saying: 'He has given me the will to go on living.' Later that year, in front of a crowd of onlookers and after an hour of gentle persuasion, he convinced a suicidal man to not throw himself off Trent Bridge. Clough made no mention of these altruistic acts in his autobiographies, but for the latter, the police gave him a Citizen of the Month award. At a time of significant job losses at the local Raleigh bicycle and Player cigarette factories, plus an ongoing slump in Nottingham's lace industry, Forest's achievements were a ray of light; a beacon of hope in troubled economic times. Unlike that other Nottingham hero Robin Hood, whose exploits in and around Sherwood Forest were purely fictional, Clough snatched silverware from under the noses of far wealthier clubs and brought it back to Nottingham, England's (then) seventh-largest city, and shared it with his adoring flock. 'CLOUGHIE WALKS ON WATER', read a Forest banner in that era. Yet Clough's powers weren't omnipotent. Just as his voiceover on the 1980 novelty record 'You Can't Win 'Em All' (a plea to end football hooliganism), performed by Canadian artist J. J. Barrie, failed to trouble the charts or stem the tide of terrace trouble, Forest's increasingly pedestrian league performances showed that Clough couldn't influence events on the pitch by force of personality alone.

Perhaps John McGovern called it right when he told me: 'Our success in Europe gave us status, and Clough's fame was enormous, but it didn't make us a big club, like a Liverpool.' There were already palpable signs even before the 1980 European Cup final that the Clough–Taylor magic was wearing off.

• • •

Clough reckoned that Peter Taylor's trusted antennae, which had served them when it came to buying players since their early days at

Hartlepools, were starting to go awry. This was perfectly illustrated when that most incorrigible of '70s mavericks, Stan Bowles, was whisked up to Nottingham for £250,000 from Queens Park Rangers in February 1980. Bowles was bought to add flair to a Forest team that, in the league at least, were turning in increasingly pedestrian performances. 'Stand up straight, get your hair cut and get your hands out of your pockets, Stanley,' was how Bowles recalled Clough addressing him when he turned up to training. Fixing me with his clear blue eyes, Bowles added: 'If he thought he could speak to me like I was a kid, he was much mistaken.' Clough and Taylor had dealt with gambling footballers all their careers, but none as inveterate as Bowles. Although Bowles scored on his debut, he recalls Clough 'looking at me disapprovingly from the minute I set foot in the place'. Peter Taylor, on the other hand, was far friendlier because, Bowles reckoned, 'he wanted to listen to my gambling tips'. Like the former Rangers man, Taylor was rarely seen without a copy of the *Racing Post* tucked under one arm. Inevitably, Bowles shot himself in the foot at Forest, going AWOL after not being selected for John Robertson's testimonial match and not turning up to join the Forest party as it prepared to fly to Madrid for the European Cup final. With Trevor Francis ruled out after rupturing his Achilles tendon, the self-destructive Bowles may well have played a role in the final, but he cared not one jot. 'Cloughie could shove it up his arse,' Bowles told me with his impudent smirk.

Despite taming colourful characters at Forest like Larry Lloyd and Kenny Burns, the recalcitrant Bowles was a breed apart. 'Pete wanted me, and Cloughie didn't. They argued in front of me about whether I should play. It was like two divorcing parents falling out. They weren't in tune,' Bowles said.

Taylor's book *With Clough, By Taylor* – released shortly after Forest's victory in Madrid – also caused ructions. Clough didn't appreciate the fact he'd been kept in the dark about the whole project. For the most part, it's an insightful journey through the pair's managerial career, and Taylor's waspishness about Ron Greenwood's England team makes for an entertaining read. The section that irked Clough was the final chapter, entitled – ironically – The Magic Formula. Taylor dared to suggest that Clough needed a crowd around him to ease his insecurities. Taylor betrayed his own inferiority complex, asking (perhaps not unreasonably) why, when Clough was awarded Manager of the Month trophies, he (Taylor) wasn't also presented with a super-sized bottle of Bells whisky. Taylor later admitted that, despite all the silverware, he had tired of Clough's increasingly choreographed and rehearsed bravado.

There were also economic pressures that all clubs, to varying degrees, were grappling with. In 1979–80, Forest's disappointing league form saw crowds sometimes dip below the 22,000 level, which chairman Brian Appleby told Clough and Taylor was the breakeven figure. The brand-new executive stand cost far more than the initial £2.8 million projection. Repaying the loan on it, just as the government hiked up interest rates to a record 14 per cent (rates ran at 10 per cent a year before) in a bid to curb inflation, would cast a shadow over Forest's transfer dealings for years. Yet by signing Trevor Francis for £1 million in 1979 (the previous record was the £550,000 West Bromwich Albion paid for David Mills in 1976), the irony was that Forest themselves had inflated English football's transfer market.

•　•　•

The capture of Francis, who'd arrived at the City Ground with his fur-coated wife Helen in his brand-new red Jaguar, represented a sea change in player recruitment at Forest. Clough and Taylor had – with the exception of Peter Shilton – previously signed players who'd been written off or underachieved elsewhere, like Kenny Burns, Garry Birtles or Larry Lloyd. Taylor had played the transfer market perfectly, buying low and (in the case of Peter Withe and Tony Woodcock) selling high. 'I was as surprised at the £1 million fee as anyone,' Francis told me in his distinctive nasal Devon accent. 'It was a sign that Forest now saw themselves at the top table. But I wasn't a natural Clough–Taylor type of character.' He was a thoroughbred: polite but confident in his own ability, not damaged goods that needed to be pieced back together. It had taken a few years to organise an interview with the former Birmingham City prodigy, but a cold call in 2021 finally did the trick. Not even his winner against Malmö in the '79 final stopped Clough from worrying about Francis, who he believed lacked genuine hunger. At first, he tried to bring him down a peg or two, instructing him to make the half-time tea for his teammates when he wasn't playing and forbidding him from bringing his own branded toiletries into training. 'Use the same gear as the others, big shot,' Clough told him.

I asked Francis to tell me a story about Clough that hadn't appeared in his 2019 autobiography *One In a Million*. After a few moments' reflection, Francis remembered one, insisting it 'wasn't that interesting'. We soon agreed to differ. Shortly after moving into his plush new detached house in Newark-on-Trent (twenty miles outside Nottingham), Francis received a visit one Sunday morning from Clough, who wasn't normally in the habit of popping into his players' houses. After telling him to 'get the kettle on', Clough took himself on a tour of the Francis household. 'Lovely place you have here, Trev. It'll be a nice place for your bairns to grow up,' Clough said, glancing at Francis's wife Helen, and then the state-of-the-art HiFi system and expensive furnishings. 'But [jabbing his finger at Francis], make sure you keep working hard for Nottingham Forest, or you'll be out the door.' Clough was always concerned that hefty wages sapped a player's desire, but none more so than in the case of Francis, who'd used a significant chunk of the £100,000 (£650,000 in today's money) he'd received for spending the summer of '78 with Detroit Express in the North American Soccer League on his Newark house. At twenty-five, Francis was already 'made'. 'I always felt that Clough reckoned I was too upwardly mobile, beyond his control,' Francis smiled. 'Too gilded for his liking?' I asked. 'Yeah, maybe,' he shrugged.

When Francis tore his Achilles tendon in the build-up to the 1980 European Cup final, Clough, as was his want, completely blanked his million-pound man for weeks on end and forbade him from attending the final, telling Francis his presence would be 'a distraction'. Clough quickly reasoned that some of his explosive pace may have been permanently lost. Francis was (unsuccessfully) hawked to Manchester United and Barcelona. There were mighty arguments about where he should play in the team. Francis wanted to play through the middle, with Clough and Taylor preferring him to operate out wide. As the '80s began, Francis reckoned: 'Clough would deliberately create conflict. It was a stressful way to run a club, as much for Brian as anybody else.' Other big-money signings quickly discovered that Clough's irascibility was growing worse.

The first of the post-Madrid new breed was Goldstone Ground hero Peter Ward, whom Brighton fans serenaded with the song: 'He shot, he scored, his name is Peter Ward,' whenever the diminutive forward found the back of the net. The player had long been a favourite of Peter Taylor, who'd managed Brighton between 1973 and 1976. But Clough wasn't so sure, and he torpedoed Taylor's plan to buy him a year earlier. In November 1980, Ward moved for a £450,000 fee in a curious triangular move, with Forest's Garry Birtles heading to Manchester United for £1.25 million (a fine return on a player who'd cost just £1,500 two years earlier) and United's Andy Ritchie moving to Brighton. Ward has lived in sunny Tampa for decades, and although his mop of permed curls is long gone, his moustache remains as verdant as ever, and his Lichfield accent is still potent. His Clough impression is unerring too. 'Do you like it?' Clough asked Ward's (then) wife, pointing to her husband's facial hair on the day he signed for Forest. When Mrs Ward replied in the affirmative, Clough shrugged and grudgingly said: 'Well, I suppose he can keep it then.'

He recalls the heady days of playing in the European Super Cup against Valencia, and Clough described his debut against Southampton as the best non-scoring debut he'd ever seen. But quickly, Ward found himself in and out of the Forest team. 'When Cloughie picked the side, I was out, and when Pete picked it, I was in,' he recalled. Ward often found himself on the sharp end of Clough's vicious tongue. On the Forest team bus after a 2–0 loss at Birmingham City, Ward asked the driver if he could drop him at a service station where he'd left his car. Clough's mood was as filthy as the weather outside. After instructing the driver to pull onto the hard shoulder a mile north of the services, Clough told Ward to get out and walk back, with the rain lashing down. 'And with any luck,' Clough barked as the doors were about to close, 'the little cunt will get run over.'

In the summer of 1981, Middlesbrough's twenty-year-old midfield starlet Mark Proctor signed for a hefty £450,000. Long since an admirer of the former England youth captain, Clough, also born in Middlesbrough, had regularly suggested that he moved to 'a decent club'. Clough's mantra remained unchanged. The ball was to remain firmly on the deck. 'Don't go playing one-twos with God,' Clough instructed Proctor, but with old stalwarts like Larry Lloyd and Kenny Burns now departing the City Ground and John McGovern no longer guaranteed a starting berth, Forest lacked leadership and consistency on the pitch. It was a volatile environment for new players. 'I was twenty years old and a bit jittery around Cloughie,' Proctor said. 'My best games came when Pete picked me and Clough popped to Spain for a break, which was starting to happen quite a bit.' Clough's unorthodox motivation techniques still burn brightly in Proctor's memory. On one occasion, he ditched training for the day and took the players to a local coalmine. As they crawled on their hands and knees in tunnels, Clough told them: 'This is what real work looks like.' Another time, Clough, on the eve of a Forest match, marched in behind a waitress who was carrying a large platter of chips. Even in the '80s, chips were a no-no the night before a game. Unusually, the whole squad was present, with Clough having not yet announced the team. Clough then told the waitress which specific players could have chips with their steak. 'It was Clough's bizarre way of telling the players who was playing the day after and who wasn't,' recalled Proctor, who – sadly for him – was allowed the largest of helpings. Frustrated with his lack of first-team opportunities, Proctor dared to question his manager about why he'd been demoted to the second team, Clough growled: 'Because you're too good for the third team, now fuck off.'

Both Ward, who later flourished in America with Seattle Sounders, and Proctor, who later played for Sunderland and Sheffield Wednesday, regret that their careers at the City Ground didn't work out better, but it doesn't stop them viewing unravelling events with a dark sense of humour. In the early '80s, Forest players had sponsored Toyota cars, with their names on the side. Thanks to enterprising local kids peeling off and rearranging the letters that spelt his title, 'Mark Proctor England Under-21 International' was quickly renamed 'ark coptor Murder-21 International.' Through gritted teeth, Ward can even smile about Clough torpedoing his FA Cup final dream. In 1983, with Ward back on loan at former club Brighton, who'd reached the quarter-finals, Clough announced he wanted him back at the City Ground pronto. When Ward protested, Clough told him: 'I've never been to an FA Cup final, Wardy, and neither will you.'

The pair well remember the travails of Forest's most expensive post-Madrid signing – the 6ft 2in. Justin Fashanu. Signed from Norwich City in 1981 for £1.2 million, Forest's new striker was signed to add a physicality up front that Forest had lacked since Peter Withe departed the club three years earlier. The signing was a disastrous flop. Initially, he was paired up front with Trevor Francis, who recalled: 'Fash had genuine presence up there. From corners, he could take out two men with his strength. He could hold the ball up. He was the original "Fash the Bash", before his brother John got that nickname.' But then Francis was sold to Manchester City in another £1 million move, and Fashanu's finishing proved way-ward. He took delivery of a Toyota jeep, which he'd park anywhere and everywhere, racking up multiple parking tickets. On the side of his jeep was painted a huge goal. The plan was that by the end of the 1981–82 campaign, the goal would be brimming with stuck-on footballs denoting his epic scoring feats. It didn't turn out that way, with Fashanu netting just three times in his Forest career. The (virtually) empty net on the side of his jeep symbolised the barren

nature of Fashanu's time at the City Ground. The issue of his homosexuality surfaced. Asked on more than one occasion whether
he was gay by his teammates ('out of curiosity, rather than malice,'
Peter Ward said) Fashanu either remained tight lipped or laughed it
off, responding: 'Give me a kiss and I'll tell you.' He also stood up to
Clough, who later admitted to asking him why he kept 'going to that
bloody poofs' club in town'. Gay rights activist Peter Tatchell subse-
quently claimed that Fashanu considered 'coming out' during the
early '80s, but given the climate of the time, opted against doing so.

Unlike Trevor Francis, Fashanu continued to use his branded
toiletries despite being instructed not to do so and brought his own
physiotherapist into the club. Peter Taylor later claimed: 'Justin
didn't want to play football.' Or rather, he wanted the ball to be
knocked long to him, which was at odds with Clough's and Taylor's
insistence that balls were played to feet. Unusually for a footballer
in that era, Fashanu emoted in front of his manager. Clough sledge-
hammered Fashanu's confidences. When the striker revealed that
he'd found God, Clough responded: 'Perhaps he'll sign off all your
fucking parking tickets then.' After disclosing that his confidence
was at rock bottom, Fashanu was told to 'Get on with it and stop
crying.' The point of no return was reached when, having being
banned from the training ground by Clough after storming out of
the City Ground because he'd been dropped, Fashanu turned up
for training anyway. The police were summoned, and Mark Proctor
recalled that the sight of Clough in the front of the Panda Car and
Fashanu in the back was 'the most bizarre and sad thing I've ever
seen.' Within fifteen months, Fashanu was offloaded to neighbours
Notts County, and his career petered out frustratingly.

For different reasons, and to varying degrees, none of Forest's
big-money moves after the Madrid final worked out. As a package,

the misfiring trio had cost over £2 million – the bulk of the debt on their new stand. Cumulatively, they'd be sold for a paltry £300,000. The Scottish striker Ian Wallace, another million-pound player who fared slightly better at the City Ground, was jettisoned to French club Brest for just £100,000 in 1984. The tension between Clough and Taylor grew unbearable. By now, they were in separate offices, the equivalent of a married couple deciding to sleep in different rooms. Some players were 'Clough' players and others were 'Taylor' players. Clough's trust in his assistant had evaporated, although he wasn't under any illusion that he could do a better job. 'Do you know what's wrong with him?' Clough asked substitute John McGovern, pointing at new Swiss striker Raimondo Ponte, signed for £250,000. 'No, boss, but I'm sure you'll tell me,' McGovern responded. 'The problem is that I bloody well signed him.' Clough, Mark Proctor reckoned, was 'full of hell'. Something had to give, and at Christmas 1981, it did.

On 27 December, whilst sweeping snow outside his house (Forest's entire Christmas programme was wiped out due to blizzards), Clough had 'a funny turn', as he later put it. Subsequent hospital tests showed no evidence of a heart attack, but it was clear that all wasn't entirely well. Following his doctor's instructions and taking a couple of weeks off, Clough stomped back into the club and sought out the player who'd recently driven him to distraction; forthright central defender Willie Young.

From the moment he was signed from Arsenal in December 1981 for £50,000, Young and Clough had been at loggerheads over the former's relocation allowance, which he wanted to spend on a stable for his wife, Linda, a keen equestrienne. Clough disagreed, arguing that the money should be spent only on a house. Just before Christmas, the pair had what Young described to me as 'the mother of all arguments, with swearing, and threats made on both sides.' Young told Clough he believed Peter Taylor was the 'brains behind the outfit', at which point Clough informed the Scot that he'd not be playing for the club again. By the time the Forest players reconvened in the new year, Young had regained his place in the team. Clough continued squaring up to the equally feisty Scot, but he appointed him captain nonetheless. After leaving Forest in 1983, Young didn't see Clough for years. In 1999, when Young was landlord of the Bramcote Manor pub near Nottingham, Clough stormed in one Sunday with a buddy of his, glanced around the pub, took one look at Young, and said: 'Oi, shithouse, I want a roast dinner.' 'Say please,' Young demanded. Surprisingly, a clearly famished Clough complied. The Bramcote did a particularly fine choice of Sunday roasts, as I discovered on a couple of occasions, and as Clough wolfed down his food, he gave Young the thumbs up for the quality of his meat and admitted that their face-offs had gone too far. 'You gave me a bloody heart attack,' Clough said, presumably not literally. Clough told Young that by that point, his and Taylor's relationship had all but crumbled. 'Bad times,' Clough admitted. Having bared his soul and devoured a pudding, Clough walked out without paying. 'Very generous of you, big man,' called Clough as he left.

•　•　•

In classic Taylor-speak, Clough's assistant flopped down in a chair and informed Clough: 'I've shot it. I'm done.' Nottingham Forest had just lost at home to Manchester United and would eventually tail off in eighth place at the end of the 1981–82 season. For the second season in a row, there'd be no European football. Despite having harangued Taylor that season for not watching as many matches as he used to, a tearful Clough nonetheless attempted to persuade Taylor to stay, but once he realised his assistant's mind was made up, there was little more to be said. There were two versions of events that followed. Clough insisted that he convinced the board to give Taylor a £31,000 pay off; Taylor insisted that he negotiated it all by himself. At that point, Taylor had effectively retired, and the already-strained relationship between the two now had grown chillier still. Then Taylor, who'd professed to being 'bored' in retirement, was tempted to return to management at – of all places – Derby County, now struggling at the foot of the Second Division, the club where Clough and Taylor had won the Division One title nine years earlier. Just as he'd found at Brighton a decade before, without Clough's sheer willpower, Taylor found it impossible to turn the Derby ship around. Yet despite Clough describing Taylor's decision to take the helm as 'crackers', he reached out to help his former partner one last time, offering him the opportunity to take Forest players Mark Proctor and Viv Anderson on loan.

The two players were instructed to report to the City Ground, where Clough told them the plan. 'I don't know what you think about this, Viv, but I'm not going,' said Proctor. Anderson concurred. Undeterred, Clough drove them out to Taylor's country pile, where a friendly but slightly embarrassed Taylor tried to convince his former charges to give it a shot at the Baseball Ground. They still refused to go, at which point Clough and Taylor retired to another room to talk. An incandescent Clough informed his two out-of-favour players that, if they weren't willing to go to the Baseball Ground, they could 'bloody well find their own way home'. The pair made a run for it, 'hurdling ditches and climbing fences in the dead of night', Proctor recalled. After stumbling on a pub, the pair had a late beer and ordered a cab. Three months after taking over at the Baseball Ground, Derby drew Forest at home in the FA Cup third round. A jittery Forest lost 2–0, and Clough must have been haunted by ghosts of Baseball Ground past. Archie Gemmill, a cornerstone of Derby's '72 title win, and now back at Derby for a second spell, scored one of the goals, and Roy McFarland, skipper when the Rams won the title in '75, was Taylor's assistant. As Derby fans invaded the pitch after the final whistle, Clough shook hands with McFarland but not Taylor and disappeared down the tunnel. A fuming Clough did what he tended to do when searching for a scapegoat: he picked on 6ft 4in. Willie Young. Prior to the match, Clough sought out Young and instructed him to play 'a blinder'. 'Clough was uptight,' Young explained. 'Usually, he never mentioned the opposition before a game, but this time he was telling me to keep tight on Kevin Wilson – their striker.' Afterwards, Clough made a beeline for Young, telling him he'd 'thrown the game'. When Young was seen by Clough talking to Peter Taylor before Forest players were bussed home, he was informed by his manager that, having 'talked to that shithouse Taylor, [he would] never play for this club again'. Clough didn't make good his threat.

The final denouement in the Clough–Taylor relationship came when Taylor signed, of all players, John Robertson prior to the 1983–84 season. By 1983, troubled by cartilage problems in his knee, his powers were waning. The deal was done whilst Clough was out walking the Pennines for charity. Robertson didn't tell Clough he was leaving, because Taylor suggested it might alert other clubs to the impending deal. 'It's something I'll always regret,' Robertson said. 'I should have told Cloughie my plans.' From that point on, Clough never lost an opportunity to castigate Taylor via the media, claiming at one point that if he saw him walking down the A52, between Derby and Nottingham, he'd 'run him over'. Perhaps fortunately, Taylor, who passed away in 1990, was long since gone when the stretch of road was renamed 'Brian Clough Way' in 2005.

Derby plummeted into the third tier of English football at the end of the 1983–84 season, but Taylor had already bailed by that point. He kept a low profile after that, although he did pop up on Central TV suggesting that, at odds of 40/1, a flutter on Derby (promoted back to the top flight in 1987) winning the Division One title in the 1988–89 season would be a good wager. They finished fifth. By contrast, an increasingly cartoonish Clough – with his (now) trademark green jersey, thickening eyebrows, 'young man' utterances and rapidly reddening complexion – remained very much in the public eye throughout the rest of the '80s as he flew solo at the City Ground. As English football became more hurly-burly, Forest were a sight for sore eyes, playing the attractive, lightning-fast passing game that Clough had always demanded. Given that City Ground crowds regularly plummeted to below the 15,000 mark, it was a minor miracle that Clough, on a relative shoestring, steered them into consistent top six finishes and guided them to a League Cup win in 1989. He remained the master of non-verbal communication, either flicking his Vs or placing his finger over his lips if he felt Forest supporters were behaving in an unsportsmanlike manner towards visiting players. And when Clough glanced at his charges and formed a circle with his thumb and index finger – indicating they'd done well – they still swelled with pride.

But it was never quite the same again. Taylor had always been a master at rejuvenating the careers of misunderstood hardmen, whom Clough had little time for. The Forest teams of the '80s were laden with skilful, home-grown midfielders and forwards like his son Nigel, with neat haircuts and lovely manners. They were moulded by Clough but lacked the bite of Derby and Forest teams in their pomp. Interestingly, given Taylor's claim in his book that his ex-partner needed company to mask his insecurities, Clough bought back several players whom Forest had sold, including Ian Bowyer (who reckoned Clough was clearly 'reduced' without Taylor's support), Garry Birtles, Peter Davenport and, much to the player's surprise, John Robertson, whom Clough rehired for a brief spell in the 1985–86 season. Several represented good business, but these were in part 'comfort' buys – familiar faces for Clough to work with. He couldn't always escape his troubled past either. Forest had gained a 2–0 aggregate lead in their 1984 UEFA Cup semi-final with Anderlecht. But when the Belgians won the return leg 3–0, there were allegations of foul play. In 1997, it emerged that Anderlecht had paid referee Emilio Guruceta Muro £18,000 to fix the result. For Clough, who'd described Juventus as 'cheating Italian bastards' after Derby lost their European Cup semi-final in '73, it was further 'proof' that Europeans weren't 'straight'. Clearly 'on the edge' more and more, Clough was fined £5,000 in 1988 after *Midweek Sports Special* cameras caught him punching Forest fans Sean O'Hara and James McGowan, who were celebrating on the pitch after Forest's 5–2 victory over Queens Park Rangers. But despite the tabloids offering them thousands to sell their stories, both men accepted Clough's apology, which showed the clout he still possessed. 'We're sorry that we caused Brian any trouble,' said a contrite O'Hara, even though he complained of a ringing ear.

During the decades that have elapsed since the Clough–Taylor partnership fractured, their former players have had plenty of time to take stock. Asked later why he'd signed John McGovern for Hartlepools, Derby, Leeds and Nottingham Forest, Clough barked: 'Because he was cheap.' 'There might be something in that,' McGovern laughed. 'It's sad how it ended. I still believe that Forest could have been successful at the top level for longer if Brian and Pete had remained together and there had been stability at the club.' Clough later admitted that the break-up from Taylor haunted him in the years that followed. From a football point of view, Forest's fall from grace left a void, not that other clubs particularly cared. When Björn Borg quit top-level tennis in 1981, John McEnroe spent several years making pleading phone calls, begging him to return to the fold to renew their rivalry. There was no such sentiment from Forest's rivals. 'They'd had an edge over us, and we weren't displeased that was no longer the case,' recalled Liverpool defender Alan Kennedy. Liverpool would power through the '80s relentlessly, but first, they faced a more unexpected challenge from fifty miles south-west, in Birmingham.

3

THE VILLA

'With a bit of luck, we might qualify for Europe. With a bit more
luck, we might win the FA Cup. And with a lorra luck,
we might win the boat race.'
Ron Saunders, August 1980

Villa Park – February 1981. Latching onto full-back Swain's back heel, Gary Shaw threads a perfect through-ball for Aston Villa skipper Dennis Mortimer to run onto, forty yards from the Liverpool goal. With the packed Holte End looking on, the bearded midfielder glances up at Ray Clemence and slots the ball past him. The scoreline reads 2–0 to the league leaders. It's a classic Villa counter attack goal. The beaming Scouser turns back to celebrate with his teammates. Some of them have imbibed a drop or two of brandy before emerging for the second half, with manager Ron Saunders telling them to 'get some fire in your bellies'. Mortimer believes that victory in front of 47,544 will knock the reigning league champions out of the title race. But Liverpool still only trail Villa by two points, and the free-flowing Ipswich Town are just a single point in arrears, with two games in hand. As they celebrate in the dressing room,

Saunders briefly addresses his team. 'Well done,' he says, with the faintest of smiles, when they're all sat down. 'But remember, there's a tough game at Coventry next week.' There's no danger whatsoever of English football's most understated boss getting carried away. Not even by a season-defining win.

• • •

'But Villa's at home to Liverpool,' protested the crestfallen new Minister for Administrative Affairs and MP for Birmingham East in the opening episode of political comedy *Yes Minister*, which first aired in 1980. Sir Humphrey Appleby had just informed him that he'd need to spend the weekend working on his red boxes, rather than go to the football. The Honourable Jim Hacker may have had an inkling that something was stirring at Villa Park as the new decade dawned, but the football fraternity didn't share his optimism. There was a feeling amongst Villa players that it wasn't just the club but England's second city as a whole that was overlooked. 'It kind of felt out on a limb,' explained striker Peter Withe. 'It wasn't seen as a fashionable football venue or a fashionable city,' agreed midfielder Gordon Cowans. Economically, the early '80s were miserable for Birmingham. As recently as the early '70s, per capita, the city had the highest standard of living in England. But the British Leyland car plant made drastic cutbacks due to shrinking demand and was beset by strikes as workers demanded to be paid more for night work. The Bull Ring, completed in the early '70s, was blighted by vandalism as increasing numbers of units became vacant. A 1980 government report noted that Birmingham was in 'a wretched state … horribly dirty, dispiriting'. 'Some of the city streets were left derelict,' recalled local boy Gary Shaw. A Hollywood existence it most certainly was not, although John Taylor and Nick Rhodes from Duran Duran, who hailed from Birmingham's Hollywood district, went on to find fame and fortune in the '80s.

One reason for Aston Villa's less-than-glamorous image lay in Ron Saunders's obdurate, media-unfriendly image. A prolific goal scorer for Portsmouth in the '50s and early '60s, photographs from his playing days invariably show the powerfully built forward, a champion shot putter as a schoolboy, preparing for aerial combat, his elbows fully weaponised. Only a temperate drinker, Saunders distanced himself from tittle-tattle and team get-togethers, preferring instead to analyse the game and improve his performance. 'Ron was odd. He was a loner,' recalled ex Pompey manager George Smith. 'But he was odd in the way Ramsey or Revie or Clough were. They saw the game differently to others.'

Saunders changed not one jot as a manager. Ask any of his ex-players to describe him and the following adjectives are listed; forensic, controlling, blunt, honest, intense, loyal, tough, single-minded, ruthless. Some also recalled his shyness, and when the occasion called for it, his tinder-dry Birkenhead sense of humour. 'It was Ron's way or no way at all,' recalled Dennis Mortimer, who, despite being Villa skipper under Saunders, never had his boss's phone number. Saunders had his, though. Having played the vast bulk of his career during the maximum-wage era, when players were effectively silent serfs, he had little truck with fellow managers developing their media profile outside the game. He'd roll his eyes and groan when Malcolm Allison whipped out his 'lucky' fedora hat for the cameras. Whilst respecting the success he brought to Nottingham Forest, Saunders disapproved of Clough's media antics. Ipswich manager Bobby Robson, always comfortable before the cameras, reckoned Saunders 'held a personal grudge against every word [he] ever spoke into a microphone.' Though he liked Robson, Saunders told Central TV's Hugh Johns that Robson was 'on the charm offensive so he [could] become the next England manager'. If that really was the case, it worked a treat.

Saunders also mistrusted players who spent their time on the town. After signing from Dundee United in 1976, Andy Gray became a Holte End hero with his physical approach and his bravery in the air. However, Saunders believed that Gray, a regular on the Midlands nightclub scene, was garnering too much attention off the pitch. When Gray won both the Young Player of the Year and Player of the Year awards in '78, Saunders forbade him from going to the ceremonies, claiming that with a League Cup final replay on the horizon, he needed him resting at home, rather than gadding about at a black-tie event in London. The final straw came when Saunders accused the injured Gray of 'cheating' the club over an injury before a European clash with Barcelona in 1978. 'That was us two done. I wasn't playing for him after that,' Gray told me. With that, he headed – unexpectedly – to Molineux to play for a Wolves team that had finished in fifteenth place the previous season. Letters of protest flooded into the *Birmingham Echo*.

Saunders cared not one bit. 'For Ron, it was all about the team,' explained Dennis Mortimer. 'No stars, no individuals, no unnecessary press attention, no pandering to crowd favourites.' It may not have seemed like it at the time, but amidst the 'million-pound madness' of the late '70s and early '80s (Saunders reckoned paying £1 million for a footballer was 'the most ridiculous thing I've ever heard') Aston Villa were arguably the prime beneficiaries, precisely because they chose not to dip their toes in that murky pool. By selling Gray and John Gidman (a crowd-pleasing full-back who loved bombing forward into attack) for a combined £1.6 million, not only had Villa's £475,000 overdraft been wiped out, but a tidy transfer kitty was also now in place. Not that Saunders was willing to let on which signings he had in mind when interviewed by the BBC's Barry Davies at the tail end of the 1979–80 season. 'Presumably you'll use the [Gray] money for signing players?' asked Davies. 'Yes, I'd like to think so,' came the terse reply. 'Which players?' probed Davies. 'Good ones,' replied Saunders with a smirk.

Like several other managers of his generation, not least Brian Clough, Saunders resented the influence – and as he saw it interference – from club directors. Yet, unlike Clough, who could at least lay on a charm offensive when the mood took him, Saunders appeared to actively seek out conflict if he felt his autonomy was being eroded. At Villa, he feuded with director Doug Ellis, who'd been chairman between 1968 and 1975 and who Saunders reckoned was probing too deeply into the playing side of the club. Ellis left the club soon after Saunders complained to other board members about him, though he'd return as chairman for a second time in 1982. With Ellis gone, Saunders's position seemed secure, although as it turned out, his relationship with chairman Ron Bendall wasn't built on the strongest of foundations either. Nonetheless in 1980, he was granted a lucrative testimonial with neighbours Birmingham City after six years at the club. To publicise the event, he appeared in an almost-other-worldly TV advert with actor Paul Henry, playing his role as the hapless Benny from Central TV soap *Crossroads*, which was set in a Birmingham motel. Saunders goes in goal as Crossroads's hapless handyman fluffs his penalties horribly. 'I was amazed when I saw it,' recalled Gordon Cowans, 'as the boss didn't tend to indulge in clowning around like that.'

I witnessed at first-hand Ron Saunders's 'otherness' when I encountered him in Birmingham city centre in 1998. Walking through town, I spotted Saunders sat on a bench, reading a local paper as he waited for his wife to finish her shopping. It was an incongruous scene. Swarms of shoppers, a good deal of whom were probably Villa fans, sauntered past, not even giving him a second glance. By then Saunders had been out of the game for over a decade. 'Hello, Mr Saunders,' I offered tentatively. Glancing up, he replied unsmilingly: 'Hello, son.' I explained that I was a freelance football writer and asked him if he might be willing to speak to me. I was unaware that Saunders hadn't spoken to the press for years. 'Not a chance, son. Anyone who has ever met me will tell you that I'm very boring, with nothing of any interest to say,' came the response. There was a slight twinkle in his eye. As I made to leave, he said: 'Look at this,' pointing to a photograph of Villa chairman Doug Ellis espousing about the state of the game. 'Chairmen reckon it's all about them. Him especially. I'm better off out of all of that.' I tried to keep the conversation going, but the seam was exhausted. Saunders buried his head back in his paper, and my brief interaction with the only manager to bring the title to Villa since 1910 was over. It occurred to me, though, that Saunders had probably given more away on that sunny May afternoon than he ever he did in his buttoned-up television interviews in the '70s and '80s.

• • •

Step by step, and with the help of talent scout Tony Barton, Saunders pieced together his team, plucking powerful defender Allan Evans from Dunfermline and Des Bremner from Hibernian. At twenty-seven, Bremner thought he'd missed his chance of the big time, but Saunders told him 'the best things come to those who wait'. Saunders was always baffled as to why his Tartan trio of Evans,

Bremner and Ken McNaught – signed from Everton – only won four Scotland caps between them. Goalkeeper Jimmy Rimmer was brought in from Arsenal. 'I was never made to feel welcome at Highbury,' he said. 'I was regarded as a bit of an outsider.' Saunders saw in Rimmer a kindred spirit, and he confided more in him than any other Villa player. He wasn't afraid to take a calculated risk on previously underachieving players. Tony Morley, a talented yet frustratingly inconsistent winger with Burnley, was twenty-five when Saunders signed him. 'Remember to play as I tell you, son,' he said, with his arm around Morley's shoulder, 'or you'll be in the reserves, OK?' he said, softly, in his passive-aggressive way. Of all the Villa players in that era, it was Morley who would be subjected most to Saunders's brand of kidology.

The youth team also proved bountiful, with midfielder Gordon Cowans, defenders Gary Williams and Colin Gibson and striker Gary Shaw making his breakthrough at the tail end of the 1979–80 season. The routine was always the same from the manager. An arm around the shoulder, a quiet word in the ear, and a quick reminder of the player's role. 'Saunders rarely shouted,' Gary Shaw explained, 'but you always knew where you stood with him.' This was mainly because Saunders's main work came on the training pitch at Bodymoor Heath. Stripped to his waist in the close season, the powerfully built Saunders 'was a fine figure of a man', as Tony Morley said. In his office, he had pairs of dumbbells and grippers, which he'd use when he had a spare moment or when he was discussing contractual issues. 'It was a deliberate show of strength from him,' laughed Gordon Cowans. He still trained as if he were a player, running regularly in local parks with a bin liner under his tracksuit. He set about making his players the fittest of their generation. With cross-country runs in the July heat a staple part of pre-season training, Saunders dotted his coaches around the Heath to ensure there was no slackening off. In the middle, there was the man himself, armed with his clipboard and pencil, missing nothing with that steely gaze of his. 'Call yourself professional footballers?' was his taunt to any stragglers. 'Looking a bit green around the gills there, son,' he'd smirk if any player was preparing to vomit. Occasionally, Saunders mixed things up and had the Villa players sprinting up the steep banks of a disused quarry near Bodymoor Heath. 'Better out than in eh, son?' he'd chide if anyone actually spewed up. Yet despite being drilled and, in some cases, almost killed in training, Villa tailed in a disappointing seventh in the 1979–80 campaign, nowhere near European football, let alone champions Liverpool, who finished fourteen points ahead of Saunders's men. In the final game of the season, Villa were demolished 4–1 at Anfield. There was little sign of the transformation that was to come. But as his team sloped off, Dennis Mortimer noticed with some annoyance that Liverpool players tossed the trophy to one another on their lap of honour 'like they expected to win it every year. The fire inside me started to burn.'

Saunders added the final piece to his jigsaw during the close season. In private, Saunders told club-record signing (£500,000) Peter Withe that with him in the side, Villa 'could win the league.' 'I quickly found out that Ron never spoke unnecessarily,' Withe said, 'and I discovered that he absolutely meant what he said.' Villa had struggled to score goals in the previous campaign, following the departure of Andy Gray and Brian Little's ongoing injury problems, which saw him retire from the game at the end of the 1980–81 season. English football in the early '80s could have turned out differently had Saunders landed his initial target, Dumbarton's Graeme Sharp, who went on to win medals galore at Goodison Park. Withe turned down Everton. 'Sharpy is a bit younger than me,' Withe told me. 'Perhaps he'd have clicked with Gary Shaw straight away or perhaps, which is what happened at Everton, he'd have taken a few years to adjust to the game in England. Anyway, our respective moves turned out pretty well for both of us.'

• • •

On the eve of Villa's first match of the season, Saunders gathered the squad and offered up a challenge. 'Sixty points would give us a great shot at the title. Reckon you're up to it?' he asked his players. To a man, they nodded. Villa made a fast start to the season, securing seven points out of eight from their opening four games. The Withe–Shaw partnership clicked. Although occasionally dismissed as an archetypal English battering-ram forward, the bearded Withe, with claret and blue sweatbands on either wrist, as Shaw said, 'had a deft touch for a big fella. He could hold the ball up, and he could also flick the ball onto me with either his head or his chest. He soaked up a huge amount of punishment and allowed me to play.' All was well in the Villa camp, until they travelled to Bobby Robson's Ipswich Town, laden with international players from the United Kingdom and Holland, in early September and lost 1–0.

'In head-to-head encounters, we always fancied ourselves to come on top, because we retained possession well and were more skilful,' striker Paul Mariner told me. 'But Villa were more consistent and resilient. Over forty-two matches, that's key.' With overlapping full-backs Mick Mills and George Burley surging forwards, and Dutchmen Frans Thijssen and Arnold Mühren in midfield, Ipswich's angled passing game was a delight, and they were fast and fluid on the eye. Yet with Terry Butcher in central defence and Paul

Mariner up front, they weren't lacking physical strength either. 'We had a good blend, with clever forwards like Eric Gates and Alan Brazil up front,' Mühren said. Ipswich lacked depth in their squad, which proved costly as they fought for the league, the FA Cup and UEFA Cup in 1980–81.

Following the defeat at Portman Road, Villa also lost to Everton before embarking on a ten-match unbeaten league run. After an indifferent spell in November and December, they used a 1–0 Boxing Day victory over Stoke City as a springboard to another ten-match unbeaten run. Across the pitch, Villa's partnerships flourished, whether it was the stable and secure McNaught–Evans partnership in central defence, the Withe–Shaw partnership up front or the midfield trio of Mortimer–Bremner–Cowans. 'Shape, keep the shape,' Saunders demanded, his iron fist punching his thigh. Adding the dash of pace and unpredictability to this most solid of teams was Tony Morley, or 'Anthony', as Saunders often called him. Saunders delighted in keeping Morley – a boyhood Everton fan – on his toes, whether by threatening to drop him for key matches or fining him for his impudent celebrations. In the lead-up to Villa's match at Goodison Park in February, Saunders tossed him a yellow bib in training, usually a sign that a player wouldn't be in the first XI, because he reckoned Morley would be 'showing off in front of [his] family and friends at Goodison'. But on the Saturday, Morley was in and scored a blistering goal. Following a superb swivel and pass from Gary Shaw, Morley ran hard and fast at the Everton defence before thundering a shot past Jim Arnold from fully thirty yards. The eagle-eyed Saunders noted that as he celebrated with teammates, Morley stuck his Vs up in the direction of his manager. It cost 'Anthony' a £100 fine.

'It was his way of keeping my feet on the ground,' laughed Morley, 'but £100 was a fair bit of money to a footballer in those days.' One unexpected beneficiary of Morley's – and Aston Villa's – rise to prominence was Central TV commentator Hugh Johns. 'It was an incredible decade for Midlands football,' Johns told me, his smoky baritone voice as rich as ever, 'with Derby winning the league in '72, Forest in '78, and then Villa in '81. Johns's ability to fire off descriptions of goals like verbal bullets remained as potent as ever. Perhaps the finest example of 'Johns-speak' was his summing up of Peter Withe's towering header in a 3–3 draw with Manchester United in March 1981. 'Withe. Goal. Beautiful. One–nothing.' A Tony Morley cracker against Arsenal, following an interchange of passes with Gary Shaw in a 1–1 draw at an icy Villa Park in December, was also given the Johns treatment: 'Morley. Shaw. Morley. Goal. Beautiful goal. Constructed by Morley. And finished by Morley.' Johns found Saunders 'hilariously unquotable'. Glancing around to ensure that his wife Joan couldn't hear, he informed me that 'getting anything out of Ron was a bit like getting shit out of a rocking horse. He took delight in giving nothing away.' On one occasion, Johns believed he'd pierced Saunders's armour. After viewing ITV's *The Big Match*, Saunders sought out Johns: 'I enjoyed your commentary of Morley's goal, Hugh,' Saunders said with a faint smile. 'Very atmospheric.' When Johns attempted to chat to Saunders about Morley's sparkling form, the drawbridge came up. 'He could be back in the reserves next week,' snapped Saunders. At no point did Johns get the feeling that Saunders was joking.

• • •

With the home side facing Ipswich Town in April's 'title decider', thousands of fans who couldn't gain access to the rammed Villa

Park gathered on a hill that overlooked Villa Park, just as they had for the packed-out Liverpool game two months earlier. From outside Aston Hall, they could peek between the Holte End and one of stadium designer Archibald Leitch's masterpieces, the Trinity Road Stand. Their team froze on the big occasion. Like in the FA Cup third-round clash between the two sides in January at Portman Road, which Ipswich won 1–0, Villa appeared hesitant. The two goals were, by Villa's high standards, shambolic. Ken McNaught's loose back pass and goalkeeper Jimmy Rimmer's reticence to collect the ball saw Mariner nip in and Brazil slot the ball home. In the second half, Eric Gates fired home into the top corner and, despite a Gary Shaw goal, Villa appeared to have blown it. Villa players certainly formed the opinion that Ipswich players felt they had all but won the title. 'We could hear them singing and dancing next door, cock-a-hoop like they'd won the league already,' Gordon Cowans told me. 'Saunders was rarely one to respond, but he looked at us calmly and said: "Let's see who's champions at the end of the season."' There is, however, another side to the story. Just four days earlier, Ipswich had been defeated at Villa Park by Manchester City in the FA Cup semi-final, thanks to an extra time Paul Power free kick. For Arnold Mühren, the celebrations were simply a way of letting off steam and exorcising the ghosts of the previous Saturday. 'We never took anything for granted,' Arnold Muhren told me, 'and it's natural for players to shout and cheer after winning such a big match.' Saunders asked the BBC's Barry Davies afterwards whether, with four matches remaining (Ipswich had five games left and were now a point behind Villa), he'd 'bet against us'? Ipswich capitulated, losing the East Anglian derby to Norwich City and then going down 2–0 at Portman Road to Arsenal ('We Are the Champions' was blasted out over the Tannoy system prior to kick-off), who were chasing a

European spot. When the Aston Villa players travelled to Highbury to play Arsenal in their final match of the season, they knew that a point would be enough to secure the title, assuming Ipswich prevailed against struggling Middlesbrough at Ayresome Park.

Precious little fazed Saunders's men. Their *Shoot!* profiles were testimony to that. The half-dozen players who participated professed to having no superstitions, enjoyed TV programmes like the *Kenny Everett Video Show* and *The Two Ronnies*, and their favourite meals were steak or egg and chips, washed down with a lager. Gary Shaw liked actress Victoria Principal (Pam Ewing off *Dallas*) and Tony Morley enjoyed Clint Eastwood movies. Only Kenny Swain pushed the boat out a little. He read *The Observer*, watched current affairs programme *Horizon* and liked news presenter Sue Lawley. Their contact details have remained virtually unchanged for the best part of twenty years, and they still enjoy one another's company on golf days (often at the Belfry) and on anniversaries of Villa's successes in the early '80s. They're just regular Villans, and always were.

But they were distinctly frazzled by the events of 2 May. For a manager who prided himself on organisation and routine, Ron Saunders miscalculated in the build-up to the Arsenal match. Reasoning that the players would be more relaxed if they spent the Friday night at home, the Villa coach set off early next morning and quickly got snarled up in traffic on the M6, partly due to the fact that the Challenge Cup final between Widnes and Hull KR was at Wembley that afternoon and tens of thousands of rugby fans headed south. Ken McNaught must have fumed, as according to his *Shoot!* profile, he got intensely annoyed by queuing. There was no police escort until it was too late, and the Villa coach spent the latter part of the journey crawling down the hard shoulder. Add in around 20,000 Villa fans about to pack out Highbury's open Clock End (not including those ticketless Villa supporters who travelled to north London simply to party), and it was little wonder that the coach arrived in N5 with less than thirty minutes to go before kick-off. The streets around Highbury were rammed, and the crowd was over 57,000. 'Saunders always liked it calm in the build-up,' Tony Morley recalled,

> with no fussing about tickets for fans or family or anything like that. But that day we got changed quickly and pretty much got straight out there for a quick warm-up. Then bloody Pelé appeared, and the pitch was covered in coloured balloons, which was another massive distraction. What the 'ell was he doing there? The crowd was going wild.

The Brazilian maestro was there to market Ingersoll Atari, which was sponsoring that afternoon's match. In the match-day programme, Pelé grins manically at the camera as he plays the Championship Soccer cartridge game, consisting of three red dots, three blue dots and a yellow dot in the middle.

Despite the Rémy Martin being handed around by Saunders in the dressing room to calm the players nerves, Villa froze on their big day. At half-time, they were 2–0 down thanks to goals from Willie Young and Brian McDermott. The news from Ayresome Park brought no respite either; Ipswich were 1–0 up courtesy of Paul Mariner's header. The mood amongst Villa players was subdued. Not only had Ipswich won all three matches against Villa that season, they'd also cleaned up at the players awards evenings, with Frans Thijssen and John Wark winning the Football Writers Association Player of the Year and the PFA Player of the Year awards respectively. It was torture for the Villa players and for the hordes of supporters decked out in claret and blue, many of whom had transistor radios clapped to their ears that afternoon. Salvation lay in the unlikely form of balding Yugoslav striker Boško Janković, whose two second-half goals for Middlesbrough, which gave 'Boro a 2–1 win, changed the course of both Ipswich and Villa's seasons entirely. 'Big' Boško, who sadly died in 1993, never seemed overly interested in being a highly unlikely Villa cult hero ('I met him once and he didn't give a monkeys,' recalled Gary Shaw), but a clutch of fifty-something Villa fans still celebrate 'Big Boško Day' if 2 May coincides with a Villa match. It's a niche event.

As news filtered through to Villa fans about events in the north-east, first of one goal and then of the other, the spectacle at the Clock End became truly astonishing, especially when viewed from a modern-day perspective, where a buzzin' away allocation is considered anything upwards of 3,000. Villa were labouring around the halfway line, fruitlessly trying to claw back the 2–0 deficit when, as Dennis Mortimer put it to me, 'the first rumble of thunder began'. Initially, small knots of the 20,000 supporters began pogoing up and down, and the movement rapidly spread across the rest of the Clock End. On the second occasion, the entire terrace erupted with joy and celebration because with Ipswich now losing, there was no way back for Bobby Robson's team. 'It was an explosion of relief, more than anything,' recalled Tony Morley. 'It was so spontaneous.' Throughout, the model of zen-like calm in the dugout was Ron Saunders, whose facial expression changed not one iota. The Buddha of the Touchline. When the final whistle sounded at Highbury, thousands of supporters flooded the pitch, and both sets of jubilant players (Arsenal finished third and qualified for the UEFA Cup) hared off to the sanctuary of the dressing room. 'Finally, Saunders let go, for a bit anyway,' said Tony Morley. Saunders offered champagne and King Edward cigars to his players and finally beamed for the cameras, despite complaining that his 'teeth are a bit loose today'. When the Villa team presented the First Division trophy to their fans the following day on a mizzly Birmingham afternoon, he went even further, pogoing up and down with joy in front of the city's mayoress. Still, Saunders couldn't help himself, setting targets for the following season and insisting that the players target the European Cup. And despite the copious amounts of alcohol that had been glugged, they heeded Saunders's advice. But trouble was brewing at the top.

• • •

'We needed two or three new players. Every title-winning side needs them to keep things fresh,' Saunders later explained. But when he approached the Villa board during the close season with a view to strengthening the squad, he was rebuffed, although he eventually signed midfielder Andy Blair from Coventry City. Chairman Ron Bendall also casually mentioned the fact that the board were reviewing the term of Saunders's rolling three-year contract, which meant that if and when he was fired (a seemingly absurd notion given the club were title winners), his contract would be paid up in full. When Saunders asked for clarification, none was forthcoming. Saunders hid all this from his players. Matters would soon come to a head, but for now, Saunders prepared his men for a distinctly unvarnished European Cup adventure.

The mood in the camp was positive. Nottingham Forest's achievements were a huge inspiration. Gordon Cowans said: 'Forest were a smaller outfit than us, but with an exceptional manager and excellent team spirit, they surpassed themselves.' The first round was the usual mix of minnows (reigning European champions Liverpool defeated Finnish side Oulu 7–0 over two legs), dark horses and giants of the European game, like star-laden Juventus, and Bayern Munich. But, as Tony Morley explains: 'We were English champions, and we feared no one.'

The first-round draw, which pitted Villa against Valur Reykjavik, afforded the players the opportunity to witness the spectacular volcanic landscape on the approach to the second leg. Villa had won the first leg 5–0 at Villa Park. 'It looked like we were landing on the surface of the moon,' Gary Shaw recalled. They faced more earthly concerns in Iceland, as an icy gale swept across the tiny stadium. There was also the pungent aroma from the nearby fish factory, which made several players heave. They won 2–0 on the day. 'The glamour of the European Cup, boys, eh?' deadpanned Saunders.

The memories of playing Dynamo Berlin away in the second round remain vivid for the players, just as they do for their Forest counterparts who played there a year earlier. Training in the empty Friedrich-Ludwig-Jahn-Sportpark stadium 'you could hear guard dogs barking', recalled Gary Shaw. The guards, armed with guns, watched us train from their watchtowers. It was like something out of an old Cold War film.' On the night, with a massive military presence in the 25,000 crowd, Tony Morley rose to the occasion in arguably his finest display in a Villa shirt. After crunching home an unstoppable volley after five minutes, he proceeded to score one of the European Cup's great individual goals shortly before the end of the match. Picking up the ball inside his own box, the confident Scouser pounded the full length of the pitch ('It was full of ruts and holes, so I had to keep it close') and slotted the ball past Dynamo keeper Rudwaleit to give Villa a 2–1 win. Morley then ran over to the Villa dugout and stuck two fingers up at Ron Saunders. It wasn't a V for Victory sign, either. 'Ron had called me a flash git in training the day before, so I vented,' recalled Morley. 'He let it pass until we got back to the UK, and then he bollocked me. "Those were the two best goals I've ever seen," he said. "And by the way, you're fined two weeks' wages."' Two weeks later, Morley's Berlin double assumed greater significance after Villa tamely lost the second leg 1–0 in Birmingham. By then, though, Saunders was gone.

The players were astonished when, in the midst of another tough training session on Bodymoor Heath, they saw their notoriously tough manager sink to his haunches, doubled up in pain. One of the Villa staff quickly drove Saunders home. It was the last training session he'd ever take. Within two days, Saunders had resigned. Talks over the nature of the manager's contract had stalled, with the highly principled Saunders arguing that altering it to a standard three-year contract meant that his position was far less bulletproof. It also made him less financially secure, something he'd always been acutely aware of, growing up as one of nine children at the tail end of the Great Depression. His players were stunned but not surprised, given the rumblings that had emanated from the boardroom. Some let him know how they felt by depositing bottles of brandy in the milk crate outside his front door in the weeks that followed. Two weeks later, he was unveiled as the new Birmingham City boss. 'Of all the places...' muttered Gary Shaw, 'but Ron took the view that football was first and foremost a profession and he had his family to feed.' By going to St Andrews, he wouldn't need to uproot them. Not that Villa fans viewed events objectively. When Birmingham faced Villa in the second city derby a few weeks later, Villa fans serenaded him with a variation of a popular early-'80s chant. To the tune of the British Airways advert, they sang: 'We'll piss all over you, Ron Saunders, Ron Saunders...'

Replacing Saunders was the softly spoken chief scout Tony Barton, who'd discovered players like Gordon Cowans. Less of a zealot than Saunders, Barton was a friendly face at a time of turbulence at the club. Barton always seemed to have the persona of a caretaker manager, but at this particular time, he was just the job. 'He didn't need to change anything when it came to the European Cup run,' said Dennis Mortimer. 'He carried on Saunders's work.' Barton oversaw Villa's daunting quarter-final clash with Dynamo Kyiv in March '82. The Soviet authorities refused to inform Villa of the venue for the match until the last minute, with the match switched due to the lingering winter. 'The industrial city of Simferopol, 400 miles south of Kyiv, was eventually chosen. Simferopol's Hotel Moscow, Gordon Cowans told me, 'was hardly The Ritz. It wouldn't have had a one-star rating in the UK.' The questionable hospitality was designed to throw Villa off their stride. Tony Morley ticked off the gripes on his fingers: 'Bowl of chicken soup with the feathers still on it, cockroaches inside the bread rolls, the windows not fitting the frames properly, and [he laughed], big Withey sleeping in a tiny fold-up bed.' Then there were the men in dark suits siting in the hotel dining room, observing the Villa players eating and chatting. None of that prevented Villa from grabbing an invaluable goalless draw. A comfortable 2–0 home win two weeks later saw Villa into the semi-finals, a feat made all the more laudable by the fact that Liverpool had failed to overcome eastern-European opposition after losing to Bulgarian champions CSKA Sofia.

A solitary Tony Morley goal at Villa Park gave his side a slender 1–0 advantage going into the semi-final second leg against Belgian champions Anderlecht. Villa were almost robbed of a final appearance after a running battle between rival fans at the Stade Emile Versé in Brussels. Three years before the Heysel disaster, the inadequacies of Belgian policing were evident. By then, English players were highly attuned to sensing when trouble was afoot. 'Segregation – consisting of pieces of red tape between fans – was a joke,' explained Gary Shaw. Riot police, with the early summer sunshine glinting off their plastic helmets and shields, were stationed behind both goals mobilised after a Villa supporter – a soldier on leave from Germany – invaded the pitch, claiming he was trying to escape the fighting on the terraces. Though Villa clung on for the required 0–0 draw, Anderlecht lodged an official complaint with FIFA and requested that the game be replayed, claiming that they were poised to score when play was stopped. A week later, FIFA decided that Villa would be allowed to face Bayern Munich, conquerors of CSKA Sofia, in the final.

As kick-off approached at the Feyenoord Stadium in Rotterdam on 26 May 1982, the atmosphere amongst Villa players remained relaxed. 'The pressure was really on Bayern,' recalled Tony Morley. 'We had huge respect for Paul Breitner, Klaus Augenthaler, and Karl Heinz Rummenigge, but we thought we could do well.' The game was hardly a classic. Tony Barton – bemused to see that in the official programme, Ron Saunders was still named as manager – was forced into making a substitution after just nine minutes, when he replaced the injured Jimmy Rimmer with Nigel Spink. For long spells, Villa's defence soaked up waves of Bayern attacks. Villa players appeared drained (a spot of late-night revelry at a local house of ill repute might not have helped), and Tony Morley recalls: 'Some of the lads were struggling because they had brand-new Nike boots on, which gave them blisters.' With sixty-seven minutes gone, Villa launched into (rare) attack mode. Morley twisted past defender Hans Weiner on the edge of the Bayern box and drilled the ball across the penalty area. Peter Withe recalled: 'Augenthaler had temporarily lost me.

When the ball came, I went to side foot it but scuffed it instead after the ball bobbled.' Withe called the shot his 'magnificent miss-hit', a shot that if hit properly would probably have been saved by Müller. Instead, it crept into the corner, via the post. His teammates reckon he shinned it. 'No I never. No way,' laughed Withe, 'but the net stopped me playing a one-two off the post.'

Villa endured several heart-stopping moments as Rummenigge went close, but the final whistle sparked jubilant celebrations from Villa players and their 15,000 travelling fans. Tony Barton recalled: 'It's the only thing I've ever won as a manager, but if you're only going to win one pot, make it the biggest of all.' After flying back to Birmingham, the Villa players enjoyed showing the trophy off (there were no replicas in those days) to their mates in various hostelries. Tony Morley grabbed it and drove up to Liverpool. 'I got fined for taking it, but I'd promised my pals they could see it if we won.' And at least it didn't get dented, like it did on Liverpool's watch on a couple of occasions...

Despite Villa's heroics, there remains a lingering feeling that the club and the players were not afforded the respect they deserved. Of Villa's European Cup final squad, only Allan Evans and Peter Withe (who didn't start a game) were called up for the 1982 World Cup. Gary Shaw missed out, despite several promising displays for the Under-21s and fine displays as Villa also won the 1982 European Super Cup. 'I felt my time would come,' Shaw told me, but a knee injury sustained in 1983 meant that, by twenty-five, Shaw's top-class career was effectively over. Within five years, Aston Villa were relegated, and many players departed under a cloud. Disgruntled supporters sang: 'We won the league, we won the cup, then Ronnie Bendall fucked it up.'

That may have been largely true, but it was Doug Ellis, chairman for a second time by 1982, who stood accused of failing to properly honour Villa's heroes. The office I met him in at Villa Park in 2005, with its striking claret and blue carpet and old oak table, oozed tradition and finesse. Ellis took pride in explaining who was who in the raft of old photographs that adorned the walls. Aston Villa's is a rich history. It was Ellis, who made his pile in the '60s selling package holidays to Spain, who sacked Tony Barton in 1984. 'He was my first sacking in my second spell as chairman. It was sad, given what he'd achieved. He took it well though. Not all of them were that amenable,' smiled 'Deadly' Doug, hirer and firer *non pareil* amongst '80s chairmen. Ellis had missed the European Cup final. Returning home from his holiday in Barbados, a porter's strike at Heathrow meant he missed his connection to Rotterdam.

I told Ellis that I thought it strange there was no visible celebration of the club's achievements in the early '80s. 'Move forwards; don't look backwards,' Ellis replied airily when I posed the question. We glanced at one another. 'Those who control the present, control the past?' I suggested. 'Ah, but those who control the past, control the future, which is excellent news! See – I know that Orwell quote too,' laughed the still-sprightly 86-year-old, who sold the club to American Randy Lerner a few months later. Perhaps a statue or a rebranded stand would simply have been too painful a reminder for Ellis that the class of '81 and '82 was as good as it was likely to ever get for his club.

4

THE SKY-BLUE SOAP OPERA

'You can't plan in football; it's day to day.'

PETER SWALES, 1981

The Shay – January 1980. 'Defeat will not be the end of the
world, but it will be bloody close to it,' says the under-pressure
Malcolm Allison before Manchester City's tricky-looking FA Cup
third-round clash with Fourth Division Halifax Town. Five months
into his second spell as manager at Maine Road, big-spending
City sit sixteenth in Division One, and fans are growing restless.
The last thing Allison's team need is a visit to the oval-shaped Shay,
with its open terracing and sodden pitch. 'It's lovely and cold up
here today,' says their manager George Kirkby. With a foreboding
backdrop of derelict factories and grey skies, the atmosphere feels
almost post-apocalyptic. City labour in the mud. Midfielder Steve
Daley – the country's most expensive footballer at £1,437,500 – fires
a shot narrowly wide, but City create little else. Then, on seventy-six
minutes, Scottish midfielder Paul Hendrie slams home a shot past
City goalkeeper Joe Corrigan, and that's how the score remains.
Remarkably, it's TV hypnotist Ronald Markham (aka 'Romark')

who claims the victory is down to him. Not only has he hypnotised some of the Halifax players in the lead-up to kick-off, but four years earlier, he placed a 'curse' on Malcolm Allison when the pair fell out. 'It's all about the mind of Romark,' he says, tapping his head in front of bewildered journalists. Allison's reign is unravelling, and soon, a groundbreaking documentary will only add to the air of farce enveloping Maine Road.

•   •   •

City's reckless spending spree in the late '70s and early '80s mirrored Allison's own profligacy when it came to money. Former City star Rodney Marsh recounted the story of how, on a champagne and caviar fuelled night out in the early '70s, a waiter nervously warned Allison that the bill had already reached £1,000. Lighting up a cigar and airily waving his hand in the air, Allison responded: 'I'd expect nothing else. Don't stop until it's gone above £2,000.' The man who spent much of the '70s as an ITV panellist and a newspaper columnist was a gambler who ended his days in poverty, living in a warden-controlled flat. In the '70s, an inverse law applied to Allison: the larger his 'Big Mal' persona became, the more his powers as a football manager waned. After leaving City (for the first time) in 1973, Allison was powerless to stop First Division Crystal Palace falling into Division Three, and subsequent spells at Galatasaray and Third Division Plymouth Argyle failed to reignite Allison's managerial career. In 1979, Manchester City chairman Peter Swales came knocking, desperate for the (once) talismanic figure who'd coached City to the First Division title, FA Cup, League Cup and Cup Winners' Cup in the late '60s and early '70s to breathe new life into a team that was mired in mid-table in Division One.

Like so many football directors in that era, the bewigged, Cuban-heeled Swales was a self-made man and dead proud of it. He first came to prominence during the 1950s through the White and Swales electronics rental chain. The televising of the Queen's coronation in 1953 and the arrival of commercial television two years later had established huge demand for television sets, which were hugely expensive and temperamental. The company soon moved into white goods as well, ending up with fifteen stores in the Cheshire and Manchester area. Swales sold out to Thorn for £500,000 in 1968, and five years later, acquired a majority shareholding in Manchester City. First and foremost, he was keen to cock a snook at Manchester United. Initially the signs were promising, when United were relegated to Division Two in 1974 and City won the League Cup in 1976. City finished Division One runners-up in 1976–77, but they then lost their impetus. Enter Malcolm Allison. Allison and Swales believed that, in order to match the large crowds that regularly filled Old Trafford, City needed a team laden with high-profile stars. The data suggested this was a risky strategy. Between the 1979–80 and 1982–83 campaigns, 6 million supporters a season stopped going to matches across all four divisions, and not entirely unrelatedly, the country was in the midst of its worst economic recession since the '30s, with Manchester one of the worst-hit cities of all. The textiles industry all but disappeared, and large areas were left derelict. Moss Side itself was beset by social unrest, including gun crime and drug problems. Allison's comment: 'It's my job at City to attract big-ticket players, which will then attract the fans...' was reasonable enough, but in an era of economic hardship for many, his prediction that 50,000 crowds would flock to Maine Road was pie in the sky. Nonetheless, the lavish spending began. First to arrive was Crystal Palace teenage midfielder Steve Mackenzie (yet to make his first-team debut) for £250,000, and Preston North End forward Michael Robinson, for £750,000.

He later found fame in Spain after he retired from playing by hosting cult Canal+ shows *El día después* and *Informe Robinson*, which celebrated the culture and passion of Spanish football. Such was his enduring popularity across Spain that when 'Robin' (as he was nicknamed in Spain) passed away in 2020 from cancer, tennis star Rafael Nadal commented: 'We woke up with the sad news of the death of one of our own. You were the one who always made us happy about sport.' When I met with the suntanned former City starlet in Southport in 2008 on one of his trips home, his famous toothy grin was in evidence in between drags on his Marlboro Light and sips from his beer glass as we sat outside looking at the sea. The Robinson smile disappeared when he discussed his tortuous spell at Maine Road.

Already tipped off that City were interested in signing him, Robinson met Allison at Deepdale. Allison told Robinson how it had been an 'education' to watch the Dutch in the '70s. 'Mal wanted Total Football, with players able to adapt to changing roles within the team,' recalled Robinson. Introducing Total Football at Maine Road might be a tall order, the player told Allison, given their league position. Allison swatted aside Robinson's doubts. 'Just you wait and see what happens,' he said, before telling him about his renumeration package. 'I went from £30 per week at Preston to £300 at City. That was before win bonuses. Not that there were many of them. I never asked for that amount. I'd have been happy on £100 a week!' Previously, Robinson had asked Allison what was in his carrier bag. Allison told him he'd find out later. After forty-five minutes, a club official popped in and told Allison that some journalists would like to speak with him. 'Immediately, Mal reached for the bag and pulled out his cigars and a bottle of unchilled champagne. "Have you got a glass, please?" he asked. One was brought for him, and he wouldn't meet the press until he'd sparked up and filled his glass with champers.' Big Mal was different from Malcolm Allison. 'He was pure Jekyll and Hyde,' Robinson explained.

The forward was soon joined at Maine Road by the country's most expensive footballer – Steve Daley. Liverpool manager Bob Paisley was puzzled. 'So Steve Daley is worth three Kenny Dalglishes, is he?' No one remains more baffled about the fee than Daley himself. Speaking after one of his after-dinner stand-up routines in 2004, he explained: 'City appeared to be bidding against themselves. No one else was in for me...' Daley was self-depreciating about his less-than-glorious spell in Moss Side. 'The first time I did a dinner there, I was dead nervous. I told the audience at Maine Road: "I bet you never thought you'd pay to see me again."' The joke could have backfired, but the audience was kind and lapped up Daley's act. Forty-four years ago, they weren't so charitable. Daley's desperately disappointing eighteen-month spell at Maine Road became a byword for failure, with *The Observer* claiming in 2010 that he was the 'biggest waste of money in football history'. An energetic midfielder with an eye for goal, Daley had been on the fringes of the England squad in the late '70s, and just before he put pen to paper for City, England boss Ron Greenwood told him he'd figure heavily in his future plans. 'I never heard from Ron again,' Daley admitted. Daley made his first-team bow in a 1–0 home defeat to Southampton. At Wolves, Daley had flourished in a triple axis with Willie Carr and Kenny Hibbitt. 'We knew each other's game inside and out,' he said. But at City, the midfield was in a constant state of flux, with Allison regularly chopping and changing the side.

Allison was starting to tap in to a rich seam of young local talent, which included the Bennett brothers – Gary and David – goal-keeper Alex Williams, midfielder Clive Wilson and forward Roger Palmer. David Bennett and Roger Palmer made their first-team breakthroughs under Allison. 'We were all born within a two-mile radius of Moss Side. The area was becoming more multicultural,' Gary Bennett told me. 'West Brom had the "three degrees", but there were five of us black players coming through at City.' It was well known that the younger players adored the charismatic Allison. 'A great man,' is how Gary Bennett still describes him. Yet disgruntle-ment amongst supporters grew quickly, especially as fan-favourites Peter Barnes and Gary Owen had been sold to West Bromwich during the close season to fund the Robinson–Daley–Mackenzie transfers. Talk in the stands quickly turned to who exactly sanc-tioned the move for Daley – Allison or Swales. Allison claimed to have spoken to Wolves boss John Barnwell and agreed a fee in the region of £500,000 in April '79. Daley said he was aware of City's interest for a couple of months prior to the move, but there was a delay when Barnwell was injured in a car crash. During this period, Swales contacted the Wolves board to ensure the deal got over the line, and – in Daley's words – 'hey presto, [the] fee gets hiked up to £1.4 million'. In later years, Swales and Allison blamed one another. On BBC TV's *Match of the Seventies*, Allison said: 'Swales told me he was a financial genius, and to let him deal with the money side. So I said OK.' On the same day that Daley arrived, City also shelled out £300,000 on Wrexham's Bobby Shinton, who ended up playing just five matches for City.

For Robinson and Daley, their big-money moves quickly became a nightmare. Shoved out on the wing by Allison, Robinson bought himself a four-bedroom detached house in Hale and pretty quickly I had rubber neckers turning up to gawp through my windows. It was an upside-down house, with the bedrooms downstairs and the living area upstairs. Whatever time of day it was, the curtains remained shut. I went to training and then hid at home. I hated my life.

I asked Robinson what advice Allison gave him. 'None, except to carry on working hard.' After one frustrating season at Maine Road, Robinson headed down south to Brighton for £500,000, where he became one of the best-paid players in the country, this time on a £1,000 weekly wage. 'Again, I never actually asked for it,' he laughed.

Daley, who'd signed a ten-year contract worth £500 per week, felt the pressure immediately. Teammate Nicky Reid – a full-back – explained: 'When a club signs a million-pound player, fans expect that player to do million-pound things.' Daley never did. 'The harder I tried, the worse things got,' he admitted. The abuse began. Disturbing letters were sent to Daley's home. There were threatening phone calls. Barracking from a minority of City fans. At away games he was showered with copper coins. 'That's all you're fucking worth, Daley,' fans shouted. His family no longer went to matches, and Daley stopped buying a daily newspaper, fearful of what he might read about himself. Then came the catastrophic FA Cup third-round loss to Halifax and Allison's fateful reacquaintance with Romark, the portly TV hypnotist with a bad combover, the day after Allison predicted that City had the 'mentality of a cup side.' At Palace in 1976 during their FA Cup run which saw them reach the semi-finals, Allison had reached out to Romark after seeing him work wonders in his stage show, helping audience members overcome long-held phobias of spiders, heights and rats, to name but three. 'Imagine how powerful that level of positivity could be amongst my players,' explained a fully convinced Allison. One youngster, future England left-back Kenny Sansom (then sixteen) was roped into a one-to-one by Malcolm Allison. Sansom – who went on to win eighty-six England caps – recalled:

Romark got me to repeat: 'I'm a winner, I'm a winner, I'm a winner,' and he told me to visualise getting the better of the winger I'd be marking. I thought it was a load of old crap, but Malcolm walked around clenching his fist shouting: 'Positive thinking, positive thinking,' at top volume.

Shortly before Palace faced Southampton in the semi-final, Allison and Romark had a spectacular falling out, with Romark claiming he was owed money by the Palace supremo for his motivational work with the squad. Allison denied the existence of an unpaid bill, so Romark took his leave of Selhurst Park after uttering a curse on Palace and Allison himself. At the behest of manager George Kirby, Romark was summoned to Halifax Town as they prepared for their FA Cup third-round clash with Allison's struggling City.

Romark informed the *Daily Express*: 'I was so affronted by Malcolm Allison four years ago that I feel fully vindicated in trying to help Halifax do their very best against his Manchester City team.' He met the Shaymen firstly as a group and then individually. In the *Lancashire Evening Post*, Halifax striker John Smith recalled that, two days before the tie:

Romark was saying: 'You will go to sleep now, John Smith, and then you'll overcome the power of Manchester City. You will play the greatest game of your life, John Smith. When I count to three, you'll wake up again.' I was trying not to laugh and I'm thinking: 'What's all this about?'

Smith laid on the winner for teammate Paul Hendrie (also hypnotised) in the dying minutes, not that Halifax players were convinced that Romark played much of a role. Smith later explained: 'All the headlines were about that bloody hypnotist, but we beat Manchester City through courage, hard work and belief.' George Kirby insisted: 'Romark worked tirelessly all week with the boys and deserves great credit for helping us win.' Local legend has it that Kirby's entirely earthly action – pumping hundreds of gallons of water on an already-terrible playing surface in order to even up the team's relative skill levels – may also have affected the outcome. As a 'thank you' to the local fire brigade for flooding the pitch the night before, Kirkby supposedly sent them a crate of brown ale.

Sportingly, Romark announced – in grandiose fashion – that he'd lifted the curse on Allison: 'I have now, on two occasions, defeated Malcolm Allison and I consider the matter closed.' Allison remained tight lipped, although given the way things panned out on his ill-fated return to Maine Road, he may well have still felt Romark's curse was in place.

Despite Maine Road crowds falling well short of the 50,000 predicted by Allison, not to mention curtailed cup runs, the mega deals kept coming. In March 1980, striker Kevin Reeves signed from Norwich for £1.3 million. Was Reeves nervous about the fee, I asked him? 'No, my arrival was fairly low-key,' he responded, 'because all the attention was still on Steve.' Quickly, Reeves realised that Allison's insistence on an intricate passing game was flawed. 'Too often, moves broke down in the middle of the park. We didn't have the players to pull it off,' he said.

City's trials and tribulations were brought into sharp focus when, in early 1981, Granada TV broadcast a fifty-minute documentary entitled *City! A Club in Crisis*. If *Treble Winners* – the Netflix series on Pep Guardiola's City in 2023 – was overly varnished and triumphalist, *City!* is the polar opposite. After an eight-match winless start to the 1980–81 campaign, the still-hugely charismatic Allison was already under huge pressure to turn around City's form. The fraught relationship between Swales and Allison lies at the heart of *City!* The furnishings at Maine Road during that era can best be described as high schlock. A smarmy and overconfident Peter Swales frequently holds court, sat behind Formica tables and framed by chipboard walls. There's an air of impending doom throughout. The sheer brownness of the surroundings adds to the sense of gloom. Clad in his polyester suits, the bewigged Swales darts across the brown shagpile carpets 'like a malevolent circus ringmaster', as David Tossell memorably wrote in his Allison biography *Big Mal*.

The most toe-curling aspect of *City!* is the desperate effort made by a frustrated Allison to coax any kind of quality from Steve Daley, who frequently looks disconsolately at both Allison and the camera and often appears to want to move out of the frame altogether. In one sequence, following a particularly chastening defeat, Daley and Allison have a prolonged argument. Daley (who hadn't tracked back against Terry McDermott) is accused by his manager of 'agreeing with me on Friday, and then going out and doing something completely different on Saturday'.

By now, Allison had already made it public that in his opinion, Daley wasn't even worth £600,000, and he had accused Swales of 'sticking his nose in with the Wolves chairman and hiking up the fee'. When asked on BBC's *Football Focus* in 1979 whether million-pound transfers were morally wrong, Swales responded:

'Possibly yes, but no one will go to the wall because only the clubs who can afford to spend big money will spend big money.'

Shortly before *City!* was broadcast, Swales was quoted in the *Manchester Evening News* as saying:

Malcolm raised no objection at the time about Steve Daley's fee and indeed assured me that [Michael] Robinson, [Steve] Mackenzie and Kevin Reeves, were worth the outlay. So, no one can suggest that I haven't backed Malcolm. But now it's down to him to get the best out of the players and mould the side.

It was abundantly clear, however, that Allison's days of nurturing talent – young or old – were behind him. Prior to a home game against Liverpool on 4 October 1980, with City third from bottom of the league, Swales was asked by journalists if Allison was one minute from the sack. Swales didn't say no, and arguably if the team hadn't salvaged a 2–2 draw at Old Trafford a week earlier, the axe might have fallen on Allison there and then. But Allison was given a temporary stay of execution, and as Liverpool headed to Maine Road, he is filmed in the dugout, attempting to convey basic instructions to the latest crop of City youngsters. Full-backs Nicky Reid and Steve Mackenzie are told to 'get in there' and defender Ray Ranson is instructed to 'move with him' (an unnamed Liverpool player). But City are powerless to stop Liverpool from romping to a 3–0 win. Crushed by disappointment, Allison appears to shrink further back in his seat, and sees out the game in sullen silence.

Afterwards, Peter Swales is now at his most cunning and menacing. 'Are we gonna stick with what we've got?' he rhetorically asks (about Allison's situation), drumming his fingers together as he speaks. Later, as both men puff away on huge cigars, Swales suggests that City should re-sign Scottish midfielder Asa Hartford ('the fella we let go'), who'd been sold little more than a year previously. 'Do me a favour,' harrumphs Allison from behind a cloud of cigar smoke.

It's akin to spying on a dysfunctional family plunging into meltdown, but the narrative tallies with what remains arguably Swales' most infamous one liner. Shortly before *City!* was broadcast, Swales claimed: 'You can't plan in football; it's day to day.' And for the best part of twenty years, with Swales at the helm, it was ad hoc.

The axe finally fell on Allison after City lost 1–0 to another fallen giant, rock-bottom Leeds United, at a half-empty Elland Road. At half-time Steve Mackenzie, who'd barely had a touch, gripes: 'I'm stuck in fucking limbo land.' Ray Ranson appears baffled by Allison's instructions, and the look of befuddlement on the players' faces ties in with an observation made by Dennis Tueart: 'He [Allison] struggled to get his grand vision across to the young players, and indeed to the rest of us. You had to have been in the game for some time to understand Mal. Often his routines were bewildering.' After a particularly complex training exercise at Platt Lane, Tueart recalled asking midfielder Tony Henry if he understood Allison's instructions. 'Haven't a fucking clue,' came Henry's reply.

In many ways, Allison was ahead of his time, and *City!* reveals that he deployed dance teachers (Lenny Hepple) to improve the players' balance, psychiatrists, university lecturers, played music in the dressing room, advocated shadow play in training and players rotating position to hone their skills. Yet after ten games, City hadn't won a league match, and the following morning, Swales informed the assembled press that he'd invited both assistant manager Tony Book and Allison to resign, which they duly had. Allison is firstly interviewed at his desk, and his deflation is clear. 'It is a very, very sad day. I thought the joy was just coming, just developing, and I was going to get some of the pleasure. Now, I am not going to get any of that pleasure.'

Later, he is shown bidding the City players farewell in Platt Lane Park. Some of the youngsters, including Roger Palmer and Gary Bennett, are genuinely upset, but the older professionals appear nonplussed. A notable absentee from proceedings was Steve Daley, who explained: 'I felt so bad about the fact it hadn't worked out that I couldn't face Mal.' Allison also disputes with his interviewer as to whether he was egotistical. 'If I had an ego, I wouldn't be sitting here with you now,' argues the man who wore a fedora for show on Crystal Palace's route to the 1976 FA Cup semi-finals, and who was photographed in the Palace players' bath with topless model Fiona Richmond in the mid '70s.

And there, *City!* might have fizzled out. Swales appointed Norwich City boss John Bond, a close associate of Allison's when they played together for West Ham, as Allison's successor (it is clear that Swales had already tapped Bond up several times regarding the job) and Bond, trots out platitudes at a hastily convened team meeting about the need for 'discipline' and 'desire' from the players in his East Anglian burr. In the months that followed, City slowly climbed the Division One table. Then, Bond's City were drawn against Crystal Palace, now managed by Malcolm Allison, in the FA Cup third round at Maine Road. The *City!* producers rubbed their hands with glee.

The verbal brickbats flew prior to the match. Allison lambasted Bond in the press by saying: 'If John Bond is so good, why hasn't he won anything in his previous years as a manager?' Bond responded: 'It's because of his behaviour... that I can never see Malcolm being a manager in his own right.' Bond also gives a revealing insight about his friendship with Allison to the *City!* film crew, claiming that

Allison viewed him as a 'country bumpkin up from the sticks'. In front of the heaving Kippax Terrace, Allison is given a hero's reception, but his team, rooted to the foot of Division One, is destroyed 4–0 by a rejuvenated City. Throughout proceedings, he's powerless to influence events, despite screaming: 'Stevie Lovell, hold your ground' on regular occasions.

After the game, he seems broken. The documentary concludes with a highly revealing boardroom interchange after the FA Cup clash between Bond, Allison and Swales. As they chomp away on their cigars, Allison is forced to listen to Bond telling him that he needs someone to manage him. Bond hits the nail on the head when, referring to Allison post-1972, he explains: 'I am not sure, honestly and truthfully, that he has the capacity to make teams better if he has the ultimate control.' Despite Allison's retort: 'I have found that fella to control me. Me', there's an unconvincing snigger from all those present.

In the years that followed, Bond's observation of Allison proved sadly accurate, and his career fizzled out amidst increasingly lurid stories of alcoholism and gambling debts. Bond quickly dumped Steve Daley out on loan to Seattle Sounders. 'I was in a very dark place, and I had to get out of the country for my own peace of mind', Daley recalled. 'No one wanted the move to work out more than me, but it didn't.' The transfer was later made permanent, and the £100,000 fee represented truly disastrous business on City's part. On Swales's instructions, Bond did re-sign Asa Hartford. City reached Wembley, where they succumbed to Ricky Villa's dazzling winner and lost 3–2. Allison, of course, insisted that it was his team that had come good, as he knew they would. But Bond lasted little longer at Maine Road than Big Mal, and he resigned in March 1983, with City destined for relegation from Division One. Swales remained at Maine Road until 1993, hiring and firing managers with (often) reckless abandon, and reflected on Allison's second coming: 'I was too obsessed with trying to match what they were doing at Old Trafford. I should have minded my own business.'

It wasn't even as if everything was going swimmingly across the city. Granada Television's current affairs programme *World in Action*, which aired in January 1980, alleged that the club had given backhanders to the parents of young players as an inducement to bring them to the club. The programme also suggested that bribes had been given to council officials by Manchester United chairman Louis Edwards to win lucrative contracts for his meat business. Edwards died from a heart attack four weeks later.

Peter Swales appeared to have learned his lesson, and the first clutch of John Bond signings were inexpensive, experienced campaigners like Gerry Gow and Tommy Hutchison, who added much-needed steel and nous to the team. But Swales couldn't resist lavishing £1 million on Trevor Francis, who was jettisoned after a season, with City's increasingly dire financial straits such that injured players complained they were having to reuse bandages.

•   •   •

Shortly after Allison was fired, Michael Robinson travelled to see his former manager in London to commiserate with him and apologise.

A while after I left City, Brighton beat them, and I scored. I slid to my knees in front of Mal and celebrated. It wasn't clever of me. Mal was lovely when I explained my feelings to him at his house. 'Don't worry, Michael. I'd have done the same,' he smiled.

Robinson found Allison, who'd just returned from his holiday in Portugal, in reflective mood. After observing the kids in the hotel arcades playing Pac-Man and Space Invaders, he told Robinson that 'screen time will be terrible for kids' exercise. You watch.' He also lamented that football directors were becoming ever-more power-ful. 'What's happened to the beautiful game?' a tearful Allison asked, perhaps rhetorically. Allison was the football equivalent of charis-matic American entrepreneur John DeLorean, whose futuristic-looking, DMC stainless steel sports car with gull-wing doors was manufactured at the DeLorean car plant in Belfast, for a pricey $25,000 each. 'The car of the future' flopped dismally in a depressed buying market, with DeLorean declared bankrupt by 1982. 'He was the last of the automotive wildcatters,' said a rival. And Allison, according to Michael Robinson, '…was the last football romantic, who couldn't get the basics right'.

The Allison spark flickered just once more – in Portugal, where he led Sporting Lisbon to the league and cup double during the 1981–82 season, a feat they wouldn't repeat for almost forty years. But English football had long since passed Big Mal by. The early '80s was no place for theorists or dreamers or profligate spenders. Pragmatism and frugality were the only ways to survive.

5

THE ENGLISHMEN AND THE IRISHMEN ABROAD

THE YANKEE DOLLAR

'The NASL was the perfect stage for showmen like Best, Marsh and Hudson, because the emphasis was largely on skill. The whole approach to soccer in America was so much more forward thinking than what we saw in the English game.'

JIMMY HILL, SPEAKING IN 1998

The Spartan Stadium – February 1982. Incensed that the referee has just allowed a Fort Lauderdale Strikers goal to stand, George Best demands the ball from kick-off. From the moment he receives it just shy of the 35-yard line, the Ulsterman – his left knee burning with pain – knows what he wants to do. The question is whether the San Jose Earthquakes forward's battle-worn body will let him do it. Mind over matter prevails. Best twists and turns, weaving and feinting past four bemused defenders, darting into space where there seems to be none. Then he drives the ball home past the Ft Lauderdale goalkeeper, and the pom-pom wielding cheerleaders behind the

85

goal jump up and down with gusto. On a big screen in the ground, a Miller Lite advert plays, starring Best's fellow '70s-maverick Rodney Marsh. 'That's the best soccer goal I've ever seen,' enthuses the TV commentator. The Earthquakes aren't sending shockwaves around the North American Soccer League though. In fact, they are one of the league's poorest teams. But for one last time, football's ultimate showman turns back the clock and shines amidst the razzamatazz and whizz bangs. Soon, several of the NASL's gizmos head across the Atlantic to England.

• • •

Keen-eyed trans-Atlantic flyers in the late '70s and early '80s might have spotted swathes of British footballers (some better known than others) strutting their way through customs at Heathrow, heading stateside. Several of the 'characters' jetted out for differing lengths of time and with varying degrees of success. Alan Hudson remained with Seattle Sounders for four successful seasons. Frank Worthington (Tampa Bay Rowdies) had a brief loan spell stateside. Worthington was presented with a limited edition 'Taking Care of Business' necklace that Elvis Presley (Worthington's hero) had made in fourteen-carat gold for his fans. Worthington reckoned it was 'the best present I ever received', although he still pined for his mum's Sunday roasts in Halifax. Stamford Bridge favourite Charlie Cooke, after finishing up at the Dallas Sidekicks in the Indoor League, ended up settling out there. So did Rodney Marsh, after he stopped playing for the Rowdies. The renumeration – particularly for creative players who'd starred in Division One – was often eye-wateringly good. Trevor Francis, who spent two close seasons on loan to Detroit Express, could expect to earn around

£100,000 each summer. Francis-themed products were all the rage. There were badges, pens and Trevor Francis tracksuits, although presumably not supplied by a mush in Shepherd's Bush. Ex-Manchester City forward Dennis Tueart became the first English footballer since the late '60s to play in the NASL full-time and spent two years with the New York Cosmos. In 1979, he flew in via Concorde, lived in a high-rise apartment overlooking the Hudson River, drove a pale-blue Cadillac and trebled the salary he'd earned at Maine Road. Tueart rubbed shoulders with Mick Jagger and Björn Borg before returning to Manchester in 1981. Tueart's wife Joan had been spooked when, due to a fire several floors below, she smelt smoke in the apartment one day, at a time when *The Towering Inferno* was a fixture on American TV. Besides, her husband missed 'the drizzle and the greyness' of Manchester.

Financial gain aside, several players headed across the pond as a way to rejuvenate themselves and seek sanctuary in a less-charged atmosphere. As well as Steve Daley, heading to Seattle to 'escape from everything and give myself a fresh start,' there was also Alan Hudson, leaving behind 'the stifling negativity and backward thinking of English football.' As well as rubbing shoulders with the likes of singer Tony Bennett, Hudson 'played the kind of football I'd always wanted to'. Despite the passing of time, George Best's tragicomic American adventure has lost none of its potency. When he decided to try his luck in the States in the mid '70s, it seemed inevitable that Best was Big Apple bound, but he resented the fact that the New York Cosmos wanted him to spend much of his 'down time' fulfilling commercial obligations. 'I liked the owner Steve Ross (CEO of Time Warner), but no one was going to control me like that,' Best told me, so instead he headed to California, which still retained some of its laid-back '60s cool. 'I signed for Los Angeles

Aztecs because it offered me a level of anonymity that I'd never get in England,' he said. But not entirely. After touching down in 1976, model Linda Cardoza greeted him. Wearing a T-shirt emblazoned with 'George does it Best', she handcuffed herself to him, which caught the attention of the local media.

In many ways, the US and Best were made for one another. He scored fifteen in his first season, including one on his debut against Rochester Lancers. Ultimately, Best's descent into alcoholism ruined his stay there, and he was traded to Fort Lauderdale before ending up with San Jose Earthquakes by the start of the '80s. 'Me and Muhammad Ali somehow staggered into the '80s in our respective sports. Me a drunk and him with Parkinson's,' Best said. 'By then, we were circus freaks. Perhaps we should both have been shot.' It's true that Best was in and out of rehab, and he described San Jose as an awful place 'because of the state I was in'. The club's name was controversial too, because of the city's proximity to the San Andreas Fault. Famously, his wife Angie saw a hunched figure stumbling down the road in the pouring rain whilst she was taking her son, Callum, to the doctor. 'It was me, looking like a hobo,' Best recalled. 'She gave me the heave-ho. I can't blame her.' But Best also enjoyed some periods of sobriety, and he recalled much of his career in California with great clarity.

We chatted in The Phene in Chelsea in 2004, two weeks after he'd appeared at the Mayflower Theatre in Southampton as Jimmy Greaves's star guest for his 'Evening With' show. Best pushed aside his cryptic crossword and consented – albeit cautiously at first – to me asking him some quickfire questions about the quirks of his American lifestyle. Favourite food? 'Um – Mexican. Fajitas. Duck or beef. I'd not had them before. Not good for the waistline though,' he said, patting his midriff. Favourite car you drove? A brief pause.

'A cream Cadillac. With the roof down.' Naturally. He was warming to the questions. Favourite thing about living in California? 'Sitting on the beach watching the sunset. Like the sky was on fire. Beautiful. No sunsets like California sunsets.' Song that reminds you of your time out there? Best nodded enthusiastically. 'The Emerson, Lake and Palmer version of' – he clicked fingers, shut his eyes and asked the table next door to help him – '"Fanfare for the Common Man?"' 'That's it, yes. Every time I hear that song it reminds me of skyscrapers and big American cars.' Any US phrases you picked up? 'My favourite phrase that I picked up was that when somewhere was a dump, it was an "armpit of a place". Like San Jose,' he laughed.

By late 1981, British tabloids were buzzing with rumours that Northern Ireland manager Billy Bingham, whose team had just qualified for the 1982 World Cup finals, might be interested in adding Best to his squad. But when Bingham came to watch Best play for San Jose, the team delivered an awful performance, and Bingham's interest cooled. Middlesbrough manager Bobby Murdoch suggested that Best could prove himself to Bingham at Ayresome Park. Best thought about it then turned down the request. 'I didn't fancy being kicked up the arse all afternoon back in England,' he told me. So arguably the finest footballer these isles ever produced never played in a World Cup finals. 'Crazy, I suppose,' Best admitted, 'but I don't think I'd have made much difference anyway. Billy had a great unit there and I wouldn't have got them past France. Not in that heat!' Northern Ireland were hammered 4–1 and knocked out of the second group stage, with 'the French George Best' – Dominique Rocheteau – having a field day.

As the afternoon shadows lengthened outside, our conversation turned to the various contrivances that peppered the NASL, some of which hopped across the Atlantic. I asked Best to list any soccer experiments he was party to; the crazier the better. He didn't disappoint.

> I played in a practice match with bigger goalframes. The match ended 8–6, I think. Another match was where hitting the post or bar counted as a goal. Thankfully, that never took off. The manager at San Jose was all for matches being sliced into four quarters, to cater for more adverts on TV, and for receiving extra points if the goal was from long range, as US audiences loved that. Everyone was shooting from sixty yards. Crazy.

One feature of US soccer that several British players reckoned was a positive feature was that if a game ended in a draw, a shootout would ensue. Not penalties, but 35-yard kick ins, where the player had six seconds to run from the 35-yard line and beat the goalkeeper. 'It was a fantastic opportunity for top players to display their skills,' reckoned Dennis Tueart. On one occasion, Tueart witnessed teammate Carlos Alberto juggle the ball insouciantly before lobbing it over the keeper's head. 'Those in the crowd would never forget what they saw,' Tueart said. Best concurred, arguing that 35-yard kicks should have become 'part and parcel of the English game, as it would have suited skilful players, whereas anyone with two feet can blast a penalty.'

Some novelties that seeped into the English game never took off. Cheerleaders were fleetingly seen at, amongst other grounds, Ashton Gate, with the 'Rockin' Robins' vainly attempting to improve an increasingly depressive atmosphere as Bristol City plummeted down the divisions from the top flight. Some of the English expats recalled 'tumble throws ins' (the act of performing a full somersault whilst taking a throw-in to gain extra leverage) in the NASL.

Southend United's Anton Otulakowski demonstrated the art of the 'tumble throw' for TV cameras on Southend Pier, but sadly, the lack of space between the advertising hoardings and the touchline at Roots Hall prevented it from catching on.

Coventry chairman Jimmy Hill's decision to turn Highfield Road into an all-seater stadium (at a cost of £400,000) proved unpopular with terrace diehards. 'I saw at first-hand how families could sit in comfort in American stadia, which you couldn't say about English football back in the '80s.' But after Leeds United fans laid waste to the seating, the club reintroduced terracing. 'We were thirteen years ahead of our time, and English football was thirteen years behind the times,' Hill argued. Coventry's tie-up with the local Talbot car factory was also based on the American business model. It saw Sky Blues players drive around in sponsored Talbots, although Hill's attempt to rebrand the club Coventry Talbot was blocked by the Football League.

• • •

But some features of US soccer started to change the face of the English game. Queens Park Rangers chairman Jim Gregory, having watched several matches in the US, mooted the possibility of placing a retractable roof on Loftus Road and pondered manager Terry Venables's suggestion to change the club's name to London FC. Neither plan made it beyond the planning stage, but in 1981, after years of seeing their Loftus Road pitch freeze solid in the winter, the Second Division promotion chasers became the first English club to install an artificial pitch. Rangers had sent a fact-finding delegation to the US, shunned the AstroTurf option, which had first been deployed at the Houston Astrodome in 1966, and plumped instead for

Omniturf, which was used in Holland. 'It was conceived in America but born in Holland,' Terry Venables said. In essence, it was a carpet rolled out onto a thick layer of concrete, with only a layer of sand acting as a cushion. Early footage showed the wild bounce of the ball, and many players struggling to control the ball's faster roll and complaining of soreness. QPR's gifted skipper Glenn Roeder, whose signature move was his clever soft-shoe shuffle, where he'd let the ball run as he feinted to control the ball, enjoyed playing on the surface, arguing that it improved his ball control. He had less than fond memories of the exquisite pain caused from sliding on what quickly became dubbed (incorrectly) as the 'drastic plastic'. The grass was actually comprised of Polypropylene fibres.

One time I was sent flying and scraped some skin off my thigh. Weirdly, the carpet burn was shaped like a map of England, Scotland and Wales. That night, it got stuck to the bed clothes. I had to cut it off with scissors. The next day, the club doctor put some spray on the burn. I screamed like a madman.

As Rangers gained promotion back to Division One in 1983, the accusations that the surface gave them an unfair advantage gained traction. Banned from playing UEFA Cup matches on the Omniturf, QPR had to decamp to Highbury for home matches during their 1984–85 UEFA Cup run. Gregory hoped to follow the American business model and ensure that Loftus Road was used for non-football activities throughout the week. To a degree it worked, with hockey matches and summer training schools taking place, although QPR had to alter the base recommended by the manufacturers, which led to a harder surface. It was low maintenance and resulted in fewer postponements. One enterprising vandal, armed with a paintbrush and a tin of white paint, broke into Loftus Road on Christmas Day and daubed 'Perry Buckland is Innocent' on the pitch, prior to Rangers's Boxing Day clash with Chelsea in 1981. After serving his prison sentence, Buckland had a trial with Portsmouth. Rival managers didn't like the surface, with Howard Kendall telling me: 'If a horse won't eat it, football shouldn't be played on it.' The controversy didn't stop other clubs, including Luton Town, who ironically were Rangers's first opponents on their new Omniturf, following suit.

By the end of the '80s, many of the business practices which were de rigueur in US sports had germinated in English football, particularly at both North London clubs. Arsenal vice-chairman David Dein was a keen student of American soccer. Throughout the 1970s and early '80s, Dein often stayed at the Florida family home of his American wife, Barbara. He attended NASL games and was bowled over not simply by the luxurious all-seater stadia but the razzamatazz and commercial elements of the game. He told me:

I thought that English football could learn a lot from US sports. The stadia were family friendly. It was designed to enhance the spectators' enjoyment and experience of the game. There was much more focus on the club 'brand' with T-shirts and caps and replica shirts on sale. Commercially, English football was light years behind.

When the former commodities entrepreneur invested the princely sum of £300,000 in a club that was mired in mid-table, the Gunners' old Etonian chairman Peter Hill-Wood dismissed it as 'dead money'. In truth it was 'new money', and Dein was amongst the first in a new breed of young executives who realised that in football, money was about to talk. Dein was convinced that by harvesting the very best of US business practice and sporting gizmos, English football could flourish once more. At Arsenal, he pushed his agenda forward with gusto.

When the Gunners faced Luton at Highbury in the opening game of the 1983–84 season, the players emerged from the tunnel individually, after new stadium MC Jerome Anderson barked out their names. Such grandiose entrances were part and parcel of US soccer, but Arsenal's new £650,000 star man Charlie Nicholas (who emerged last for dramatic effect) was sceptical. 'I didn't want that kind of hype,' he recalled. 'I just wanted to be part of the Arsenal team.' Dein's notion to temporarily erect a giant Diamond Vision video screen in 1984 – which showed highlights and replays and blasted out Bronski Beat's 'Smalltown Boy' at ear-splitting volume and with monotonous regularity – was initially thwarted by the authorities due to noise pollution concerns in N5. As Arsenal vice chairman, he would control 41 per cent of club shares and was carnivorous in his approach to gaining more. He oversaw the expansion of Arsenal's commercial outlets, which he'd likened to a 'Manchester bus shelter' when he first arrived at the club.

After becoming Tottenham chairman in 1984, Irving Scholar pioneered the introduction of categorised matches, where games against Arsenal, Liverpool and Manchester United were more expensive to watch, and the Dial-A-Seat facility, where fans phoned up for tickets and paid via credit card. He also worked closely with fellow property developer Paul Bobroff, with whom he started to diversify Tottenham into areas such as computing, and the clothing firms Hummel and Martex to provide funds for the club. Initially this proved beneficial, making Tottenham a market leader, but when losses were incurred, they were a drain and eventually forced

Scholar to sell the club to Alan Sugar in June 1991. Football consult-
ant Alex Fynn, who'd work closely with Tottenham throughout the
'80s, told me: 'Irving Scholar was a true football visionary, but he
moved too fast and too far for the times.'

• • •

Although the corporate side of the game – based in no small part
on the US model – was increasingly clear and present in English
football by the end of the decade, the NASL folded in 1985. Several Englishmen continued to ply their trade in the Indoor Soccer
League, but superstars like George Best had long since deserted the
sinking ship. 'They never nurtured local American talent,' Best explained. 'Although many more high-school kids now played soccer.'
The business model was also flawed, with only a handful of fran-
chises making a profit. In the end, even the New York Cosmos made
a loss. There was no happy homecoming for the likes of Hudson and
Best either. Hudson was invited to return to Stamford Bridge, but
he failed to make a first-team appearance for John Hollins's Chelsea
side. For Best, a spell in prison, a divorce and an infamous drunken
appearance on *Wogan* ('I indulged myself in the green room and
behaved like a big wanker,' he told me) awaited, as well as a brief
spell with Bournemouth and occasional appearances in testimoni-
als and veterans matches, before which he trained like a demon and
stopped boozing for weeks at a time. 'But I always knew I'd fall back
into my own ways,' he said. The NASL gave the '70s showmen a final
opportunity for a dollar-laden last hurrah amidst the razzamatazz,
before the rudest of awakenings back home.

In many ways, the NASL was a portent of things to come for English football: cosmopolitan stars with their names on their backs,

gargantuanly wealthy owners, music blaring as the teams emerged and family-friendly all-seater grounds. But that was some way off in the harsh world of '80s football in England.

THE ITALIAN JOB

'I looked at the Italians in the tunnel. We were in our nylon England Admiral tracksuits. There they were in their beautiful Azurri silk-blue tracksuits, suntanned and looking a million dollars.'

RAY WILKINS

San Siro Stadium – October 1984. A charged atmosphere at the Milan derby, with 80,000 supporters chanting, lighting Roman candles and unfurling banners on both the Curva Sud (Milan fans) and Curva Nord (Inter fans). The stakes are high. Milan haven't defeated their local rivals for six years, which have seen them relegated twice. With Liam Brady in midfield and West German superstar Karl-Heinz Rummenigge up front, Inter are hot favourites to win. When Alessandro Altobelli gives Inter the lead, the match appears to be going to form. It's been eighty years since a team that had gone behind in this derby have come back to win. Milan's two Englishmen are about to turn history on its head. Agostino Di Bartolomei volleys home after intricate build-up play between midfielder Ray Wilkins and burly forward Mark Hateley. With twenty-five minutes left, Hateley, plucked from Second Division Portsmouth during the close season, stamps an indelible mark on Italian football history. Hovering around the penalty spot, he soars above Inter defender Fulvio Collovati to meet Pietro Virdis's curled cross and powers a header past Walter Zenga's flailing dive. The game ends 2–1. Italy's finest writers heap praise on the Englishmen. Screenwriter Ugo Tognazzi describes Wilkins and Hateley as 'two rare and refined English species in a divine fish'. Injuries disrupt his Milan career, but Mark Hateley's legend grows stronger with each passing year.

• • •

In 1980, with Italian football reeling from the Totonero betting scandal, which saw AC Milan demoted to Serie B and striker Paolo Rossi banned for two years, the Italian FA decided to lift the fourteen-year ruling that had seen foreign players banned from plying their trade in Italy. It had been introduced following the national team's dismal showing in the '66 World Cup, which saw them defeated by North Korea and eliminated at the group stage. Serie A attendances were plummeting and national manager Enzo Bearzot reckoned that 'top foreign players would help raise the bar quality-wise'. From the start of the 1980–81 season, Italian sides could add one foreigner to their squad. From the start of 1982–83, it was two. Some of English football's leading lights were ripe for picking, but were encouraged to think twice before playing in Serie A.

Presumably scarred by the alarming TV images of murdered five-time Italian Prime Minister Aldo Moro being located in the boot of a Renault in central Rome, Jean Keegan told husband Kevin that he most certainly would not be accepting an offer to move from Hamburg to Juventus in the summer of 1980. Moro had been kidnapped by activists from the Red Brigade, and violence between left- and right-wing groups surged in the early '80s. Much to the surprise of pretty much everyone, Keegan accepted Southampton manager Lawrie McMenemy's offer and opted to head for the rather more sedate environs of Hampshire instead.

Thwarted in their bid for the England captain, Juve turned their attentions to Arsenal's talismanic midfielder Liam Brady. Although he'd made his intentions to leave clear a year earlier, executive Ken Friar made a last-ditch effort to keep the Irishman, reminding him that the new Conservative government had recently axed the top tax level from 80 per cent to 60 per cent. But keen for a new adventure, and with his salary several multiples of what he earned in north London, Brady headed to Turin regardless.

A clutch of former players, including Denis Law and Jimmy Greaves, who'd plied their trade in Serie A in the early '60s urged caution. As he prepared to put pen to paper for AC Milan in 1984, Manchester United's Ray Wilkins was warned by Law – who'd suffered a miserable year at Torino in 1963, about the ever-present paparazzi. 'I listened carefully to what Denis told me,' Wilkins recalled, 'but the thought of sampling a new culture and playing a different style of football appealed enormously.' Through the medium of his *Shoot!* column, Jimmy Greaves, who'd struggled to adapt to life in Milan in 1963, wished Luther Blissett all the best with AC Milan after his 1983 transfer, but warned him to look out for the 'sharks' in Italian football who would 'delight in seeing him fail.' There were also English managers who, fearful of the detrimental effect a talent drain would have on the domestic game, suggested that leading stars shouldn't represent their country if the lure of the lire proved irresistible. 'All that spaghetti will make you fat, Trev,' Brian Clough (who wasn't even the winger's manager anymore) told Sampdoria-bound Trevor Francis. 'If I was England manager, you wouldn't be in my team.' In the *Sunday Mirror*, former Liverpool manager Bob Paisley outlined his two-point plan. It stated that no British player should be allowed to go abroad before his twenty-eighth birthday, and that once they'd gone, the player should be banned from playing for their country.

The Paisley Plan was never implemented, and for the players, the thrills easily outweighed any potential spills. Arriving in Turin to an ecstatic welcome, Liam Brady was carried shoulder-high as he left the airport. 'I felt like I was one of the Beatles,' he told me. And the photographs of the expats (aside from the obligatory shots that showed them wearing headphones during their less-than-successful linguaphone courses) invariably suggested they were living glamorous lives. Sampdoria's Trevor Francis and Graeme Souness – neighbours in an upmarket Genoan suburb – were snapped posing outside their luxury villas, with its lemon tree-lined gardens, and posing in their budgie smugglers on a speedboat in fashionable Portofino. After England duty, Wilkins and Hateley were seen being whisked back to Milan's training camp via private jet. Cultural opportunities abound. During one close season, Wilkins went to watch *Aida* in Verona's reconstructed Roman coliseum. 'It was such an uplifting and wonderful experience. Quite superb,' he said in classic Wilkins-speak. As for Trevor Francis, he enjoyed frequenting cafes with wife Helen, and 'watching the world go by'. He even acquired a thoroughly metrosexual man bag, which he clutched under his arm. 'It wouldn't have gone down well in England,' he admitted. Invariably, eating out late – generally after 10 p.m. – took some getting used to, as did drinking wine rather than beer. Chain smoking amongst Italian players was far more common than in England. When Francis and Souness treated themselves to a cold bottle of beer after a Sampdoria match, they were hauled before the club president for 'dragging the club's image through the mud'. Not every novel cultural experience was uplifting, however. Signed as a pair by Bari in Serie A in 1984, Paul Rideout and Gordon Cowans witnessed a gangland murder on the outskirts of the impoverished southern city as they cruised by in their air-conditioned coach. 'You heard a pop from the gun, and then a man fell straight to the floor,' Cowans said.

The story of how four British players brought some stability to AC Milan in the era before Silvio Berlusconi helicoptered into the San Siro with 'Ride of the Valkyries' blaring resonates forty years later. After Milan's first relegation, Joe Jordan headed there from Manchester United. Nicknamed 'Lo Squalo' on account of his missing front teeth, the robust Scottish forward scored twelve goals in fifty-two appearances. Hardly prolific, but Milan fans admired Jordan's physical courage. Despite Jordan claiming that Milan fans only recognise him now due to his infamous touchline flare-up with Gennaro Gattuso at the end of Tottenham's Champions League clash with Milan in 2009 ('Fuck around and find out,' the once-fearsome frontman snarled as Gattuso got up close and personal), the Joe Jordan fan club only officially folded in 2013, thirty years after he departed the San Siro.

Luther Blissett's lonely stint up front for Milan during the 1983–84 season eventually took on an air of absurdity. On the face of it, the former Watford man's record of five goals in thirty games is instantly forgettable but despite that, he's fondly remembered. His twenty-seven goals for Watford in 1982–83 made him the top scorer in European football that season and club legend Gianni Rivera presented him with his award before a Milan match in 1984. 'Platini scored the most goals last year with eighteen. Milan, I will score more,' Blissett told la *Gazzetta dello Sport* after signing. 'With his boxer's physique, how many teams will he knock out?' a headline asked. Yet as Blissett failed with alarming regularity to find the back of the net, the tone of the headlines changed. 'Blissett, when will you score?' asked *Gazzetta* on 3 September. He broke his duck against Verona later that month, but, whereas at Watford he'd thrived on seizing onto long passes, too often the ball appeared to bounce off him as Milan mounted their attacks. The English press delighted in mischief making, dubbing him 'Luther Missett'. Stories in Italy, the product of flames fanned on Fleet Street, suggested that Watford had sent Blissett's brother to play instead, or that Milan had accidentally signed Blissett rather than their initial target, John Barnes.

As he discussed these issues during our interview, Blissett shook his head. 'What they were saying, in a roundabout way, is that black players – black people – all look the same.' His legendary miss against rivals Inter from five yards out was – frame by frame – pored over by the hypercritical Italian media like it was footage from JFK's assassination. 'If that had gone in, things might have been very different,' Blissett said. Blissett wasn't alone amongst foreign signings in struggling to adapt to the demands of Serie A that season. Ludo Coeck and Francisco Elói also lasted a single season. At least Livorno fans loved Blissett, dedicating a banner to him after his late winner against Pisa relegated their Tuscan rivals. It wasn't a surprise when Blissett returned to Vicarage Road at the end of the season to be reunited with Graham Taylor, after Milan scored just thirty-seven goals in thirty matches, finishing eighth in the process. Ridicule was heaped upon him after his complaint that it was impossible to buy Rice Crispies in Milan. 'I did say that,' Blissett told me, 'but it was a jokey way to end a long interview. It's all anyone remembers. And I didn't really miss them that much.' Instead, Blissett's apparent pining for his favourite Kellogg's breakfast cereal appeared to reinforce his uncultured approach to Serie A and his inability to adapt to life in Italy.

By the time I interviewed Blissett for the first time in 1997, his name had already been hijacked by a collective group of militants and writers in Genoa. Seven years earlier, an urban myth circulated that when a group of people on a Rome bus were questioned by police over nonpayment of fares, they collectively gave their name as Luther Blissett. 'Yes, I'm aware of it, and it's a bit weird,' Blissett shrugged. The truth got steadily weirder. Some twenty years after the player left Milan, a group of four Italian writers working under the pseudonym Luther Blissett published a bestselling historical novel, Q, in 1999, which sold well in the UK. When asked why they'd adopted Blissett's name, one member insisted: 'We needed the name of a person who had been stupidly underestimated and misunderstood.' Blissett the player remains cagey about discussing the group who've hijacked his name. 'Sometimes I feel flattered, sometimes annoyed. I try not to let it bother me, because really, what can I do?'

Ray Wilkins, derisorily labelled 'the crab' in some quarters for his supposed predilection for the sideways pass, relished playing in Serie A, where as he put it, 'the emphasis was on retaining possession and close control'. He also helped launch the career of Paolo Maldini, who spent twenty-five years at the San Siro, lending him a pair of his boots so the sixteen-year-old could make his debut away at Udinese in January 1985. 'That boy would be nothing without me,' smiled Wilkins. As for Hateley, his stock rose immediately. In the days before the Milan derby, he'd been locked in talks with the club over his car. 'I was pootling around Milan in a hired Fiat,' he said. 'Then that goal went in, and my silver family Mercedes estate car was delivered the following week.' Hateley's sheer physical power, combative nature and long dark hair saw him dubbed 'Attila', after the infamous warrior leader of the Huns. 'The Attila nickname was perhaps because Italians couldn't pronounce my surname properly,' he admitted. The *Gazzetta dello Sport* ran numerous stories about 'Mark Attila'. One reporter wrote: 'He is like Conan, the mythical, invincible barbarian … and like a barbarian, he celebrates when his rivals are destroyed.' Hateley's superhuman strength was written about widely in the Italian media. A worker at the Legnano apartments, where Milan's Englishmen lived, claimed to have seen a bare-chested Hateley rip a telephone directory in two. 'I think I'd remember if I'd done that,' Hateley laughed. In his home, he has two photographs of his famous header, one in colour and one in black and white. Despite seeing the image almost every day, he was rendered speechless when, during the Milan derby in 2016, supporters unfurled a giant display, showing Hateley soaring above Collovati. The accompanying banner read 'sovrastiamoli' ('we tower above them'). 'The power and size of the image humbled me,' Hateley said.

Outside the San Siro in 2018, a fan stall was dedicated to Hateley's historic goal against Inter Milan. On sale were posters, pens, badges and T-shirts showing 'Atilla's' header. Aldo, the Milan fan running the stall, had written a musical about the goal and its place in club history. 'I'm going to invite Mark along on opening night,' he told me. 'It will play to packed houses in the city on and around the fortieth anniversary.' Sadly, that anniversary has now come and gone, and Aldo's dream appears not to have transpired.

By 1987, Hateley and Wilkins had headed to Ligue 1 – Monaco and Paris Saint-Germain respectively, as the Berlusconi era got into full swing. Nonetheless, the hullaballoo that still surrounds Hateley, and the other '80s Englishmen of Milan remains as intense as ever.

6

THE COGS IN THE
RED MACHINE

'The only thing that really matters is winning.
Everything else is secondary.'
BOB PAISLEY, 1981

Parc des Princes – May 1981. On a bumpy pitch, rutted and roughed up by the French rugby team, Liverpool toil against a far-from-impressive Real Madrid in the European Cup final. Real winger Laurie Cunningham complains afterwards that 'the ball had a mind of its own'. Terry McDermott said that it 'bounced up at crazy angles'. With the game seemingly heading for extra time, left-back Alan Kennedy storms forward. Controlling the ball on his chest from a Ray Kennedy throw-in (the latter is always at pains to point out that, despite their Geordie roots and shared surname, they are most certainly not brothers), Alan Kennedy allows the ball to bounce down, and on the edge of the box, Real centre-half Gattuso swipes wildly at the ball but misses. Kennedy now has a clear path to goal. Bursting through, 'Barney Rubble', as teammates nickname him, drills a left-footed shot past bewildered goalkeeper

Agustín. Kennedy glances around furtively to check that he isn't offside. The goal stands. Kennedy's exhausted teammates are slow to catch the jubilant full-back, who's galloped to celebrate with the Liverpool fans behind the goal. When Terry McDermott gets to him, he screams 'you lucky fucking sod' in his ear. The underrated Kennedy's decisive intervention has landed his club the cup with the big ears once again.

• • •

In the eight seasons after he took over from Bill Shankly, Bob Paisley took Liverpool to new heights, winning five league titles and three European Cups. The Boot Room boys; Joe Fagan, Ronnie Moran, Roy Evans and Tom Saunders, moulded initially by Shanks, remained present and correct, as selfless and as dogged and committed to the club as ever. Nottingham Forest and Aston Villa emerged as challengers, both domestically and in Europe, but the red machine continued to purr, despite its component parts changing over time.

As the '80s dawned, even English football's most successful club was feeling the cold winds of economic recession. Anfield crowds – down by an average of 10,000 on '70s figures – were dwindling, and Liverpool chairman John Smith announced that, despite the club having a turnover of £2.5 million in 1979–80, their net profit was only £71,000, which he deemed 'ridiculous considering the size and achievements of the club'. Liverpool became the first English club to announce a sponsorship deal, and the two-year Hitachi deal netted them £100,000; Smith described it as 'useful, but not game changing'.

By the early '80s, the majority of Liverpool players had gravitated to Southport, typically living in four-bedroomed detached houses in upmarket cul-de-sacs with double garages and club-sponsored Fords parked on the drive. They lived next door to doctors, bank managers and businessmen. The area was also replete with golf courses, not that the Boot Room boys approved. 'They were concerned that we'd injure ourselves lugging our clubs around,' said midfielder Ray Kennedy.

The players' geographical distance from the city centre didn't mean they were unaware of the increasingly dire economic situation in which many fans found themselves. Kirkby-born forward Terry McDermott, famous for his permed ringlets and moustache, knew this all too well. The dressing-room prankster – who delighted in impersonating some of Bob Paisley's indecipherable Hetton-le-Holisms ('Can you do us a one, son?') spoke of the decimation facing England's fourth city at the start of the '80s. 'I had family and friends who'd worked as dockers and in the Bryant & May and Triumph factories. Now that was all gone, with nothing to replace it. They could hardly put food on the table, let alone afford to go to football.' Unlike the rabblerousing Shankly, Bob Paisley usually swerved politics, but he'd occasionally remind his players of the privations their fans were enduring and urge them to 'do it for the crowd'.

By Liverpool's almost-serene standards, the 1980–81 campaign was a year of turbulence and tension. Twenty-three players were called upon to contribute; a sizeable number in the era before squad rotation became the norm. This was in contrast to the sixteen deployed in the season directly before and after. Bob Paisley's team finished fifth in Division One, their lowest league position for a decade. Sceptics suggested that, with the emergence of Ron

Saunders's Aston Villa side, the Anfield party might be coming to an end. Yet not only did Liverpool win the European Cup, they laid the foundations for the plethora of trophies won between 1982 and 1984.

There was a definite pecking order at Anfield, with the 'three Jocks' – Alan Hansen, Graeme Souness and Kenny Dalglish – setting the standards both on the pitch and in the dressing room. Goalkeeper Ray Clemence, who'd been at Liverpool for over a decade, explained: 'They were untouchable on the pitch, and merciless and cutting when it came to humour off it. They were a cut above – right down to the fact that they had McVities chocolate biscuits with their tea before training, and the rest of us ate digestives.' Along with the three Scotsmen, Clemence was one of the few Liverpool players whose place in the team appeared guaranteed. Another was Ray Kennedy, who joined Liverpool in 1975 from Arsenal and was transformed from a burly striker into a languid and visionary midfielder by Paisley. Although usually laid back and affable, Kennedy was a perfectionist and looked down on those whom he felt possessed a lower skillset. One of those – in his opinion – was Alan Kennedy. On one occasion after a beer or two, Ray Kennedy lamped a barman who called him 'Alan' by mistake. Pranking teammates delighted in disguising their voices, phoning the players' lounge, asking for (Ray) Kennedy, and when he answered, saying: 'Could I speak to Alan please?'

I wrote to Ray Kennedy in 2002, some twenty years after he was diagnosed with Parkinson's disease, on the very slim chance he might agree to speak with me. To my surprise, he rang me back and invited me to meet with him at his home in the north-east for a rare interview. It was done on the understanding that he might cancel at the last minute if he wasn't feeling up to it. It took almost two years to finalise a date. The tanned Kennedy was still an impressive physical specimen, but his eyes were puffy and tired. His shuffling gait as he led me into his lounge revealed the devastating effect that Parkinson's had taken on his body. 'I've put my teeth in for you,' he grinned, explaining that, in order to boost his energy levels, he was guzzling copious amounts of Lucozade, which had a detrimental effect on his dental health. At different times during our interview, Kennedy's speech sped up and then slowed down to a slur, and he took a couple of breaks to self-medicate. We chit-chatted about his conversion into a left-sided midfielder and Kennedy also laid bare how his body began to break down in his final months at Anfield: 'When I see footage of myself, I'm clearly lumbering about more.'

Kennedy was honest about his temperament. 'I was critical of certain players.' I asked him about his namesake, Alan Kennedy.

I don't think I'm being out of order when I say that he didn't possess much of a footballing brain. He frustrated me. He was brave and fearless, which is why he was good at taking penalties, and he charged forward like a lunatic, because he never thought through the consequences of his actions. He won a shitload of medals, though, so fair play to him. We were like chalk and cheese mind.

'But you combined at the right time in Paris, didn't you?' 'I suppose we did,' Kennedy tersely admitted.

• • •

During the period between 1981 and 1984, some unlikely cult heroes seized their moment in the limelight and impacted the club's history in multiple ways, a trend that continued throughout the decade.

Their recollections are every bit as compelling and revealing as those of more-established luminaries in a period when Liverpool were at the height of their powers.

In our 2004 interview, to coincide with the release of his autobiography, I figured that I might as well ask Alan Kennedy the inevitable question about his debut for Liverpool first. 'Did Bob Paisley really say what people say he said?' The answer, the affable Geordie confirmed with a grin, was yes. After a distinctly shaky first-half display on his debut for Liverpool against Aston Villa at Anfield (he'd shanked a couple of clearances), Paisley sauntered over to his new £300,000 signing from Newcastle United, looked at him and said: 'I think they shot the wrong Kennedy, son.' Paisley's *bon mot* had been trotted out in after-dinner speeches down the years with such regularity, often by people who weren't even there, that I was concerned it might just be an urban myth.

But Kennedy confirmed it was true. The vignette illustrates perfectly the fact that from the off, Kennedy was an unlikely hero, who was often unsure of his place in the team during his seven-year spell at the club. 'I ended up winning tonnes of medals,' he told me, 'but I was always looking over my shoulder, and I was never totally confident that I fitted in.' Kennedy questioned me when I referred to him as a Liverpool 'star' from the early '80s. 'A star? More a cog in a machine, I'd say.' Perhaps, but a cog whose nerveless temperament proved decisive in two European Cup finals. 'I would hardly describe my time at Anfield as a bed of roses,' said Kennedy, 'and I think Ronnie Moran barked at me from the touchline more than he did at any other player.' Kennedy initially struggled to adapt to Liverpool's short passing game. After telling Graeme Souness that he didn't see him calling for the ball during a match, the midfielder punched him square in the face. 'Can you see me now?' Souness asked a shocked Kennedy.

At the height of the club's success, Anfield could be the harshest and most unforgiving of environments, rigidly sticking to the Boot Room philosophy that had guided the club towards so much success since Bill Shankly's arrival in 1961. There were tensions and problems to solve, like at any other club, but Anfield's wise men solved them better than anyone else in the game. The Boot Room remained a bastion of continuity and – to newcomers at least – curious customs. Players who weren't certain of their place in the final XI were still forced to go through the agony of the 'boot routine' if the team hadn't already been confirmed on the Friday. Thirteen pairs of boots were lined up underneath the treatment table before a match, at which point Joe Fagan would send the team out to inspect the pitch. When they returned, the starters' boots would be nestled under the shirts, with the remaining two pairs left underneath the table. More often than not, one of the pairs belonged to David Fairclough, still the 'supersub' – much to his annoyance – who described the system as 'unenlightened'. Israeli defender Avi Cohen, who made a dozen appearances in 1980–81, always struggled to understand why players were allowed to eat toast but not bread rolls. 'Ronnie Moran told me later it was because they thought rolls were more stodgy,' said Cohen, who was taken to task by Moran for daring to have a roll with a bowl of soup on an away trip.

Cohen recalled that on one occasion, annoyed that he'd been left out of the team again, he had the temerity to knock on the famous Boot Room door. 'Piss off,' came the reply. He complied, but half an hour later, an agitated Ronnie Moran asked him what he wanted. Puzzled, Cohen asked: 'How did you know it was me?' 'Because the knock lacked conviction,' came the sledgehammer response. The players still ate fish 'n' chips after matches and downed bottles of Higson's Pale Ale, distributed by Moran on the team coach. The only one who didn't partake was Graeme Souness, who had a penchant for goujons and champagne – hence the 'Charlie' nickname. Players were encouraged to drink beer instead of spirits, because the Boot Room boys reckoned beer was easier to sweat out in training.

The Boot Room's approach rarely changed, even when it came to European competition. The emphasis was still on high-octane, two-touch five-a-side matches. From the touchline, Ronnie Moran would yell 'pass and move' at the players, and a free kick would be awarded to the opposition if they failed to do so.

The identity of Liverpool's next European opponents was always a matter of great interest at Melwood. After receiving confirmation via phone, Paisley hobbled out onto the training pitch to convey the news. If his head was down, the players knew they were heading behind the Iron Curtain and – as Ray Clemence recalled – 'facing a night in a cramped and crappy hotel, with basic food and miserable faces.' Liverpool players in the '80s were used to heading east. Three of their European Cup campaigns foundered in Tbilisi, Sofia and Lodz as Paisley's team came up against skilful passing teams and gifted playmakers like Dynamo Tbilisi's Aleksandre Chivadze, who destroyed the myth that eastern-bloc players were all endeavour and muscle. The Liverpool party spent as little time behind the Curtain as possible, often spending just a single night there prior to the game, and (if possible) flying home immediately afterwards. This approach harked back to the Shankly era. Legend has it that the Scot, fearing Cold War espionage, would hunt around his room for recording devices, shouting: 'I know you can hear me, you bastards.' Apparently.

A trip to western Europe, with decent food, plusher accommodation and training sessions at a local sports club was deemed by Paisley to be far more palatable. Excursions to what are now considered European glamour parks were rare. In 1980–81, Liverpool thrashed the Finnish minnows AP Oulu 11–2 on aggregate in the first round and then overcame the brickbats and hostility they faced at Pittodrie by thrashing Alex Ferguson's Aberdeen 4–0, winning 5–0 on aggregate. They cruised past CSKA Sofia in the quarter-finals, setting up an appetising semi-final with Bayern Munich, whose side contained the core of the West German side that won the 1980 European Championships, including Paul Breitner and Karl-Heinz Rummenigge. After failing to make a breakthrough at Anfield in a goalless first leg, the writing appeared to be on the wall for Paisley's side, particularly after Kenny Dalglish went off injured early in the second leg.

Faced with the prospect of playing eighty-three minutes without his star striker, Paisley cast his eyes over the substitute's bench for options. Opting against bringing on Ian Rush, his young £300,000 signing from Chester City who'd thus far failed to impress in a Liverpool shirt, Paisley threw on Toxteth-born winger Howard Gayle, who'd previously made just one first-team appearance but who became the first black player to appear in the Liverpool first team by doing so. Rush and Gayle knew first-hand how vicious the atmosphere could be in the Anfield dressing room. During this formative time in his Liverpool career, Rush avoided Kenny Dalglish as much as possible due to the merciless ribbing he received from the Scot for his dress sense (skinny jeans and sweaters) and his inherent shyness. Gayle had fallen foul of Alan Hansen in the game of 'ricks'. Whenever a player used an unfamiliar phrase or 'misspoke', Hansen would pounce. On one occasion, Gayle accidentally said: 'Don't bush around the beat,' rather than: 'Don't beat around the bush,' and Hansen and co. never let him forget it.

Gayle's other trials and tribulations at Anfield were rather more serious, though. At the tail end of the '70s, he'd had an infamous run-in with former Liverpool skipper Tommy Smith, who'd racially abused Gayle in training. On one occasion Gayle snapped, squared up to Smith and warned him: 'One day, Tommy, when you're taking a piss, I'll be there outside the bathroom waiting for you with a baseball bat. Then we'll see how much you've got to say.' Smith backed off. Gayle recalled that only Graeme Souness spoke up for him. The others turned a deaf ear and a blind eye to events. There was another incident at one of the players' Christmas parties, which weren't exactly bastions of good taste anywhere. Photographs from the era show players from a raft of clubs dressed as serial killers, Nazis, Klansmen, and (now) disgraced DJs. Roy 'Chubby' Brown was compere, and when a stripper, covered in talcum powder, put Gayle's head between her breasts, Brown took one look at him and said: 'Try walking through fucking Toxteth now.' Gayle laughed along with the others, but the incident left him feeling uncomfortable, partly because the Boot Room boys had suggested to him on more than one occasion that he might want to move out of Toxteth, or specifically Norris Green, where the price of substantial Georgian properties had fallen to as low as £4,000. 'It suggested to me that they didn't fully understand my ethnic roots. Liverpool has the oldest black community in Europe. I was part of a culture that didn't understand my culture,' Gayle told me. Within a few months, as the neighbourhood burnt during the '81 Toxteth riots, which were sparked by the arrest of Leroy Cooper, Paisley would ask Gayle once more to move out.

But in Munich, he had his chance. 'Get in behind them,' Ronnie

Moran told him. Underneath the Olympic Stadium's futuristic slanting roof, Gayle's impact on the match was sensational. Bayern forward Karl-Heinz Rummenigge later admitted that Gayle's name wasn't mentioned once in their team talks. With almost his first touch (from an Alan Hansen pass), Gayle accelerated past Wolfgang Dremmler in the Bayern box and was summarily scythed down. It was as cast-iron a penalty as could be, but the referee waved Gayle's protestations aside.

The athletics track created a gap between the pitch and the crowd, but Gayle could hear – and see – exactly what was happening. 'There were the monkey chants every time I received the ball. Hate on their faces. More than the occasional *sieg-heil* salute from fans at the front,' he told me. 'It wasn't anything I'd not heard or seen before in England, but it was on a far-bigger scale.' Did the volume of abuse put Gayle off his game? 'No,' Gayle responded in his softly spoken Scouse accent. 'It just made me want to run at them harder and faster.' Which he did.

Gayle wasn't the only bit-part player making his mark that night; defender Richard Money, whose departure from Fulham to Liverpool in 1979 for £300,000 was mentioned on *Minder* by Dennis Waterman's character, Terry McCann, and Colin Irwin also starred as Liverpool pressed. After sixty-one minutes, having tortured the Bayern defence for almost an hour, Gayle fouled Dieter Müller and received a yellow card. Fearing that Gayle's frustration might boil over, Paisley hauled his winger off and threw on the experienced Jimmy Case. The disappointed Gayle would come to regard this as further evidence that Paisley didn't trust him, but for the Liverpool manager, individuals' feelings were of secondary importance when it came to the team ethic. Bayern themselves had already goaded the visitors. When Paisley's men walked out onto the pitch before kick-off, they were mystified about the A5 flyers that were littering the side of the pitch and were being used as paper aeroplanes by Bayern fans. The flyers contained travel instructions for Bayern fans to the final in Paris. The team talk took care of itself. 'This is what they think of you,' ranted Moran, clutching a fistful of flyers. The players were incandescent.

The match was tight and tense, and it was settled by the most insouciant of Liverpool goals. From a David Johnson pass, an unmarked Ray Kennedy controlled the ball on his thigh, allowed it to bounce once and stroked it home. It appeared to take the Geordie an age to score. 'There's no point in rushing these things, is there?' Kennedy laughed during our interview. Despite a furious Bayern onslaught in the dying minutes, and Rummenigge's goal, the away goal took Liverpool into their third final in four years.

With Paisley's injured players restored to fitness, the Liverpool boss did what he always did and ruthlessly discarded Gayle, Money and Irwin for the final. Alan Kennedy, who'd broken his wrist, was reinstalled. In keeping with Liverpool's tricky season, the build-up to the match was – like the flight to Paris from Speke Airport – uncharacteristically bumpy. FIFA officials insisted that the Umbro signs on the Liverpool shirts were covered over with what looked like giant white Post-it-notes, which are clearly visible on the footage, and that the three white Adidas stripes on the players' boots were enhanced. 'So, Joe Fagan, cursing and swearing, had to use white paint on eleven pairs of boots,' Kennedy said. 'You should have heard the language....'

Much was made in the press about Kennedy's imminent battle with Real's English winger Laurie Cunningham, but Kennedy recalled that little was said about the England winger by Liverpool staff prior to the match, other than to warn him to 'keep his feet' against the former West Brom player. As it turned out, Cunningham had a poor match. When Kennedy's moment with destiny arrived in the seventy-sixth minute, he briefly noticed that Kenny Dalglish and David Johnson were in a better position in the penalty box, but he drove on regardless and lashed the ball home. 'Was that a fucking cross or what?' yelled Ray Clemence in the dressing room afterwards. 'It was a playground goal, really,' Ray Kennedy scoffed during our interview. 'Real's defending was awful.' But the jubilant Alan Kennedy didn't mind. Liverpool's final XI each received £5,000 for securing Liverpool their third European Cup and were greeted as heroes upon their return to Speke Airport. 'I'm delighted for Alan. Footballers come in all shapes and sizes,' Paisley said. Three years later, Kennedy applied the finishing touch in a European Cup final again, to the bemusement of his teammates once more.

•　•　•

The churn of players at Anfield was never ending, and new signings continued to find Bob Paisley as idiosyncratic as ever. Defender Mark Lawrenson, signed for £900,000 from Brighton in July 1981, recalled:

> I was staying at the Atlantic Tower Hotel, when a receptionist rang up to say that Bob was waiting downstairs. I went down, suited and booted, and there he was waiting in an old gold Ford Granada, which looked like a pimp-mobile, wearing a cardigan that had yellow fried egg stains on it, and carpet slippers on his feet. I thought – 'And you've just won the European Cup?'

Lawrenson later settled in next to Alan Hansen in central defence, but initially he played in several defensive positions. On one occasion, Paisley asked Lawrenson if he could 'do a left one?' 'Pardon, boss?' asked the perplexed Republic of Ireland international. 'A left one,' Paisley repeated. 'I had to go to Joe Fagan and ask for clarity,' Lawrenson told me. 'He means left-back,' Fagan responded with a grin.

Prior to Christmas, Liverpool languished in mid-table, with defenders struggling to adapt to playing alongside the new man between the sticks – Bruce Grobbelaar. Ray Clemence had departed to Tottenham, giving the Zimbabwe international a chance to establish himself in the first team. It was far from a straightforward process. The acrobatic showman infuriated his defence with more than a few ricks and howlers during those early months. Against Manchester City in December, Grobbelaar dropped several crosses and allowed a shot by Kevin Reeves to squirm under him in City's 3–1 win. After the match, Joe Fagan lambasted the entire team for letting their standards slip. The captaincy was stripped from Phil Thompson and given to Graeme Souness. Young Irish midfielder Ronnie Whelan gained a regular berth in midfield and relentlessly pressed opponents in the middle of the park. The Boot Room stuck with Grobbelaar – who'd failed to convince his teammates that he was a worthy successor to Clemence – reasoning that on too many occasions, he had been left exposed by teammates not doing their jobs properly. 'Bob did tell me to cut out the hand stands though,' laughed Grobbelaar. With the sandblastings over, the reorganised defence and midfield functioned superbly, and Paisley's team went on an unbeaten run in the new year to secure another league title.

● ● ●

'It was where the Anfield outsiders tended to live, the ones whose faces didn't always fit,' said striker Michael Robinson of his Wirral residence. Bruce Grobbelaar lived there, after firstly tucking himself away in north Wales. So did Craig Johnston, the tenacious midfielder whose strong Australian accent (he was actually born in South Africa) saw him given the predicable nickname 'Skippy' by teammates. 'We thought a little bit differently from the others,' Johnston recalled. 'After matches, I liked to walk the streets of the city and take photographs, which I kept quiet from the others. Imagine the piss-taking if they'd have known...' Johnston had come over from Australia as a teenager, and as a youngster at Ayresome Park, had been told by Middlesbrough manager Jack Charlton that he was the 'fucking worst player [he'd] ever seen'. On Charlton's orders, Johnston was instructed to train in the car park, away from the other players, but he fought his way into the 'Boro first team after Charlton left. His formative experiences in England led him to describe himself as 'the worst player at Liverpool' following his £400,000 move to Anfield in March 1981. But Johnston's fitness levels and sheer determination made up for any other shortcomings he may have had.

Other Wirral residents David Hodgson (signed from Middlesbrough for £450,000 in 1982) and Michael Robinson (a £250,000 purchase from Brighton in 1983) were bought to bolster competition for places up front. They never even remotely threatened to oust Dalglish or Rush from the team. When the *Guardian*-reading Robinson scored a hat-trick against West Ham on one of his rare runs in the first team, Dalglish wrote 'I don't believe it' on the match ball. Hodgson – ribbed mercilessly for wearing leather trousers, instead of the traditional slacks favoured by teammates – told me: 'From the outset, I never had the self-confidence to succeed at Liverpool.

I didn't have the mindset of many of the others.' Perhaps fittingly for two players who never quite felt like they belonged, they viewed the unsparing Boot Room culture rather differently from Anfield's Southport residents, or the 'sand crunchers' as Robinson described them. 'At Brighton, I was used to praise being heaped on me. At Anfield, there was none of that. They'd have got more out of me had they put an arm round my shoulder a little more. But they did OK anyway, didn't they?' Robinson said.

The pair were amongst the most handsomely renumerated in English football. Although player wages were never openly discussed at Anfield, when details of Hodgson's Middlesbrough contract was leaked to the tabloids by his former chairman, it caused consternation in the ranks, because the players knew that Liverpool always matched incoming players' salaries. Hodgson can still rattle off the finer points of his bumper contract. '£1,000 per week basic. £250 per appearance. A £33k signing-on fee spread over a four-year contract. A £15k car allowance, and a £2,500 allowance for moving house. I didn't have an agent. I negotiated that myself,' he told me in his crisp north-eastern accent. Kenny Dalglish was less than impressed. 'Is this true, Hodgy?' he asked his new team as he read about it in *The Sun*. When Hodgson confirmed that it was – except for the car allowance, which Liverpool refused to honour – Dalglish rolled the newspaper under his arm and stomped off. 'Presumably to see the chairman,' Hodgson laughed.

Perhaps more than any other Liverpool player of that era, Robinson (on £1,000 a week), whom teammates nicknamed 'Cat' thanks to his excellent reflexes in goal during training sessions, enjoyed soaking up the gritty ambience of Liverpool in the '80s and took himself off to various gigs in the city centre. 'I saw Echo & the Bunnymen, Julian Cope's band [The Teardrop Explodes]... You name it. There was an amazing creativity about the place.' Robinson described the majority of players as being 'apolitical', and they looked with curiosity at Robinson as he devoured *The Guardian*.

I was very good friends with Graeme Souness, but despite the fact he appeared in *Boys from the Blackstuff* [Alan Bleasdale's drama set in recession-hit Liverpool] and had an encounter with Yosser Hughes [Bernard Hill's antihero character], he was an admirer of Thatcher. Footballers often tend to be conservative by nature.

Robinson briefly featured in the ITV comedy *Scully*, which charts the life of a Scouser in his early twenties who has *Walter Mitty* fantasies of running out with the Liverpool team and scoring at the Kop End. In some ways, Hodgson and Robinson accepted their bit-part roles with good grace, with Hodgson likening it to 'a cameo role in an Oscar-winning movie'. Robinson recalled that, although he failed to establish himself as a regular,

underneath all the sarcasm and the barbs, there was a warmth amongst the players. I arrived when the players were having dinner, and when I walked in, Graeme Souness called out: 'I saved you a chair, Michael; come and sit next to me.' And he was fantastic company then and afterwards.; a wonderful captain.

Hodgson recalled how the likes of Dalglish and Souness immediately offered to help him look for property in the local area. 'The players had each other's backs,' he explained. In their own way, the duo also made a valued contribution as Liverpool completed a treble in the 1983–84 campaign.

As Liverpool embarked upon another European Cup adventure

during the 1983–84 campaign, they did so with Joe Fagan at the helm, following Bob Paisley's retirement during the close season. There was little fuss as England's most successful manager stood down. The squad was informed early in the new year that Paisley would be leaving and that Fagan would step in. 'It wasn't much of a surprise, given Bob's age,' Mark Lawrenson explained. 'The Boot Room philosophy would continue, and it was done with the minimum of fuss and emotion. The Liverpool way.' Unusually, Paisley joined his players on the pitch after Liverpool beat Tottenham in the League Cup final at Wembley in March and then at Anfield after wrapping up the 1983 title, cajoled into it by Graeme Souness. Then Paisley disappeared down the tunnel and was gone.

Under Fagan, 'absolutely nothing changed', according to Mark Lawrenson. That was hardly surprising. It had been Fagan – along with Ronnie Moran – who'd always espoused Paisley's no-frills approach, believing that players should solve tactical issues themselves. When a nervous Michael Robinson asked Fagan how he should approach his debut, a grinning Fagan responded: 'Either put the ball in the back of the net, Michael, or give it to someone who can. Improvise.' En route to the European Cup final in Rome, Liverpool players improvised and problem solved like never before.

Overcoming the Danish part-timers Odense, Liverpool then eased past Spanish champions Athletic Bilbao and their hatchet man Andoni Goikoetxea (who'd gained the nickname 'the Butcher of Bilbao' after snapping Diego Maradona's ankle like a twig during his side's clash with Barcelona in 1983) and swatted aside three-time European Cup winners Benfica. The home legs were notable for low attendances. Only 30,000 watched Fagan's team beat Benfica, and there were yawning gaps on the terraces and in the stands for the Odense game. Liverpool faced the skilful-yet-spiky Dinamo București in the semi-final. It was the club's most toxic European encounter. 'Dinamo went over the top from the off; flying elbows, late tackles, leaving their foot in,' explained Mark Lawrenson. 'Their captain set out to wind up Souness. Big mistake.'

Sammy Lee had given Liverpool a 1–0 lead, but Dinamo pushed forward as the game entered its final quarter. When a Liverpool attack broke down, Lica Movila found himself alone next to Souness. Incensed by Movila's niggling approach, Souness threw a right hook, breaking Movila's jaw in two places. The referee didn't see it. Neither did the Kop, nor the TV cameras. Alan Kennedy did, describing it as a 'red blur, followed by a thud'. By the time the official noticed Movila prostrate on the turf, Souness was thirty yards away, with hands on hips; a picture of innocence. The upshot of Souness's punch was the most hostile of receptions in Bucharest.

'Charlie' revelled in his notoriety. At Bucharest Airport, with stony-faced officials glaring at Liverpool's 'ultra-alpha male', as Craig Johnston described him, Souness simply stared back. On the team coach to the stadium, fans pointed at him and gestured to Souness that he'd get his throat cut. Souness flashed back a puzzled smile, shook his head and pleaded mistaken identity, pointing to the similarly dark haired and moustachioed Alan Kennedy. 'I thought he might get me killed,' Kennedy recalled. When the Liverpool players ran out onto the pitch for the warm-up, the boos and whistles began. As the ball came close to him, Souness either dummied it, or hoofed the ball up the pitch, just to wind the crowd up more. 'Graeme was standing there laughing and smirking,' said Mark Lawrenson. 'He revelled in it. You have to have a certain mindset to behave like that.' Souness used the catcalls to fuel another superb performance in which two Ian Rush goals gave Liverpool safe passage to a fourth European Cup final. The atmosphere at the final in Rome was no less toxic.

• • •

Liverpool's captain looked at Michael Robinson as if he were mad. 'We're the best team in Europe,' Souness insisted, 'and we want to beat Roma in their own back yard.' Robinson had just suggested to Souness that it might be better if they met Jim McLean's Dundee United, who'd conquered Roma 2–0 at Tannadice in the first leg of their European Cup semi-final, in the Rome showpiece match. But for a series of questionable refereeing decisions in the return leg, Robinson may have got his wish. Instead, Roma ran out 3–0 winners to set up a clash with Fagan's side. The two sides approached the final in hugely different ways. Coached by the methodical Swede Nils Liedholm, the Italian champions secreted themselves away – monk like – in a hilltop retreat and were subjected to a regime of early nights, white meat and fish and mineral water. Meanwhile, Liverpool headed to Israel, ostensibly to play in a friendly match but also, as it turned out, to sink copious amounts of beer. A night out took a turn for the worse when an inebriated David Hodgson urinated all over his teammates' feet as he lay under the table. Words and then punches were exchanged. The Israeli press got to hear about the incident, and word quickly reached the Roma players. The bust-up was quickly forgotten, but one upshot of Liverpool's Israeli tour was that the players – with Hodgson acting as official MC – adopted Chris Rea's 'I Don't Know What It Is but I Love It' as their unofficial anthem. 'It got sung on the coach, wherever we travelled,' Hodgson explained. It demonstrates to perfection the conservative musical tastes of most '80s footballers. A cursory glance at *Shoot!* focus pages from the era reveals Liverpool players' love of Billy Joel, The Eagles, Barbara Streisand, Stevie Wonder and Phil Collins. Although Bruce Grobbelaar went left of field with his love of hardcore Canadian rockers Doug and the Slugs and Michael Robinson loved Liverpudlian new-wave acts, Chris Rea's catchy midway route prevailed, and proved to be the unlikeliest of war cries.

In the press conference before the match, Joe Fagan joked that his team talk would be 'longer than usual for this one – about five minutes'. He ordered his players to shoot on sight and not to allow Roma's Brazilians Falcão or Cerezo to dictate the pace of play. When the players walked out to inspect the pitch and smell the atmosphere, they were greeted by a tidal wave of catcalls from the Curva Sud, where Roma fans had gathered hours before the game. Alan Kennedy recalled: 'The noise was like nothing we'd heard before. Graeme Souness told us to walk close to the Roma fans, look them in the eye.' Liverpool fans were hugely outnumbered. Given 17,000 tickets, the club were only able to sell 10,000 of them; a far cry from Liverpool's first European Cup final seven years earlier, when more than twice that number made the pilgrimage to the Eternal City.

As they headed back down the tunnel and filed past the Roma dressing room, David Hodgson decided it was time for the first Chris Rea salvo. 'I sang the first verse, and then the other lads joined in on the chorus,' Hodgson said. 'Pretty loud, although not quite as loud as it would be later.' Word later reached the Liverpool camp that, to a man, the already tense Roma players had looked nervously at their coach Niedholm. 'We heard that the colour drained out of their faces,' Mark Lawrenson said, 'because they realised that, despite the press dubbing us as underdogs, we were in a relaxed mood.' As the Liverpool players lined up in the long, dark tunnel before

kick-off, Roma kept them waiting. It was an old trick deployed by
teams to give them a slight advantage prior to big matches. When
they eventually emerged from the sanctity of their changing room,
Roma began some warm-up exercises. It was time for another blast
of Chris Rea: 'This time, our singing was so loud that it drowned out
the noise of the crowd outside,' David Hodgson explained. 'We were
banging on the walls, and when the Roma players finally lined up
next to us, we looked them in the eyes and belted it out even louder.
They looked at us with a mixture of fear and disbelief.'

As both sets of players emerged for the kick-off, the Curva Sud
exploded as smoke bombs, flares and Roman candles were detonat-
ed by Roma fans. 'Silencing the home fans' – as Fagan instructed his
players to do – would be extremely difficult. Nonetheless, Liverpool
soon slipped into their usual pass-and-move game; the tempo of the
match was dominated by Souness. World Cup winners Bruno Conti
and Francesco Graziani struggled to disrupt the unflappable cool of
the Liverpool back four. Right-back Phil Neal was the only one who
hadn't been ever-present in the league that season, and it was he
who stabbed Liverpool ahead after a mix-up in the Roma defence.
The Liverpool fans standing on the Curva Nord went wild. Around
the rest of the Stadio Olimpico, there was stunned silence. Shortly before half-time Roma got an equaliser, with Roberto Pruzzo
heading home from a Conti cross. The Curva Sud jolted back to life
with a guttural roar. The second half was a tense affair. Liverpool
were happy enough deploying their passing game and keeping the
ball. When Roma substituted Pruzzo after sixty-four minutes, Alan
Kennedy knew where the game was headed. 'Their players started bollocking the ball boys if they threw the ball back too quickly.
They were already playing for penalties.' Just before the Liverpool
first team departed to Rome, they'd taken on the reserves in a spot

kick shootout. 'It wasn't taken very seriously, and the kids won 3–2,' Mark Lawrenson recalled.

The penalty shootout was played out in front of the Curva Sud. The ultras did their level best to distract the Liverpool spot kick takers, ably assisted by the clustered paparazzi behind the goal, whose flashbulbs popped just as the opposition made contact with the ball. A nervous Steve Nicol skied the opening penalty, as did Bruno Conti with Roma's second spot kick. The scores were tied up at 3–3. Grobbelaar and Graziani had a dig at one another right at the end of extra time, and when Grobbelaar saw Graziani put his arm around the referee's shoulder as he prepared to take Roma's fourth spot kick, he decided to improvise. Liverpool players from the era still find Grobbelaar's rubber-legged routine amusing. Michael Robinson described it as his 'puppet-on-the-string act'; Kennedy called it the 'spaghetti-leg scene.' Whether or not Grobbelaar's theatrics put Graziani off to any degree remains a mystery, but only the showman between the sticks would have had the audacity to pull it off. Graziani's penalty clipped the top of the crossbar, leaving Alan Kennedy with the opportunity to win the European Cup for Liverpool.

'My legs were really heavy as I approached,' Kennedy said. 'I was very nervous, and when I placed the ball, I span around quickly to give myself some leverage. Otherwise, I'm not sure that my legs would have had the power to get me to the ball.' Kennedy's teammates weren't entirely convinced that Kennedy was up to the job. Grobbelaar playfully exclaimed: 'Not fucking you!' as the full-back walked past him, and Mark Lawrenson recalled that in the centre circle there were 'raised eyebrows and furrowed brows' as it dawned on the players that it would fall to 'Barney' to decide the outcome of the final. But as Kennedy prepared to strike the ball, he opened up his body and, as Tancredi dove to the right, he fired the ball to the left. Once again, Liverpool were European champions.

The players partied the night away, belting out 'I Don't Know What It Is but I Love It' for the hundredth time. 'Bruce was full of it, telling us how he'd put Graziani off,' Michael Robinson explained. '"But you didn't even bloody save it. Graziani missed," Graeme Souness told him.' No one was allowed to get above themselves.

There was an unpleasant postscript, with Liverpool supporters running the gauntlet of the Roma fans' fury in the streets afterwards. Rocks were thrown and some Liverpool supporters were stabbed, leading them to dub the Eternal City 'stab city'. At the tail end of the 2023–24 campaign, Liverpool announced that their new home kit would be styled in the fashion of the class of '84. The slick advert shows modern Liverpool stars sipping cappuccino, sitting on vespas and looking moody against a classical Roman architectural backdrop. That certainly wasn't the experience of many terrified Liverpool fans that night, and the bad feeling between Italian and English fans festered in the lead up to the European Cup final at the Heysel Stadium a year later.

7

THE REVIVALISTS

'I reckoned that if we finished ahead of Liverpool,
everything else would fall into place.'

HOWARD KENDALL

Anfield – October 1984. From a speculative Gary Stevens punt, Everton's Scottish striker Graeme Sharp controls the Adidas Tango ball, which league champions Liverpool use in their home games, on his left foot. Toffees players have been practising with it all week at Bellefield, with manager Howard Kendall urging them to accustom themselves to its extreme bounce and swerve. Sharp drags the ball away from Liverpool defender Mark Lawrenson ('There was no point in trying to outpace him,' Sharp later said), allows it to bounce once and volleys home from thirty yards with his right foot. The Tango ball flies past Bruce Grobbelaar into the top-right corner, and Everton fans go berserk. They've not seen their team win at Anfield since March 1970, when The Beatles were (officially at least) still in business. When the referee blows his whistle, confirming the fact that the FA Cup holders have finally sunk their rivals from across Stanley Park, the travelling supporters, wedged into the corner of the Kemlyn Road End and dotted around the rest of the ground, chorus: 'Hand it over, hand it over, hand it over, Liverpool.' Sharp – the beaming goal scorer, haring for the tunnel, has the distinct impression that the tide in the city may just have turned. There's a long way to go in the Canon League Division One title race yet, but from now on, Liverpool's ever-noisier neighbours will always be in the ascendancy.

• • •

At the conclusion of the Anfield face-off, Everton supporters also sang Howard Kendall's name raucously. Only nine months before, many of those same fans wanted him gone. I interviewed Kendall, under whom the Toffees won two league titles, the FA Cup and European Cup Winners' Cup between 1984 and 1987 late last century. We met at his favourite Chinese restaurant in Sefton Park, shortly after he'd departed Goodison Park for a third time. Everton had narrowly avoided relegation from the Premier League during the 1997–98 season. He was in a slightly introspective mood, but his spirits rose when he reflected on Everton's glory years. Sipping on his wine and munching on a prawn cracker or four, he looked around and said:

> We had no-holds-barred lunches in here, paid for by players' fines for lateness. They could eat and drink all they liked. They could get things off their chests. There was even the odd scrap. But what happened in here stayed between us, and taught the players to have each other's backs. 'Look out for one another in the restaurant, in the bar, and on the pitch,' I'd tell them. They listened.

But Kendall's first three years in the Goodison hot seat were tortuous.

As a player, Kendall was a member of Everton's midfield 'Holy Trinity'. Alongside Colin Harvey and Alan Ball, his intelligent play in the centre of the park helped Harry Catterick's side win the league title in 1970. After spells at Birmingham City, Stoke City and then Blackburn Rovers, Kendall returned to Goodison Park, initially as player–manager in June 1981. Under Gordon Lee, Everton had just finished fifteenth in the league and were in urgent need of rejuvenation. In order to 'make a bang', as Kendall put it to me, he unveiled his – as it turned out – not-so-*Magnificent-Seven* signings during the 1981 close season, of whom goalkeeper Neville Southall was the only success. The 'ghosts of Goodison past' – as he put it – rattled Kendall. Everton's greats from yesteryear regularly attended matches: Joe Mercer – skipper of the golden team from the pre-war era, the 'Golden Vision' himself; Alex Young; and the tough and uncompromising Harry Catterick still gave his former charge the benefit of his experience – 'whether I bloody wanted it not,' Kendall said. When Everton lost 5–0 at home to Liverpool in November in the 1982–83 season (Ian Rush plundered four goals), Kendall recalled that all three visited him in the days after the game.

There were tears in Joe's eyes, Alex was speechless and Harry Catterick said it was the worst thing he'd ever seen. There were portraits of all the old stars like Dixie Dean everywhere, looking at me. I wanted to put the whole lot on a bloody big bonfire and burn them ... but that wouldn't have solved anything.

Kendall's men finished eighth in 1981–82, then seventh in 1982–83, before results and Goodison Park attendances went off a cliff in

1983–84. There were two matches that Kendall described as 'the lowest of the low'. On 27 December, Everton were hammered 3–0 by Wolves, who'd finish in bottom place that season. 'I received death threats,' Kendall told me, gently shaking his head. 'My car had graffiti scrawled all over it.' Four days later, a miserable 13,479 crowd watched the team labour to a 0–0 draw with Coventry. 'Not only could you hear what the crowd was singing ['shit' and 'crap' seemed to be the most popular words], but you could also see which individuals were barracking us,' recalled Graeme Sharp. Kendall was also made acutely aware of the dire financial state in which the club, and the city, found itself. Chairman Philip Carter continued to back his manager, but warned Kendall that crowds were crashing well below the breakeven level. After walking around the Everton area, essayist Lincoln Allison wrote about 'deserted streets, surrounded by factories and warehouses and occasional heaps of rubble. The silence is eerie, frightening.' Kendall was also shown a Liverpool chamber of commerce report where one local businessman commented: 'We have survived two world wars, the Blitz and the Depression of the '30s. I wonder whether we shall last out the next twelve months.' Kendall was in a similarly perilous position, admitting to me: 'If I hadn't been a former Evertonian who'd done well there, I'd have been out on my ear. It bought me a little time.' The domestic cups would prove to be his salvation.

The Everton players who took to the field at the Manor Ground on 18 January 1984 for the Milk Cup quarter-final with Oxford United retain vivid memories of the smells that greeted them. There was the scent of fried onions, which always drifted across the ground from the burger vans outside, and cigarette smoke drifted across from the terraces which were close to the pitch. Conventional wisdom holds that the game changed the entire course of Everton's modern history and Kendall's managerial career. For the majority of the match, Everton were massively under the cosh from a side that would be promoted as Third Division champions at season's end and, after eighty-two minutes, led through a Bobby McDonald goal. Adrian Heath, who since his hefty £700,000 transfer from Stoke City in 1981 had been frustratingly inconsistent, was instructed by his manager to push forwards and see if he could grab a goal. Headline writers suggested that Kendall's P45 was in the process of being penned just as 'Inchy' seized on a stray back pass by Kevin Brock, rounded goalkeeper Steve Hardwick and slotted the ball home. 'Everyone talks about Brock's back pass,' said Heath during our interview, 'but I still had a bit to do. One game by itself can't alter the course of a club's season, but the relief we felt was huge.' Kendall acknowledged he owed Heath an enormous debt of gratitude. 'Here's to Adrian,' he said, raising his glass and smiling. 'But things were already starting to click by then.'

•   •   •

Following a 3–0 humbling by Liverpool in November 1983, Kendall had gone to the pub with his reserve-team coach Colin Harvey. A gifted midfielder – nicknamed the 'white Pelé' by Everton fans – Harvey was as tenacious and exacting with young players as he was once creative and skilled on the pitch. His passion for the club bordered on the ferocious. After he was signed from Dumbarton, Graeme Sharp struggled to secure a first-team berth, and Harvey regularly took him to task, reasoning: 'If I didn't think you had a chance, I'd let you piss off in the afternoons and play snooker.' Over a beer or two, Kendall told Harvey that he wanted to promote him to first-team coach, because he 'needed those eyes and ears of yours across the first team.' Harvey – who accepted Kendall's offer in an instant – was a zealot. Immediately after matches, he watched video replays and discussed with players what they needed to do to improve their game. His was a computer like mind in an analogue age. Harvey instructed Graeme Sharp on the subject of how forwards were the first line of defence, urging him to close down space more effectively.

Also present and correct by now in the team were former Bolton Wanderers midfielder Peter Reid and ex-Wolves forward Andy Gray. 'About bloody time,' Reid said to Kendall when he rang him about a proposed £60,000 transfer in July 1982. The tenacious midfielder had seen his market value drop due to a succession of knee injuries, and initially struggled to gain full fitness at Goodison Park. At the start of the 1983–84 campaign, Kendall and Harvey prepared to write him off, but then Reid enjoyed a decent run in the team, and Harvey altered Reid's role within it, instructing Reid to move forwards and press the opposition rather than drain his legs and drop back to support his own defence. 'It changed the whole dynamic,' Kendall explained to me, 'and it made us a much more effective pressing team.' Looked at another way, Adrian Heath's dramatic equaliser at the Manor Ground is due to Reid's relentless harrying of Brock, forcing the Oxford man into a careless ball. 'Reidy had been doing that for a while,' Kendall explained, 'but this was proof that his approach worked.'

Gray had arrived from Wolves in October '83 for a hugely cut-price £250,000, due to combination of the player's ongoing knee injuries and Wolves' dire financial situation. 'They needed the money sharpish,' Gray told me when I interviewed him at the Sky Sports studios in the '90s, 'and Howard Kendall convinced me that Everton had great potential.' The question of Gray's giant medical file – crammed with X-rays and reports on his troublesome knees – was dealt with by Gray throwing some of the incriminating evidence onto the open fire in his home and watching it burn. Former teammates vouch for Gray's vivacious personality and his ability to inspire those around him. 'In some ways, Andy was our saviour, a fact he often reminded us of,' laughed Graeme Sharp. Kendall appealed to Gray's sense of frustration that despite winning individual awards like Young Player of the Year, two League Cup victories (with Aston Villa and Wolves) was a fairly poor return for a player who was fond of describing himself as a 'winner'. 'I couldn't wait to get stuck in,' Gray told me. His trophy haul was about to increase.

• • •

Tall, raw and lanky, forward-turned-central-defender Derek Mountfield had spent two seasons at Tranmere Rovers before making the short journey to Goodison Park for £30,000 in 1982. After morning training was finished, Colin Harvey set up intensive afternoon sessions for the moustachioed Mountfield that focussed on the player's heading and range of passing. 'I take my hat off to Colin,' Mountfield told me, 'because without him I'd never have broken through.' With his £150 per week contract in hand, he became a first-team regular just as Everton's fortunes improved. Present and correct for the replay against Oxford, which was won at a canter with an orange ball in a Goodison snowstorm, Mountfield also played in both legs of the Milk Cup semi-final against Aston Villa. Everton's 4–2 aggregate win saw them reach Wembley, and he recalled the manic scenes on the motorway as the all-Merseyside Milk Cup final approached. En route down south in the Everton team coach, Mountfield recalled seeing some fans sat in a mocked-up living room in the back of a moving lorry. 'They were sat there in armchairs with beers toasting us as we cruised past,' he said. Many of the cars and coaches had red *and* blue flags fluttering from the windows. In the stands and on the terraces that afternoon, supporters mixed freely. Mountfield later discovered that it wasn't all bonhomie when it came to the red/blue divide. After becoming a first-team regular, he took delivery of a sponsored Ford Toyota from a local garage, with 'Mountfield' written in bold letters down the side of the car. 'It was asking for trouble,' he admitted. 'Everton fans beeped me and waved and put their thumbs up when I stopped at traffic lights. Liverpool fans beeped and stuck their fingers up. One time, they smeared dog shit all over my car, which was nice of them.'

Everton forced a goalless draw at Wembley in a match they arguably should have won. Alan Hansen clearly guided Adrian Heath's goal-bound shot away with his hand ('The most blatant bloody handball you'll ever see,' fumed Graeme Sharp), but Everton's furious penalty claims were waved away by the referee. A Graeme Souness winner settled matters in the Maine Road replay, but although Kendall was disappointed, he later reflected: 'Anyone could see the strides we were making.'

His team forged ahead in the FA Cup, knocking out Notts County at Meadow Lane thanks to Andy Gray's memorable half-volley header. 'The ball came to me with a low bounce,' Gray recalled. 'I had a split second to decide whether to head it or volley it, and I chose the former, although generating power on it like that is tricky.' Adrian Heath's late headed winner in the semi-final at Highbury against Southampton sparked wild scenes of jubilation from Everton fans. 'I can only describe it as an outpouring of emotion,' Derek Mountfield explained. 'Many of our fans had had tough times in the

'80s, and our job was to give them something to smile and cheer about.'

Having not played at Wembley for sixteen years, Everton would now play there no less than seven times in the space of three seasons. Mountfield concluded that finally playing in the showpiece matches was 'a welcome relief from all the rigmarole surrounding the event.' By 1984, the build-up to the final began at breakfast time, with cameras trained on the players tucking into their cornflakes and poached/scrambled eggs on toast. Holed up in their Buckinghamshire hotel, Everton's players were awoken by an almighty racket on the lawn underneath their rooms. 'There was Freddie Starr falling down a manhole and doing some funny walks,' recalled Graeme Sharp. Howard Kendall found the Scouser Starr's manic performance bizarre, admitting to me: 'I never knew what the bloody hell he was talking about.'

In their memoirs, several Everton players have claimed that Starr was dressed as Adolf Hitler, but they're mixing up their FA Cup finals. Starr paraded in full Nazi regalia and threatened to blow host Dickie Davies's head off before the '75 final between Fulham and West Ham. Nine years later, Starr (an Everton fan) contented himself with wearing a flat blue and white cap and an Everton scarf. 'Is that your wife, John?' Starr yells up to full-back John Bailey, who's hanging out of his window, with roommate Andy Gray. 'Yes, and we've had a lovely evening,' Bailey replies, patting Gray on the head. Bailey – or 'Bails', as his teammates called him – was at the centre of much of the '80-style banter before the game. It transpired that prior to the Milk Cup final, he'd hired Howard Kendall a kissogram. To get his own back, Kendall arranged for a 22-stone kissogram to give 'Bails' a smacker before the team headed down south for the

FA Cup final. Via video link-up, Bailey then spoke to his family on the Everton Express, which was speeding down from Liverpool; his sister-in-law sported a pair of joke goggly eyes to demonstrate that she hadn't slept because she was worried about him.

The slapstick dispensed with, Everton set off for Wembley on their team coach, with an onboard BBC camera for company. 'The mood was relaxed but focussed amongst the players, and the Milk Cup final had got them used to playing in a big game at Wembley,' Howard Kendall explained. Whilst TV footage showed Watford chairman Elton John overcome with emotion during the National Anthem and 'Abide with Me', Everton were doggedly focussed on the job in hand. As soon as Graeme Sharp put them ahead with a neat finish in the thirty-seventh minute ('The feeling of scoring at Wembley with all your family watching is indescribable,' Sharp told me), the outcome was never in serious doubt. Andy Gray doubled Everton's lead after appearing to head the ball out of Watford keeper Steve Sherwood's hands. Finally, Everton had broken their fourteen-year trophy duck. 'It was the springboard for everything that came next,' Howard Kendall said.

• • •

Kendall could be withering and cutting. Graeme Sharp remembered Kendall pulling him into his office and making scathing comments about his lack of recent goals. When Sharp argued that he'd just scored the equaliser against Coventry City, Kendall insisted the goal didn't count because it came from a dead ball, which 'isn't the same as a goal from open play'. Representatives from Hafnia – the Danish canned meat company that sponsored Everton between 1979 and 1985 – invited Kendall to try their tinned ham; he told them that it 'tastes dry and too crumbly'. 'I wouldn't eat it. The chairman [Philip Carter] wasn't too pleased with me.' Fed up with the players shoving their hands into their tracksuit bottoms, Kendall saw to it that the pockets were sewn up. 'He was ruthless and pernickety,' said Adrian Heath, 'but that's what made him such a good manager.'

Always keen to upgrade his squad, Kendall signed midfielder Paul Bracewell from Stoke City and Birmingham City left-back Pat Van Den Hauwe at the start of the 1984–85 campaign, with Kendall reasoning that the latter would give Everton a dash of '80s hard-man menace. The acquisition of the player whom Everton fans soon nicknamed 'Psycho-Pat' confirmed that his side could be as physical as any other when the occasion demanded it, which Kendall argued was 'essential for any successful team.' A highly skilled and accomplished defender, who was equally at home in central defence, Van Den Hauwe – clad in his classic '80s Hafnia kit, complete with plunging grey neckline, pin stripes and vinyl sheen – looked every inch the '80s hard man. With smouldering eyes and his dark mullet splayed out behind him, the Welshman listened intently to Kendall's instructions to 'look out for each other on the pitch'. Infamously, he waded into an altercation between Queens Park Rangers striker Simon Stainrod and Peter Reid during a fiery 0–0 draw at Loftus Road, punching the Rangers man and, for his pains, receiving two black eyes and a sending off. The incident was reported on ITV's *News at Ten*. But this was an exception, because the tough Welsh defender, like the majority of his teammates, largely stuck to Kendall's philosophy of 'controlled aggression', with the emphasis on skill, pace and a never-say-die attitude.

Everton made a poor start to the 1984–85 season but then quickly hit their stride. The victory at Anfield in late October 'gave the players the belief that they could win the league', Kendall said, and they followed up that victory with arguably their most eye-catching league win of the season a week later in the 5–0 thrashing of Manchester United. 'Everything clicked that day,' recalled Graeme Sharp, who netted Everton's fourth goal. His side were 3–0 up within a quarter of an hour, thanks to a brace from the in-form Kevin Sheedy and Adrian Heath sliding in a third. For Howard Kendall, the fact that Everton greats from yesteryear now queued up to pay homage to his team was clear evidence that his team was a force to be reckoned with. Joe Mercer visited the dressing room and told Kendall's men that he'd 'watched Brazil play in blue that day.'

Not even the loss of Adrian Heath to a broken ankle sustained during Everton's clash with Sheffield Wednesday (the Sharp–Heath pairing was the most potent in the country at that stage) could derail the side's ascent to the top. Andy Gray now donned the No. 9 shirt alongside Sharp and produced a string of performances that quickly turned him into a Goodison icon. 'I could feel the breath of history on me,' Gray recalled. 'Dixie Dean wore that shirt. So did Bob Latchford and Joe Royle. It acted as an extra spur to me.' When Everton visited White Hart Lane in April to face third-placed Tottenham, the match was billed as a title decider. Gray had previous with Paul Miller and Graham Roberts – Spurs' formidable centre-back pairing – and Graeme Sharp recalled how he quickly got pulled into an almighty scrap with the pairing that ran for almost the entire ninety minutes: 'There was punching, kicking, flying elbows, you name it. And it wasn't even my bloody argument.' It was Gray who, on the stroke of half-time, cracked home a sweetly struck half-volley past Tottenham goalkeeper Ray Clemence, and when Trevor Steven rounded Clemence to put his side 2–0 up, the match and the title race was to all intents and purposes over, despite a Roberts thunderbolt giving his side late hope.

In the midst of a 25-match unbeaten run in all competitions, Everton reached peak performance level. Televisually, the 4–1 victory over relegation bound Sunderland is arguably the most memorable, with two flying Gray headers and Paul Bracewell's superb volleyed pass for Trevor Steven to run onto and drive the ball past Chris Turner. They lifted the title on 21 April with Derek Mountfield, who scored a remarkable fourteen goals that season, volleying home the opener and Graeme Sharp heading home a second. Although Everton reached both the FA and European Cup Winners' Cup finals that season, it was their semi-final performances against Luton Town and Bayern Munich that embodied their fighting spirit.

For eighty-six minutes against David Pleat's team, they laboured horribly. Luton took a deserved lead, with midfielder Ricky Hill firing past Neville Southall from the edge of the box. 'We always felt that we could find a way,' said Andy Gray, but Southall's fine save from Hill was all that stopped Luton grabbing a second. The game was notable for Derek Mountfield's running battle with towering Luton striker Mick Harford. 'We were punching, kicking and elbowing each other throughout,' Mountfield explains. Occasionally, the pair still bump into one another on the golf-day circuit and laugh about the sulphurous nature of their clashes forty years ago, but with the clock showing eighty-six minutes, Harford had already given Mountfield two black eyes and a broken nose. 'Mick's flying elbows were the sharpest I ever encountered,' recalled Mountfield.

Given the mortal combat that had come before, it was ironic that Harford's relatively gentle shove on Graeme Sharp led to the eighty-sixth minute free kick from which Kevin Sheedy squeezed a shot past goalkeeper Les Sealey. 'We'd got ourselves out of jail, and on balance we probably didn't deserve it,' Howard Kendall explained.

At half-time in extra time, Mountfield paid homage to the patron saint of central defenders when Mick Harford, who'd also clobbered the Everton defender in his knee, was substituted. Freed from battling with Harford, Everton's 'black and blue hero', as a tabloid labelled him, trotted forward and powered home the header that steered his side into a second consecutive FA Cup final.

In the Cup Winners' Cup, Everton had drawn 0–0 away against fellow treble-chasers Bayern Munich despite being denied the services of forwards Andy Gray and Graeme Sharp due to injury. Describing it as a 'superb result,' Howard Kendall vowed to 'throw everything at Bayern at Goodison.' It wasn't just hyperbole. A fortnight later, with Gray and Sharp fit once more, Kendall urged his team to 'bomb them. By that, I meant use any means necessary to get at them and progress to the final.' The Everton players I spoke to, and Kendall himself, concurred that the atmosphere at Goodison that night was the most crackling they ever played in. 'It's what you go into football for,' Graeme Sharp said. 'Just talking about it now, I can feel the electricity of it all.' Fellow forward Andy Gray likened the mood to a 'roll of thunder, which exploded as we came out of the tunnel before the game started.' The feuding between the players was vicious. Hans Pflügler scythed down Gray, Sharp and Reid, with the latter needing stitches in his leg at half-time. Andy Gray lashed out at midfielder Wolfgang Dremmler twice, and Kevin Ratcliffe cynically chopped down winger Ludwig Kögl. The visceral atmosphere was temporarily halted when Bayern's target man Dieter Hoeneß put his side ahead just before half-time, giving his team a vital away-goal advantage, despite Everton dominating the game in terms of chances created.

At half-time, a confident Kendall simply told his side to 'keep doing what you're doing and let the Gwladys Street [End] suck the ball in.' Cliched and hackneyed though it may appear, his home-spun advice worked perfectly. Shortly after half-time, Graeme Sharp flicked the ball home with a deft header, and Andy Gray bundled the ball home after Bayern goalkeeper Jean-Marie Pfaff was baulked by his own defender. Both goals came from Gary Stevens's long throws, teed up for him by the Goodison Park ballboys who had been instructed to get the ball to him sharpish on the right occasion. Trevor Steven finished the job as he thumped the ball past Pfaff to make it 3–1 on aggregate. 'I hope I take that atmosphere with me to the grave,' Kendall told me.

In contrast with the raw emotion of the semi-final at Goodison, the final, played three weeks later in Rotterdam, was almost an anticlimax, despite the presence of around 25,000 Evertonians in the crowd. It was partly because unlike star-laden semi-finalists Bayern Munich, the opposition – Rapid Vienna – were a relatively weak side with striker Hans Krankl their only big name. A wholly dominant Everton ran out 3–1 winners, with Gray, Steven and Sheedy scoring the goals. Nottingham Forest manager Brian Clough gushed: 'They've got a superb young manager, a magnificent young team and I'm of the opinion they'll be a force for many seasons to come.' The players insisted they had plenty left in the tank for the FA Cup final against Manchester United three days later. Howard Kendall grew mildly irritated with me when I asked him whether the rumours that the players had over-celebrated following the victory were true. 'Oh, that's all a load of crap,' he frowned. 'It was put out there by Derek Hatton.' Hatton, the militant Liverpool councillor who was a thorn in Labour leader Neil Kinnock's side throughout the '80s – accusing him of 'doing Margaret Thatcher's work for her' by expelling the city's militants from the party – also happened to be a fanatical Everton fan. Depending upon who one speaks to, Howard Kendall either ordered the players, accompanied by Hatton, out to a Chinese restaurant for a party that went on until daybreak, or it simply never happened at all. As it was, a rather leggy Everton missed several chances and ultimately lost to Norman Whiteside's curled winner, despite United being down to ten men following defender Kevin Moran's sending off. The punishing fixture schedule finally caught up with Kendall's men, and not even their appearance on *Wogan* in their pastel-blue tracksuits to sing 'Here We Go', their FA Cup final song, which reached a lofty No. 14 in the charts, could alleviate the disappointment that they'd lost out on being regarded – as Andy Gray put it – 'not just a special team, but a very special team'.

Five days after losing to United, Everton won the Merseyside derby on 23 May in front of another gargantuan Goodison crowd, with reserve striker Paul Wilkinson scoring the winner. 'It was further evidence that we were emerging from Liverpool's shadow,' Kendall explained, 'and I was already looking forward to the opportunity of playing in the European Cup.' But that never happened, because six days after the Merseyside derby, Liverpool would face Juventus in the European Cup final, the match that knocked Everton, and English football, clean off its axis.

8

MENSIS HORRIBILIS

THE LAST GAME

*'It wasn't just that going to games was unsafe for families;
it was unsafe for everyone.'*

<small>GEORGE KENDALL, BIRMINGHAM CITY FAN</small>

S t Andrews – May 1985. The final match of the season. From
late morning onwards, as Leeds United fans stream out of Birmingham New Street Station, the feeling of moodiness and tension
escalates. Pubs near the ground have their windows put through.
Street fighting rages. The game is played, despite skirmishes between rival Leeds and Birmingham supporters and missiles being
thrown from the terraces and the stands. There are stoppages due
to crowd behaviour. Already promoted, Birmingham win 1–0, but
events after the final whistle worsen. Hordes of Birmingham City
fans at the Railway End invade the pitch. Shoehorned into a corner
of the Tilton Road End at the opposite end, many of the caged
6,000 travelling Leeds fans, kept behind by the police, attempt to

rip down the fences that pen them in. The steel structure holds firm. Two thin blue lines of policemen separate the supporters. On the Tannoy, Blues manager Ron Saunders implores: 'For the sake of football, go home.' Ignoring him, several hundred Birmingham fans immediately surge onto the pitch, throwing torn-up advertising hoardings and ripped-out seats. 'I couldn't get my head around it,' Saunders later said, 'that on what should have been a day of celebration, Birmingham fans were actually destroying their own stadium.'

11 May was not destined to be a day remembered for the football.

• • •

Birmingham City had the chance to end up as Division Two champions if they beat Leeds United at St Andrews *and* if league leaders Oxford United dropped points. The visitors could also have gained promotion if results went their way. There was all to play for in front of a healthy 24,847 crowd. But in the week leading up to the match, the police received intelligence that there was likely to be trouble between the two sets of rival hooligans, dubbed Birmingham's Zulu Warriors and the Leeds Service Crew. It's curious, then, that an Operational Policing Unit (OPU) was present at the Hawthorns, thirty miles away, for a dead-rubber First Division clash between already-relegated West Bromwich Albion and Arsenal, a match that attracted fewer than 10,000 fans to the game, but not at St Andrews. The OPU was diverted from the Hawthorns to St Andrews after half-time.

Birmingham's Zulu Warriors attacked around thirty away supporters, as well as a dozen or so regulars, drinking in the Australian

Bar, in Hurst Street, a few hundred yards from New Street Station. In the ground, although the two sets of fans were (largely) kept apart, the subsequent Popplewell report, which investigated events at St Andrews, described the scenes as being more like 'the Battle of Agincourt than a football match'. It's worth pointing out though that amidst the carnage at Agincourt, pound coins weren't used as weapons. Nor were sawn-off plastic seats, kettles or bottles. Neither was a catering van disassembled, nor its contents strewn everywhere. Popplewell claimed that National Front literature was discovered littering the ground, and that some Leeds fans had given the Sieg Heil salute. Birmingham fan George Kendall recalled:

> It was total anarchy. Chaos. They always said that a minority caused trouble at matches, but thousands were either charging on the pitch, throwing stuff, screaming like madmen at the police or egging the whole thing on. I didn't go to a football match after that for nearly five years. The game had literally gone mad.

Fifteen-year-old Ian Hambridge travelled from Northampton to watch his first Birmingham match that day. Late on in the game, during another skirmish between supporters, he became separated from his friends and took cover behind a wall – just one brick thick – at the Tilton Road End. As the police pushed the Leeds fans back into their area, a six-foot wall collapsed under their weight, burying several policemen, a line of parked cars and Ian Hambridge, who died in hospital the next day from head injuries. Dozens of police and supporters were treated for injuries that weekend. At a now largely-rebuilt St Andrews, there is a plaque that reads:

To the Memory of
IAN HAMBRIDGE
aged 15 years, of Northampton,
who lost his life resulting from
a tragic accident here
at St Andrews (near this spot)
On Saturday 11th May 1985.
As a Football Supporter,
One of us, never to be forgotten

The Hambridge family are still unclear as to how their son died, and whether it was due to a structural fault or whether the wall was pushed over. Sadly, Ian Hambridge was one of many innocents to lose their life on what should have been a day of celebration during May '85.

• • •

In contrast to the Wild West feeling around St Andrews, the mood before the match at Valley Parade, some 128 miles further north, was one of celebration. By some distance, Bradford City, managed by ex-Leeds star Trevor Cherry, were the best team in Division Three and were looking forward to their first season in the second tier for half a century. An expectant crowd of 11,031 – twice the average figure that season – flocked to Valley Parade to watch Bradford take on Lincoln City, saw skipper Peter Jackson hoist the trophy aloft at 2.30 p.m., bought the souvenir programme and belted out 'We Are the Champions' with gusto. Supporters dressed as bantams strutted their stuff on the pitch, much to the players' amusement. Shortly before kick-off, the Bradford players held up 'THANK YOU FANS' placards to their supporters and took applause from all sides of the ground.

The first half was nothing to write home about, and with just minutes left, a majorette troupe was already lined up on the touchline, ready to entertain the crowd in the break. At the match that day was James Perry and his son, who took their place in the main stand, four rows from the front. Constructed in 1909, the wooden stand was compact and bijou. Visually, it was notable for the twenty-two wooden struts in front of the seats and its distinctive orange and red paintwork. Work was scheduled to begin on the following Monday. Chairman Stafford Heginbotham told the press that the old wooden roof would be replaced by a steel one. In the 1984 reprint of his book *Football Grounds of England and Wales*, author Simon Inglis compared the limited view from the old stand with that of a Sopwith Camel. There was no perimeter fence at the front, which later proved to be a blessing. He also noted that underneath the seats, there were shutters that, when opened, revealed heaps of accumulated debris. Apprentices had long been in the habit of sweeping litter into the gaps under the seats. Inglis informally alerted the club to this fact. He was told that it was scheduled to be cleared during the close season. That same year, Bradford council warned that the (litter) problems 'should be rectified as soon as possible. A carelessly discarded cigarette could give rise to a fire risk.'

A few minutes before half-time, James Perry became aware of an odour that reminded him of 'burning plastic'. Screwing up their faces, Bradford fans speculated what the smell might be. A little time went by. James Perry then became aware of a kerfuffle behind him. Turning around, he saw wisps of smoke appearing at the back of the stand. Perry recalls the reaction of the crowd at the front being one of jocularity. 'Piss on it, Piss on it,' chanted some supporters. As the moments passed, others sang: 'Bradford's burning, Bradford's burning, call the engine, call the engine,' in the style of the popular nursery rhyme. To Perry's left he could see that some fans were already scrambling to the front and escaping to the sanctuary of the grass. 'The smell was now a proper burning smell,' Perry said.

We were out of there. Everyone in our section was fortunate enough to be able to head for the safety of the pitch. But there was quickly mass panic around us. There was quite a big dip at the bottom and you had to climb over a boundary to climb onto the pitch. Some older fans needed a hand. I moved onto the pitch and grabbed my son's hand. I held him tight. And then we turned around.

Perry watched as the blaze metastasized at terrifying speed through the entire stand, which was now like a tinder box. Within two minutes, fire engulfed the entire structure. The low roof caused the flames, fanned by a northerly wind, to spread horizontally.

The intensity of the flames was incredible. It reminded me of the fire storms you see on film during the Blitz. The plumes of black smoke billowed into the sky. I never let go of my son's hand. Some fans who got onto the pitch had been burnt by the asphalt, which was used to seal the roof and which now dripped down. Their hands got burnt, because they were trying to protect their heads from the asphalt. Some of their clothes were smoking. The timbers from the roof began to buckle and collapse. To me, it seemed inevitable there must be deaths, because the fire was moving that bloody fast.

For many supporters in the main stand, there was no easy access to the pitch. Those at the back, who had initially felt warmth under their feet and could then see flames through the slats, were sat behind a high yellow wall. The only option for them was, under direction from the police and the stewards, to head to the concourse, where they found locked exit doors (to prevent ticketless fans from gaining entry), more panic-stricken fans and smoke-filled tunnels. There were no fire extinguishers to be found. Many of the fifty-six died there. Eventually, the wails of the ambulances could be heard over the chaos at Valley Parade, but by then, the stand had been utterly consumed by fire. One Bradford fan, who had been fifteen years old at the time, told me:

> I was on the point of losing consciousness, due to the thick smoke. It was pouring into my lungs. I thank God that in front of me were these three hefty chaps, who put their shoulders into it and smashed a door down. Someone behind me shoved me through. We stumbled clear and onto the street. I threw up.

The local community rallied, opening their front doors to survivors who were desperate to telephone their families to let them know they were safe or begin the (sometimes fruitless) process of locating those from whom they'd become separated as the inferno took hold. The fire brigade worked until dawn the following morning to douse the fire and locate the victims. Several died in their seats, overcome by a combination of smoke and flames. Others were asphyxiated by the smoke as they struggled desperately to prise open the bolted exit doors. As well as the dead, a further 256 suffered injuries. Many more were traumatised by what they witnessed.

I didn't go back to Valley Parade for ten years. Couldn't face it. I got sweaty and panicky just thinking about it. I never said a word to my mum or dad about it after I'd been checked out at hospital and discharged. I figured that it would be selfish, given that a boy in my class at school died that day. I was still here, after all. No one talked about it. I internalised the whole thing. 'I'm fine,' I said. Told them I was bored with football and didn't want to go. 'Not interested,' I said. I don't think they believed me, but I was a closed book. I had nightmares, awful flashbacks of choking and blackness. It was PTSD. Of course it was. I started getting counselling around 2000. It helped. It still helps. I go to most home games now. Valley Parade has been totally rebuilt, but I always look at the plaque to those who died before I go in, to count my blessings and to remember. Sometimes, it helps to talk about it. This [talking to the author] has helped. I'm happy to speak with you. But don't mention my name in your book. I don't want fuss or publicity.

The local community and the football world rallied. The Bradford Fire Disaster Fund raised £3.5 million, and in July, English and West German veterans from the 1966 World Cup final faced off at Elland Road to further top up the fund. In the same week, a multi-denominational memorial service took place in the shadow of the burnt-out stand. Two giant charred pillars formed a Christian cross, and sections of the ceremony were conducted in Urdu and Punjabi, an acknowledgement of the help offered by ethnic communities to supporters in the hours and days after the fire.

The Bishop of Bradford, the Right Reverend Roy Williamson, expressed hope that 'the long process of healing can now begin'. Justice Oliver Popplewell was appointed by Home Secretary Leon

Brittan to investigate the circumstances surrounding the Bradford fire, the riot at St Andrews and the events at the Heysel Stadium.

THE HEYSEL DISASTER

'To this day, I have to be reminded who won the match.
That's the bit I don't remember.'
CHARLIE BURGESS, FORMER *GUARDIAN* JOURNALIST

Heysel Stadium – May 1985. The morning after. Lifeless bodies have been removed. But the distorted metal and detritus in Section Z tells the grim story. Shattered beer bottles and scrunched up beer cans litter the scene. Mangled metal fence posts are twisted at grotesque angles. Crush barriers are bent over; their concrete bases ripped open. The chicken-wire fencing that was supposed to have separated Liverpool fans and neutral supporters during the European Cup final lies flattened and crushed. In Section Y, makeshift holes have been kicked out of the perimeter wall, to allow ticketless supporters outside a route in. Two English journalists, the *Daily Mail's* Jeff Powell and Charlie Burgess from *The Guardian*, stare uncomprehendingly at the desolate scene. They spot a crumpled-up postcard of Brussels' futuristic silver Atomium glinting in the sun and turn it over. In Italian, it reads: 'As you will see, we are always present with the lads. Black and white greetings. We hope to come home with the cup. Love to all. Stefano.' Written by a Juventus fan, the postcard is unstamped. To the left is the rubble from the wall that collapsed the night before under the weight of terrified football fans. Thirty-nine people died. As the true extent of the Heysel disaster slowly sinks in, the recriminations for English football are about to begin.

• • •

On a balmy May morning the day before, thousands of Liverpool fans streamed down the hill into the centre of Brussels from Jette Station, waving their chequered red and white flags, and from the coach parks located a few hundred yards away from Heysel Stadium. There wasn't a cloud in the sky. Many of the travelling fans were now veterans of European Cup finals, this being their fifth in eight years. Attuned as they were to the ambience of showpiece matches, fans quickly formed the impression that the city itself wasn't fully braced for the influx of supporters. The Belgian police were present, but not entirely correct. 'In Rome and in Paris, police were watchful. In Brussels they looked disinterested and detached, chatting between themselves and often looking the other way,' Liverpool fan Chris Maudsley told me. The feeling amongst supporters, some of whom wanted to exact revenge on Italians for the trouble in Rome a year earlier, was that they could pretty much do whatever they wanted.

Many headed for the historic Grand Palace and its surrounding streets. In some cases, rival supporters drank together and swapped memorabilia. Throughout the afternoon, impromptu football matches between the English and Italian supporters took place across Brussels. 'There was a lovely, convivial atmosphere,' Chris Maudsley said. 'After we finished our game, we exchanged scarves.' For others, events unfolded rather differently. Loaded up with beers from coaches and trains, a good number had been drinking for hours. Now, they were about to indulge themselves in quaffing far stronger Belgian beers in the full glare of the hot sun. Many vomited, doubled up in front of horrified locals. 'You always got drunken arseholes following English teams in Europe back then,' explained (then) *Guardian* journalist Charlie Burgess. 'But this was beyond. There were so many Liverpool fans with their heads in the gutter that day.' *Daily Express* writer John Keith, who worked for the paper for thirty years, was following up a reliable tip-off that Joe Fagan was about to retire. He'd soon be writing about non-football matters. 'The mood was sinister, and strange, different from anything before or since,' he told me.

Broken glass was everywhere, as beer bottles were lobbed, dropped and smashed. 'It crunched and splintered under our feet as we walked across the coach park,' Liverpool fan John Harmer told me. Inexplicably, some bars still sold beer in glasses. Shop windows – minus grilles – were put through. Terrified shopkeepers and shocked checkout girls looked on helplessly as crates of beer were plundered from shops. A jewellers was looted. Petty cash boxes were lifted from souvenir stalls. As vendors vainly gave chase, the scarves and shirts also vanished into thin air. Robbing was nothing new when it came to Liverpool fans in Europe, but as well as the Scouse accents, there were some different dialects in the mix this time. A new crowd.

Liverpool fans spoke to me of the lax ticketing arrangements for the match back in England. 'Any Tom, Dick or Harry could get a ticket,' said Chris Hawkins, who lived in London throughout the '80s and bought his tickets from a bucket shop near Kings Cross Station. In front of him, two men bought a travel package. 'You Liverpool fans?' the cashier asked. 'Nah, West Ham,' came the response. 'Going for the beer and a fight,' they laughed. They left with their coach and match tickets, having paid in cash and shown no formal identification. John Harmer went to Smith's travel agents in Liverpool and asked for two match tickets, with travel included. As he prepared to hand over his passport for proof of identification, the agent shook her head. 'She just wanted the cash,' Harmer said. 'There was no loyalty scheme in place. I didn't need to prove who I was. I really could have been anybody.'

There may be conflicting memories about the build-up to the match, but there's no equivocation that the Heysel Stadium, built for the 1935 Brussels Great Exhibition, was unfit for a match of this gravitas. Despite previously hosting three European Cup finals – the most recent of which had been in 1974 – Liverpool players and fans were singularly unimpressed when they clapped eyes on the dilapidated ground. 'It wasn't an elite stadium,' striker Paul Walsh told me. 'The front of it was crumbling. Flaky paint. It looked very dated.' John Harmer, who has travelled across Europe with Liverpool over the past forty years, looked around and thought: 'I'm in the right place, but it doesn't *look* or *feel* right.' Aesthetics aside, the security outside was clearly inadequate. Walsh noticed that flimsy chicken-wire fences that were there to keep the rival fans separate were 'curled up at the bottom. Anyone could crawl underneath them.' Around the ground, despite a supposed ban, alcohol was openly sold via pop-up shacks and vendors with portable beer fridges. Some supporters, who still have their complete tickets to this day, recall being waved through into the ground with crateloads of beer.

Outside, some supporters picked or kicked away at the breeze-block edifice. 'Loads of fans wore Doc Martens,' Chris Maudsley told me. 'The breezeblock literally splintered every time you kicked it. Some chipped away at it using bottles.' Bigger pieces of masonry were later used as missiles inside the ground, but for some ticketless fans, the object of the exercise was to gain access to the stadium via the improvised tunnels. John Harmer explained: 'I got frisked outside. Fine. No problem with that, but one fan behind rushed past me and headed straight through a hole in the wall. He got in for nothing, and he could have been anybody. Also we were going in with Juventus fans. There was no segregation where I went in, which was completely unlike previous finals.'

Inside, Liverpool supporters were designated Areas X and Y of the terrace, with Area Z set aside for neutral supporters. The 'neutral' element was the aspect that especially alarmed Liverpool chief executive Peter Robinson, as it was open to so many variables. Subsequent investigations found that many tickets for Area Z were snapped up by Italian expatriates living in Brussels or found their way onto the black market and were purchased on the day of the match. 'Anybody with determination or money, or both, could gain access to the ground,' Mark Lawrenson explained. The jerry-built chicken-wire fences between the Liverpool sections and Area Z (like the fences outside the ground, they curled up at the bottom) simply added to the worries.

•   •   •

In the build-up to the match, Jimmy Hill, who'd host BBC's coverage of the show in London, met with the channel's top brass to discuss the tone of the programme.

It had been a terrible few weeks for English football, and it was hoped that a splendid final between two such illustrious clubs would lift the nation's mood, especially if Liverpool retained their European crown. There were rumours this would be Joe Fagan's last match. It was hoped that we could focus on the football, and just the football. But I had a bad feeling about the whole thing.

To set an upbeat tone for the show, which was scheduled to start at 7.05 p.m., Hill was to have some golfing banter in a five-minute slot with chat-show host Terry Wogan (the genial Wogan would then host his show after the football finished) and guest Bruce Forsyth. The former *Generation Game* host and Hill were due to have a chin-measuring contest before the action cut to Hill and studio pundits Graeme Souness and Terry Venables. But that never happened, because, as Forsyth and Wogan larked about in a golf buggy, Hill was aware that – as he described to me – 'English football was going to hell in a handcart at Heysel'. Playing along, Hill chuckled at Wogan's and Forsyth's light-entertainment antics, whilst he was receiving updates about the ensuing carnage in Brussels in his earpiece. 'I wasn't surprised by the turn of events,' the well-connected Hill told me,

> because I'd received a tip-off a few days before that the Liverpool chief executive, Peter Robinson, had lodged complaints about the poor state of the Heysel Stadium and inadequate ticketing arrangements. He always knew what he was talking about, did Peter. Factor in what occurred between Roma and Liverpool fans a year before, and trouble was always likely.

The Liverpool players certainly realised something was awry when, as they trooped around the outside of the pitch to 'test the wicket' (as manager Joe Fagan put it), they were pelted with pieces of masonry by Juventus fans. The unfit Alan Kennedy, who travelled to Brussels with the Liverpool party, surmised the situation immediately, telling Alan Hansen: 'They're throwing the bloody stadium at us.'

An hour or so before the game began, missiles – mainly cans, bottles and breezeblock chunks – were lobbed to and fro between the Liverpool supporters shoehorned into Area Y and the 'neutrals' in Area Z. Liverpool supporters, looking enviously at the considerably less crowded Area Z, started to destroy the flimsy fencing and encroached on the neutral zone. There was posturing, gesturing, missile throwing and skirmishes. Metal poles from the now-trashed fence were brandished. Groups of Liverpool supporters charged at the neutrals. Then – a full stampede. Terrified supporters headed to the corner of Area Z. Crush barriers buckled. The collective weight of the fleeing supporters caused a retaining wall to collapse, which led to many deaths.

Perhaps the most affecting of the shocking images that were viewed across the globe was that of a large, moustachioed Italian man, his eyes wide with terror as his friends lay dead or dying around him. He holds his hand forlornly in the air, desperately crying for help. Several were taken by photographer Eamonn McCabe, who was working for *The Guardian* and *Observer*. He later recalled: 'My remit changed from sports to news photographer in an instant.' The images were more akin to a warzone than a football match. In the Liverpool dressing room, situated close to Area Z, the players heard the ominous rumble of masonry as the wall collapsed. Alan Kennedy was dispatched to investigate. When he conveyed the news to his teammates, and as confirmation of the growing list of confirmed dead began to filter through, Mark Lawrenson recalled that Joe Fagan 'appeared to age ten years as the news got worse'. There was still a huge amount of confusion about exactly what had transpired inside the ground, with many fans not realising the extent of the horror until well after the match.

Journalists began processing what was going on. Brian Glanville (*The Times*) told me: 'Eamonn McCabe signalled to me with both hands three times. Thirty people. Then he drew his finger across his throat. From his expression, I knew that was a minimum number. It took some time to gather my thoughts and begin writing.' Venturing down from the press box, Charlie Burgess viewed the dead lying in rows, covered in Juventus flags and their jackets. At this stage, he counted twenty-seven corpses and immediately rang *The Guardian*'s news desk to tell them he was now reporting from a disaster zone. On BBC1, Barry Davies said:

> One cannot but feel that the time has come and – if I can express a personal opinion – that the time has long since passed when we have to concentrate on the majority and if that means we have to take some steps to prevent the minority from coming abroad and dragging the name of our country into the gutter, then we have to do it.

Mark Lawrenson recalled the 'sense of disbelief' in the dressing room. Liverpool players glanced at one another uneasily as they were told that the match would be played: 'The reasoning from the Belgian chief of police was that if it wasn't, and the crowds were released onto the streets, the situation would explode once again.' With corpses still piled up near Area Z, riot police now forming a line next to the Liverpool fans in Area Y and mounted police on the running track, the match began. It was as subdued as Barry Davies's commentary. 'We played with reduced intensity,' substitute Jan Mølby recalled. 'It was almost pre-season friendly pace.'

Lawrenson's damaged shoulder popped out of place after just two minutes, at which point he was taken to hospital, in full kit and boots. After being checked out by a doctor, he was given a painkilling injection and placed in an empty ward, where he briefly dozed off and awoke to see an armed guard at his doorway, to keep any agitated Juventus fans out. A message was sent out requesting that Roy Evans bring Lawrenson's civvies. The next morning, Evans brought along a Liverpool tracksuit top and bottoms. 'I asked Roy what the bloody hell he thought he was playing at,' Lawrenson said. 'Wearing Liverpool gear was not a clever plan.' The player was smuggled out – via a service lift – in his tracksuit, which was turned inside out. Verbally abused en route, Lawrenson, with his arm in a sling, noticed at the airport that the skips containing the Liverpool kit had been graffitied: 'They'd scrawled "killers" and "murderers" on them.'

Juventus had displayed slightly more urgency and won the match thanks to a fortuitous penalty, awarded after Zbigniew Boniek was brought down by Liverpool defender Gary Gillespie yards outside the box. The Liverpool protests were half-hearted at best, and Michel Platini slotted home the decisive penalty. The Frenchman's frenzied celebrations and his bare-chested parading of the trophy with team-mates afterwards were a jarring sight, given the tragic events before the match. When everyone had gone and the floodlit Heysel Stadium was deserted and eerily quiet, Charlie Burgess walked in silence with Peter Robinson to survey the scene once again. 'It looked like something from a holocaust museum. There were shoes, discarded clothes and glasses strewn everywhere. It was ghostly.'

Liverpool players flew home to Speke Airport, where they'd landed to adulation with the European Cup on four previous occasions. The now-retired Joe Fagan openly wept on the tarmac. His players' heads were bowed. Nowadays, when Liverpool players from that era meet up in Southport, the subject of Heysel isn't discussed. 'Whether it's shame or embarrassment, I'm not sure. But it's not talked about,' Mark Lawrenson said. Many Liverpool fans were unaware of the full extent of the disaster until the following day.

There were wild rumours of gun shots being fired and even of IRA involvement. Liverpool chairman John Smith claimed the National Front had infiltrated the ranks of Liverpool fans. The heavily policed ferries, which took fans back to Dover, reflected the extent to which English football fans were now *persona non grata*. 'The police stared at us. They glared at us. There were no cocky comebacks from us for once. We kept our traps shut. Most of us felt we deserved the cold shoulder,' said Chris Maudsley.

The press headlines were suitably apocalyptic. 'Bloodbath – Soccer Hits the Ultimate Depths' (the *Mail*) and 'The Final Shame' (the *Mirror*) certainly captured the mood. But it was *The Guardian* lead: 'Quarantine Our Sad, Sick Game' that was a portent of things to come. In the years that followed, European commentators tried to make sense of events that evening. French media theorist Jean Baudrillard, in his book *The Transparency of Evil to Heysel*, argues that, as well as the unfolding images of the disaster being a gripping and early form of 'interactive television', they were further evidence of the violent nature of Britain in the '80s. Baudrillard suggests that, in the wake of the inner city riots of the early '80s, the Falklands conflict and the graphic footage of violence during the long-running miners' strike, it was no surprise that violence exploded in Brussels. 'It was a cultural reflex conditioned by circumstance and environment,' Baudrillard claimed.

It was also the long-term consequence of dilapidated grounds, inadequate policing, poor security, cheap alcohol, the culture of taking ends, verbal barbs and hatred between supporters; this was a disaster waiting to happen since the late '70s. The collapsed retaining wall at the Heysel Stadium was the inevitable self-destructive climax to the arc of violence and toxicity that had been endemic for years.

• • •

Seven Fleet Street journalists who'd been present and correct in Brussels were invited to meet with Margaret Thatcher and Sports Minister Neil Macfarlane to discuss the tragic events on Friday morning. In advance, they were forbidden from taking notes or recording conversations. The meeting gave the journalists a crash course into Margaret Thatcher's businesslike manner. 'She was electric, with those piercing blue eyes of hers,' recalled Charlie Burgess. 'Thatcher was fantastically well briefed, greeted us all individually ("Welcome, Mr Burgess from *The Guardian*"), radiated energy and listened to our accounts of the night.' Her cards were placed well and truly on the table. Describing the Heysel disaster as 'a national shame', the issues of a football ID card scheme and an impending ban on English clubs playing in Europe were openly discussed. 'It was obvious where things were headed after the meeting,' Burgess explained.

The Times's Brian Glanville's memory of the Downing Street meeting – and Thatcher's manner – remained vivid when I interviewed him in 2004. Like Charlie Burgess, he believed that Thatcher had already decided on her course of action:

In her unique way, she was highly impressive. I glanced at her on a couple of occasions during the meeting. She was studying us all rather haughtily, as if she were a bird of prey. I also got the impression that, although she wanted our views on Heysel and possible solutions, she took a very dim view on football, and the forthcoming European ban was a done deal, and nothing we said would have changed her opinion.

Thatcher listened intently to the journalists' tales of the farcical security and the shoddy state of the Heysel Stadium, but her repeated message – that the main cause of death was due to 'misbehaviour, charging and an awful lot of drunken fans' – remained unequivocal.

A solemn mood hung over the meeting, but there was a moment or two of farce. 'Of course it's not Chelsea, it's Tottenham,' Thatcher barked, rolling her eyes at her Sports Minister after Neil Macfarlane had erroneously complained that Chelsea (the team he supported) would miss out on a UEFA Cup slot due to the impending ban on English clubs in Europe. The gentlemen of the press quickly corrected him. 'These men actually *know* what they're talking about,' Thatcher told McFarlane. During tea and biscuits, the talk had turned to the general issue of behaviour in sporting contests. 'Denis [Thatcher] was a rugby referee. Awful lot of trouble in the scrums,' Thatcher said, much to the bemusement of her guests, who sat on two long white settees and had just witnessed a full-scale riot a matter of hours earlier.

• • •

The expected bans came quickly. UEFA placed an indefinite ban on English clubs playing in European fixtures, which FIFA followed up by banning English clubs from playing football matches of any kind on foreign soil (although within a fortnight the law was adapted so friendlies could be played), leading Margaret Thatcher to describe the move as 'a proper opportunity to put our own house in order'. Liverpool had already withdrawn from the following season's UEFA Cup, and then the Football Association pulled out the rest of its representatives for the 1985–86 campaign – Everton (European Cup), Manchester United (Cup Winners' Cup) and Tottenham, Southampton and Norwich City (UEFA Cup). The reaction to the

indefinite ban on English clubs from the press was broadly supportive, but within the game, responses were far more mixed. The most
emotive and layered responses tended to emanate from those who
lost most from the ban.

'Most of us thought Liverpool and maybe Juventus should be
banned. No one else,' opined Manchester United manager Ron
Atkinson. New Liverpool manager Kenny Dalglish later said: 'She
[Thatcher] probably got all the English clubs banned. If she'd kept
her mouth shut, the rest of them might not have suffered.' Apart
from themselves, the club which lost out most from the ban were
Liverpool's neighbours from across Stanley Park. Throughout the
time it was implemented, Everton were denied the chance to com-
pete in the European Cup (twice) and the UEFA Cup (twice).

When I spoke with Howard Kendall, thirteen years after the ban
was imposed, the previously chirpy former Everton boss immediately wore an air of sad resignation. 'Firstly, no one should die
going to watch a football match. Plain and simple. But… The impact
on English football, and Everton Football Club, was enormous. A
sliding-doors moment, I believe it's now called,' Kendall said.

A clearly pained Kendall referred to 'races not run and paths
left untrodden' due to his team missing out on the European Cup:
'Every manager and player wants the chance to prove themselves
in the top European competition and we were denied that chance.
The ban didn't teach Everton supporters a lesson. They'd never been
in any trouble in the first place.' Kendall didn't accept that Everton
were nailed-on winners of the '86 European Cup, arguing that Juventus ('Imagine the controversy if we'd been drawn against them?')
had more European know-how and citing the example of Steaua
București winning the '86 final as an example of the 'dangers always
lurking behind the Iron Curtain'.

The European ban immediately affected Everton. Kendall said that he'd have liked to have kept fan-favourite Andy Gray to add competition for places after signing Leicester striker Gary Lineker, but given the projected reduction in income streams due to the ban, that proved impossible. Kendall drove round to see Gray on the day he was moving into his new house in Formby to tell him he was no longer needed at the club. Spotting a handyman who was fixing the kitchen plumbing, Kendall told him to down tools immediately. 'The chap looked as miffed as Andy did,' Kendall said. After leading his team to a second title in 1987, Kendall accepted an offer to manage Athletic Bilbao. 'I wouldn't have left but for the ban,' he said. His great Everton team aged and then disintegrated. 'Races not run. Paths left untrodden,' Kendall repeated. 'And lives lost.'

From a purely football point of view, the fallout from the European ban abruptly ended the unprecedented period of success English clubs had enjoyed across European competitions since the late '70s. International pariahs, English clubs now entered a seven-year hiatus of introspection, sterility and worsening finances, with sharp-suited executives looking for ways to somehow make their clubs profitable again. Perhaps it's a miracle that English football, with a trail of wreckage, destruction and death left in its wake, even survived 1985. Yet somehow, it staggered on.

THE POPPLEWELL REPORT

'There was the suggestion that to require a card or pass at a football ground was interfering in some way with the liberty of the subject. This I have to say is simply emotional nonsense.'
POPPLEWELL REPORT, 1985

1985 was English football's *mensis horribilis*. It was a punctuation mark in English football history. Within the space of just twenty days, ninety-six people lost their lives at three different grounds; thirty-nine at the Heysel Stadium, fifty-six at Bradford City's Valley Parade and one at St Andrews. Many more suffered life-changing injuries and trauma. The alarming truth was that any of the three tragedies could have occurred in the years preceding it. In the '70s, Tottenham, Leeds United and Manchester United supporters had, on different occasions, gone on the rampage in Europe. As English and French fans skirmished in Bilbao during the two countries' match in the '82 World Cup, a metal fence collapsed. Commentator John Motson was instructed to focus on the game. In Liverpool's League Cup semi-final clash with Walsall at Fellows Park in 1984, the low wall at the front of the away end collapsed with a terrible thud under the pressure of surging away fans celebrating Ronnie Whelan's equaliser. Fortunately, there were no fences, meaning injured supporters could spill onto the pitch. There was no hooliganism involved, but images of Graeme Souness carrying a stricken young fan away for medical attention were a disturbing portent of things to come. The fact that no one died at Kenilworth Road in February '85, with an estimated 10,000 away fans squashed into a terrace whose capacity was half that, and which had fences at the front, was a miracle.

• • •

The Popplewell report – published in January 1986 – set a blueprint that marked the beginning of the end of 'old' football, with its antiquated stadia, crumbling infrastructure and the virtual absence of customer care. The conclusion of the Popplewell report was that a lighted cigarette, casually discarded between wooden planks onto a heap of inflammable rubbish under the wooden seats – had most likely caused the fire. A crushingly ordinary thing to do during that era, when smoking was permitted at matches, this seemed the most insidious option.

In the decades that have followed, the inquiry, which controversially addressed all three of the tragedies which occurred in May 1985, has been criticised for the undue haste in which it was carried out. The testimonies were received over the course of just five days. No women were interviewed, despite eleven of the victims at Valley Parade being female. Martin Fletcher, in his 2015 book *Fifty-Six: The Story of the Bradford Fire* (the author lost several close family members that day), reveals that, stretching back to the 1960s, there had been eight previous fires at business premises owned by Stafford Heginbotham. The Valley Parade fire was the ninth. This 'mountain of coincidences' – as Fletcher put it – was not investigated by the Popplewell inquiry. Heginbotham had wrongly claimed that a smoke bomb, thrown by a fan, had started the fire at Valley Parade. Simon Inglis's informal tip-off to the club about the flammable litter under the stand could not used in the inquiry. 'I was called as a witness to the Popplewell inquiry and retold the story as part of my evidence. However, I was quickly given to understand that my tale could not be used as evidence because it was essentially "hearsay",' Inglis told me. To show how lax the club had been, in the aftermath of the fire, a copy of a local newspaper was found from November 1968, which somehow survived the inferno.

On the thirtieth anniversary of the fire, Detective Inspector Raymond Falconer stated that the police were aware of an Australian man who claimed to have inadvertently started the fire when his cigarette was casually discarded onto the detritus below the seats. A number of news organisations named him as Eric Bennett, who was visiting his nephew in Bradford from Australia and attended the game. His nephew Leslie Brownlie described Falconer's comments as a 'cock-and-bull story'.

Several areas of the report specifically focussed on tightening up on rules and regulations surrounding fire safety at grounds. Stewards were to be trained in fire prevention and evacuation procedures, fire extinguishers would be readily available, and exits would remain manned – and unlocked – at all times. The days of 'stewards acting like cinema usherettes' were over. So was the era of wooden stands. Popplewell recommended that any new stands built should be constructed from non-flammable materials and that moving forwards, smoking should be banned in wooden structures. Fire authorities now had the authority to restrict the use of any stand at any level of football they deemed a risk. This quickly had a disproportionate – and often near-catastrophic – effect on lower division clubs. Lincoln City, Bradford's opponents on the day of the Bradford Fire, saw the capacity of their compact Sincil Bank ground slashed and their seating capacity briefly reduced to zero. The late '80s saw many older timber structures torn down.

Beyond the focus on stadium safety, the report also recommended that grounds introduce CCTV in order to monitor the behaviour of fans. Previous use of CCTV at grounds had been sporadic, although the grainy footage of the St Andrews riot was used to prosecute supporters of both Leeds United and Birmingham City. In his final report, Popplewell acknowledged that his recommendation that 'urgent consideration' be given by football clubs to introducing membership systems had caused a great deal of angst on the terraces and in boardrooms across the country. Although at pains to point out that this was not the same as a national identity card system (Popplewell reckoned a football membership card would be the same as a driving licence), he was still clearly of the opinion that such schemes would improve law and order at matches and to enable clubs to harvest the information for commercial and marketing reasons. The government soon pushed hard for compulsory membership card schemes at all clubs. Many chairmen felt that the government wished to go further. 'I believed that by the mid '80s, Margaret Thatcher was of the opinion that football clubs should act as guinea pigs for a national ID scheme,' Aston Villa chairman Doug Ellis told me.

The final report is, to some degree, nuanced. On the suggestion of membership schemes, Popplewell points out that clubs including Brentford and West Ham had already partially deployed such schemes during the 1984–85 campaign. He acknowledged that many fans, not all of whom fell 'into the rough working-class category', as he put it, tended to arrive late at the turnstiles, which would put a strain on the system and could cause issues outside grounds. He also noted that the computer systems required to run a membership scheme would cost a great deal of money and that such schemes might spell the end of the 'floating supporter'.

Many of the elements that, for better or worse, had defined the experience of football by 1985 were on the way out. With CCTV cameras now actively encouraged, and Popplewell's point that membership schemes should be tied in with clubs' commercial activities, the report, despite its many faults, provided an inkling of where football was headed. But it wasn't sufficiently root and branch to prevent another stadium disaster in 1989.

9

THE BLACKOUT AND THE BLOND BOMBSHELL

'Football rates itself far too highly. It has no
God-given right to be on television.'
BBC HEAD OF SPORT JONATHAN MARTIN, MAY 1985

Upton Park – October 1985. Unbeaten in eight matches, John Lyall's West Ham side are pulverising visitors Aston Villa. With fifteen goals between them already that season, the Hammers' dynamic striking partnership of Tony Cottee and Frank McAvennie have a field day. Cottee – a home-grown academy starlet – fires home from twenty-five yards for his second of the afternoon. McAvennie, a peroxide blond plucked from St Mirren, also grabs a brace, and his outrageous lob over Villa goalkeeper Nigel Spink has the Hammers fans salivating. He's quickly become an Upton Park icon. Within a couple of months, he'll become a TV celebrity too, with appearances on *A Question of Sport* (as the mystery guest), *Wogan*, and *Saint & Greavsie*. The former milkman will net twenty-six league goals that season as West Ham enjoy their best-ever league season. Cottee's and McAvennie's virtuoso display in the

4–1 demolition of Villa, lives only in the memories of the 15,034 fans who watch the game in person though, due to a complete TV blackout on all league and cup matches. Peak West Ham this may have been, but the vast majority of the dynamic duo's goals before Christmas are consigned to the black hole of history.

•   •   •

It seemed that English football had reached its lowest ebb. But in the summer of '85, as the English press continued to run stories about the Heysel disaster and the likely ramifications of the subsequent ban, another crisis was already well advanced. In February 1985, the Football League rejected a joint BBC–ITV four-year deal worth £3.8 million per season. A sticking point was over the number of live matches that should be televised. Television companies wanted nineteen live matches broadcast, with the Football League insisting that the ceiling should be set at thirteen league games and three Milk Cup games, including the final. Negotiating on behalf of the Football League subcommittee were Ken Bates (Chelsea), Robert Maxwell (Oxford), Irving Scholar (Tottenham), committee chairman Sir Arthur South (Norwich City) with Alex Fynn from the advertising agency Saatchi & Saatchi present in an advisory capacity thanks to Scholar's invitation. Wary of the impact on crowds that live football would have on attendances (especially in the case of Bates and South), negotiations stalled. With attendances at matches about to fall through the floor and English stadia in desperate need of renovation after the findings of the Popplewell inquiry, there were already fears for the future of many clubs. 'Give us your fockin' money,' ordered Bob Geldof that summer as Wembley hosted Live Aid, and the nation responded. Getting punters to do the same at

Sealed with a kiss. Kevin Keegan (*left*) and Emlyn Hughes (*right*) get up close and personal with Prime Minister Margaret Thatcher as the England team prepare to fly out to the 1980 European Championships in Italy. Phil Neal (*second right*) looks unconvinced. The bonhomie won't last long.

© PA Images / Alamy Stock Photo

Tear gas explodes. A week after the cocktail party at No. 10 Downing Street, Italian riot police in Turin fire tear gas cannisters at England fans warring with locals after Belgium score an equaliser in England's opening match in the European Championships. Thatcher said that English football had been 'shamed abroad'.

© PA Images / Alamy Stock Photo

All smiles in the Nottingham Forest dugout between Brian Clough (*left*) and assistant Peter Taylor (*right*), with European Cup winners Nottingham Forest in their pomp. By the early '80s, the relationship between the pair was becoming frayed around the edges. © Trinity Mirror / Mirrorpix / Alamy Stock Photo

Steve Daley (*centre*), flanked by cigar-chomping manager Malcolm Allison (*right*) and assistant Tony Book (*left*), signs for Manchester City in September 1979 for £1,437,500, becoming the most expensive player in English football. The move was a failure, with Daley claiming that City were 'bidding against themselves' for his signature.

© PA Images / Alamy Stock Photo

From a Tony Morley (*far right*) cross, Peter Withe's 'magnificent mis-hit' (his words) wins the European Cup for Aston Villa in May 1982.

© PA Images / Alamy Stock Photo

Paul Mariner, who lost twelve pounds in weight in the searing heat of Bilbao, celebrates scoring his team's third goal in the 3–1 win over France in England's first match of the 1982 World Cup. 'We were all totally spent,' he said.

© Trinity Mirror / Mirrorpix / Alamy Stock Photo

ABOVE Liverpool's Alan Kennedy fires home the winner in the 1981 European Cup final against Real Madrid. He said that he was never a star in that team, more a 'cog in a machine'.
© PA Images / Alamy Stock Photo

LEFT Everton celebrate their first title success in fifteen years after defeating QPR 2–0 in May 1985. *Left to right*: Kevin Sheedy, Andy Gray, Graeme Sharp, Derek Mountfield.
© Trinity Mirror / Mirrorpix / Alamy Stock Photo

Carnage at Kenilworth Road in March 1985, as supporters riot after Luton Town defeat Millwall 1–0 in an FA Cup sixth-round clash.
© PA Images / Alamy Stock Photo

ABOVE As Liverpool and Juventus players contest the 1985 European Cup final, the detritus on the terraces at the Heysel Stadium, Brussels, tells a grim story. Earlier, thirty-nine supporters died after a wall collapsed in Area Z.
© Süddeutsche Zeitung Photo / Alamy Stock Photo

LEFT All smiles as Oxford United skipper Malcolm Shotton holds aloft the Milk Cup in 1986, following his side's 3–0 win over QPR. Oxford owner Robert Maxwell (*right, in natty bow tie*) beams with pleasure.
© PA Images / Alamy Stock Photo

Diego Maradona wheels away from Terry Butcher after scoring arguably the World Cup's greatest ever goal, in the quarter-final between England and Argentina in 1986.
Source: Wikimedia Commons

At Stringfellows in 1989, West Ham's Frank McAvennie poses with his model girlfriend, Jenny Blyth.
© MediaPunch Inc. / Alamy Stock Photo

Ricky Villa scores Tottenham's winner in the 1981 FA Cup final replay against Manchester City. 'Instinct took over. I just headed towards goal,' Villa said. © David Bagnall / Alamy Stock Photo

Keith Houchen's spectacular flying header levels the score for Coventry City in the 1987 FA Cup final. Tottenham defender Chris Hughton appears less than impressed. © Trinity Mirror / Mirrorpix / Alamy Stock Photo

Goalscorer Lawrie Sanchez (*left*) and captain Dave Beasant, who became the first goalkeeper to save a penalty in the FA Cup final, celebrate Wimbledon's shock victory over Liverpool in 1988.

© Trinity Mirror / Mirrorpix / Alamy Stock Photo

When **S**aturday **C**omes

The Half Decent FOOTBALL Magazine

June 1989 No. 28

50p

Hillsborough: Unanimous Verdict

It wasn't our fault

It wasn't our fault

It wasn't our fault

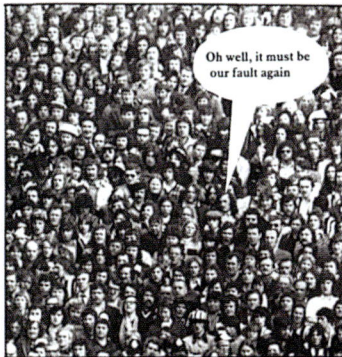

Oh well, it must be our fault again

When Saturday Comes's front cover after the Hillsborough disaster in April 1989.
© *When Saturday Comes*

Banner maker and Hillsborough survivor Peter Carney made this evocative tribute to the ninety-seven Hillsborough victims. © Peter Carney

'Football-wise, the banana craze happened in a different universe,' said former Manchester City star Ian Brightwell. © James Wright

Kit-design guru John Devlin produced these images of some vintage '80s shirts. Clockwise here is England '82 with the classic epaulettes, the plunging collar of Everton, the pinstripes of Liverpool and the bright colours of Watford.
© John Devlin

Michael Thomas's dramatic late goal wins the title for Arsenal at Anfield in 1989. Thomas later said: 'At the time, I didn't think about what rested on that shot.' © Paul Marriott / Alamy Stock Photo

the turnstiles would prove far harder. Now, all clubs would miss out on their slice from a TV deal. *The Express*'s Alan Thompson summed the situation up succinctly: 'Lost in the quagmire of petty argument and bloated self-importance are the two things that really matter – the future well-being of football and the entertainment of the public.' TV viewers were denied the opportunity to enjoy the spectacle of the most captivating title race for years. But the blackout also meant that the 1985–86 season's surprise package – Frank McAvennie – acclimatised to English football almost undetected.

The omens for West Ham's season were hardly positive. In recent years, club stalwarts Billy Bonds, Trevor Brooking and Frank Lampard had all recently retired, and that summer, 21-year-old Paul Allen had left for Tottenham for £400,000. After narrowly avoiding relegation in 1984–85, manager John Lyall signed midfielder Mark Ward from Oldham (£250,000) and Frank McAvennie (£350,000) from St Mirren. 'I'd never heard of either of them. Nor had most of the fans,' Tony Cottee told me. There then followed a disastrous pre-season friendly defeat to Orient, which saw fan demonstrations and one irate Hammers supporter storm the dressing room and harangue the players. The precise wording varies according to which player one speaks to, but his tirade, according to Tony Cottee went along the lines of: 'What the fuck is going on here? Sort it out, you bunch of useless wankers.'

Following the arrival of McAvennie, Tony Cottee, who always set himself the target of being the club's top scorer that season, was concerned. 'Frank and I were both strikers. I felt that Frank might have been bought to replace me. But John Lyall reassured me that wasn't going to be the case.' Lyall told Cottee that he would continue to partner Paul Goddard up front (the pair had netted a healthy thirty-eight goals between them in 1984–85), with McAvennie playing in the 'hole' behind them. 'That was quite revolutionary for the '80s,' Cottee explained, 'and John (Lyall) told me that we'd be playing attacking football on the floor, the West Ham way.'

McAvennie's 'false nine' role ended after just forty minutes of the Hammers' first match of the new season at St Andrews, which had now been repaired after the carnage of the match against Leeds United on the last day of the previous season. A paltry 11,086 saw West Ham go down to a 1–0 defeat against Birmingham in a match which kicked off at 11.30. The authorities were keen to avoid fans going to the pub beforehand, and with alcohol now banned from being sold in the ground, fans were, to all intents and purposes, 'dry'. As well as losing the season opener, Paul Goddard (nicknamed 'Sarge' by his teammates) left the field due to a shoulder injury; he wouldn't return to the first team until the spring. So McAvennie was pushed up front to partner Tony Cottee. Although the pair couldn't save West Ham in the Midlands, they dovetailed well during West Ham's first match at Upton Park that season. McAvennie scored twice in a 3–1 defeat of Queens Park Rangers. Unusually for him, Cottee didn't score until the seventh game of the campaign, in a 2–2 draw with Sheffield Wednesday. Throughout his long career, Cottee diligently kept a scrapbook of newspaper cuttings describing all his goals. 'It drove me crazy that it had to stay in the drawer throughout August. Frank had already scored five goals before I got my first.'

When I met McAvennie in the late '90s, he'd recently retired from the game. His life was at a crossroads, and tough times lay ahead. In 2000, after he was cleared in court of an incident involving the supply of controlled drugs, McAvennie found himself in dire financial straits, and he sold the medals he won at Celtic to a fan in order to raise some much-needed capital. The time when he could pull designer suits off the peg was long gone, but when I met him, he appeared to have lost none of his self-confidence. I was reassured to see that his peroxide hair was as blond as ever, and his capped teeth (he'd had them done before he came down to London) still dazzled. 'It's always important to look the part,' he grinned. After walking away from contract negotiations with Luton Town, he soon put pen to paper for the Hammers. During negotiations, he found himself in a black cab with John Lyall.

I asked him to drive me down Kings Road. I wanted to get a feel for London and see where I'd be shopping. There was a motorcade holding up the traffic because Princess Diana was on the move. I took one look at the police motorcyclists and said to John: 'I see they've been expecting me.' John looked at me as if to say: 'What the bloody hell have we signed here?'

McAvennie delayed his start at pre-season training in order that he could attend the Live Aid concert at Wembley on 13 July. 'We were right down the front dancing to Queen and The Who. I was pretty anonymous. Eventually, a few West Ham fans recognised me and I had a great time with them at the concert.' When he finally did start training, it was a revelation. 'John Lyall made sure we actually trained and ran with a ball. I loved it there from the off.'

There was nothing in McAvennie's *Shoot!* profile – published shortly after his arrival at Upton Park – to suggest that he was anything other than a run-of-the-mill '80s footballer. He lived in a 'nice house near the training ground', enjoyed watching the American series *Cheers* and *Miami Vice* and played the occasional frame of snooker. The only clue that the Scot was a mould breaker emerged when he professed an admiration for the hell-raising Alex 'Hurricane' Higgins 'because he plays the game with flamboyance'.

At first, though, McAvennie's teammates were unsure of the new recruit. It was mainly down to his strong Glaswegian accent. In training, West Ham players thought he was growling at them, spoiling for a fight. 'Giveitheremate' and 'lookinforthepasspal' – delivered with bewildering speed – were two classic McAvennieisms. 'I was just being friendly,' he grinned. By early October, with ten games gone, the Hammers had found their gear, and the Cottee–McAvennie partnership was flourishing. 'We just clicked,' Cottee said. 'We had an excellent understanding of what the other was doing.' Off the pitch, though, the pair were chalk and cheese. 'I'd go out for a few beers and then head back to my flat where I lived with my girlfriend,' Cottee said. 'Frank – on the other hand – was part of the London scene almost immediately.' McAvennie found his bearings quickly, but if ever he was in need of a little local knowledge, he could always call on the services of fellow Scot Charlie Nicholas. Two years earlier, the (then) Celtic striker eschewed interest from Liverpool and Manchester United and opted to join Arsenal for £650,000.

He'd failed to deliver consistent match-winning performances for the Gunners, although his knack of scoring against Tottenham endeared him to the Arsenal crowd. Nicholas's public persona made him arguably the most *à la mode* of all '80s players. With his mullet haircut, black perm, earring, leather trousers and penchant for wearing jackets that he pulled up to his elbows, 'Champagne Charlie' looked like a member of Duran Duran or Spandau Ballet. His much-publicised basic weekly salary of £2,400 saw a clutch of top players demand a pay rise from their clubs. 'Arsenal play in London and they're paying him a west-end salary. It's different down there,' Joe Fagan had told some of his disgruntled Liverpool stars. With regards to his New Wave musical tastes, Nicholas certainly broke the mould. A fan of the Psychedelic Furs, and A Flock of Seagulls, Nicholas listened to 'We Will Follow' by U2 to prepare for games and appeared on the front cover of the thoroughly right-on *New Musical Express*. He didn't wear socks, and he sported expensive custom-made Italian man bags. Modelling contracts from Burtons and Littlewoods came his way, too. In fact, Chelsea winger and Cocteau Twins fan Pat Nevin, who'd signed for the Blues in the same week Nicholas arrived at Highbury, was even more entrenched in the music scene, sharing a flat with *NME* writer Adrian Thrills and striking up a friendship with John Peel that saw him acting as an unofficial, unpaid production assistant on the legendary DJ's BBC show. Nevin had also dated Altered Images singer Clare Grogan. But unlike Nicholas, Nevin was happy to move around the capital virtually undetected, flitting in and out of clubs and gigs, museums and art galleries 'that other footballers wouldn't be seen dead in', Nevin later said.

When Charlie Nicholas headed up west, though – to swanky Highgate bars or Blondes nightclub in Mayfair, a phalanx of photographers inevitably followed. 'Playboyeurism' was how Culture Club singer Boy George referred to the media's obsession with wealthy footballers and pop stars. Nicholas smiled when I suggested that he'd have slotted in well on the 'Rio' pop video, where coiffured Duran Duran stars prance about on a yacht with a sorority of supermodels drinking champagne. As for the suggestion that he was indulging in a spot of 'conspicuous consumption' – the act of showing off his material wealth by frequenting the best night spots – Nicholas countered: 'Most weekends I'd stay in with a bottle of wine on my own and rent a video, but that doesn't make the headlines, does it?'

By the time McAvennie arrived in London two years after the

Bonnie Prince headed south, the Arsenal man had grown weary of press intrusion. They'd run numerous stories about his private life, including relationships with TV presenter Suzanne Dando, Flake advert model Janis Lee Burns, and Dollar singer Thereza Bazar. The warning signs were there for McAvennie, but the former milkman was determined to enjoy himself in London regardless. Nicholas may have earned a good deal more than McAvennie – who was on £600 a week basic at the start – but it didn't stop him heading to Stringfellows and living it up. Following Nicholas's lead (Nicholas was paid £10,000 to pose in a pair of budgie smugglers with two glamour models), McAvennie was soon cosying up to Page-3 girls in the capital. The '80s was the heyday for the likes of Maria Whittaker, Samantha Fox and Linda Lusardi. 'I was mates with lots of them and married one too – Jenny Blyth,' McAvennie said. 'Apart from West Ham fans, Page-3 girls and nightclub owners, literally no one knew who I was for the first few months,' he said. That was about to change.

McAvennie made his TV breakthrough on the newly created *Saint & Greavsie*, hosted by Ian St John and Jimmy Greaves, on 15 October. McAvennie was paraded up and down London Bridge, with Martin Tyler asking passers-by if they recognised the First Division's top scorer. No one did. Not even a West Ham fan they spoke to. Some had heard of him, but that didn't mean they could pronounce his name properly. McElhenny, Marconie, McVitie… By coincidence, comedian Billy Connolly, leaving a nearby TV studio, was collared by Tyler and asked if he recognised the West Ham goal getter. 'Of course I do,' replied the Big Yin. 'It's the football writer Hugh McIlvanney.' His appearance on *Wogan*, with an audience of 22 million, saw McAvennie finally become a household name in the area of light entertainment. Clad in a grey suit, he appeared alongside football legend Denis Law. The West Ham man appeared shy and slightly overawed. 'Why is it that no one knows who you are?' the Irish smoothie asked him. 'Perhaps it's because my name is so hard to pronounce,' McAvennie responded bashfully. 'What do you do away from the pitch?' Wogan asked. 'Enjoy myself,' came the (not untruthful) response. McAvennie's explosion onto the scene would soon attract newspaper headlines galore, but the 1985–86 title race was replete with other intriguing subplots.

• • •

Buoyed by his side's FA Cup victory over Everton at Wembley, Manchester United manager Ron Atkinson was determined to end the club's eighteen-year hoodoo of not winning a league title. He was 'obsessed with finishing above both Everton and Liverpool. If we do that, we'll be the 1986 league champions – no question.' 'Big Ron' reckoned that United owed it to football to play in an attacking style, particularly given the pit of gloom in which the national game found itself. 'There's little doubt that football stands at a crossroads. At Old Trafford, we're aiming to put the smile back on people's faces,' Atkinson said. Permatanned, bejewelled, Mercedes-driving, fond of a glass of champers and with a combover that will echo through the ages, Atkinson was afforded more nicknames than any of his contemporaries. 'Goldfinger', 'Romeo Ron' and 'Bojangles' (to name three) was also the most high-profile of all '80s bosses, although not the most successful. His 1984 utterance that 'I've always liked the good things in life, and I've always been prepared to graft hard for my luxuries' was classic working-class-boy-makes-good speak. His players say that in private, rather like Malcolm Allison, Atkinson was quiet and thoughtful and preferred sipping from a teacup to a champagne flute. But, with United now benefitting handsomely from a classic Thatcherite piece of anti-protectionist engineering – the abolition of sharing gate receipts for league games with the visiting team – his United team appeared to be in the ascendancy. He'd spent the past four years assembling an expensive squad. They had a strong, if slightly static, defence, with the combative and skilful Paul McGrath at its heart; their midfield possessed a blend of Gordon Strachan's skill, the power of young Norman Whiteside and the talismanic presence of skipper Bryan Robson. Up front, there was the combative duo of Frank Stapleton and Mark Hughes.

On reflection, Atkinson realised there was one main problem at the heart of United. 'We lacked genuine pace up front, which made it difficult to get in behind teams. I tried to sign Gary Lineker, but Everton nipped in first.' At the start of the 1985–86 campaign, United won their opening ten fixtures. An expectant 49,743 packed Old Trafford for the first game of the campaign against Aston Villa and saw the Red Devils run out 4–0 winners, with Hughes grabbing a brace. 'To be so rhythmic early in the season is very pleasing,' Atkinson purred. The Red Devils followed this up with victories over Ipswich, Arsenal, West Ham and Norwich. Five more league victories in September saw Atkinson's United blaze a trail out front. Some footage of United during the blackout has survived, because even though matches weren't being broadcast in England, they were televised in Ireland and other Western European countries. Some of these were then sold on VHS. 'No one was getting carried away,' blond goalkeeper Gary Bailey told me, 'but when I saw [fullback] Arthur Albiston score a goal from miles out at Maine Road in the Manchester derby, even I thought: "This might be our time."'

Just to show that United weren't having it all their own way on the winning-streak front, Third Division Reading – with striker Trevor Senior in fine form – triumphed in their opening thirteen matches.

The tabloids were convinced that the title was heading to Old Trafford. 'JUST GIVE IT TO THEM NOW', barked the *Mirror*. Such headlines didn't impress Norman Whiteside. 'The real test was how we'd respond when the winning streak ended,' he said. After drawing with Luton, United then won three more games and drew against Liverpool, before the problems began. The primary cause was that in mid-October, Bryan Robson got injured and missed the next three months of the season. 'He was 50 per cent of our team,' Gary Bailey admitted. 'Robbo was our beating heart, our rock, our pillar. When he was absent, our foundations were rocky.' The midfield lost its edge and ability to harry opponents, and United's form slumped alarmingly. They suffered their first loss of the season, a 1–0 defeat at Sheffield Wednesday, and then after a home 0–0 draw against Tottenham, they were unexpectedly hammered 3–0 at struggling Leicester.

The *joie de vivre* which lit up United's play in the early stages of the campaign evaporated, although United still had a decent cushion and remained top of the table at new year. Down the other end of the East Lancashire Road, Everton and Liverpool remained nonplussed about United's pole position. Toffees manager Howard Kendall had an inkling that United would stumble. 'When we won the league the season before, we'd lost our first two matches. The pace you set at the start of the campaign didn't dictate where you'd end up.' In late November, a month after a 1–1 draw at Anfield against Kenny Dalglish's team in the league, the two north-western giants jousted once again in the last sixteen of the Milk Cup. Two Jan Mølby goals settled the issue in favour of the home team. After signing from Ajax in August 1984, the 'Great Dane' was shocked at the lack of coaching at Melwood. 'It took a while for me to hit my groove,' Mølby said. 'You found your own way, whereas at Ajax they had a very prescribed way of playing.' Mølby quickly embraced life at Liverpool. The drinking culture was as vibrant as ever. 'The philosophy was that you wanted to be the best team on the pitch and the best drinkers in the bar. We were,' he said. Mølby's distinctive Scandi-Scouse accent was down to born-and-bred Liverpudlian Sammy Lee. 'I spent a lot of time with Sammy when I arrived at the club. It's all thanks to him,' Mølby said.

The aura surrounding the Great Dane's first goal was heightened because – apparently – there were no cameras at the game. So, it was left to Liverpool supporters' fevered imaginations to tell the epic tale. Describing the 'action', Mølby told me:

Rumour had it that I took out Norman Whiteside with a flying tackle, left him in a crumpled heap then stormed forwards with the ball at my feet, with United players bouncing off me as I did so, and then unleashed an unstoppable shot from around forty yards that almost burst the net open, with Gary Bailey cowering for cover because I hit it so hard.

In fact, a rogue camera did capture the action and the goal, whilst pretty darned good, wasn't quite the figment of Liverpool fans' fevered imaginations. The Great Dane cleverly whipped the ball away from Whiteside and risked life and limb by running past him. 'He could have broken me in two,' laughed Mølby, 'but the clobbering never came.' Instead, a static United defence allowed Mølby to saunter to the edge of the area, unchallenged, and let fly. 'It was my first goal at the Kop End,' he explains, 'and it was a great feeling to see it sail in.' Not only had Liverpool made a point against their fierce rivals, they clocked that Ron Atkinson's side were running out of steam. As Mark Lawrenson put it: 'Jan Mølby was never going to be a sprinter, was he? But he tore through their defence like they weren't there. It suggested to us that without Robson, United had a soft centre.'

• • •

Late in '85, the 'big five' – consisting of Tottenham, Arsenal, Everton, Manchester United and Liverpool announced their plan to form a Super League outside the jurisdiction of the Football League. That is, unless the League's rules were changed to grant them greater elbow room. Tottenham director Irving Scholar and Arsenal vice chairman David Dein were the main instigators behind the move, with Manchester United chairman Martin Edwards and Everton's Philip Carter also keen to push for more clout. What stuck in the executives' craw more than anything was that TV money had to be shared equally between all ninety-two league clubs. 'Why should – say – Hartlepool, who hadn't had any matches televised in a season, receive the same amount as Manchester United, who'd been on television eighteen times?' Manchester United chairman Martin Edwards said. 'The tail often wagged the dog.'

'We were the young ones; all fans of our respective clubs, and we simply wanted the best for United, Arsenal, Tottenham or whoever. Most executives were much older than us,' Edwards told me. He balked at my suggestion that 'the new breed' were Thatcherite disciples. Edwards was at pains to point out that he vehemently opposed the proposed identity card scheme and 'fundamentally disagreed with Thatcher over her handling of the ban on English clubs in Europe'. Whatever private views they held, in public at least Edwards and co. remained staunchly apolitical. Over dinner in Swaziland during a pre-season tournament in 1984 in which United and Tottenham competed, Edwards and Scholar had discussed their shared frustrations of running a top club ('It was a meeting of minds. We discussed the fact that bigger clubs have bigger problems, like stadium overheads and the cost of policing grounds,' Edwards said), and they soon discovered that executives at other leading lights thought in much the same way. One grumble was that the First Division was too big and that it should be cut from twenty-two to twenty clubs. Another was that the league's egalitarian voting structure (each of the ninety-two clubs had one vote apiece) wasn't suited to the modern game. 'It hadn't changed in almost a century, but the football landscape was changing,' Edwards pointed out. How many other clubs the 'big five' would have taken with them is unclear, but a breakaway was averted following an intense six-hour meeting at a Heathrow hotel just before Christmas. A ten-point agreement emerged that included the three-quarters majority necessary for rule changes being reduced to two thirds, and the number of votes for all First Division clubs being increased from one to one and a half. Additionally, top-flight clubs would now receive 50 per cent of all centralised TV and sponsorship money. 'It was a precursor to the Premier League,' Edwards explained. 'Of course it was. It paved the way for the '92 breakaway.' The Football League was powerless to prevent the big five getting their way. A precursor indeed.

In December, it was announced that football would return to screens early in the new year. Once again, the Football League came off second best, forced to accept an almost-derisory £1.3 million joint package from the BBC and ITV that would see six live League matches, two Milk Cup semi-finals and the final, plus live FA Cup ties from the third round until the quarter-final. 'John Motson can dust off his statistics and Brian Moore can polish his hyperbole,' joked Football League secretary Graham Kelly. The pair were mightily relieved. Moore had spent some of his gardening leave recording voiceovers for matches broadcast in Europe and Ireland. Motson told me that he spent much of his enforced sabbatical 'pacing up and down [his] study, worrying about what might happen.' The message that rang loud and clear from the whole saga was that, rather belatedly, football authorities realised that they needed football rather than the other way around. 'Speaking fifteen years later,' Jimmy Hill told me, 'it's astounding to think that five months of football coverage was only considered to be worth £1.3 million. The product simply wasn't attractive. The TV companies had the football authorities on the ropes.' The BBC–ITV 1986–88 joint package was still only worth £6.2 million. 'The figure still reflected that football was in the dark ages when it came to negotiation and sorting deals,' Hill said.

On Saturday 4 January, *Big Match* viewers watched highlights of Arsenal winning 4–3 at Grimsby Town in the FA Cup, thanks mainly to a brace of Charlie Nicholas free kicks, and an entertaining 2–2 draw between Portsmouth and Aston Villa. Ten goals in two games wasn't a bad advert for a sport that desperately needed a shot in the arm. The following day, all eyes turned to Selhurst Park, as West Ham prepared to take on Charlton Athletic in BBC *Match of the Day* live. Finally, television audiences would be able to watch Frank McAvennie in action on the field.

In truth, the match was an absolute stinker. Having done precious little for most of the match, McAvennie sprung into life in the dying minutes, seizing on a miscued clearance from John Humphrey and lobbing Charlton goalkeeper Bob Bolder. With Bolder trying desperately to hook the ball away, Tony Cottee snaffled it home to make absolutely sure. 'I thought Frank had scored enough already. I'd have that one,' Cottee said. The *Wogan* appearance a few weeks before had hugely boosted McAvennie's public profile. When he picked his mother up from Gatwick airport the following week, he recalled 'women – young women and older women – staring at me. I was under no illusions why. It was because I was a footballer, not because of my looks.' In the same week, he was bundled out of the side entrance at Stringfellows, having been tipped off that the paparazzi were clustered outside, anxious to snap him out on the town. He played head tennis with actor Leslie Grantham, aka 'Dirty Den' Watts on the set of BBC1's new soap opera *Eastenders*. 'You're the best striker in England,' Grantham claimed. 'And you're the best soap actor,' responded McAvennie.

McAvennie appeared to embody the 'get rich quick' philosophy that was espoused by the Thatcher government. The London stock market was deregulated, and previously nationalised industries, including British Telecom and British Gas, were floated on the Stock Exchange, giving speculators the chance to buy shares in companies and often make a killing by selling them off for a quick profit. The fabric of London was changing, with the derelict docklands rebuilt and newly gentrified, with some of the proceeds from the Brink's-Mat gold robbery ploughed in. The 'in crowd' of London footballers, Page-3 girls and soap stars demonstrated that working-class boys (and girls) could make it just by putting themselves out there. 'I was just a footballer who wanted to have some fun,' shrugged McAvennie. He was certainly having fun on the pitch, although there wasn't too much fun to be had in January, due to the big winter freeze. The Hammers only played once.

McAvennie reckoned that the harsh winter ruined the Hammers' title chances. 'Not because we lost form, but because we barely played.' After seeing their busy Christmas schedule decimated, West Ham played only four league games in ten weeks. Lyall's men weren't alone in seeing the winter programme disrupted, but they suffered more postponements than any other title-hunting team. 'We were always chasing,' Tony Cottee said. 'The gap was always a bit much to bridge.'

Nonetheless, by late March, they were still in with a chance as they prepared to face Chelsea at Stamford Bridge. Some forty years later, the vibrancy of West Ham's flowing play still resonates. Midfielder Alan Devonshire, restored to full fitness after missing the entire 1984–85 campaign due to a knee injury, opened the scoring with a glorious 25-yard effort, and Tony Cottee slid home twice from close range following flowing Hammers moves. Inevitably, the final flourish was provided by the blond bombshell; McAvennie thumped home and performed the prancing pony celebration favoured by several '80s strikers. After the clobbering, Chelsea's title challenge disintegrated, and they picked up just nine more points before season's end.

It left Chelsea free to concentrate on Wembley glory; not in the FA Cup or League Cup but in chairman Ken Bates's brainchild the Full Members' Cup, which, in the post Heysel landscape, was an additional competition for clubs in the top two English League divisions. Neither the Full Members' Cup nor the Screen Sport Super Cup – for those teams that missed out on European football due to the ban – were regarded favourably by either fans or clubs. 'They were the *Albion Market* [a short-lived, low-budget '80s ITV soap opera that was set in Salford] of cup competitions,' said Howard Kendall. Attendances across both competitions were awful, with just 4,000 fans turning up to watch a West Bromwich Albion v. Charlton Athletic clash in November. Arsenal declined to enter the competition, with

Ken Bates suggesting that perhaps the Gunners thought the competition was 'beneath them'. 'It *was* beneath us,' manager Don Howe told me in an interview. The Super Cup also turned out to be anything but. Attendances were well below the average, and Everton's benched striker Graeme Sharp recalls mockingly 'gesturing' at those who were playing. 'What a waste of time this is,' Howard Kendall told his players as they prepared to face Liverpool in the first leg of the final in May 1986. 'Now get out there and play.' The final of the Screen Sport Super Cup was carried over into the following season, due to fixture congestion, just to show what a half-baked concept it turned out to be. *The Times* declared it to be 'regarded by the public as a larger version of Trivial Pursuit'. Liverpool defeated their neighbours 2–1 over two legs, but after the trophy went into a crowd of Liverpool fans, it went missing, never to be seen again.

In the Full Members' Cup, Chelsea and Manchester City, two decades or more before the petrol dollars started to flow in, squared up to one another at Wembley. The match was played the day after both sides had played their respective league games. 'The competition itself was Mickey Mouse,' recalled former striker Colin Lee, 'but the final was an absolute cracker.' Lee scored twice as the Blues beat City 5–4 in front of a surprisingly healthy 65,000 crowd. David Speedie had the honour of scoring the first Wembley hat-trick since Geoff Hurst's treble in the '66 World Cup final. The Full Members' Cup was later renamed the Simod and the Zenith Data Systems Cup. At the business end of the campaign, it was left to Merseyside's two reluctant Screen Sport Super Cup finalists, Everton and Liverpool, to fight it out for the top prizes.

•　•　•

'There was practically nothing to separate us that season,' said Mark Lawrenson. '[The gap] was wafer thin. Had Everton won the double, we couldn't have had any complaints.' The prospect of Liverpool winning only the third double of the twentieth century appeared remote when, for the second time in two seasons, Everton won at Anfield in January in the league. Before kick-off, Howard Kendall told his players not to be fearful of shooting from distance. 'Bruce Grobbelaar was a tremendously athletic and spectacular goalkeeper,' Kendall told me. 'But he was always liable to an occasional error.' Kendall's instincts were spot on. On a chilly day, Grobbelaar allowed Kevin Ratcliffe's daisy cutter to squirm under his body. 'Brucie wanted the earth to swallow him up, and so did we,' Mark Lawrenson said. Everton's second was all about Lineker's searing pace and dinked finish over Grobbelaar. 'We used his blistering pace to good effect,' said Graeme Sharp. 'We could go long with Links if we needed to, because we knew he'd seize onto chances.'

In 1984–85, five players reached double scoring figures for Everton: Sharp, Heath, Mountfield, Steven and Sheedy. Fast forward a year, and there were just three. Lineker hit thirty, Sharp nineteen and Heath – who spent the latter part of the 1985–86 campaign on the bench – was stuck on ten. In late spring, Kendall's men spluttered, and Lineker temporarily stopped scoring, drawing blanks against Chelsea, Manchester United and Nottingham Forest. Those matches would prove costly, but despite their tribulations in front of goal, they still went into the final three games of the season with the destiny of the title in their own hands. The initiative was lost at a febrile Manor Ground. After Lineker missed a hatful of chances, Oxford's Les Phillips gleefully slammed home the U's winner. 'It was a bloody nightmare,' said Graeme Sharp. 'One of those nights where the ball was never going to go in for us.' Sharp attached no blame to Lineker ('The best finisher I ever played with') but observed that, unlike Heath or Gray, he was rarely part of the build-up to goals. In our Chinese restaurant interview, Howard Kendall put his head in his hands at the mere mention of the Oxford match. 'We weren't clinical enough,' he sighed. Then he paused for some time. 'Because of the way Gary played, if he wasn't scoring, he wasn't contributing very much to games. It was a matter of style,' he added with a shrug.

Lineker then gave a slightly tetchy post-match TV interview, where he grumbled that the backroom staff had left his battered but trusted old boots in Liverpool. Instead, Lineker toiled in a new pair. 'It's true that it was their job to remember to pack Gary's old boots,' Howard Kendall said, 'but it was Gary's responsibility to remind them.' On the final Saturday of the league season, Everton ran amok, with Lineker finding his shooting boots (literally) and scoring a hat-trick in a 6–1 win over Southampton. But Liverpool were in. If they won at Stamford Bridge on the same afternoon, the title was theirs.

'There was lots of talk of pressure,' explained Mark Lawrenson, 'but this was a team that had played in European Cup finals and won plenty of league titles before.' On a rutted pitch, the game was tetchy and tense. Flurries of fake news spread to Goodison Park and the Hawthorns (where West Ham were taking on the relegated West Bromwich Albion) that Liverpool had conceded an early goal. The romantics wanted it to be so. In the *Daily Express* that morning, Steve Curry wrote of his wish that Liverpool would falter 'and open the door for West Ham to clinch the title for the first time in their history'. The Hammers beat West Brom 3–2, but Liverpool also did their bit. After twenty-three minutes, Kenny Dalglish latched onto a Jim Beglin chip, cushioned the ball on his chest allowed it to drop, and calmly slotted the ball home. It was a sublime piece of skill; Dalglish's face radiated pure joy as he ran in front of travelling Liverpool fans at the north end of the ground. Thanks to dogged defending and the age-old tactic – instilled by Shankly and modernised by Paisley – of keeping the ball, Liverpool held out for a 1–0 win. At the Hawthorns, ecstatic West Ham players left the pitch convinced that Liverpool had drawn. 'Our fans were delirious. For a while, anyway. In that scenario, the title would be ours if we could win at Goodison on the Tuesday night,' explained Tony Cottee. When word filtered through that Liverpool had in fact won, the mood hit rock bottom. 'There were so many grown men in tears,' said Frank McAvennie. 'We might have been the best team that year, but Liverpool knew how to manage their season.' In case Everton fans needed reminding that Liverpool were back on top, travelling supporters at Stamford Bridge composed a little ditty to the tune of 'Ten Green Bottles': 'The Blue-nosed bastards aren't champions anymore, cos they went to Forest and only got a draw, then they went to Oxford and the bastards couldn't score, so the Blue nosed bastards aren't champions anymore.' Howard Kendall's men had a chance for revenge in the all-Merseyside FA Cup final the following weekend.

Much of the build-up to the showpiece match was fairly standard. In a *Pot Black*-type scenario, Gary Lineker defeated Mark Lawrenson by two frames to one as they tried to outwit one another on a full-size table. The cameras visited both team hotels and travelled with them on the coach trip to Wembley. Dressed in half red and blue, Scouse comic Roger McGough read out his poem on divided loyalties ('I'd be bisexual, if I had time for sex, but it's Goodison one week and Anfield the next') and some media outlets played the record 'Red and Blue Together.' Headteacher Frank Ravey wrote

the lyrics and comedian Ken Dodd sang the song, with the proceeds going to charity. But there was an edge to the build-up too.
On ITV, Liverpudlian comedian Jimmy Tarbuck held a pre-match
party that was attended by several *Brookside* stars. Ricky Tomlinson, who played Bobby Grant on the Channel 4 soap, wasn't invited.
'Tarbuck appears on Maggie Thatcher's political platforms and I am
a member of the Labour Party. He is operating a Jimmy Tarbuck
blacklist and it is not on,' Tomlinson said. Over on the BBC, Warren
Mitchell's character Alf Garnett – who usually appeared post-9 p.m.
watershed – ranted about the European ban. 'And all because of a
load of drunken Scouse gits, we're banned out of Europe,' he argued.
'It's not a European Cup without us, is it?'

For the players, though, it was all about the match. With chants of
'Merseyside, Merseyside' booming out, the match began at a frenet-
ic pace. It was physical too. 'The game was meatier back then. It was
part of the ritual that teams kicked the crap out of each other early
to test each other's mettle,' said Everton defender Derek Mountfield.
Peter Reid scythed down Craig Johnston and was in turn taken out
by Ronnie Whelan. Everton scored first. From a precision pass by
Peter Reid, Gary Lineker outpaced Alan Hansen and slotted the
ball past Bruce Grobbelaar at the second attempt. Everton's tactics
were working a treat, with Graeme Sharp deliberately jumping for
headers early into Lawrenson and Hansen. 'They didn't like it when
you were on top of them,' Sharp said. Liverpool's centre-backs didn't
much like Lineker's pace either. 'He was like a knife through hot
butter when he was in the mood,' Lawrenson said.

'We were so much second best it was embarrassing,' said Jan
Mølby. But then he began to control the game. Despite being a far
cry from the svelte, pyrotechnic footballers of today, Mølby moved
with a certain grace on the pitch. His slide rule pass set Ian Rush up

for his first goal, and Mølby's cross put Johnston in for Liverpool's second. From his own half, Mølby then orchestrated the move that saw Rush put the match out of Everton's reach. 'One of my better days,' Mølby said modestly.

In a show of Liverpudlian togetherness, the majority of Everton fans stayed in their places to watch Alan Hansen hoist the FA Cup aloft, and the 'Merseyside, Merseyside' chants could still be heard. But whilst the Liverpool players got stuck into the celebratory beer and champagne in their dressing room, Everton players merely drowned their sorrows. It got worse for them. The next morning, both teams flew back on the same plane to Speke Airport, with Toffees stars sitting in sullen silence as Liverpool players horse played on the seats opposite them. Then there was the teams' joint bus ride through the streets. 'Us up front with both trophies, journalists in the second bus and Everton in the third bus. It can't have been much fun for them,' laughed Jan Mølby, none too sympathetically.

It certainly wasn't, as Derek Mountfield recalled:

It was bloody awful. We sank a few cans and needed a piss. There were no toilets on board, so we stopped outside this house and Sharpy knocked on the door to use the loo. The wife let him up. We all queued up. Turned out the bloke inside was a Liverpool fan, saw the whole event unfolding on TV and told us all to bugger off. Only Sharpy got to empty his bladder. So much for Scouse solidarity.

Conspicuous by his absence was Peter Reid, who refused to participate in the parade. 'I told Reidy I'd fine him two weeks wages if he didn't show,' said Howard Kendall. '"Done," he said. I didn't see him until pre-season training. He was a Scouser but first and foremost he was an Evertonian.'

In the wake of the disasters of 1985, English football was in the doldrums. The twists and turns of 1985–86 showed that at its best, football could thrill crowds and, to some extent, even unite rival sets of fans. West Ham players tried to alleviate their disappointment at missing out. Tony Cottee sold his Fiat Uno, which he'd won for being named Young Player of the Year for '86, and splashed out on a Ford XR3i, which he had on order for 1 August. 'It was the ultimate '80s boy-racer car,' Cottee said. 'Kenny Dalglish reckoned West Ham were the best team in the league that season,' said Frank McAvennie, who reminded me that whilst ten of Gary Lineker's goals came from penalty kicks, all of his were from open play. Even though the wider public didn't clap eyes on the Scot for the first five months of 1985–86, he was a much-needed shot in the arm; a hybrid of a '70s maverick a la Bowles and Marsh and a Premier League star ten years in the future. Later that year, McAvennie's buddy Nick Berry shot to No. 1 with 'Every Loser Wins'. McAvennie didn't feel that way. 'It was West Ham's best-ever season, but I'm still gutted we didn't win the league,' he said.

Both the player and his club fell to earth with a bump during the following season, but in 1985–86, his star turn in E13 was just the tonic English football needed.

10

THE *VERY* '80S RIVALRY

'Both clubs were a kick up the '80s – a blast of much-needed fresh air.'
JOHN MOTSON

Vicarage Road – January 1984. Four days after the two sides battled to a 2–2 draw at Kenilworth Road, Graham Taylor's Watford and David Pleat's Luton go head-to-head again in a blood-and-thunder FA Cup third-round replay. There's skill, steel and some slapstick defending. Under the Hertfordshire floodlights, Taylor's men draw first blood, racing into a 2–0 lead thanks to winger Nigel Callaghan's lob and George Reilly's towering header. Mal Donaghy pulls a goal back for the visitors, before the hosts' John Barnes latches onto a long diagonal Callaghan pass and drills home to put his side 3–1 to the good. Two Paul Walsh goals take the tie to extra time before a header from Scottish striking sensation 'Mighty Mo' Johnston (Taylor insists on calling him Maurice) gives Watford a dramatic 109th-minute winner. 'That was pure, raw entertainment,' Taylor gushes after seeing his side run out 4–3 winners. 'We lost, but I couldn't keep my eyes off the game for a minute,' acknowledges David Pleat. It's cavalier and carefree stuff. Watford favour long, sweeping passes from the back for wingers Barnes and Callaghan to run onto. Luton's passing is crisp, fast and accurate, with the balls played to the feet of forwards Brian Stein and Paul Walsh, who'll soon partner one another up front for England. The clash of styles crystallises the (often) fierce debate about just how the game should be played in England in the '80s.

Yet both clubs also have much in common, with a community focus and multicultural lineups. They have strong links to show business too. It's a uniquely '80s rivalry.

• • •

As early as 1982, Graham Taylor and David Pleat were both touted as future national team managers, showing just how far they had come in the previous decade. Once a whole-hearted full-back with Grimsby Town and Lincoln City, Taylor had led the Imps to the Fourth Division title in 1972–73 and turned down a chance to manage West Bromwich Albion before Elton John came knocking in 1978 and offered him a £20,000 salary (the envy of many top-flight bosses) to manage his collection of Fourth Division misfits. Pleat had been a winger with Luton and then Exeter City, but a succession of injuries meant that he looked towards coaching from a young age. At just twenty-three, he'd already qualified as a Full Badge FA Coach in 1968. He managed Nuneaton Borough until 1973, before becoming Luton manager in 1978. With singer Elton John as owner of Watford and comedian Eric Morecambe director at Luton, both Taylor and Pleat had the opportunity to rub shoulders with two celebrity A-listers in an era when football and showbiz rarely mixed.

'It wasn't just the salary that attracted me to Watford,' Taylor explained during our interview, 'although that was obviously a factor.

It was Elton's love of the club and passion for the game that sold the project to me.' Conservative in his musical tastes, Taylor was a Vera Lynn and Perry Como fan. He knew next to nothing about Reg Dwight, save for occasional glimpses on TV. He was unaware (initially anyway) of John's homosexuality and substance abuse. 'I wasn't very worldly. I'd seen the big hair and the platform shoes, and that was it. He was a rock star, but at least where Watford was concerned, his head wasn't in the clouds. If it had been, I wouldn't have come.' That said, when John told him that he wanted Watford to play in Europe one day, he could be forgiven for thinking that Watford's owner had lost the plot. 'But there was something steely about him. It wasn't pie-in-the-sky thinking,' Taylor said. Neither did Elton John baulk when Taylor told him it would take in the region of a £1 million outlay to get Watford into the promised land. 'We'll give it a go,' came the response. Taylor admired John's homeliness. When he went around for initial talks at John's Windsor mansion, mum Sheila cooked them lunch, and his stepfather Dave helped fix up the Taylors' house in Berkhamsted. 'Elton didn't need the fame,' Taylor told me. 'He got enough of that on stage. Like me, he was fiercely ambitious for the club.'

Comedian Eric Morecambe's role at Luton was rather different. Morecambe resigned as a director in 1975 but remained an ambassador for the club. Like Elton John, who famously pulled out a Watford FC membership card from beneath a red box on the top of his piano for the cameras in his 1973 hit 'Step into Christmas', Morecambe was also fond of a spot of product placement when it came to his favourite football team. Playing a Roman soldier in the 1973 *Morecambe and Wise* Christmas show, Morecambe turned a sign around that read 'Luton Town' on the back. 'Do you think you can resist me?' Morecambe was asked by Vanessa Redgrave's

Empress Josephine in the same show, as she revealed a Luton Town knee garter. Pausing, Morecambe responds: 'We're going up the league,' as the pair embrace on the chaise lounge. Morecambe knew his football, having watched the Hatters since moving to the area in 1970. 'He was a lovely guy, very enthusiastic,' David Pleat told me. 'He was especially interested in the development of the reserve team.' On one occasion, Morecambe asked Pleat why he couldn't convey his instructions to them via a series of handheld boards in the dugout. 'Footballers can't follow one instruction, Eric, let alone half a dozen,' Pleat responded. Jealous of the attention he received, Luton board members weren't entirely comfortable with Morecambe on the board, but as Luton gelled in the late '70s, Morecambe 'was as encouraging as ever' towards Pleat.

Convincing lower-division players to move down south often proved tricky. 'Many of them took one look at house prices and headed back to the hills,' Taylor said. There was also the unprepossessing nature of the higgledy-piggledy Vicarage Road and the cramped and asymmetrical Kenilworth Road. 'We always showed new signings around *after* they'd signed on the dotted line,' laughed Taylor. Until 1979, the elliptical-shaped 'Vic' had a dog track running around the pitch. Greyhound racing added a much-needed revenue stream to the football club, but Taylor said that 'having piles of dog shit around the place wasn't the best marketing tool.' He received abusive letters when the dog racing stopped, but by the start of the '80s, Vicarage Road was for football only. His Bedfordshire counterpart would tell potential signings that Kenilworth Road was a platform they could use to 'prove themselves'. The Luton and Watford managers were often reliant on their network of spies and scouts to unearth young gems. 'My man in Ireland, Eddie Cochran, tipped me off about Mal Donaghy. We paid £15,000 for a player who turned out 488 times for Luton. Fantastic,' said Pleat, who himself had a great eye for a player, nabbing striker Brian Stein from under Watford's noses and midfielder Ricky Hill after he played a schoolboys game in Hitchin. Taylor received a tip-off about John Barnes – a talented winger who was playing for Sudbury Court. 'We got John for the price of a set of kit,' Taylor smiled with that toothy grin of his. 'Not bad business, I suppose.' There were no 'Hollywood wages' – as Taylor put it – on offer at Vicarage Road. 'We ran a tight ship,' Taylor said. Hornets winger Nigel Callaghan recalled how, after telling his players to bring their passports, Taylor took his players to a less-than-exotic Isle of Wight training camp. 'He properly wound us up,' Callaghan told me. 'And it rained all the time we were there, too.'

By the early '80s, both clubs were well and truly on the up. The nation's commentators loved both the Hatters and Hornets, promoted to the top flight at the end of 1981–82 campaign. Luton were champions with a (then) record points tally of eighty-eight points, as their fans are keen to point out, with Watford in runners-up spot. 'Refreshing and easy on the eye. Their kits were made for colour TV!' smiled *The Big Match*'s Brian Moore. Luton's classic white shirt had sunset orange strips down both arms, with three Adidas stripes added for good measure. 'It looked sleek and modern. A wonderful design,' reckoned David Pleat. Watford's was the more eye-catching, after Graham Taylor decided to add red to the classic yellow and black design. 'The kit was a visual feast,' Taylor gushed, 'and it reflected the way we played. Lively, exciting and buzzing about. After all, we were hornets, were we not?'

Both sides scored – and conceded – hatfuls of goals in the 82–83 season. Luton found the net sixty-five times but conceded a whopping eighty-four goals. By some distance, theirs was the most porous

Division One defence. Watford struck seventy-four times, but conceded fifty-seven times. Two televised matches in particular reflected their varying approaches to football. Watford travelled to Highbury in November to face Arsenal. The Hornets made a strong start to the season and were perched in third place. 'I'm not worried about them putting the ball in our net – as long as we get more at the other end,' Taylor said. 'I'd rather win 5–4 than 1–0.' Things didn't always go to plan. In September they hammered Sunderland 8–0 at home, but they had recently lost 3–7 to Nottingham Forest in the League Cup. Undeterred, Taylor warned the Gunners before the game that they 'would go right at them and chase them down'. They did just that. Winger John Barnes's opening goal came from a monstrous kick from goalkeeper Steve Sherwood, and a flicked header from 6ft 4in. striker Ross Jenkins. The eighteen-year-old Barnes scored a brace in Watford's 4–2 win, with Arsenal players harried at every opportunity. Watford's goals came courtesy of the set pieces and signature moves that Taylor drilled his players in during training. So, did this make Watford the arch purveyors of the long-ball game? 'Absolutely bloody not,' exploded Taylor during our interview, knocking over his coffee. It was the only time he lost his charm and his bonhomie. As he wiped up the spillage with his napkin, he explained:

> I got bloody sick of the media and the football hoi polloi saying that. If you study our matches carefully, we were adept at precision long passing. Long ball is lumping the ball aimlessly into space, which we didn't do. Our defenders and midfielders could deliver balls accurately for our strikers [Jenkins and Blissett] to head and our wingers [Barnes and Callaghan] to run onto.

At the risk of further annoying Taylor, I asked him about his connection to Charles Reep, often dubbed the 'father of the long-ball game'. In the process of analysing thousands of games, Reep used a system of shorthand to note down every cross, pass and shot. His conclusions were that most goals were scored from three passes or fewer and that if a team had twenty shots in a match, they had an overwhelming statistical chance of winning the match.

> He sent me his report, and I met with him. I incorporated the bits I agreed with – that the more shots on target we had the better and the need to get the ball forward quickly – but disregarded his rigid targets about winning the ball back in the final third so many times and playing the ball in the final third a certain number of times. Too rigid, too inflexible. Now, can we please move on?

We did.

Not everyone looked down on Watford's direct style. George Best – working as a studio pundit for ITV – argued that 'Graham Taylor has done a fantastic job, and Watford are simply maximising their assets'. But others in the game poured scorn on the Hornets' style. Tottenham manager Keith Burkinshaw, after watching his side lose 1–0, said: 'All they do is help the ball forwards. For us to play that way we may as well get rid of Glenn Hoddle, Ricky Villa and Mike Hazard, because you don't need any sophistication at all in midfield.' In the *Mirror*, Kevin Mosely described them as 'wholesalers, because they don't need middlemen'.

In finishing runners-up to Liverpool in their first season in the top flight, Watford completed the double over Arsenal and defeated Liverpool and Tottenham too. 'The win at Highbury meant the world to me,' Taylor told me. 'It was one of the classic English football venues, and to give them a bit of a hiding filled us with pride.' For Pleat's men, vindication that their free-flowing passing game could reap dividends came at Anfield on a sunny September day, in a breathless 3–3 draw. 'We went there thinking we could win,' striker Paul Walsh told me. Brian Stein fired the visitors ahead, but the highlight of the move was Walsh's Cruyff-like turn, which had Liverpool defender Mark Lawrenson swiping at thin air before setting Stein up for his goal. 'We put Lawrenson and Hansen on the back foot all game. Rarely if ever did you see them struggling in that way,' Walsh recalled. Luton drew 3–3 and the Kop sportingly applauded after firstly Kirk Stephens and then Mal Donaghy replaced the injured Jake Findlay in goal. Despite the fact that Luton had conceded three goals, skipper Brian Horton recalls Pleat urging his troops to continue playing in the same expansive manner. 'With the team struggling against relegation, it would have been very easy for David to instruct us to tighten up at the back, but we weren't defensively minded like that,' said skipper Brian Horton.

Both Pleat and Taylor were convinced that they were right in their respective visions. 'The fact we finished runners-up, suggested that we got it right most of the time,' Taylor said. His pragmatism was in marked contrast to Pleat's. 'Some called us idealists, but we were in the entertainment industry, and I don't think we let anyone down in that regard,' Pleat said. The Hatters trained (much of the time) with the ball at their feet, practising angular passing and shadow play (the training art of maintaining shape without the ball). 'We were encouraged to play our natural game,' midfielder Ricky Hill told me. Watford drills focussed on cross-country runs and dead-ball scenarios from crosses, corners and throw-ins. 'We harried our opponents relentlessly. It required our players to be extremely fit,' striker Luther Blissett told me. 'Everyone had to buy in, otherwise it wouldn't have worked.' Was Waford's style of play more suited to the top flight than Luton's, I asked Graham Taylor? 'The league positions in that first season would indicate that, yes,' Taylor said with a smile, 'although Luton stayed up.' Just.

Due to an end-of-season slump, Luton went into the final game – against Manchester City at Maine Road – knowing that only victory would keep them up. The Hatters' form had collapsed like a pack of cards in the final throes of the campaign. Hammered 5–1 at home by Everton, in the penultimate match they lost 3–0 to Manchester United. On the Tuesday before the City match, Pleat honoured his promise to send a full-strength team to Vicarage Road for Ross Jenkins's testimonial. Jenkins had played for Watford in all four divisions and was about to depart the club. Some players questioned whether that was a good decision. Pleat reasoned it would be a welcome distraction and a chance to forget about the Maine Road clash. It wasn't much of one, because the Watford fans' chants of: 'Going down, going down' were so relentless in the first half that Graham Taylor grabbed the microphone at half-time and told his fans to shut up. They complied – for the most part. 'That was a classy gesture on Graham's part,' Pleat acknowledged. The players were allowed to have a glass of wine with their evening meals as the Luton players gathered at a health spa in the days leading up to the match. The atmosphere was relaxed, but deep-down Pleat was well aware that if Luton, with the smallest average gates in the top flight, went down, 'we might well have never come back'.

On the journey up to the game, hundreds of cars crammed with Luton fans, their orange scarves and balloons fluttering outside the windows, gave their players the thumbs-up sign. The team coach blasted out Spandau Ballet's 'True' and Duran Duran's 'Is There Something I Should Know?' Midfielder Raddy Antić, a substitute that day, recalled: 'Players were arguing about which of the two bands were better, rather than talking about the game.' He paused. 'I preferred Duran Duran.' As his players prepared to run out at a packed Maine Road, Pleat urged them to press forwards but not to concede, because City required only a point to stay up. If they lost, City would go down. The game was goalless when Pleat subbed Antić on after 80 minutes and said to him: 'Good luck, Raddy, and if you get a chance to shoot, take it.'

The atmosphere was unbearably tense. 'You're going down, you little cunt,' City defender Nicky Reid told Paul Walsh as the clock wound down. 'In fairness – at that point, we were,' Walsh said during our interview. Playing out wide – because City defenders kept stamping on his left foot, which had been broken when the two sides played in January – Brian Stein crossed the ball on eighty-seven minutes. After City goalkeeper Alex Williams punched it clear, Antić fired the ball home with his right foot from just outside the box. The 34-year-old galloped towards the Luton bench. Pleat and coach David Coates urged their players to keep calm. 'It was very good advice,' recalled skipper Brian Horton, 'because we had an allergy to keeping clean sheets.' Given that Antić was Athletico Madrid coach when club president Jesús Gil rode through the city on an elephant after Antić's team completed the double in 1996, it's remarkable that he reckoned Pleat's celebration after the final whistle was 'the most incredible thing I ever saw in football'.

At the final whistle, the City players sank dejectedly to their knees and Luton players hugged one another and saluted their fans. A jubilant David Pleat, clad in his brown suit and slip-on shoes, staccatoed across the Maine Road turf like a week-old foal, or as he put it, 'like a crazy kangaroo'. Antić shook his head and laughed. 'I liked the fact that as he began to run, he did up his jacket – like a true Englishman.' The symbolism was irresistible; little Luton had cocked a snook at one of English football's establishment clubs and shoved them through the relegation trapdoor. After the game, Pleat sought out City boss John Benson to commiserate with him but was a little nonplussed at the presence of comedian Eddie Large. 'I didn't quite know what to say,' said Pleat. It would be nice to think that every 5 May, Pleat fishes out the (now) famed garments and recreates his iconic celebration. But he gave the suit to a charity shop and the shoes were auctioned off a few years ago for £4,000, the proceeds from which went to Luton's academy. 'It seems to be all people remember me for,' Pleat said, 'but in the three seasons before I went to Tottenham, we improved every year.' For pure drama, though, nothing could match the Hatters' Maine Road heroics.

During the close season, Raddy Antić received a message asking him to pop into Kenilworth Road, because Eric Morecambe, now only an occasional watcher of Hatters matches, wanted to meet with him. Morecambe told Antić that, as he listened to the game on Radio 2, he was worried that he would have another heart attack. 'Except he didn't actually use the phrase "heart attack", but he whistled and squeezed where his heart was. I laughed a lot.' Antić had met Morecambe before, and the comedian nicknamed him 'Antics, Raddy Antics.' After chatting about how the English game was becoming more cosmopolitan, Morecambe expressed pride that Luton Town were at the forefront of that change. As Morecambe prepared to take his leave, he smiled at the player, thanked him once more, and repeated the phrase: 'Antics. Raddy Antics.' As he did so, Morecambe waggled his glasses (Antić borrowed mine to demonstrate) and the pipe in his mouth. 'I don't know why it was so funny,' Antić said, 'but I laughed all the way home just thinking about it. And I still laugh when I think about it now.'

• • •

Light industry remained fairly buoyant in the south, which helped lend both clubs a modernist edge. Bedford Trucks, a subsidiary company of Vauxhall, sponsored Luton, and Iveco, a company whose headquarters were in Berlin, had its name plastered all over Watford shirts. The fact that both were transportation companies merely emphasised that Luton and Watford appeared upwardly mobile, at a time when a clutch of traditional 'giants' like Chelsea and Newcastle United were stalled in the second tier.

The club's hi-tech electronic scoreboards also created great excitement. Watford got theirs first, unveiling it to their fans in 1978 for a friendly against Wolves. By the early '80s, the 'Enjoy The Game' motif, flanked by 'Pac-Man'-style figures, became synonymous with Watford's family-friendly approach. 'There were some who came to watch us just because of the scoreboard, particularly from Germany,' laughed Taylor. 'A group of them grilled me for an hour about microchips. I just shrugged. I still haven't got a bloody clue what they are.' Luton's, believed to be the biggest in Europe, was unveiled two years later, and the £100,000 cost of installation was met by local firm Wallspan Bedrooms. 'It was a fantastic way to interact with our fans,' said Brian Horton. 'It mentioned births, marriages, christenings and the like.' It also meant that Wallspan kitchens got plenty of exposure. After the club had won the Second Division championship in 1982, keeper Jake Findlay was chosen to appear in a televised advert for the company. The advert had a touch of *Tales of the Unexpected* about it and took four and a half hours to shoot. But at least Findlay and his wife got a complimentary set of bedroom furniture for both bedrooms out of it. Or so Findlay thought.

Six years after Wallspan tanked, Findlay received an unwelcome £300 tax bill as the receivers audited the company's accounts.

Community work continued apace. In common with many clubs, the Junior Hatters and Hornets clubs were hugely popular, and during the close season both clubs hosted summer schools, with players involved in the coaching role. 'It was part of our mantra. We tried to build it into players' contracts, but the PFA blocked us,' Taylor said. Both managers were aware of the importance of nabbing fans young, with more fashionable London clubs in proximity. Whenever a shop, wine bar or sports centre opened in or around Luton or Watford, a beaming player would usually be present and correct, ready to cut a ribbon with an oversized pair of scissors. Nigel Callaghan, who now DJs for a living, was MC at multiple school discos and social events in town. John Barnes refereed the annual pancake race around Watford. Some of the stories are bizarre. Raddy Antić recalled judging at a local fete and a scrap ensuing at the end of a 'measure off' during a giant cauliflower growing competition. During a comedic *This Is Your Life*-style sketch for supporters, John Barnes dressed up as Graham Taylor's pregnant lover. 'Yes, it really did happen,' Taylor told me, head in hands. For the Watford staff, there were parties at Elton John's house, where everyone, from players to tea ladies, was cordially invited. 'It fitted in perfectly with the kind of club Elton wanted,' Luther Blissett told me. 'Our kids were welcome, and there was also a five-a-side pitch set up. Everyone piled in, including Elton himself. He liked doing normal things.' After a Christmas party at the Hilton in Watford, John treated his players to an impromptu one-hour concert on a battered old piano. 'It was an unforgettable show,' winger Nigel Callaghan recalled. Only Graham Taylor and wife Rita got the invite to the famous fancy-dress parties at Elton John's manager John Reid's house though.

> The first time, I didn't really know what to expect, so I went in a shirt and tie, and Elton greeted us in a giant wig and full makeup, dressed as Louis XVI. Or perhaps it was his wife [Marie Antoinette]. With him, you never knew. I looked at him, and said: 'Well, Elton, one of us has got it wrong.'

• • •

Reinvesting some of the money they received from Luther Blissett's £1 million move to AC Milan, Watford signed two forwards: 6ft 4in. Cambridge United striker George Reilly, and the rather more diminutive striker Maurice Johnston, signed from Partick Thistle for £200,000. The towering Reilly looked much older than his twenty-four years. Perhaps it was because many of his front teeth were missing, thanks to the sharp elbows of Bradford City defender Steve Baines. 'I was only eighteen. I swallowed a few, and when I was crawling around looking for the rest on the floor, the referee booked me,' Reilly told me. More or less a straight swap for the departing Ross Jenkins, Reilly was already a veteran of aerial combat. He listed the techniques used by central defenders and midfielders to put him off his game. 'The main one was deliberately heading the back of someone's head. It smashed right through you. Elbowing was another one, as was standing on your ankle. All the tricks of the trade. I got targeted because I was usually the tallest.' He quickly became a drinking buddy with Maurice Johnston. 'He was an entirely different kettle of fish, was Mo. Something that Watford and Graham Taylor hadn't seen before,' Reilly explained.

Living in the flat above the club shop for an extremely modest £5 a week, after training had finished Johnston often played snooker in town. But, sporting his white-leather suit and blond highlights, 'Mighty Mo', as the press soon nicknamed him, always had his eyes on big-city nightlife. He soon became a regular on the London club scene. It never curtailed Johnston's prodigious goal scoring (he plundered twenty-four goals during the season), but his nocturnal activities in London caused Taylor concern from the off. 'I always took care to call him "Maurice". If I'd called him "Mo", I'd have merely been adding to the media feeding frenzy that quickly developed around him,' Taylor said. A natural finisher, Johnston occasionally came into training the worse for wear, and Taylor's coaching staff did their best to patch him up before it began. 'Have you sorted out Maurice?' Taylor would ask them, never missing a trick.

Watford quickly discovered their mojo in the FA Cup. After knocking out Luton in a replay, Watford eased past Charlton and Brighton before heading to St Andrews to face Birmingham City in the quarter-final. Since crossing the second-city divide from Villa Park, manager Ron Saunders had been unable to revive the Blues' fortunes. In part, he was convinced it was due to the curse that travellers had placed on Birmingham's ground after they were evicted from the site in 1889. Saunders believed that victory over Watford would symbolise that his strenuous efforts to rid St Andrews of the centuries-long curse had been successful. He'd invited healers onto the pitch, liaised with a 'horoscope person' (as he described her) called Madam Rozina, ensured the players wore red socks and that the soles of their boots were painted red and ordered the ground staff to hang crucifixes from all four floodlights in a bid to 'keep the spirits at bay'. John Barnes's first goal in Watford's 3–1 win – a drag back past two defenders and a beautifully curled finish – was bewitching to behold. 'We're trying to keep bad spirits at bay,' said Ron Saunders, 'but you can't keep a talent like John Barnes at bay.'

In the semi-final at Villa Park, Watford ended the Wembley dream of Third Division Plymouth Argyle, with a diving header from George Reilly settling the match. Understandably, there was a great deal of reference to Argyle's gallantry and fighting spirit, but for Graham Taylor, the build-up to Reilly's goal perfectly encapsulated the uglier side of English football in the '80s. 'Barnes' jinking run was wonderfully skilful, but the backdrop was the monkey chanting that rained down. And there was nothing he could do about it. Despicable,' Taylor said. Twenty-five years after netting the winner and now employed in the building trade, George Reilly got involved in an altercation with a coworker who bit part of his ear off. 'Remember Plymouth Argyle,' his assailant hissed, before sinking his teeth in. 'The thing was, that I doubt the kid was even born when we played them, so I don't really know why he held such a grudge,' Reilly said. Before Watford could focus on Wembley, though, the Beds–Herts derby was about to boil over.

After forty minutes of a full-blooded Division One clash, there was a thud and a flurry of limbs as Watford skipper Wilf Rostron and Luton defender Paul Elliott crunched into one another. The pair quickly scrambled to their feet and went chest to chest. There was some pushing and shoving, and Rostron asked Bristolian referee Roger Milford exactly when he planned to clamp down on Elliott, whom, he reckoned, had committed three or four bookable fouls already. 'It was just handbags – something out of nothing,' reckoned Graham Taylor. 'That type of thing went on in most games,' agreed David Pleat. To the general astonishment of all those inside the ground, Milford showed both men a red card. Annoying though it may have been for Elliott, it was a tragedy for Rostron, who was now poised to become the third FA Cup final captain in successive years to miss out on the showpiece match due to a suspension. This followed Queens Park Rangers' Glenn Roeder in 1981, and Brighton's Steve Foster in 1982. Rostron's furious manager rounded on Milford in the tunnel after the match ('I went nuts at him. I totally lost it,' Taylor recalled), and during the ensuing media storm, there was even talk of Rostron's case being referred to the High Court. It wasn't such an absurd notion, given that Foster's suspension had ended up in the highest court in the land a year before, although it was ultimately thrown out. The football fraternity were appalled. Pundit Jimmy Greaves described it as 'yet another diabolical injustice perpetrated by Lancaster Gate'. But the Rostron ban was upheld, and Les Taylor was appointed in his place.

For the final, Watford, in association with Benskins Brewery, produced 12,000 bottles of commemorative ale and sold over 39,000 rosettes and 8,000 flags. 'The town went absolutely cup final crazy,' recalled Graham Taylor. 'It wasn't always easy to stay focussed.' There was one glaring omission from all the hullaballoo; no FA Cup final song. Taylor and Elton John, who was on a European tour, took a dim view of such ditties, with the manager believing it to be a 'waste of time and money'. The Watford team stayed at a hotel just off the A41, and for the benefit of the BBC TV cameras, comedian Michael Barrymore joined them for breakfast. His 'hilarious' Basil Fawlty routine seemed to go down well with the players, but not so well with the manager. 'I found him bloody annoying, to be honest. I wasn't up for a load of noise when I was trying to focus,' Taylor recalled.

He was sent a DVD of the 1984 final, but he never watched any of it, not even the clip of Elton John crying during 'Abide with Me'. The Hornets were swatted aside by Howard Kendall's resurgent Everton during the Merseysiders' comfortable 2–0 win. One of the problems was Watford's inexperienced defence. Trevor Steven gave Neil Price a torrid afternoon down the right-hand side. Watford players still feel aggrieved at the manner of Andy Gray's goal, insisting the ball was headed out of Steve Sherwood's hands. But Watford's frontline of Barnes, Callaghan, Johnston and Reilly performed poorly. Elton John threw a party afterwards for all the Watford staff at his house. Nigel Callaghan danced with Kiki Dee, with whom John released the song 'Don't Go Breaking My Heart' that year. There was plenty of singing, although 'Sad Songs' and, in particular, 'I Guess That's Why They Call It the Blues' were off the menu. George Reilly blasted out 'I'm Still Standing', with the chairman–owner clapping along. The following morning, Reilly served John eggs and bacon. 'It was hard not to feel a bit bloody miserable though,' Reilly explained.

•   •   •

In 1984–85, it was Luton's turn to knock Watford out of the FA Cup, with Wayne Turner's finely crafted goal settling the tie after a second replay. Whenever the Beds–Herts derby loomed, both managers went out of their way to dampen down any potential trouble between the two rival clubs' sets of supporters. 'Graham and I would write slightly sycophantic programme notes and be generous about one another's clubs in interviews,' David Pleat recalled. By and large, there was relatively little crowd trouble between the Home Counties teams, but when Luton drew Millwall at home in the quarter-finals, there was a palpable sense of nervousness amongst Luton officials. The notorious clash, played on 13 March, became infamous on a night of destruction and violence.

There wasn't time to make the game all-ticket, because Luton had only sent Watford packing four days earlier in the second replay. Processing all the tickets was impossible. Kenilworth Road immediately became a beacon for hooligans from several London clubs. The yobberati arrived in Luton town centre during the early afternoon, after the police received intelligence of mass gatherings at Kings Cross Station. By 3 p.m., the Arndale Centre in the town was closed after gangs of youths, all headed 'for a day out in the country', as club historian Roger Wash puts it, made nuisances of themselves. 'The police were aware of huge numbers of unruly supporters heading into the area,' recalled David Pleat, 'but as I remember, Bedfordshire Police didn't have any horses, I'm afraid, only dogs.'

By late afternoon, Luton resembled a warzone. Hooligans rampaged down Oak Road near the ground smashing terrified residents' front windows. 'There were "Millwall, Millwall" chants, but I heard "Chelsea, Chelsea" too,' local resident Brian Kendrick told me. Kendrick was struck by flying masonry, his own car's windscreen wipers, and a full can of Heinz tomato soup: 'I threw the can back at the little bastards. It hit one of them. He shouted that he'd come back for me. Thirty years later, I'm still waiting.' Violence and menace were all pervasive. Publicans tried desperately to close the doors to their hostelries and shove out miscreants. As they did so, their windows were put through. 'It was like a tornado had hit Luton,' explained one barman.

The feeling amongst many Luton fans before the game was that it would have to be postponed, but no such intervention happened. An hour before kick-off, visiting supporters stormed the Kenilworth Road End gates. The open terrace, which was supposed to accommodate 5,000 fans, soon held double that number. It was a miracle that none were crushed to death. Literally squeezed out, hundreds climbed onto the pitch and began to maraud across the ground, lobbing bottles, nails and coins at home fans in the Oak Road End, before violently shoving out Luton supporters in the Bobbers Stand. Some terrified home fans sought sanctuary in the tunnel. Concerned players looked to their families in the directors' box, which was being pelted with snooker balls. 'Who the fuck is that?' one hooligan asked another when Millwall manager George Graham strode over to appeal for calm. 'We knew straight away they weren't all Millwall fans,' Roger Wash said. The game began on time, but referee David Hutchinson was forced to take the players off after fourteen minutes due to more fighting. 'Whatever happens, we're going to finish this game,' Hutchinson told David Pleat, whose team led 1–0 thanks to a smart Brian Stein finish at half-time. Pleat remembers little of the game, but he recalls: 'When the ball went out of play in the second half, it literally bounced off the policemen ringing the pitch.'

At the final whistle, the players hared down the tunnel, as the worst of the fighting ensued. Forty years later, the scenes have lost none of their capacity to shock. Hooligans swarmed across the pitch, using the ripped-out orange seats as weapons that they hurled at (retreating) police officers. The 'English disease' appeared uncontainable. And given the plethora of 'Pride of London' sweatshirts, mullets and grey leather jackets and the smashed-up Argos and Vauxhall advertising hoardings, this was a quintessentially English dystopia. It was every inch as bleak and depressing as the stark 'Don't Die of Ignorance' AIDS advert, or *Threads*, the BBC's harrowing account of a post-nuclear holocaust world. Given the level of chaos and the fact that a policeman was pummelled whilst reviving a colleague, it's remarkable that no one died that night.

In the cold light of day, as stoic residents counted the cost and swept up the glass shards, Luton players trained on the Kenilworth

Road pitch, once the detritus had been removed. That snooker balls and darts were removed was grimly ironic, given that, as discussed, those two TV friendly sports were in the ascendancy at the time, in marked contrast to football. Naturally, the discussion turned to ways in which hooliganism could be stopped. One couple, having seen their son (a Chelsea fan), run amok the night before on the television, threw his bedding into their front garden, informing him that if he behaved like an animal, he could sleep like one. It was hardly a long-term solution. The mental scars amongst Luton fans ran deep. A third of season-ticket holders in the Bobbers Stand – according to Pleat – stopped coming to games.

In the House of Commons next day, Margaret Thatcher blamed football hooliganism on 'a lack of parental and teacher discipline'. Luton North MP John Carlisle adopted a stronger tone, arguing: 'The only answer is to inflict on those the physical pain that they inflicted on others last night.' Luton chairman David Evans, a Thatcher acolyte and Tory MP for Welwyn Garden City, concurred with John Carlisle, telling me in our rather prickly 2000 interview that the hooligans should have been 'birched in Luton town centre in front of local residents until their backsides bled'.

Over the coming months, Evans and other Tory ministers mooted controversial long-term plans about how to end the scourge of hooliganism at Kenilworth Road and far beyond. Evans had been none too keen on Chelsea chairman Ken Bates's scheme to install an 11ft perimeter fence, complete with the 'ultimate deterrent' for pitch invaders. Barbed-wire at the top of the fence would be added, with an electric section as Bates's cherry on the cake. 'Any fan touching the fence will immediately have to let go and fall 15ft,' Bates explained. 'My God, how awful,' David Evans commented. 'The next step is he will issue SS helmets to his stewards.' Politicians from both sides seemed to agree. 'It's a terrible idea, Stalag Stamford Bridge,' Labour's Reg Prentice stated. The Greater London Council (GLC) squashed Bates's plan. After another series of skirmishes during an FA Cup match with Bristol Rovers at home in January 1986, Evans made up his mind. Luton would become the first club in England to formally ban away fans from Kenilworth Road. At a cost of £250,000, only fully vetted, card-carrying Luton fans could pass through the electronic turnstiles. 'We didn't want scum at Luton matches. This eradicated the problem,' said Evans, who'd made his fortune in the industrial cleaning business. There were in fact various ways of circumnavigating the away-fan ban – which lasted until 1991 – if one had a friend who lived within the vicinity of the town. I asked Evans whether the implementation of the away-fan ban was for the benefit of the club or to further his own career in a government that was notoriously tough on crime. Evans called me a 'bloody idiot', in his barrow-boy accent, although he softened a little, saying: 'With an accent like this, I wouldn't have progressed far.' Evans lost his seat at the 1997 general glection. He never did answer my question, though.

At a cost of £335,000, the En-Tout-Cas artificial surface had been laid at Kenilworth Road in the summer of 1985, with the bounce of the ball regarded as 'truer' than Queens Park Rangers' Omni-turf laid four years previously. Luton reckoned the surface pulled in around £150,000 in revenue per season, with American Football team the Luton Flyers playing at Kenilworth Road. Hockey, bowls and dog training sessions took place too. Another bonus for the club was that the cost of the surface was largely met by their new sponsorship deal with Bedford Trucks. A 1986 segment of *The Money Programme* highlighted Luton's efforts to sell match-day packages to local businesses, which was made possible by the conversion of the Bobbers Stand into corporate boxes. Fans who were willing to pay the money gained access to the dressing room close to kick-off, and they were able to hear the wit and wisdom of chairman David Evans, who often joined guests at their pre-match meal, sharing his staunch views on immigration and capital punishment.

The press quickly dubbed the artificial pitch 'drastic plastic' and the corporate boxes were unlovingly called 'chalets' by visiting supporters. 'There was negativity towards us. David Evans was naughty about the away-fan ban. He pushed it through without any consultation. Luton became pariahs,' David Pleat told me. The surface suited Luton's passing game, although statistically, their home form hadn't markedly improved from when the pitch was all grass. Rival teams' managers huffed and puffed about the surface. Kenny Dalglish, whose Liverpool side was demolished 3–0 in a second FA Cup replay and 4–1 in a league match during the 1986–87 season, insisted: 'I still believe that if you have an artificial surface, you have an artificial game.' By then, though, David Pleat had left Kenilworth Road for Tottenham. John Moore then steered Luton to their best top-flight finish (seventh) before handing over the reins to Ray Harford. In 1987–88, Harford steered Luton to a thrilling 3–2 Littlewoods Cup final victory at Wembley over George Graham's emerging Arsenal side. The sunny Sunday was replete with ironies. Luton's away form on grass had been abysmal that season and they were clear underdogs against the holders. But their passing game won the day, and it was one of David Pleat's favourite sons, Brian Stein, who swept home the late winner. Broadcast live on ITV, David Pleat was Brian Moore's co-commentator. Moore recalled that Pleat 'was like a father at a wedding; proud and emotional, but sad that his adored child was all grown up and gone'. Others were less poetic. 'It's bloody Lu'on, innit?' ranted Stavros, Harry Enfield's

Arsenal-supporting Greek kebab-shop owner with fractured English on *Saturday Night Live* a week later.

As captain Steve Foster and his teammates paraded the trophy around Wembley in front of their delighted straw boater-clad fans, chants of 'Are you watching Elton John?' could clearly be heard. Watford were already condemned to relegation from Division One. Graham Taylor and John Barnes had departed the club in the previous close season, with the Hornets' star winger putting pen to paper for Liverpool and Taylor heading to the Midlands to rejuvenate Second Division Aston Villa. Ironically, it was Watford's 4–1 FA Cup semi-final defeat to David Pleat's Tottenham in April '87 that convinced Taylor it was time to seek pastures new: 'The fact that David was in charge of Spurs intensified my feeling that I could achieve bigger things at a bigger club with bigger resources.'

For much of the '80s, Luton and Watford had crossed paths and locked horns as they sought to survive in the unforgiving arena of top-flight football. That they ultimately thrived was due to the two clubs' willingness to innovate. But it was also due to the contrasting philosophies espoused by their rival managers.

11

THE MAXWELL MANOR

'Eventually, even Bob Maxwell lost count of the huge number of pies he'd stuck his fingers into.'

JIM SMITH, SPEAKING IN 2004

Oxford – March 1982. 'Welcome to the biggest council house in the country,' booms Robert Maxwell, the imposing tenant of Headington Hill Hall, in his rich baritone. 'Thank you,' says new Oxford United manager Jim Smith, who's just been ushered into Maxwell's giant oval office. 'I hear you like a glass of Scotch,' says the business tycoon, pouring two glasses. Glancing around, Smith is immediately struck by the oak panelled walls and leather-bound volumes on the bookshelves inside the nineteenth-century residence, which is also the headquarters of the Maxwell-controlled Pergamon Press. As they puff their way through several Cuban cigars, Maxwell pontificates on the various ills surrounding English football and recounts his scarcely credible life story. Early on in proceedings, Maxwell, his dyed jet-black hair tapering into a widow's peak, leans in towards Smith, stares at him with his big solemn eyes and asks: 'Are you with me, Jim?' Smith nods. Words are unnecessary, because as Smith later explains: 'When Bob Maxwell asked you a question, it was really an order.' Maxwell tops up the Scotch, the pair clink glasses and, after Maxwell instructs Smith to delay the start of his holiday to Majorca by a day, start to plot how they will steer Oxford United, who've been in the football league for a quarter of a century, into the top flight of English football.

• • •

'A festival of shit,' was how Maxwell described the financial state of football to Smith on their first proper get-together in Headington. 'He literally sand-blasted me with examples of mismanagement at clubs,' Smith said. Maxwell certainly had a rich seam of disaster stories to draw on. In 1982, Bristol City remained in existence only after tearing up the contracts of eight of their leading players. The unfortunate 'Ashton Gate Eight', as they were known, were the most infamous martyrs to the meltdown football was facing. In the same year, Norwich City purged their backroom staff in order to try to deal with a £327,000 debt. 'There will be hundreds of players on the dole by the end of the season,' City chairman Arthur South predicted. Fourth Division Halifax Town put their entire playing staff up for sale. The beleaguered Rochdale chairman said the club would cease to exist unless their home attendances doubled. Even Manchester United, the best-supported club in the country, saw their crowds plummet by 25 per cent in the early '80s. 'The game's dying on its feet, Jim,' Maxwell boomed. But that wouldn't be happening to Oxford, he reassured his new manager, as he proceeded to shove what Smith described as an 'entire plate of sandwiches in his gob'.

What Oxford United needed to do, Maxwell insisted, was to think outside the box. 'How else will we reach the First Division?'

he asked Smith. The former Birmingham City boss smiled, believing Maxwell was 'bloody mad'. But he was impressed with Maxwell's forensic knowledge of how other clubs had attempted to reduce their costs and overheads. Reading from his list, Maxwell told Smith that Bolton Wanderers, Hull City and Crystal Palace had sold off portions of their now largely deserted terraces to supermarkets. He mentioned that Leeds United and Wolverhampton Wanderers were considering selling their grounds to local councils. They both eventually did so. Maxwell believed that ground sharing and mergers would become commonplace. Smith piped up that such measures wouldn't go down well with supporters. 'But they know nothing about business,' snapped Maxwell. 'It's time that football got its house in order and streamlined.' Since paying £130,000 for his debt-ridden home club in 1982, when it was mired in the lower reaches of Division Three, Maxwell had already made waves. There had been little immediate improvement on the pitch under manager Ian Greaves, whom the spectacularly foul-mouthed Maxwell fired in 1984 after Greaves swore in a board meeting. 'I won't have my fucking managers swearing in the boardroom,' Maxwell told Smith.

'My life seemed pretty boring and dull compared to his,' Smith said. Most people's did. Born Ludvík Hoch in eastern Czechoslovakia in 1923, he escaped the Nazis' clutches as they annexed chunks of Europe. Many of his family members perished at Auschwitz. 'Bob told me from that point onwards, he'd do whatever it took to survive. "Get the fuckers before they get you," was his motto,' Jim Smith said. He then morphed into Private Leslie du Maurier after transferring from the Czech refugee division to the British Army. Then came his final name change. As Captain Robert Maxwell, he developed an upper-class English accent and won the Military Cross.

In the post-war era, Maxwell became a publishing tycoon and

represented the Labour Party as MP for Buckingham between 1964 and 1970. However, he lost control of Pergamon Press following a 1971 Department of Trade and Industry report that stated he was not 'a person who can be relied on to exercise proper stewardship of a publicly quoted company'. 'Bob told me it was all a witch-hunt by toffs who didn't like the fact he was a foreign millionaire,' Jim Smith said. After a decade of exile, he reacquired Pergamon and breathed new life into the British Printing Corporation, a separate acquisition. Maxwell was now a multi-millionaire but professed to being bored. 'He was a business genius, or so he was fond of telling me,' Jim Smith said, 'but business can be quite dull.' Bob was always looking for the next risk. He missed out on buying *The Sun* and the *News of the World* in the late '60s, beaten to it by Australian Rupert Murdoch, who became a sworn enemy of Maxwell's. In fact, Smith had initially thought that Murdoch owned Oxford. 'They even had the same initials. I'm glad I never called him Rupert by accident. It wouldn't have ended well for me.' Unlike the more restrained Murdoch, however, Maxwell wanted to get off the business pages and increase his profile. He certainly achieved that, and much more besides, over the course of the '80s.

He wasn't the only colourful, high-profile lower-league club supremo on the scene. Don Robinson replaced Harold Needler at Fourth Division Hull City in 1981, immediately proclaiming that the Tigers would be the first club to 'play football on the moon'. Robinson, who'd previously been chairman at Scarborough, quickly reached out to fans, meeting and greeting them at matches and handing out bottles of champagne at games. Robinson outlined his grandiose plans for Boothferry Park. He wanted to turn it into an 'entertainment bowl' that would host pop concerts and add a hotel/ gymnasium complex. He vowed that the club would reach the top flight by the end of the century. None of those plans materialised, but Robinson, who once rode a horse onto the pitch dressed as a cowboy, did make good on his promise to produce Tiger Cola, which once sold 20,000 cans in a year. Maxwell to Smith reiterated the story of Lincoln City chairman Gilbert Blades, who took over as Lincoln City chairman in 1982. Blades, who'd vowed that the Red Imps would live within their financial means, received death threats from supporters when, with Lincoln chasing a promotion slot, he refused to sanction new signings for manager Colin Murphy, ultimately deciding that it would place the financial state of the club in 'mortal danger'. Blades stood down, lamenting: 'I understand that fans will complain, but calling me a wanker all game is going too far.'

Then there was the fur coat-clad, cigar-chomping Essex butcher Anton Johnson, who'd dabbled in music promotion and had brought acts like Fleetwood Mac to Purfleet. Johnson purchased – at different times from the late '70s onwards – Rotherham United, Bournemouth and Southend, and he gave Harry Redknapp his first management job. Unsurprisingly for a man who kept two caged alligators in a nightclub he once part owned, Johnson enjoyed the spotlight, despite being a divisive figure at both Roots Hall and Millmoor.

But over time, it was Robert Maxwell who mastered the dark arts of meddling and interfering – both inside and outside football.

• • •

Oxford narrowly missed out on promotion from Division Three in Smith's first season, and Smith quickly saw the different facets to Maxwell's personality. After agreeing to make good on his promise to put £750 into the players' pool for the 1983 end-of-season trip to Spain, Maxwell opened up a briefcase stuffed full of £50 notes. In the process of counting out the full amount, he accidentally dropped two on the floor. 'These are for your holiday too,' Maxwell told Smith, slipping them into his top pocket and tapping Smith on the chest as he did so. Maxwell was also a sentimentalist and loved spending time with Oxford's veteran trainer Ken Fish, who insisted that the Oxford players wolf down a Mars bar prior to matches for energy. 'One time I came in to meet Bob but couldn't find him. Finally, I heard his laugh, and there he was, slapping his thigh, with Ken regaling him with stories about old football,' Jim Smith said.

But Maxwell always had an eye on the future, and in '83, Oxford almost ceased to exist as an independent club. One afternoon, Maxwell phoned Jim Smith and boomed: 'Congratulations, Jim, you're the new manager of Thames Valley Royals.' Rather than pepper his boss with questions, Smith responded with the comment: 'Thanks for letting me know, Bob,' before the phone went dead. 'I was so amazed that I couldn't speak,' Smith said. Maxwell had purchased a stake in Reading and proposed buying them for £220,000 and merging the local rivals in a brand spanking new stadium at Didcot. 'In Bob's world, the whole scheme made perfect sense,' Smith told me. 'Mergers, takeovers, sharing the running costs of an all-purpose ground, publicity, better sponsorship deals, hiring the venue out to local schools and colleges...' But Smith sensed what was about to happen. 'The fans will go ape shit at both clubs, Bob,' he told Maxwell. 'Fuck the fans,' came the response. 'It's my club and I make the decisions.'

With the story now splashed on the back and front pages of most newspapers, Maxwell deployed classic double-speak. 'I'm not a dictator trying to urge my will on fans,' he insisted, before reminding supporters: 'The alternative is no Oxford United.' At home to Wigan the next weekend, Oxford fans, one of whom brandished a banner that read 'OXFORD LOYAL, NOT THAMES VALLEY ROYAL', spat at Maxwell and yelled 'Judas' at him. In Reading town centre, Royals supporters also arranged protest marches. It wasn't the Football League that torpedoed the plan – chairman Jack Dunnett had argued: 'I think it's a good viable alternative if done in the intelligent way that Oxford and Reading are doing it.' It was Royals director Roger Tranter, who obtained a high court injunction preventing chairman Frank Walter from any more negotiations without the board's knowledge. A rival consortium led by former Reading player Roger Smee purchased Walter's stake. Maxwell was incandescent: 'He's fucking murdered two clubs, Jim. That man [Tranter] has blood on his hands.' Except that was very far from the case. Reading would be promoted to the Second Division within three years and Oxford reached the top flight within two. But before that, Maxwell also threw his considerable 22-stone weight behind an audacious deal to buy Manchester United.

He used his recent £120 million acquisition of the *Daily Mirror* and sister paper the *Sunday People* to publicise the pending deal. The red-top tabloid announced that 'within a week', he would buy United for 'the staggering transfer fee demanded by Martin Edwards... £10 million'. Ultimately the deal never happened, because, apparently, Edwards added another £3 million to the fee. Maxwell's apocryphal version was that, as United thrashed Luton 5–0 the weekend before the deal would have gone through, Edwards added another million each time one of his players hit the back of the net, which in any case, would have made the final price £15 million. The former United chairman told me that during his meeting with Maxwell about a possible sale, a final price was never formalised, and that in any case, Maxwell was distracted as Soviet President Yuri Andropov had died that day. 'Get me the Kremlin,' he repeatedly instructed his minions. 'I'm not sure that he was ever fully serious about buying,' Edwards argued. Thwarted in his Thames Valley Royals plan and his deal to purchase Manchester United, Maxwell now turned his attention to raising the profile of Oxford United.

Ramshackle it may have been, with its rickety, asymmetric stands, sloping away terrace and notoriously claustrophobic underground toilets for travelling fans, the Manor Ground was certainly an intimidating experience for visitors as Oxford built a head of steam in the mid '80s. 'One feature of the ground was that it sloped from end to end. If we were storming downhill in the second half,' former skipper Malcolm Shotton told me, 'we always felt we would win.' Oxford had the formidable centre-back pairing of Shotton and Gary Briggs. As well as sporting spectacular moustaches, the double act, who'd often high-five after repelling an opposition attack, were arguably the toughest unit around. 'It was like running into a block of concrete,' was how Manchester United striker Norman Whiteside described clashing with Briggs. Luton striker Mick Harford reckoned Shotton 'possessed the sharpest elbows in football'. The Oxford duo believed that skilful rivals should be neutralised by whatever means necessary. 'We were hard but very much unfair,' Shotton laughed. Briggs was perhaps the more effective in the air out of the two, as Shotton discovered to his cost when Briggs accidentally headed his captain during a match. 'His nut was rock hard. Briggsy completely wrecked it. It took an operation or two to fix it,' said Shotton, pointing to his (now) reconstructed nose. Oxford served notice of their rise to prominence with some headline-grabbing Milk Cup victories in front of the cameras, including a 1–0 victory over Manchester United in 1983 and a remarkable 3–2 defeat of First Division leaders Arsenal the following season. By the time they sent the Gunners packing, Oxford were also top of the Second Division, having signed the powerful forward Billy Hamilton from Burnley and striker John Aldridge from Newport County for £75,000. It should have been £80,000, but Maxwell sliced £5,000 off the fee by agreeing to have the cash motorbiked to south Wales that evening. Maxwell always completed the deals himself 'because he intimidated 90 per cent of people he met, so he could barter chairmen down', Jim Smith said. He also insisted on paying for every transfer in full. Or 'on the nose', as he put it.

Maxwell was rarely so prompt in paying his debts outside football. By the mid '80s, Jim Rosenthal, who'd begun his journalistic career with the *Oxford Mail* in the early '70s, was a regular on TV screens. 'I knew a few people in Oxford in different jobs who had to wait a long, long time before Bob Maxwell paid them for work they'd done,' Rosenthal told me. But Jim Smith grudgingly admired the club owner's belligerence in those days. In 1983, under pressure from leading chairmen, the Football League decreed that clubs would now keep 100 per cent of their gate receipts, rather than share them. Such a rule change clearly benefitted the bigger clubs, with bigger stadia. 'See – these rich bastards don't want the likes of us pissing on their parade, Jimmy,' barked Maxwell, who, of course, tried to buy one of the 'rich bastards' (Manchester United) a year later. 'But we'll show them, won't we?'

• • •

After the *Mirror* purchase, Maxwell synergised his assets. Oxford shirts carried the *Sunday People* logo, and advertising hoardings around the Manor Ground publicised the *Daily Mirror*'s Spot the

Ball competition. Embroiled in a circulation war with *The Sun*, and owner Rupert Murdoch, Maxwell ensured that both the *People* and the *Mirror* were crammed with news and views from the Manor Ground. Senior writers often challenged Maxwell on this, arguing that Oxford didn't warrant such publicity. They never won. On one occasion, the *People's* sports editor thought he'd triumphed, only to find that although the sports section was left as he'd edited it, the final news page before the sports section, hastily penned by Maxwell himself, was all about Oxford. The *Mirror's* chief sportswriter Harry Harris, who'd been appointed by Maxwell, often found himself in an invidious position. Summoned to Maxwell's office in the mid '80s, the meddling supremo instructed Harris to write an exclusive story that Johan Cruyff would be taking the reins as manager forthwith. The following day, with Cruyff vehemently denying the story was true and Jim Smith apoplectic, Maxwell sandblasted Harris. 'That's another fine mess you've got me into, Harry', he complained.

Maxwell's public image grew. On the 1984 Christmas *Paul Daniels Magic Show*, the diminutive TV magician vanished one million pounds under the watchful eyes of Owen Rout (the general manager of Barclays Bank) and Maxwell, described as 'a man of integrity' by Daniels. Maxwell's later misdeeds lend this illusion a bleak sense of irony. Like any oligarch worth his salt, Maxwell also indulged in a spot of nepotism, appointing his daughter Ghislaine as director in 1984. The appointment was publicised on *TV-am*, hosted by Anne Diamond and anchorman Mike Morris. She was certainly more of a football fan than her father and was fairly proactive, establishing a United supporters' club at Balliol College, where she had studied modern history with languages, and participating in protests to push forward development of a new stadium. The Balliol club attracted 160 members, allowing them to gain entry to the Manor

Ground with a 10 per cent discount. She believed that the sport wasn't realising its own potential: 'There are hundreds of families out there – a huge, untapped market. There are a lot of people for whom football is the core of their life. I'd like to make the club as successful as I can for their sake.'

Speaking well over a decade before Ghislaine Maxwell became notorious for her involvement in the Jeffrey Epstein affair, Jim Smith said that she was 'a genuine fan of the club who knew her stuff'. Clad in her yellow and blue scarf, she became a regular presence at games alongside her father. Consistent with the spate of recent documentaries about her, Smith noted how 'Bob's voice changed when he spoke to her. He softened a bit, and actually listened to her when she spoke, which I don't think Bob did with anyone else.' She in turn, would take the mickey out of him. 'I always found it ironic that when Bob did his thing [Smith threw his arms wide and made a giant splashing sound, referring to Maxwell's drowning in 1991], he fell off the yacht [Lady Ghislaine], which he named after her.'

Perhaps with good reason, Oxford players from that era are reluctant to discuss the disgraced father and daughter and point out that the club's rise to the top flight was a remarkable story in its own right. And so it was, but the Maxwells' presence lends the story several degrees of seedy glamour. Players' contract negotiations dragged, because after being summoned to Headington Hill Hall to discuss terms, Maxwell, who always headed up the talks himself, would pop in and out of talks, as he had multiple ongoing meetings in different rooms in the building. 'He'd start the meeting, then disappear for two hours. He'd come back and say 'Now – where were we? The answer was right back at the start,' midfielder Ray Houghton told me. And then there was Maxwell's apparent inability to remember names. After Oxford won the Second Division, Maxwell grabbed the microphone, and when attempting to introduce the players to the crowd, failed to get beyond Malcolm Shotton (the captain) and George Lawrence – the only black player at the club. 'It was embarrassing,' Jim Smith said. Worse was to follow. When the team paraded the Second Division trophy around the city in 1985, they were on an open-top bus, whereas the club owner, with a reluctant Jim Smith, travelled ahead in his white Rolls Royce with the trophy. 'The irony was that some fans made the "wanker" sign at Bob because he'd sacked them from Pergamon Press,' Jim Smith told me. Maxwell abandoned the celebration halfway through, telling his driver to take him to lunch and instructing Smith to alight and rejoin his team on the bus.

Yet whether he knew the Oxford players' names or not, skipper Malcolm Shotton would occasionally use Maxwell's influence, ushering Oxford's owner into the dressing room at half-time if things weren't going well, because he knew that Jim Smith, who possessed a volcanic temper if things were going badly, 'would tone down his language and calm down a bit if Mr Maxwell was there'.

But Oxford would play in the promised land of Division One without Jim Smith. Looking to double his Manor Ground salary from £25,000 to £50,000, he was invited to Maxwell's Holborn residence to discuss terms after the season ended. On the evening of the Heysel disaster, Smith had verbally nudged his chairman up to £47,000, at which point one of Maxwell's aides ran in with news of the unfolding carnage in Brussels. Maxwell promptly walked out, and Smith claimed not to have heard from him again, during which time he was tapped up by Queens Park Rangers chairman Jim Gregory. 'Perhaps Bob realised that with the incoming ban, the economic climate in football was about to become even more depressed, and he didn't fancy paying me more,' Smith said. Rangers promptly doubled Smith's salary. The *Mirror* initially described Smith's salary as a 'handsome pay rise', but thanks to Maxwell's editing, it was later altered to 'excessive remuneration'. In a scenario replete with irony, former Reading manager Maurice Evans, who'd supported blocking the Thames Valley Royals plan two years earlier, took over as the new Oxford boss, having been appointed first-team coach at the Manor Ground a year earlier.

Stranger still was that when relegation threatened, Oxford fought their way to the 1986 Milk Cup final at Wembley, and their opponents were none other than Jim Smith's Queens Park Rangers. Via the medium of the tactics board, the club chairman had imparted his limited tactical knowledge before the second leg of the semi-final against Aston Villa, instructing Ray Houghton to stand on the sixteen-yard line (cue gales of laughter from the players), run the entire length of the pitch after latching onto an opposition corner and cross for John Aldrige to head home. The Us released a cup final song, purloining Slade's 'My Oh My', which failed to make inroads into the charts. More successful was the mass sale of bull hats with horns protruding from the top. Heading up ITV's commentary for the game was Oxford fan Jim Rosenthal, who wore a gigantic rosette throughout proceedings as he traded banter with Ian St John and Jimmy Greaves. Rosenthal's partisan garb didn't go down well with the channel's top brass. Neither did his refusal to interview Robert Maxwell, who owned a sizeable stake in Central TV. 'I was asked to conduct a pandering interview with Maxwell, which I wasn't prepared to do,' Rosenthal told me. 'It all meant that for quite a while, my presenting duties were somewhat curtailed.'

On the day, Rangers were no match for a vibrant Oxford team, and goals from Jeremy Charles, Ray Houghton and Trevor Hebberd gave Maurice Evans' men a comfortable 3–0 victory. 'I knew we'd win, Jimmy,' gloated Maxwell afterwards. 'Your players' hands were all sweaty and nervous when I shook them.' The rotund Maxwell himself worked up quite a sweat when, clutching the Milk Cup, he lumbered around Wembley on a solo lap of honour. The jubilant Oxford players failed to lift Maxwell to throw him into the communal bath. 'Water displacement would have been a problem if they had,' Jim Smith said. It was Oxford United's greatest day, but the great dictator insisted that one of the *Mirror*'s goal pictures was removed and replaced by an image of him embracing the chairman of Rangers' sponsors Guinness, Ernest Saunders, who would be convicted for fraud a few years later. Maxwell confided in Smith that he was irked by the fact that Oxford were denied a European berth because 'bloody Liverpool can't control their murdering fucking fans'. The underrated Evans kept Oxford in the top flight thanks to a last day 3-0 shellacking of a lacklustre Arsenal at the Manor Ground. They stayed up the following season, too. By then, though, not only had Maxwell – football wise – cast his gaze elsewhere once more, he'd also made quite an impression on directors from other clubs.

• • •

Maxwell took a lead in persuading clubs to push for a better TV deal. As the owner of Mirror Group Newspapers and the main shareholder in MTV Europe, his was a powerful voice. When an offer for £19 million over four years arrived in 1985, the Football league's TV negotiating committee endorsed it, but Maxwell memorably described it as 'mad, bad and sad', suggesting that football on TV was worth a minimum of £50 million per season. ITV head of sport John Bromley was furious, arguing: 'They have hooligans kicking each other on the terraces, lousy facilities, and boring players and

they say its television's fault nobody goes to the game anymore...'
The TV blackout for the first part of the 1985–86 campaign (see
Chapter 9) further damaged the image of the game, and it was only
when Maxwell stood down from the front line of negotiations that
the dispute was resolved, albeit with the Football League accepting
just £1.5 million for the rest of the season. It was another humiliat-
ing climbdown on the part of the Football League. Ironically, Sky's
first contract to show live games, which was signed in 1992, was £61
million per season, not that Maxwell lived to see it.

Commissioned by the Football League at Irving Scholar's bidding
to evaluate the true worth of football to the TV companies, Saatchi
& Saatchi – under the guidance of Alex Fynn – produced a report
entitled 'Football and Television: It's Influence on Programme Cost
And Advertisement'. The report stated that per season, the rights
were worth £6 million – considerably less than Maxwell's projection.
The advertising agency also produced the first plans for a Premier
League. There were three permutations – a breakaway league of ten
clubs playing each other four times a season, a Premier League of
two divisions of forty clubs and a showcase division of twenty clubs
with the rest of the league comprising both national and regional
divisions.

As for Maxwell, Fynn recalled: 'He was interested in the future of
the game, and he had an insight that football was undersold, but he
didn't appreciate the extent to which it was perceived as damaged
goods in those days.' To Maxwell, Alex Fynn was 'Mr Saatchi'. Fynn
argued that 'Mr Tottenham' – Irving Scholar – was the first senior
football figure to understand the potential of TV. 'He grasped that
the event, like nature of the sport, be it at a local, regional or national level, could be marketed and turned into a TV spectacle.' Maxwell
called Aston Villa chairman Doug Ellis 'Mr Villa'. Ellis didn't buy

the belief that Maxwell could never remember names. 'It's an old business trick, David,' Ellis told me. 'Pretend you've forgotten their name in order that they never feel at ease with you.' 'I'm Jon,' I reminded Ellis. 'Of course you are. My apologies,' smiled Ellis. We both laughed. 'Deadly' Doug had 'got' me. Alex Fynn and Doug Ellis both recalled Maxwell's gargantuan appetite for food. 'He was a giant of a man. He devoured a whole bowl of crisps in one go, scooping them out with his hand,' Fynn explained. Ellis looked on aghast as Maxwell hoovered up a plate of Jaffa cakes. 'It really did put me off the man even more,' Ellis recalled, 'especially as he spat bits of chocolate over me as he talked during the meeting.'

Maxwell moved to increase his stake in Derby County, taking overall control there in 1987, whilst appointing son Kevin as Oxford United chairman. Initially, he was regarded as a hero in the east Midlands, buying the heavily mortgaged Baseball Ground and bringing Southampton goalkeeper Peter Shilton to the club. Maxwell then agreed to buy yet another top-flight side, meeting Watford chairman Elton John's £2 million asking price. It was another case of him attempting to synergise his assets. Maxwell had just purchased the giant Oldham's plant in the town, where the *Mirror* would be printed. Owning the Hornets would enable him to centralise his attention on one geographical area. His proposal was that he would run Derby and keep Kevin Maxwell as Oxford chairman, and although he'd own Watford, he wouldn't take any kind of administrative role there. The league management committee blocked the deal, with a fuming Maxwell dismissing them as 'the mismanagement committee'.

The Watford fiasco was a symptom of how Maxwell's businesses were, bit by bit, faltering. His purchase of London News failed to the tune of £25 million, and biographer Tom Bower reported that by the late '80s, his investors were casting more critical eyes on his proposed business deals. His football clubs began to suffer, as Maxwell slowly started to retreat from public life. 'He's fat, he's round, he's never at the ground,' sang Oxford United fans, a ditty that would be echoed at the Baseball Ground by the end of the decade. With Oxford headed for relegation in March 1988, Maurice Evans was replaced by former Liverpool defender Mark Lawrenson. Although Kevin Maxwell was chairman ('The unpleasant way Bob spoke down to him was embarrassing', Lawrenson told me), his father still pulled the strings. Lawrenson was summoned for Sunday lunch at Headington Hill Hall, where Maxwell, clad in a silver shirt and with a serviette tied around his neck, proceeded to grill his sons about every topic under the sun and devour his food with his hands. 'Bob's table manners weren't the best,' Lawrenson admitted. Exasperated by what he considered underwhelming responses from his sons, Maxwell pointed at Ghislaine and told Lawrenson: 'She's the only one with any balls here.' The Lawrenson–Maxwell relationship didn't last long, with the former accusing Maxwell of reneging on his promise not to sell striker Dean Saunders to Derby County. 'At the end of the day, it's got fuck all to do with you,' Maxwell barked, storming out of the room. The two men never spoke again.

Jim Smith had one final meeting with Maxwell, at a Chinese restaurant in Holborn in late 1990, where his former chairman scoffed a plate of noodles without the need for cutlery. 'He'd piled on weight by this time, and he looked under huge pressure,' Smith said. By now, he was plundering the *Daily Mirror*'s pension funds in order to prop up his various other businesses, although that wouldn't come to light until years later. Despite his dishevelled appearance and his ballooning weight, he told Smith that he was about to invest in the Bulgarian toothpaste market, broker a deal with President

Mikhail Gorbachev about mass investment in Russia after the end of the Cold War *and* buy Tottenham from Irving Scholar. By now, Oxford United were stalled in the second tier of English football, and Derby were heading for relegation from the top flight. 'Bob was a bit sentimental that night. There were tears in his eyes when he talked about Oxford's success.' Within a year, he was dead. Former Prime Minister Margaret Thatcher paid generous tribute to him.

The irony is that as a football director, the former Labour MP embodied the worst elements of Thatcherism: untrammelled individualism, pure unadulterated consumption, corporate greed and a loathing of any restraint of trade. His former football associates were unconvinced that his drowning was entirely accidental. Mark Lawrenson suggested that vengeful debtors somehow pierced the security ring around him. Harry Harris – whom Maxwell had told would be the new *Daily Mirror* editor shortly before his death – is convinced that the Israeli secret services got to him. Jim Smith insisted: 'I don't believe Bob jumped from the yacht. He'd never have given up trying to save his businesses. Anything was possible in his eyes.'

At Oxford United in the mid '80s, that was most certainly true.

12

THE IMPOSSIBLE JOB?

They gulped down the thin air of Mexico City as they gave chase,
but even without the heat, they'd never have caught him.'
DON HOWE

Azteca Stadium – Mexico City, July 1986. At pitch level from forty yards away, England manager Bobby Robson knows what he's just seen. Assistant Don Howe has seen the same thing. From the bench, both men have tracked the run of Diego Maradona, who's pounced as Steve Hodge's sliced back pass hangs for fractionally too long in the rarefied air. The squat little Argentinian has a run on goalkeeper Peter Shilton and, with a little thrust of his hand, knocks the ball into England's net to give Argentina the lead. Most players on the pitch reckon Maradona used his head. Robson looks towards the referee, expecting him to disallow the goal. There's nothing, despite the protestations of Terry Fenwick. 'You know what, Don – I think he's going to give it,' he tells Howe. The pair shake their heads in frustration. England are 1–0 down to Argentina in the World Cup quarter-final. If there's one thing that Robson has learnt during his four years in charge, it's that his capacity to control the outcome of events is somewhat limited.

• • •

Looking out of the window, the former England manager puffed out his cheeks. I'd just asked Bobby Robson to describe the main difference between managing Ipswich Town, which he did between 1969 and 1982, and the national team. We met at the PSV Stadion at the very end of last century. He'd just returned for a year to PSV Eindhoven, where he'd first headed in 1990 after departing the England job following the World Cup in Italy. His office was functional and featureless, but his avuncularity and charm enlivened the room. He took a few seconds to answer my question. Spreading his arms to the edges of the table that separated us, he said: 'The main difference is that when I was in charge of Ipswich, which was a small club, I could control what was in front of me. With England, I had to try and control everything out there,' he said, pointing beyond the confines of the room. 'And that was often impossible.'

After arriving for work at Lancaster Gate in July 1982, his salary for managing the national team and acting as head of coaching for English football was £65,000 a year.

I talked to the Italian and West German coach and it was two or three times below what they earned, and they didn't have the additional coaching role on top, and they had a driver to take them around the grounds. It was a pay cut from Ipswich, but that wasn't the real problem. The issue was the lack of awareness of the demands of the role, and the poor structure in place.

Robson pushed hard for Don Howe to be appointed as his full-time No. 2 and to undertake scouting duties for the numerous junior England teams. But Robson was baulked in appointing a second in command and spent hours and hours driving himself up and down motorways locating stadia. 'It was gruelling work, the part that the public didn't see,' Robson said. 'It was a relief when matches came around and I could focus on the team and the match. Sometimes, anyway,' he grimaced. During his eight years in charge, Robson only lost one qualifier, to Denmark in 1983. It ultimately cost England a place at the 1984 European Championships. 'The level of hysteria shocked me,' Robson said. 'I was as disappointed as anyone to miss out, but to be spat at, verbally abused in the street, to have abusive letters sent… It went well beyond constructive criticism.'

Robson cited two figures in particular whose criticism stung him. The first was the *Mirror* sportswriter Nigel Clarke, who was a constant critic throughout the '80s. In a television segment before a match away to Greece, Clarke is filmed against a backdrop of journalists about to clamber on the bus, and promises that 'Robson will get fried' if England failed to win. 'I tried to look at the bigger picture. There was a tabloid war raging between *The Sun* and the *Mirror*. I was caught in the crossfire of that, but ouch – so many bullet holes,' Robson smiled, clutching his stomach in mock pain. 'It was everywhere – a more vicious, more prying media, where any sort of muck raking was considered acceptable.'

Robson's other arch critic was former Ipswich and England manager Sir Alf Ramsey. 'Ah, Alf,' said Robson, throwing his hands up in exasperation. 'Inscrutable, stony-faced Alf. He had a face like a sphinx and was impossible to read in conversation.' Yet through the medium of his *Mirror* column, ghosted by Nigel Clarke, he let it be known that he thought very little of Robson. When he was in charge at Portman Road, Ramsey repeatedly snubbed Robson's offer that he could attend Ipswich matches and sit in the directors' box whenever he wished. When Robson offered Ramsey a lift home after a function, a po-faced Ramsey informed Robson that he'd arrived by train and would return home via the same mode of transport. 'If there was one person in the country who you'd have thought would have some empathy with the struggles of being in the role, it was Alf. Yet he completely blanked me – or criticised me in print. I'll never understand why. It was tough to take.' Before the 1986 World Cup, Ramsey, who often announced his loathing of the Scots, met with Alex Ferguson to advise him about travelling to Mexico but point-blank refused to meet with Robson. Once in Mexico, there were none of the run-ins with the press that had occurred under Ramsey in 1970. Ramsey aside, Robson got on with pretty much everyone.

Robson was often gregarious and self-deprecating company in our interview. His boundless enthusiasm for the game – and for life – shone through. He laughed about his inability to remember players' names but messed up the anecdote that illustrated his point. 'I went down one morning to breakfast, saw Bryan Robson and said: "Good morning, Bryan."' I cut in: 'You mean you called him Bobby.' 'Ah yes, that's it. I said: "Good morning, Bobby," and he said: "No, you're Bobby. I'm Bryan."' Luther Blissett just laughed when Robson repeatedly called him 'Bluther'. Terry Butcher recounted how the entire England bench was in stitches when Robson became frustrated with debutant Stuart Pearce because the Nottingham Forest player failed to respond to repeatedly being called 'Gary' by the irate England manager. Robson was often late for his own meetings. 'Timekeeping wasn't Bobby's strong point,' Ray Wilkins said. Robson spoke of his pride at setting up the Lilleshall centre of excellence and of handing international debuts to 'players like Lineker and Gascoigne, who became icons of the English game, and of working once again with Terry Butcher, whom I managed at Ipswich. It was always wonderful to have that continuity in the dressing room.' Robson spoke with admiration of the fighting qualities embodied by his 'warriors' – as he called them – Butcher and (Bryan) Robson. 'They possessed what players of that era needed – heart, fight, aerial strength and physical strength. And they could both play a bit too. Often on awful pitches. You'd want them on your side in combat.' Terry Butcher spoke of the nature of the game in the '80s:

> I loved the combative nature of football back then, when there was much more contact than there is now. We took pride in our skill at heading the ball and practised and practised in training. Football was a far more aerial game in the '80s, a different game to what it is now. Aerial duels were part and parcel of the game, and we were very proficient at them.

· · ·

Robson had two main regrets. The first, as he put it, was that 'the language and attitudes surrounding black players in the England team changed little in the eight years I was in charge'. After Viv Anderson became the first black player to be capped for the senior team, black England players were still being subjected to abuse and threats. When Cyrille Regis received a call-up to the squad in 1982 (under Ron Greenwood), he received a bullet through the post, accompanied by an anonymous letter that read: 'If you put a foot on our Wembley turf you'll get one of these through your knees.' How, I asked Regis, did he respond to the threat? 'Simple,' he said.

I brought it along to the match, showed it to Viv [Anderson] and said: 'I got a bullet, and you got nothing. 1–0 to me.' I laughed it off, like I always did with that kind of thing. There'd have been no point in taking it to the FA, or whatever. Nothing would have got done. Besides which, I figured I'd got far worse with monkey chants and bananas being thrown at me.

Regis recalled the 'banter' of the era, which he described as 'white noise'. 'A lot of other players would ask me if I'd been busy rioting, or they'd do an impression of Chalky White [comedian Jim Davidson's persona] and say "Morning, Cyril" in a fake West-Indian accent.' Off the pitch, Regis was often stopped by the police. 'They'd see a black man driving a decent car, and they assume it might not be legally his. They were often apologetic when they recognised me, but… you know.' Even official publications normalised the fact that racist language directed at black players was part and parcel of the game. In the 1980 *FA Soccer Book for Boys*, Mick Channon is quoted as saying: 'I suppose in the heat of a game some players may have a bit of a go at an opponent. If that opponent happens to be black, then that fact might just creep into the conversation.' Racist language always went unpunished, on and off the pitch. Could black players have complained to the police, I asked Regis? He grinned at me. 'I can imagine how that conversation would have gone,' he said. '"What – someone calling you a name are they, son?" they'd have said, smirking at me.' At West Ham, supporters nicknamed black players Bobby Barnes and George Parris 'super coons'. It was meant to be a term of endearment.

On television, black figures, like comedian Lenny Henry and newsreaders Moira Stuart and Trevor McDonald, were becoming more prominent. That was certainly the case in English football, with more multicultural teams. When Bobby Robson took over, he awarded several black players their first senior caps, including Luther Blissett (Watford), Mark Chamberlain (Stoke City) and Ricky Hill (Luton Town). The predictable tabloid headlines were very much of their time. 'Black explosion', 'Black power', 'Black Flash' and 'Black Invasion', to name four.

Early on in his time as manager, Robson was buttonholed by an FA representative, whom Robson didn't name: 'A few black lads in there [the squad] Bobby,' he told Robson. 'Make sure they don't take over.' Standing his ground, Robson retorted: 'If they're good players, the colour of their skin is irrelevant.' That particular FA suit never raised the issue with Robson again. As for the players, proud though they were to represent their country, the abuse and threats they received were a sad reflection of the times. Shortly after he made his debut as a substitute against West Germany, Luther Blissett received a letter saying: 'Pull on the white shirt again and we'll shoot you.' As was the case with Cyrille Regis two years earlier, Blissett, who grabbed a hat-trick against Luxembourg in a European Championship qualifier, remained quiet about what had happened. 'To complain would make me seem like I had a chip on my shoulder, which would have been bad news,' he said. In Blissett's early days at Watford, Graham Taylor himself weighed in if members of the crowd verbally abused the striker. 'Once he came out onto the pitch at half-time and told whoever was doing it that that wasn't how fans behaved at Vicarage Road, and Graham had him removed. But that wasn't a realistic course of action during England games,' Blissett said. The only saving grace from Blissett's point of view was that, in the days before social media, 'at least those people couldn't spread their views to others via the click of a mouse'.

Ricky Hill, the first player of Indian origin to represent England (his father came from Lucknow in the Indian state of Uttar Pradesh) was also awarded his first cap in 1983: 'Many fans echoed what they heard on TV at the time. Programmes like *Love Thy Neighbour* and *Til Death Us Do Part* trotted out racist language and racist slang for laughs. Hill believed that if a black player was a forward or a creative player, they were at particular risk of verbal abuse: 'Wingers especially, because you were closer to the terraces, and forwards, because they could be criticised if they missed a chance.' Hill, a clever and cerebral midfielder, won three caps under Robson. 'I didn't quite fit the stereotype of a black player at that time. I wasn't a quick, tricky winger, like a John Barnes or a Tony Daley, and I wasn't a big burly centre forward like Cyrille [Regis] or Garry Thompson.' In 1986, after having a fine season for Luton Town, Hill believed he had a good chance of making the final cut for Bobby Robson's World Cup squad. In the build-up to Robson's squad selection, he was disappointed to read Alf Ramsey's description of him as: 'A talented player, but not someone I'd want to go to war with.' For Hill, Ramsey's comment perpetuated the myth that black players lacked 'bottle'. 'I'll never know whether Alf's comment impacted on Bobby Robson's thinking,' he told me, 'but when someone with his (Ramsey's) kind of clout speaks, it makes you question whether some views are institutionalised.'

A (now) infamous scenario played out in front of Robson's very eyes; he described it as the 'beauty and the beasts' episode. Following a loss at home to the Soviet Union, and with England not at that year's European Championships, Robson again came under pressure from the media to resign. On the face of it, his decision to take his side to South America and play Brazil at the cavernous Maracanã Stadium appeared potentially suicidal, against a team which had so bewitched viewers at the '82 World Cup. But Brazil were going through one of their customary mid-tournament dips, and Robson's team, deploying a daring 4–2–4 formation, defeated Telê Santana's team in their own back yard. John Barnes's meandering run, which took him past five Brazil defenders before slotting the ball home, remains arguably the most iconic goal of the Robson era. 'I wish I could tell you that I was cheering John all the way and marvelling at his skill,' Robson told me, 'but instead I was screaming: "Pass it, pass it," every inch of the way. The goal was a thing of sheer beauty.' Which is more than can be said about events on the Uruguay-bound flight afterwards. A group of far-right supporters, chanting 'England is white' and '1–0, 1–0' (thus suggesting that they didn't recognise Barnes's goal), harangued Robson and his players. 'There was no point in arguing with them,' Robson said, 'because you can't reason with ignorance.' In his autobiography, Barnes questioned whether Mark Hateley's goal, which made it 2–0, should therefore have stood, given that he supplied the cross. Having later managed multicultural teams at PSV and Barcelona, Robson looked back with sadness at the reactions England's black players received when they were selected for their country. 'There was no mechanism in place to help these players in the '80s, and there should have been. We tried to ignore the issue or tell them to keep their chins up. But that was never enough. Not by a long way.'

• • •

I'd spoken to Robson for nearly an hour, segueing between his playing career with Fulham and the various stops on his managerial career. But we hadn't discussed his other main regret yet. 'Come on then, let's talk about bloody what's-'is-name,' Robson sighed. Before the notorious Mexico City quarter-final clash in 1986, 'bloody what's-'is-name' had occasionally shot like a zephyr across English skies. Diego Maradona introduced himself during a prestige friendly at Wembley in June 1980, when the reigning World Champions took on Ron Greenwood's England prior to them departing for the 1980 European Championships. England won 3–1, with David Johnson scoring twice and Kevin Keegan grabbing the third, but the match is mainly remembered for Maradona's star turn midway through the first half. The Boca Juniors star pirouetted in minimal space and lasered his way towards goal, leaving four England players flailing in his wake. As he slipped his shot past Peter Shilton, the ball flicked the outside of the post and went fractionally wide. It was the most bewildering piece of skill I'd ever seen,' Kenny Sansom told me. 'The whole move was over in around four seconds. But the approach and the way he ran into the box – it was spookily like what happened in Mexico in '86. Except this time he got it fractionally wrong.

In the second half, Sansom brought down Argentina's No. 10 for a penalty, after Maradona threatened to slalom past England's entire defence. 'By then, we're all thinking: "What the fuck have we got on our hands here?"' Sansom said. When defender Dave Watson later deployed Anglo-Saxon defensive prowess on Maradona, leaving him in a crumpled heap after raking his studs down his ankle, Leopoldo Luque chastised him. 'David Watson was huge. He looked like a heavy metal star,' Luque told me. 'I told Watson that Diego was just a kid, and to leave him alone. Watson said that if he was big enough to play in the match, he'd be treated like a man. Then he told me to fuck off and get on with the game.' At the end of the match, Maradona sportingly applauded all four corners of Wembley, along with his teammates.

His sporting approach was also in evidence after Barcelona beat

Aston Villa in the first leg of the 1982–83 Super Cup, and Maradona, though absent from Barca's line up, made a beeline for Gary Shaw, asking if he could swap shirts with him and telling the Spanish press that Shaw would become a future star of world football. After Barca's 3–0 defeat at Old Trafford against Manchester United in the 1985 UEFA Cup quarter-final, he saluted 'the sheer passion and intensity of English fans'. And at White Hart Lane a few weeks before the '86 World Cup began, after borrowing a pair of striker Clive Allen's boots, Maradona put on a dazzling show during Ossie Ardiles's testimonial, even apologising to a mesmerised crowd when one of his clever overhead passes failed to pay off. Such was the mutual love between the Tottenham crowd and Maradona, there was talk of him leaving Napoli for north London, with sponsors Holsten Pils fronting up most of the money. 'Imagine if that had happened… Maradona playing in England after the '86 World Cup,' muttered Bobby Robson.

For the first time in over a generation, England's qualification for the World Cup finals was fairly straightforward. Robson's men didn't lose a single match, finishing top of their group ahead of Northern Ireland, who also reached Mexico. Robson had one main concern: the state of skipper Bryan Robson's damaged shoulder. 'It was a classic case of club v. country, and I felt that poor Bryan was caught in the crossfire,' Bobby said. He urged Manchester United manager Ron Atkinson to push through the player's operation, which would stop it popping out of place, but Atkinson refused, reasoning that he needed his skipper for United's title challenge, which ultimately foundered anyway. 'So we took Bryan, whom I felt was now playing within himself, to protect his shoulder. It was never going to end well.' Thanks to a little bit of investigative work from Don Howe, Robson was also aware that his players played more competitive matches per season than those from other nations.

> We played forty-two league matches. In Serie A and the Bundesliga, it was thirty-four. Plus we had two domestic cup competitions, with replays, which other countries didn't have. There was no Europe for our clubs due to the ban, but instead the authorities brought in those bloody silly competitions like the Full Members' Cup, which no one really wanted. I implored the league to give me more time with England players, but it wasn't to be.

Before the start of the World Cup qualifiers, Robson had bumped into Argentina coach Carlos Bilardo, who raised doubts as to whether Maradona would play at the '86 World Cup. He'd not played for the national team since being sent off against Brazil in '82 as Argentina crashed out against their bitter rivals. The Argentinian public didn't trust Maradona anymore, Bilardo said. His ankle wasn't the same since Antonio 'the Butcher of Bilbao' Goixotchea snapped his ankle like a twig back in '83, resulting in Maradona needing to wear different size Puma boots on either feet. His cartilage was playing up too, apparently. Even when Maradona returned to the fold, his national coach, whom Robson reckoned had 'the best poker face of all', told anyone who cared to listen that Maradona wasn't the player he'd once been. So when Robson watched Maradona provide all three assists in Argentina's 3–0 win over South Korea and then half-volley Argentina's equaliser against reigning champions Italy once the tournament started, he knew that 'Bilardo had been having us on, not that I especially believed him anyway'. The fateful quarter-final clash in Mexico City would prove conclusively Maradona's genius, but England came perilously close to not making it at all.

Bobby's boys from '86 maintain that, despite the 1–0 defeat against Portugal in the first game and the 0–0 draw with Morocco in the second, which saw Bryan Robson leave the field – and the tournament – with his arm in a sling and Ray Wilkins sent off for throwing the ball within the vicinity of the referee, the mood in the camp was still positive. It's true that neither the team's official song – the unmemorable 'We've Got the Whole World at Our Feet' – and the plain white shirts with pinstripes could hold a candle to the 1982 vintage, but the camp was a unified one. Terry Butcher insists that despite what some tabloids alleged, there was no rebellion in the ranks after the draw with Morocco and that the new 4–4–2 formation which would be deployed against Poland in the third and deciding group match was entirely the work of Don Howe and Bobby Robson. In the first two matches, with Gary Lineker and Mark Hateley up front and Chris Waddle out wide, England deployed a lopsided 4–3–3 formation. For the Poland game, England would go with a midfield quartet of Glenn Hoddle, Peter Reid, Trevor Steven and Steve Hodge. Hateley, England's leading scorer in the qualifiers, was dropped and replaced by Peter Beardsley. The reaction of the players to the tactical change was one of relief. 'We thought: "Thank God,"' Terry Butcher told me, 'as Bobby explained it on his flip chart. You could tell by all the scrawling across pages and pages that Bobby and Don had given the whole thing a great deal of thought.'

Also written on one page of Bobby Robson's flip chart was the list of dates that England would fly home on if and when they exited the competition. According to Terry Butcher, the first date – the day after the Poland match (12 June) – 'was later crossed off joyfully by Bobby' thanks to an inspired hat-trick from Gary Lineker in England's 3–0 win. The mood certainly lifted amongst the chortling ITV panellists, as they chit-chatted about the stomach bug known as the dreaded 'Montizumah's revenge'. Swigging only bottled drinks and having a dedicated chef seemed to be the way to avoid copping an unfortunate dose. The buzz-phrase of the tournament was 'The Group of Death,' trotted out increasingly monotonously by British pundits discussing Group E, which contained Scotland, West Germany, Denmark and Uruguay. Jimmy Greaves told me that he'd coined it, but in fact he'd merely borrowed it; Uruguay coach Jorge Omar Borras first used it. Brian Moore found it hilarious that Mick Channon, with his broad Hampshire burr, was unable to pronounce man of the moment Gary Lineker's surname correctly. 'Loinaykrrr,' was the closest Channon got to nailing it. England fans, congaing around semi-deserted stands, chanted: 'Two Gary Stevens, there's only two Gary Stevens,' whenever the Everton/Tottenham players who shared the same name were on the pitch. But things were about to get serious for Bobby Robson's team, as Argentina and Maradona hove into view.

In the build-up, both managers asked their teams to ensure they didn't discuss the Falklands conflict. 'It was an unofficially official request,' Terry Butcher told me. Both nations' players complied. Bobby Robson told journalists that if they asked him about the Falklands War, he'd walk out. Even the forthright Maradona kept quiet. 'Look, mate, I'm here to play football. I know nothing about politics, nothing,' he told English journalist John Carlin. Tabloids in both countries certainly did not remain apolitical. 'Argies, Here We Come!' ran *The Sun*'s headline, and the Argentinian *Crónica* barked: 'We're Coming to Get You, Pirates!' Both Robson and

Bilardo considered carefully their tactical options. England elected not to place a man marker on him, believing it would destroy the shape of the team. Maradona played in the centre of a disciplined five-man midfield, with the instruction to rove and destroy. He was, as teammate Jorge Valdano put it: 'A genius who was granted the privilege of freedom.'

As the teams lined up under the noon day sun for the national anthems, the players stood upright and to attention, facing the front. All bar one. Maradona, who'd later describe Robson's men as 'a bunch of toilers', glared contemptuously up and down the English line. It was difficult to know precisely whom he was glaring at – presumably not Glenn Hoddle – whom he'd raised his thumb to and winked at in the tunnel a few minutes earlier. Skill-wise, Hoddle was the only England player whom Maradona believed was on his level, and Hoddle had graciously allowed Maradona to wear his No. 10 shirt at Ossie Ardiles's testimonial a few weeks before.

The first half was tight. Argentina's defence easily smothered England's long passes and England strikers Gary Lineker and Peter Beardsley were blocked out by Argentina's impenetrable defensive wall. Terry Fenwick was booked early on for a foul on Maradona, which slightly inhibited the team's dogged approach afterwards. The pitch, which consisted of hundreds of pieces of turf that moved under the players' feet whenever they accelerated away, was a nightmare. Bobby Robson reckoned the Tunisian referee was nervous, with the potential for 'going a bit easier on Argentina than us'. Whether or not that was genuinely the case, Argentina's first goal in the fiftieth minute appeared to confirm Robson's fears. In the ensuing confusion following a Maradona attack that had broken down, Steve Hodge's lofted back pass was intercepted by Maradona, who leapt and deflected the ball into the net with his fist. There was certainly a flurry of bodies and arms, but Robson knew what had happened and so did the normally ultra-cool Peter Shilton, who harangued the referee. All to no avail. The goal was given. 'Hug me before they disallow it,' Maradona told his teammates.

It was the perfect example of what is known in Argentinian football as *viveza* – the art of taking the short cut to success. 'He'd behaved like a rascal, an urchin,' Bobby Robson sighed, and to the satisfaction of all Argentines, Maradona had pickpocketed the English pirates. '*Viveza* is hugely celebrated in our psyche,' Jorge Valdano told me. 'When one uses cunning like that and gets away with it, you celebrate. But in other cultures, it's considered a crime.' When Maradona scored his second goal five minutes later, there were still few English players who realised that Maradona had used his hand to put Argentina into the lead. His slaloming solo strike, which left a raft of tough-tackling First Division players – Fenwick, Reid and Butcher – trailing in his wake, made an indelible mark on the Englishmen who couldn't possibly contain the puckish genius of Maradona. 'I'd seen wingers like John Barnes, who could go past two or three opponents,' Terry Butcher told me, 'but not four or five, like Maradona could. He was something else. A force of nature. I was disgusted with myself for not getting to him.' Peter Reid gamely gave chase but was never going to catch the will-o'-the-wisp streaking ahead of him. 'He was only heading to one place...' Reid tailed off. Terry Fenwick spoke of 'an object disappearing into the distance...to do what he did, on such an awful surface, was pure genius.' Maradona's brother Hugo claimed that his brother's mind had flashed back to Wembley in 1980, where he'd slipped the ball agonisingly wide of Shilton's post. In Mexico City, he'd made a nanosecond decision to take the ball round Shilton, rather than risk making the same mistake again. Little wonder that in his famous commentary of the goal, Víctor Hugo Morales described Maradona as a 'cosmic kite' and asked which planet he came from.

England pulled a goal back from Gary Lineker after John Barnes's exquisite cross, and but for defender José Luis Brown's intervention, Robson's men would have equalised. But Argentina held on. Afterwards, Terry Butcher and Diego Maradona were selected to provide urine samples. In a claustrophobically tight room, a triumphant Maradona indicated (rather wisely) to Butcher that he'd used his head to score the goal. 'If he'd pointed to his hand, I don't know what I'd have done,' Butcher told me.

A year later, Maradona played for a Rest of the World XI against a Football League XI at Wembley, after being flown in by private jet and paid an appearance fee of £100,000. The showpiece match kick-started the centenary celebrations for the formation of the Football League. Despite running on to the theme of Superman, the reception Maradona received was poisonous, although there were ironic cheers when Bryan Robson clattered him to the floor as he prepared to conjure some magic in midfield. 'We needed Bryan's toughness in Mexico City,' lamented Bobby Robson, who managed the Football League X1. It was estimated that Maradona's presence had added another 20,000 to the disappointing 61,000 attendance. 'No one in English football at that time had anything like that kind of allure,' he admitted. In the years that followed, Maradona was dismissive of those whom he'd vanquished at the '86 World Cup, describing Peter Shilton as 'thermos head', Peter Reid as 'the slow one' and Terry Fenwick as 'that one with the long hair'. When Argentina, now coached by Maradona, took on Scotland – for whom Butcher was assistant manager in 2008 – Maradona claimed not to know who Terry Butcher was. Maradona also vacillated on the symbolism of the match against England. When the occasion suited him, he'd insist that politics never came into it. However, in his 2000 autobiography, he wrote: 'We knew a lot of Argentinian kids down there, shot down like little birds. This was revenge.' The one thing that he and the England players concurred with was that forcing footballers to play matches under the burning Mexican sun to suit European viewing schedules was morally reprehensible. 'Football is, more and more, being portioned off and sold to the highest bidder,' Maradona complained.

Ironically, as the Maradona cult grew over the ensuing decades, ephemera from the England match – both fake and real – was indeed sold to the highest bidder. A lock of his hair, apparently clipped on the day of the game, almost sold for around $30,000 before the eBay seller was flushed out as a fraud in 2012. But some Maradona memorabilia netted the sellers a fortune. In 2019, England midfielder Steve Hodge, who'd swapped shirts with Maradona after the game, sold it for £7.1 million at auction. The shirt had a remarkable backstory. Ruben Moschella, Argentina's technical assistant, was dispatched to various sports shops across Mexico City after the players complained that their cotton shirts were too hot and heavy. Moschella returned with two blue shirts. 'Which one?' he asked Carlos Bilardo. Maradona strolled in, saw the lightly striped, blue number, and said: 'We'll beat England in that one.' A seamstress hastily sewed on eleven team badges. Hodge's roommate Peter Reid recalled that Hodge hung up the shirt in their room the night before they flew home next day. 'There it was, torturing me whenever I looked at it. I told Hodgey to take it down,' Reid said. The match ball, collected by referee Ali Bennaceur, was sold for a fee of around £2–3 million in 2023. The classic 'Hand of God' photo, which photographer Daniel Motz told me 'is blurred and artistically lousy', has made him a tidy sum in royalties down the years.

Bobby Robson took the defeat against Argentina hard, and when, with a forward line of Lineker, Waddle, Barnes and Beardsley, England flopped dismally at the 1988 European Championships, losing all three group games, he once again found himself on the end of fierce criticism. 'It didn't help that Lineker played with hepatitis and that players like Sansom, who'd always been top-drawer for me, made individual mistakes that cost us. I looked for a spark, someone off the cuff, a Maradona – if you like – who could ignite us. But the spark wasn't there.'

The chances of Robson remaining as coach for the 1990 World Cup appeared unlikely. Ironically, perhaps the nearest thing English football has ever produced to a Maradona was about to explode onto the scene. Paul Gascoigne would be a saviour not just for Robson's England but also a catalyst who dragged English football into a new era.

13

THE CONTINENTALS

THE YUGOSLAVS

'For me, Southampton was heaven on earth.'
IVAN GOLAC

The Dell – February 1981. As Southampton central defender Dave Watson lofts a ball towards forward Mick Channon, Ivan Golac, motoring down the right wing, senses what's coming. 'That old bastard and I could read one another's thoughts on a football pitch,' said Golac of Channon, who taught him to swear in English. Channon flicks the ball towards Golac, now on the edge of the area and, without breaking his stride, the Yugoslav half-volleys the ball home from fully twenty-five yards past a helpless Tony Godden. It's the cleanest of strikes. Golac's fellow Saints have since used various adjectives to describe the Yugoslav's wonder strike. Channon said that it 'screamed' past Godden. Kevin Keegan reckoned the ball 'arrowed' into the West Brom net. Twenty years later, Golac preferred a more Anglo-Saxon phrase: 'It went in like a fucking rocket,' he explained to me. Those sweary English lessons with Mick Channon obviously proved a roaring success.

•   •   •

By the early '80s, a raft of Yugoslavs plied their trade in English football. They came in different shapes and sizes and enjoyed varying degrees of success in English football. There was 'big' Boško Janković of course, (see Chapter 3), the balding Middlesbrough striker who became an unlikely cult hero for Aston Villa fans when he scored a brace of goals against Ipswich in a 2–1 victory in the final game of the 1980–81 season, as Bobby Robson's men conceded the title to Ron Saunders's team. Gigantic defender Nicola Jovanović, a £300,000 purchase from Red Star Belgrade, became the first non-Brit/Irishman to play for Manchester United. A back injury meant that Jovanović was jettisoned by United after just thirty often-underwhelming displays. Midfielder Ante Miročević scored for Sheffield Wednesday in the loss to Brighton in the 1983 FA Cup semi-final. He loved going fishing with manager Jack Charlton near Barnsley and enjoying copious amounts of ale and whisky chasers. 'I'd drink ten, twenty a night and then we'd train the next day. That's what England taught me, how to drink and play,' he told Charlton's biographer Colin Young. Full-back Džemal 'Jimmy' Hadžiabdić – signed from Velež Mostar – is still fondly remembered by Swansea City fans, after playing a starring role in John Toshack's team which reached the First Division in 1981.

Some cultural hurdles were tricky to overcome. 'Jimmy' initially believed that the parking fines on his car's windscreen were requests for autographs from Swansea fans. Understandably, Notts County goalkeeper Raddy Avramović was baffled as he observed manager

Jimmy Sirrell's curious habit of licking the rim of the tomato ketchup bottle before passing it round to his players at the meal table. Some, like Norwich City defender Drazen Mužinić, struggled hugely with the language, despite manager John Bond hiring an interpreter from the University of East Anglia to help his £300,000 signing acclimatise, although Martin Peters recalled Mužinić wailing Kate Bush's 'Wuthering Heights' 'in almost perfect English'.

The Yugoslavs came in different guises. There was Petar Borota, Chelsea's eccentric 'sweeper-keeper' who dabbled in fine art and alarmed teammates and Blues fans by bouncing the ball off his own cross bar when it was still in play and dropping crosses. 'I played with Petar at Partisan. He was superbly gifted but liable to drop clangers,' said Ivan Golac in classic English footballer speak of the goalkeeper who insisted that *Homes & Gardens* was his favourite reading material. Vladimir Petrović, a delicate and somewhat pallid-looking playmaker, both delighted and frustrated Arsenal fans in equal measure during his four-month spell at Highbury in the second half of the 1982–83 campaign, following his arrival from Red Star Belgrade.

Until the age of twenty-eight, the state's footballers were contracted to play within the Federal People's Republic of Yugoslavia. Beyond that, they were permitted to ply their trade abroad, as long as the authorities deemed that they were loyal to the Marshal Tito-led regime. 'It was not ideal,' explained Golac, whose father was a member of Tito's national guard, 'but many other eastern-European players, who'd have added much to the game in the west, were forced to spend their entire career behind the Iron Curtain.' Politics and football were intertwined in Yugoslavia. When Tito died in May 1980, the clash between Hajduk Split and Red Star Belgrade was paused just before half-time. Split's President and a local politician announced Tito's passing to the crowd, and the lined-up players either sobbed or looked uncomprehendingly into the distance. 'We'd been told that life without Tito was impossible,' explained (then) Red Star midfielder Vladimir Petrović. After Tito's death, the Communist authorities tightened their grip on the sport. Petrović was poised to join Arsenal for £250,000 after the 1982 World Cup, but due to Yugoslavia's poor displays (they failed to progress through the first group stage), the authorities delayed his move to N5 for six months. 'We were punished, and when I eventually arrived I was thrown in at the deep end in January, with Arsenal struggling in mid-table,' Petrović told me. 'It was tough to acclimatise.' A photograph of Petrović appeared in the Arsenal programme, with the Yugoslav, wife Zaga and daughters Kristina and Marina looking nervously at the camera. Arsenal fans were told that Petrović 'enjoyed sight-seeing in London,' but on the pitch, Petrović often appeared bewildered, with the ball flying over his head.

It was the imposing Golac, whose mane of long hair gave him the appearance of a rock star, who proved the most adaptable of the Yugoslavs in English football. Unlike the other Soviet satellite states, the republics of Serbia, Croatia, Bosnia and Herzegovina, Montenegro, Slovenia and Macedonia had been granted autonomy over some of their affairs. Citizens had greater access to foreign travel, and Yugoslavia became a popular tourist destination for westerners. The cultural flow between east and west was also freer. 'We were very much aware of English football and music – the two most important things in life,' Golac laughed. 'I had hundreds of vinyls,' Golac told me. 'I loved The Kinks, The Who, The Rolling Stones, The Beatles… anything that English '60s music had to offer. I learnt to speak English through music! My taste in music was far more English than any English footballer I ever met.'

Golac believes that he slotted in so well at The Dell because apart from the fact he understood basic English, he was allowed to play his natural game. At The Dell, he delighted fans with his swashbuckling runs up the right wing. He noted the differences between the game in England and Yugoslavia:

In Yugoslavia, the style of play was far more technical. The emphasis was on passing and moving. Full-backs were expected to attack. It was much more physical in Division One, and that's why so many of my countrymen struggled in England. I was lucky in the sense that I played a more physical style anyway, and I liked to tackle. But at Southampton, there were also so many technically gifted players.

Golac arrived at The Dell in the same month as World Cup winners Ossie Ardiles and Ricky Villa signed for Tottenham. Six months earlier, the European Community had ruled that the Football Associations of its member states could no longer deny access to players based on their nationality, and that summer, the Football League lifted its 47-year ban, with the number of foreign players at any one club capped at two. In contrast with the fanfare of publicity that surrounded Tottenham's Argentinians, Golac remembers only 'mild curiosity' about his signing. Golac was always faintly amused when quizzed on whether he could withstand the ferocity of the English game. 'I'd played in Belgrade derbies, with 90,000 lunatics letting off fire crackers and smoke bombs and flares. I wasn't intimidated.' Keen to impress his teammates straight away, he set about them in training with gusto.

Alan Ball was brilliant, and I quickly formed a great partnership with him. But he wasn't impressed when I tackled him too hard in training a few days into my Southampton career. As he lay on the floor, I thought he was going to get up and punch me, so I said: 'Welcome to English football, Bally,' to make him laugh.

The Balls made Golac and his family feel welcome in their Hampshire surroundings. Ball's wife Lesley took Golac's spouse to the butcher's and helpfully oinked and mooed to help Bratislava Golac order the meats she wanted. Golac loved the Hampshire countryside, smiling as he recalled the long walks he enjoyed taking along the River Itchen near Shawford, 'where I could see herons and kingfishers'.

Southampton finished a creditable fourteenth in Golac's first season. Aware that his side couldn't lavish huge transfer fees on players, manager Lawrie McMenemy opted to bring in older players. Club icon Mick Channon returned from Manchester City, and Charlie George arrived from Derby County. 'Mick, Bally and myself formed a beautiful partnership on the pitch, and they occasionally got me to go to the horse races with them too,' Golac recalled. Channon also tried to get Golac in trouble, encouraging him to call 6ft 4in. former guardsman Lawrie McMenemy a 'big miserable bastard'. 'But the smirk on Mick's face was a warning that I shouldn't go there,' Golac explained. The team's profile grew further when Kevin Keegan was unveiled as a new signing in August 1981. 'No one knew anything about it,' Golac explained. 'The press and the players didn't have a clue what was happening until Kevin walked out at the press conference with his wife and young baby.' Golac believes that midfielder David Armstrong, a goal scoring midfielder who weighed in with fifteen goals a season, was the most underrated of all the Saints players he appeared alongside: 'He was often overlooked because he was bald and looked older than he was.'

In 1983–84, with Peter Shilton now in goal and Danny Wallace starring as a goal scoring winger, Southampton finished in runners-up spot behind Liverpool. 'We were always two players short of a title-winning side,' Golac admitted. He threw his hands up. 'But we played some beautiful football.' Golac loved to throw in the word 'beautiful' to conversation. The Dell, with its eclectic mix of skew-wiff and asymmetrical stands and terraces was a 'beautiful stadium'. He and the supporters, he said, had a 'beautiful relationship'. Then there was the goal that he'll always be remembered for. 'I struck it on what the English call the belly of the ball. From the second I connected with it, I knew it was going in. It was… beautiful.'

The Yugoslav players' paths rarely crossed, either on or off the pitch. Džemal Hadžiabdić left Swansea in 1983, following his team's relegation from the top flight. 'He was the most skilled of all of us,' Golac said. 'He lost his life savings in the civil war and started coaching in the Middle East.' 'Jimmy' – a Muslim by birth – now goes by the name of Jamal Haji. Golac never faced Arsenal with Petrović on the pitch, but he reckons that 'English football wasn't ready for him at that time'. Petrović, given precious little protection from referees, flitted in and out of the team, and by the time he practically burst with joy after scoring an excellent goal for Arsenal at Highbury in the spring sunshine as they defeated Aston Villa in the FA Cup quarter-final, manager Terry Neill had already opted against paying the full £400,000 for the player. 'I doubt that many Arsenal fans will remember me,' Petrović told me. Not true. Those of a certain vintage smile wistfully when they remember 'the pigeon' gamely trying to pass his way out of trouble in the hurly-burly First Division. As for Petar Borota, by the early '80s, Chelsea were mired in Division Two, and Borota – who was still swinging from the cross bar and talking to fans during breaks in play – lost his place in the

Blues team after his side suffered a 6–0 shellacking at Rotherham, with Borota culpable for three of the Millers' goals. His teammates remain convinced that Borota, who went missing before kick-off, played whilst under the influence of vodka that day. 'Who knows with that one?' Golac laughed. Borota was later jailed after being implicated in a theft of Serbian painter Paja Jovanović's work, before dying in 2010 after a long illness.

Golac was the last of the original 'band of Yugoslav brothers' – as he put it – to last in English football. After departing Southampton in 1986, he went on to manage Partizan and won the Scottish Cup with Dundee United in 1994. Before our interview ended, I asked Golac whether he ever convinced his Southampton teammates to read the poetry of Yevgeny Yevtushenko, a Russian beat poet. His eyes widened. 'How do you know I like Yevtushenko?' he asked. 'You said so in your *Shoot!* profile,' I replied. 'No, I couldn't interest them,' he smiled, before pondering the question a bit longer. 'I did lend Mick Channon a copy of *One Day in the Life of Ivan Denisovich* [by Aleksandr Solzhenitsyn], but he told me he preferred the *Sporting Life*. These days, Golac flits between Vienna and Belgrade and is delighted when older Saints fans still recognise him. They've long since forgiven him his brief loan spell with arch rivals Portsmouth. 'My heart is still at The Dell,' he admitted, with a wistful smile.

THE DIMINUTIVE DANE

'Allan Simonsen was a big name in football,
but perhaps not a big name in South London.'
RICK EVERITT, CHARLTON FAN

The Valley – March 1983. In a cavernous ground that once held seven times that number, 10,000 hardy souls watch a tense Division Two clash between Charlton Athletic and Chelsea. With the scores tied up at 2–2, the hosts, hammered 7–1 by Burnley a week earlier, spark into life. The star attraction, Danish forward Allan Simonsen, who moved to The Valley from Barcelona five months before, steals the show. Firstly, he weaves past two bewildered Chelsea defenders and drills the ball past Blues goalkeeper Steve Francis. Four minutes later, his deft header makes it 5–2. Valley regulars are ecstatic. The problem is, there's nowhere near enough of them. Not even for a London derby. The painful truth is that Charlton simply can't afford Simonsen, despite chairman Mark Hulyer's prediction that the 1977 Ballon d'Or winner's arrival would galvanise Addicks fans into re-turning to the dilapidated Valley. Like everything connected with the Simonsen transfer, nothing quite adds up.

• • •

After being alerted that Simonsen was less than impressed with the prospect of sitting on the bench at the Nou Camp, following the ar-rival of Diego Maradona from Boca Juniors, a host of top European clubs courted him. Just three months after scoring Barcelona's third goal in their 2–1 win over Standard de Liège in the Cup Winners' Cup final, thereby becoming the first player to score in all three European club finals, Simonsen fell victim to the Spanish Football Association's 'two foreign player' rule. With Maradona's much-trumpeted arrival and West German midfielder Bernd Schuster a firm favourite with coach Terry Venables, Simonsen realised that three into two simply didn't work. 'At that point, I decided that it was time for a new challenge,' he explained. Real Madrid and Tottenham had advanced talks with him. There were rumours of interest from America and West Germany, where he'd starred with Borussia Mönchengladbach in the '70s and pipped both Kevin Keegan and Michel Platini to the Ballon d'Or in '77. But, after insisting that he wanted 'a more stress-free environment,' Simonsen opted to join Charlton. It was perhaps the most eye-catching and startling of all transfers in the '80s. It wasn't entirely stress-free, though.

Throughout our conversation, the Dane, described in 1982 by Danish Prime Minister as 'our country's finest export, along with bacon and Carlsberg', was diplomatic in the extreme. At twenty-eight, chairman Mark Hulyer was the youngest in the league. Having wrested control of the club away from Michael Gliksten, Hulyer reckoned he needed a sprinkling of stardust in order to increase Charlton's 6,000 average crowd. Thwarted in his attempts to sign Newcastle United bound Kevin Keegan, Hulyer turned his attention to Simonsen. 'I liked Mr Hulyer's positive attitude and the offer of a new challenge in a new environment,' Simonsen told me. Hulyer was aware that Simonsen was friends with Addicks youth coach Ernst Netuka, who'd known the player since his teenage years. His £324,000 transfer fee wasn't unreasonable for such a talented player, but it was twice what Barcelona had paid for him two years before, and Charlton's annual income was just £270,000. Simonsen's weekly wage was around £1,500, at a time when his teammates earned an average of £200. Wary of Charlton's perilous financial situation, Barca demanded £100,000 up front, with the other instalments paid at agreed intervals. It was a massive gamble on Hulyer's part. Despite a niggling hamstring injury and the Spanish FA's failure to clear him to play for a month after he arrived in SE7, he made his bow for the club as a substitute in a reserve-team clash against Swansea City, scoring on his debut. 'There were lots of people there for what was only a reserve match,' he recalled. 2,000, in fact, ten times the norm. 'I hope that Allan's arrival will give first-team fixtures a similar boost,' Hulyer explained. But there was a whiff of desperation too. 'I'd be heartbroken if people do not come and support the team now that we have signed Allan. We couldn't have done any more to show our ambition to get back into the First Division,' Hulyer explained. That wasn't entirely true. Young defender Paul Elliott and striker Paul Walsh were both sold to Luton Town in order to raise some much-needed capital. In a rare moment of candour, Simonsen admitted: 'It all revolved around me.' Hulyer had well and truly placed all his eggs in one basket.

Amidst popping flashbulbs, director Malcolm Webster flew Simonsen north to watch Charlton play at Carlisle, and the Dane finally made his first-team debut against Middlesbrough, with his hamstring still troubling him. He scored a deflected free kick after coming on from the bench, but couldn't stop his team from losing 3–2. The attendance of 10,807 was an improvement, but some way short of the 20,000 crowds required for the deal to work financially. Manager Ken Craggs looked on in bemusement.

'Allan was a superbly gifted footballer,' he explained.

But the whole thing was surreal. I watched Allan closely when he came on, and he spent most of his time looking at the sky, as the ball flew over his head. After playing for Mönchengladbach and Barcelona, who prided themselves on attractive, attacking football, I wondered what Allan made of it all. He must have found the whole experience a bit… agricultural.

If that was the case, Simonsen never let on. Not then and not since.

Simonsen always insisted he was 'delighted to be Charlton' and that he was 'very happy with the situation at the club'. He towed the party line even when the club (allegedly) defaulted on his wages in the spring. By then, Craggs had been fired in late November, following Charlton's 5–1 defeat at The Valley in front of a miserable 6,731 crowd, with Simonsen looking on from the stands, as the club's directors fidgeted anxiously in their seats in the near-deserted stadium.

With Lennie Lawrence appointed as manager in November, Charlton struggled to find consistency. There were some high spots. Almost 17,000 turned up for Charlton's FA Cup third-round clash with Ipswich Town, but Lawrence's team lost anyway. Watched by an estimated 60 per cent of Danish TV viewers, Simonsen played a key role as his side defeated Newcastle 2–0. The match had been dubbed as 'the battle of the Ballon d'Or winners', but Kevin Keegan, who won the award in 1978 and '79, withdrew from the match due to injury. Striker Derek Hales reckoned Simonsen 'thought two or three moves ahead, whereas many of our players didn't know what they were going to do even when they got the ball'. By season's end, he'd triggered the clause in his contract that allowed him to move if the Addicks couldn't pay his wages, and headed home to Vejle, his first club, on a free transfer. For all sorts of reasons, the player who lost a fair proportion of his weekly wage playing cards on the team bus was never a fit. In training, he'd regularly enquire of midfielder Steve Gritt 'why we don't pass the ball'. 'A fantastic talent who struggled to adapt to the fact that he wasn't at Barcelona anymore,' was Gritt's assessment.

Lawrence kept Charlton in Division Two by the skin of their teeth on the last day of the 1982–83 season, sending down Bolton Wanderers instead after hammering them 4–1. Looked at positively, without flashes of Simonsen's trickery, Charlton would have been relegated. But the wolves were at the door. Leeds United took Charlton to court for failing to pay the £150,000 they owed for winger Carl Harris. By 1985, the East Terrace was closed permanently, and a year later, the cash-strapped Addicks had departed The Valley entirely for a six-year Selhurst Park exile before returning to SE7 in 1993.

Simonsen remained a force to be reckoned with well into the '80s. A few months after leaving Charlton, he scored a vital penalty in a European Championships qualifier against England at Wembley, which helped the Danes qualify for their first international tournament at the expense of England. Three years later, he was a member of the Danish squad for the World Cup in Mexico. He was a pioneer for other Danes who would ply their trade in English football in the '80s, including Jesper Olsen, John Sivebæk and Jan Mølby. 'We saw that Allan had come to England and wanted to do the same. He inspired us,' Mølby told me.

Simonsen's brief sojourn at Charlton was a surreal experience for all concerned, but the Dane was always a symptom rather than the cause of the Addicks' growing financial woes.

THE BOY FROM BRAZIL

'We've got Mirandinha, he's not from Argentina.
He's from Brazil, he's fucking brill.'
NEWCASTLE UNITED FANS' CHANT, 1987–89

Anfield – October 1988. Despite an early Gary Gillespie goal and incessant Liverpool pressure, struggling Newcastle United are level at

Anfield, thanks to John Hendrie's equaliser before half-time. With just seconds left, Mirandinha, the Toon's Brazilian striker, is bundled over in the box, and the referee points to the penalty spot. After a short run up, he calmly side-foots the ball past Bruce Grobbelaar to give his side a remarkable 2–1 win. It's one of the few bright spots in a season when Newcastle will go down. In the moments after his successful spot kick, Mirandinha trots over to the Kop and proceeds to give supporters what can only be described as a 'come on then' gesture with his hands. Less than impressed with Mirandinha's celebrations, Koppites make hand gestures of a rather different nature with either one or two digits. Years later, Mirandinha claimed the Liverpool supporters 'rose to a man to sportingly applaud me after I scored'. Like much of the diminutive striker's stay on Tyneside, his Anfield celebration appeared to be lost in translation.

• • •

The conversation pauses as Mirandinha, his eyes closed in thought, racks his brains to remember the name of the comic that late '80s Newcastle players enjoyed reading. It had 'lots of large people eating too much and farting'. We looked at one another for a moment, and then the translator, during our 2009 interview in Brazil. 'Was it *Viz*?' I asked. 'That's it, *Viz*,' Mirandinha smiles, tapping me on the arm. 'I think it was very English humour,' he says. 'It's what we call "toilet humour",' I added. Both Mirandinha and the translator found the phrase hysterically funny.

I'd asked him to explain to me the elements of English culture that surprised him the most after he put pen to paper for Willie McFaul's Newcastle side in 1987, making him the first Brazilian to play in English football. First and foremost, there was the weather. 'It seemed to be freezing most of the time,' he winced. 'Once, against Tottenham, I wore gloves when it snowed, but then I fell over and they were instantly soaking wet.' There was the food. 'Potatoes, green vegetables. Overcooked. Battered fish. Ketchup on everything.' There was also Paul Gascoigne, with whom Mirandinha played for a single season before he headed south for £2.2 million to play for Terry Venables's Tottenham. 'There was no one like him in Brazil.' Pause. 'In fact, there was no one like him in England either,' explained Mirandinha, who saw at first-hand the early stages of 'Gazza-mania' before the shell suits, the false breasts and the tears.

Gascoigne was Mirandinha's unlikely friend and faux translator, who'd try to land the Brazilian in trouble by teaching him 'very, very bad words.' In one sense, Gascoigne was himself the living embodiment of a *Viz* character; a football version of Biffa Bacon perhaps. The media hyped up Gascoigne's distinctly '80s tomfoolery. He concealed a dead fish inside defender Peter Jackson's car in order to stink out the automobile. He booked black striker Tony Cunningham onto a course of sunbed sessions. On *Saint & Greavsie*, Jimmy Greaves nicknamed him 'Fat-Boy Bamber' (after *University Challenge* presenter Bamber Gascoigne) and suggested he ate 'Mars bars and popcorn for breakfast'. Gascoigne was more than happy to play along with the image and claimed that, apart from himself (of course), 'brown ale and *Viz* were the best things ever to come out of Newcastle'. His linguistic pranks on Mirandinha were cartoonish in the extreme. 'Mr Willie, I'm fucking starving,' Mirandinha informed Willie McFaul as the Newcastle team waited for their fish and chips before embarking on the long journey back to the north-east from Carrow Road after Mirandinha made his debut against Norwich in August '87. Gascoigne put the Brazilian striker up to it, of course. Mirandinha was persuaded that Wednesday was pronounced 'wank day', and when Mirandinha met Gascoigne's friend Jimmy 'Five Bel-lies' Gardner for the first time, Gazza encouraged him to greet him with: 'Hello, Jim, you are a fat bastard.'

Amusing though Mirandinha sometimes found Gascoigne, he also witnessed at first-hand his recklessness and inability to know when to call it a day. 'He couldn't stop eating black beans, which formed part of my diet. He'd come around to my house and eat so many that he was nearly sick,' he explains. Gascoigne also crashed Mirandinha's club-sponsored Vauxhall, writing the vehicle off, although the Brazilian was keen to play down ongoing rumours that it caused a rift between them. Behind the outlandish behav-iour, Mirandinha saw in Gascoigne someone who craved company. 'He spent a lot of time with me, and when he wasn't performing in front of a crowd, he was sensitive and caring. He seemed to be at his happiest when he went fishing, and he loved being in the fresh air.' The pair were recruited by the Variety Club charity and pre-sented north-eastern schools with the keys to Sunshine coaches. Gascoigne's story was 'always fascinating', Mirandinha explained.

The tale of how Francisco Ernandi Lima 'Mirandinha' da Silva ended up in the north-east of England is equally compelling. Born in poverty in Aerolândia, a neighbourhood in Brazil's fourth city – Fortaleza – Mirandinha's father sold salt from evaporated sea water as he worked tirelessly to feed his seven children. 'As a kid, I did anything I could to bring money into the house,' Mirandinha said. 'Selling citrus fruits, grapes and washing people's windscreens when they were stuck in traffic jams.' Football was always an escape. A diminutive and pacy forward, he plugged away at several clubs before a fine season at Palmeiras during the 1986–87 campaign. It drew the attention of Brazil manager Telê Santana and talent spot-ters outside Brazil.

One of Mirandinha's close friends, Humberto Silva, was on a university exchange scheme in England. He had a good relationship with Bev Walker, who was also close to ex-Newcastle legend Malcolm Macdonald. 'Supermac' began singing the player's praises to Newcastle and even arranged for VHS tapes of Mirandinha in action to be sent to Willie McFaul. They were impressed with what they saw, and his profile was raised further when he made the breakthrough for Brazil in the Rous Cup in May 1987. Mirandinha scored in a 1–1 draw with England at Wembley. Brazil then beat Scotland 2–0 at Hampden Park and he was voted man of the match. Willie McFaul, present and correct at both Wembley and Hampden, made the decision to sign the Brazilian. 'There were no agents involved at all,' Mirandinha said.

Newcastle-born Peter Beardsley had just departed to Liverpool for upwards of £2 million. Three years earlier, Chris Waddle had left for Tottenham. The Toon couldn't keep their Gallowgate heroes in the north-east, so they decided that a dash of South-American panache was just the ticket. Mirandinha's signing was made official at the city centre Swallow Hotel. A film crew asked Malcolm Macdonald about the player's (apparently) 'suspect' temperament when the going got tough. Macdonald's diplomatic response was: 'He's so quick that defenders won't actually be able to kick him anyway.' Mirandinha moved into a club house at Bedlington, a former mining village. He very quickly became a local celebrity and even enjoyed kickabouts in the street with local boys. 'Street football was exactly how I developed my skills as a child. It was home from home for me,' he said. He also grasped the economic difficulties of the era. 'It was the same in Brazil. Mines shut down, or the work was done with machines. People suffer. Football can help.'

He was a big hit with his teammates. It was said that Mirandinha needed his own ball as he was notoriously unwilling to part with it, either in training or during matches. 'It was a joke, but it later became a problem,' ex-Newcastle star Glenn Roeder admitted, 'and it was occasionally a source of tension within the team.' Mirandinha, impressed by Roeder's famous shuffle, told him that he must have been born in Brazil. 'Actually, my dad taught me in our back yard in London,' Roeder responded.

Mirandinha preferred to do his own thing, ordering rice with his meals instead of potatoes, eschewing the delights of Newcastle Brown ('One bottle occasionally, but that was it,') and sticking to his own fitness regime, including running on his own and doing warm-downs, which were almost unheard of during that era. On the pitch, the goals that he scored from open play were always eye-catching. There was a thunderous free kick in the Tyne–Tees derby against Middlesbrough and a smart finish at Old Trafford, which brought Newcastle victory against Alex Ferguson's Manchester United. He latched onto Paul Gascoigne's exquisite lob to net his first home goal in a victory against Everton. But even though Mirandinha plundered an impressive nine goals in seventeen matches during his first season, there was always the feeling that he was too much of a virtuoso performer for the rough and tumble of Division One. 'He got frustrated when he didn't get the ball,' Glenn Roeder said. There were rumours that he wanted to return to Brazil, and transfer gossip linking Gascoigne with a move away appeared to unsettle the Brazilian further. When Gascoigne's departure to Tottenham was announced in the summer of '88, Mirandinha was crushed. As a present, Gascoigne presented him with a cat, which he instructed Mirandinha to name 'Gazza'. 'But it's a girl cat,' Mirandinha insisted. Despite Gascoigne's grumblings, the cat was eventually named 'Belly' – after Jimmy. Newcastle, and Mirandinha's form, quickly went into free fall. McFaul was sacked in September and replaced by Jim Smith. Apart from his penalty at Anfield in the shock defeat of Liverpool, Mirandinha sank without trace. 'Mr Smith favoured the direct approach. I hurt my neck' – he looks to the skies for dramatic effect – 'watching the ball fly overhead.' There were furious rows between the pair, with Smith eventually declaring: 'I hope he rots on his São Paolo pig farm.' The Toon were relegated to Division Two where they stayed for five years, before Kevin Keegan's galvanising influence saw them return to the top flight. By then, Mirandinha was long gone, returning to former club Palmeiras during the 1989 close season.

'I tried to be a hero for the fans,' Mirandinha said, 'but results were not always so good.' Culturally, though, Mirandinha made his mark. Inspired by his arrival, local dance schools reported that Samba classes grew in popularity. Fans sported sombreros on the open Gallowgate End to serenade him. 'They're Mexican, but who cares?' he laughed. Following Mirandinha's lead, his teammates began to order rice instead of potatoes with their meals. Playing in England touched Mirandinha deeply. His daughter was born in England and is named Sarah – after Sarah Ferguson. His favourite moment came not on the pitch but when he was asked to switch on the Christmas lights in 1987 on Northumberland Street. 'I left on a Santa sledge,' he said. 'When I think of it now, it brings tears of joy to my eyes.'

14

THE GIANT KILLERS

THE NEW TOWN BOYS

'Win your battles on the pitch. All of 'em.'
STAN STORTON TO TELFORD UNITED PLAYERS

Buck's Head Stadium, February 1985. Telford United are doing what they do best: making football league clubs suffer. Today, Fourth Division opponents Darlington are in for it. In front of a feverish 8,040 crowd, the Stags follow manager Stan Storton's instructions to the letter and take the game to their hapless opponents during the FA Cup fourth round clash. From a gigantic clearance by goalkeeper Kevin Charlton, forward Dave Mather, who works at Vauxhall during the week, latches onto a flicked header and thunders the ball past the Shakers' keeper. Shortly before half-time, full-back Eddie Hogan drills home a swerving free kick from fully thirty-five yards. 'Rivellino himself couldn't have done it better,' beams Stan Storton afterwards. Finally, just twenty-seven seconds into the second half, John Alcock latches onto another monstrous punt by his goalkeeper and half-volleys the ball home to make the score

3–0 and propel his side into the last sixteen of the cup, a feat not achieved by a non-league club since Blyth Spartans reached the fifth round seven years earlier. Telford are arguably the most progressive non-league outfit in the country, but much to the irritation of those involved in the Shropshire club's rise to prominence, recognition of their achievements is thin on the ground.

•   •   •

'Is there anywhere more invigorating than the state of Telford?' barked Stephen Fry's Gordon Gecko yuppie type. It wasn't the only new town to be lampooned on *A Bit of Fry and Laurie* in the late '80s (Stevenage also got a hard time), but when Rik Mayall's Alan B'Stard claimed Telford was a 'place where people from Liverpool go to lose the accent and have a bath', in an episode of *The New Statesman*, it was abundantly clear that whether or not Telford was a prime example of soulless urban planning (Fry's character also refers to the plethora of 'executive breakfast lounges in the town'), it was certainly worthy of comedic attention. The '80s was also boom-time for Telford's light industry and its football team.

Two unequivocal truths affixed themselves to Telford during the decade: it had the highest concentration of mobile phones outside London, and its football team were the most feared FA Cup giant killers of all. The two facts aren't entirely unconnected. Assorted blue-chip and light industries had invested in Telford from the late '70s onwards, its population mushroomed to 120,000 and with the M54's completion, the town's connections with northern cities improved drastically. Telford United drew on players from a fifty-mile radius, its fanbase grew and Maxell – the company that manufactured cassettes – sponsored the club. One of the most famous '80s adverts saw Pete Murphy – lead singer with Bauhaus – reclining in a chair and listening to a recording of Mussorgsky's 'Night on Bald Mountain', as the narrator whispers: 'Maxell – break the sound barrier.' Goalkeeper Kevin Charlton told me that he once approached Murphy in London 'after a bevvy or two, invited him to a Telford game and asked him whether he had a load of Maxell tapes at home. He literally ran off.'

In its previous guise as Wellington Town (founded in 1879), the club had occasionally shone in non-league competitions. Trophies garnered by the club included the Shropshire Cup and the Welsh Cup – with Swansea Town defeated 4–1 in the 1940 final. Wellington Town fans saw direct parallels between the club's rebranding as Telford United in 1969 and the new town development. One disgruntled Wellington fan claimed in the press that it was 'a soulless amalgamation of towns and villages'. But whatever misgivings Wellington Town loyalists had, the rebranded Telford United quickly became hugely successful on the pitch, reaching the inaugural FA Trophy final in 1969, losing 2–0 to Macclesfield and one year later lifting the trophy by defeating Hillingdon Borough in the final.

United qualified for membership of the newly founded Alliance Premier League in 1980 (the fifth tier of English football), and club directors spoke ambitiously of achieving league status, but manager Stan Storton sounded a note of caution: 'Altrincham have won the Alliance Premier League for two years running. They've been knocking on the door and haven't got in. Gaining league status will mean bucking the entire system.' Storton's realism didn't prevent him from assembling a vibrant and robust team that excelled itself in cup competitions. Full-back Antone Joseph recalled: 'Before matches, Stan instructed us to win our individual battles across the pitch. "Match them for their work rate. Roll your sleeves up, fight, harry them and out shove them if you have to," he'd say.' Telford played the game at high intensity. Kevin Charlton reckoned they 'upped the ante even more against league sides', with Storton giving his players a gentle tap on the shoulder and a nod of the head afterwards if they'd done their job.

But it wasn't all about wars of attrition. Antone Joseph recalled that Storton's training regimes focussed on short passing. And he was also a deeply caring manager, aware that, like him, his players had day jobs. 'Once, during a few days of blizzards,' Joseph explained, 'Stan drove through the snow to where he knew the players from Liverpool would meet to come down for training, to tell them it was cancelled. He then had to drive all the way back to Telford.' In 1982–83, Telford served notice of their giant-killing potential by defeating Wigan Athletic in the FA Cup. The club also won the FA Trophy after defeating Northwich Victoria. With his £250 win bonus, Antone Joseph bought a state-of-the-art, smoked-glass stack stereo system. A year later, Telford reached the FA Cup fourth round after beating Stockport County, Northampton Town and Rochdale, before being squeezed out by the odd goal against Second Division Derby County at the Baseball Ground in a 3–2 thriller. 'Telford were incredible,' said Rams manager Peter Taylor, 'and they were as good as any league team we've played.'

In the following season, the Lilywhites went further still. Third Division Preston were hammered 4–1 at home in the second round (Deepdale fans gave Telford a standing ovation whilst screaming 'pub team' at their own players), and Bradford City, who'd go up as Third Division champions that season, were beaten 2–1 in the third round with striker Colin Williams and midfielder Mark Hancock providing the finishing touches. Following Telford's 3–0 defeat of Darlington in the fourth round, Shakers boss Cyril Knowles didn't hold back in his criticism of his team or his praise for Telford:

I feel almost suicidal tonight but Telford, in my opinion, would be a huge success in league football. Maybe it's time the league looked at restructuring to allow clubs like this into the football league. But that would mean cutting out some of the dead wood, and that could be us.

Division One leaders Everton awaited in the fifth round at Goodison Park.

After the Darlington victory, Telford had lost just twice in fifteen meetings with league clubs in the FA Cup, and yet their profile remained relatively low. When another new-town team – Harlow Town – defeated Second Division Leicester City (and a very young Gary Lineker) in the third round in 1980, the Essex team bagged themselves a slot on *Nationwide*. Presenter Sue Lawley patronisingly described them as a 'super little team'. But apart from a brief *Football Focus* piece and a *Saint & Greavsie* cameo before the trip to Goodison, there was virtually nothing else. It still irks Antone Joseph: 'I think that it almost became expected of us – that we'd progress to the third round.' Goalkeeper Kevin Charlton added: 'Other non league clubs like Hereford and Sutton defeated First Division sides, and that created the headlines. We were more consistent over time, but we only defeated Third and Fourth Division clubs. It wasn't as much of a story.'

Victory at Goodison Park would likely have sent Telford's profile into the stratosphere, but Stan Storton's team were brought back down to earth in a 3–0 defeat, although they went in goalless at half-time. 11,000 Telford supporters travelled from Shropshire, which at the time was the largest away following ever recorded in the FA Cup. The game ended on a sour note, with Everton's Peter Reid being stretchered off just before the end following a clash with Antone Joseph, and some home fans lobbing coins at the Telford players.

Despite the spiky ending, Toffees boss Howard Kendall said: 'I fully expect to see Telford in the football league within a couple of years.' Yet despite reaching the third round the following season (where they lost to Leeds United) and winning the '89 FA Trophy, Telford were dogged by relatively disappointing league finishes, and league football never did become a reality. Goalkeeper Kevin Charlton admitted: 'Those amazing cup runs probably distracted us from finishing higher in the Gola League.'

Telford United's financial collapse in May 2004 (the phoenix club AFC Telford is back in the Vauxhall Conference and plays at the New Bucks Head), came two years after a government report that cited growing social deprivation in the town and a lack of high-er-education opportunities and concluded that, since the '80s, 'a number of ambitious ideas in the town have come to nothing'. Once again, the town's economic fortunes were tied up with those of the football club. MIRAS Contracts boss Andy Shaw – whose firm kitted out numerous blue-chip companies in the town – had ploughed in over £1 million of his own money. But when MIRAS tanked, so did Telford United. It was a stark reversal of the situation in the '80s when, thanks to the town's economic prosperity and the club's FA Cup heroics, the sky appeared to be the limit.

THE MULTIPART MEN

'It gushed it down out there.'

KEN WRIGHT, FORMER CHORLEY MANAGER

Molineux – November 1986. Drenched for ninety minutes, Chorley Town goalkeeper Ian Senior is playing the game of his life, making several last ditch saves to deny Wolves' Andy Mutch and Steve Stoutt, to keep the score at 1–1 in an FA Cup first-round replay. At half-time, he changes his sopping-wet green shirt, playing in blue for the second half. Like some of his teammates, Senior is slightly discombobulated, because the ground that once thronged to 60,000 plus crowds is a shadow of its former self. A meagre 4,419 have turned up to watch the Fourth Division hosts toil against the Multipart Leaguers. Those fans who are present are either dotted around the bright orange John Ireland stand, fully thirty yards away from the pitch, or huddled under the roof of the crumbling South Bank terrace. The other two sides of the ground stand silent and condemned. When striker Paul Moss chips Vince Bartram to grab Chorley's goal that night in front of a ghostly north terrace, he admits: 'I didn't know where to run to.' At the final whistle, the Wolves diehards boo their team off. New Wolves boss Graham Turner reckons his team have weathered the Chorley storm and will prevail in the second replay, but things are about to get worse for the Fourth Division club. For sixth-tier Chorley, though, who've never progressed beyond the first round, their fifteen minutes of fame are upon them.

• • •

Chorley's three-match saga with the four-time FA Cup winners almost never happened. Ken Wright's men were initially paired with Halifax Town, but much to the FA's embarrassment, Darlington had mistakenly been placed in the southern section of the draw. Chorley were hastily re-drawn at home to Wolves, which the players discovered via Ceefax. The Magpies' compact Victory Park stadium, with one side of it grass banked, was deemed inadequate to stage the tie, so Bury-based Wright quickly reached out to his contacts and it was played at Bolton Wanderers' Burnden Park. 'There was huge excitement when we drew Wolves,' recalled Ken Wright during our interview. 'They were one of the biggest names in English football.' By 1986, their good name appeared to be all they had going for them. Six years after Andy Gray had scored the winner in the 1980 League Cup final against reigning European champions Nottingham Forest, Wolves were scraping the bottom of the barrel after suffering three successive demotions. A crisis didn't appear to be in the offing in the summer of 1979, when Gray signed on the dotted line for an English record fee of £1.49 million in front of the brand-spanking-new John Ireland stand, complete with 10,000 seats and forty corporate boxes. But it was an illusion that Wolves could invest both in bricks and mortar *and* star players. The Gray money came from the proceeds of Wolves selling Steve Daley to Manchester City earlier that week.

'We are proud to unveil this ultra-modern new stand,' the club said in 1979, 'because it will give fans the opportunity to watch this wonderful team in style and comfort.' It was an impressive construction that represented the first stage of an ambitious plan to redevelop the ground. The cost was around £3 million and repaying the debt depended upon, in manager John Barnwell's words, 'long cup runs, European football and strong attendances'. Despite winning the 1980 League Cup, Wolves' UEFA Cup run was brief, and the team was relegated from Division One in the 1981–82 season. Ex-forward Derek Dougan was the leader of a consortium that purchased the club in a bid to save it, but the real players behind the deal were two brothers from Saudi Arabia, Mahmud and Mohammad Bhatti of the company Allied Properties. They secured promotion, but as three sides of Molineux rotted, the Bhatti brothers' plans for a new stadium and leisure park in the centre of town were rejected by the council.

Managers who tried and failed to stop the decline used multiple analogies to describe Wolves' plight. Tommy Docherty, who failed to stop Wolves tumbling into Division Three in May 1985, described Wolves as 'the Miss Havisham of football clubs, with nothing to do but sit and wait to die'. By now the club was watched by Molineux crowds averaging around 5,000. Former chief scout Sammy Chapman took over from Docherty, and following ground safety regulations that were introduced following the Valley Parade fire of May 1985, the north and east stands were closed. 'In one day, I saw cockroaches in the dressing rooms, and rats scuttling around on the terraces,' Chapman said in our interview. With Wolves preparing for its first ever season in English football's bottom tier, their planned close season trip to Belgium was cancelled, and instead the team travelled to Southport. Chapman told the press: 'If the players want fish and chips and a stick of rock, they'll have to bloody buy it themselves.' The team made a sluggish start to the campaign, and then Chorley hove into view in November.

The '80s were tough times for the town. The last working mine closed in 1985, and the skyline changed dramatically as derelict textile mills were either pulled down or converted. 'In such difficult times,' said manager Ken Wright, 'the FA Cup run was a welcome distraction.' His team, which was plodding along in mid-table, edged out Horwich RMI, Penrith, Armthorpe Welfare (a mining team) and Bishop Auckland in the qualification rounds. Life was busy for Wright, who worked in the motor trade and who later became Chorley chairman: 'We'd train on Tuesday and Thursday evenings, and then I'd be out watching games and scouting for play-ers on Monday and Wednesday evenings. It was full on. But there was such excitement when we drew Wolves.'

The 1–1 draw at Molineux proved to be goalkeeper Ian Senior's defining match as a footballer. 'Almost everything went my way that night, despite the gusting wind and the horizontal rain,' he said. A fireman by day, Senior often had to miss training due to his shifts and simply play games. But he was well prepared for Wolves. He could do little about Matt Forman's goal for Wolves, but from then on, he kept everything out. First, he clawed away Andy Mutch's left-footed shot, then he plunged down to his left to smother Mutch's header. His best save came in the second half, when he was able to tip Mutch's goal-bound header over the crossbar. By that time, Chorley had grabbed a Paul Moss equaliser, which Wolves claimed was offside. 'We used to have ball boys around the pitch in yellow tops behind the barriers,' explained Graham Turner. 'One kid was nearer the pitch than the barrier and the linesman glanced across. The Chorley forward [Moss] was offside, but the "lino" thought he saw a yellow shirt, but it was a ball boy, he admitted it afterwards.' The goal stood.

In contrast to the backs-to-the-wall performance at Molineux, Ian Senior's kit remained almost pristine during the second replay at Burnden Park, during which Wolves were comprehensively out-played by the Multipart men. Running onto a slide rule pass, Charlie Cooper collected the ball, rounded Wolves keeper Vince Bartram and gave Chorley a first-half lead. As the Magpies continued to pile on the attack after the break, Mark Edwards lobbed Bartram for a second, before Cooper scored his second in the dying minutes. Chorley had done it, reaching the FA Cup second round for the first time in their history. The Chorley players partied long into the night in a basement disco at the house of one of Ken Wright's work colleagues. Captain Phil Marsden told me:

> We had lots of '80s hits going on. I remember dancing to 'Don't You Want Me' by The Human League and 'New Rose' by The Damned, which was a bit more to my taste. But we drank all the booze this fella laid on for us, so I can't recall much beyond that.

As the Chorley boys threw their shapes and pondered how to spend their £120 win bonus (Ian Senior put it towards buying a car, and Phil Marsden shelled out on a heated serving trolley – which were all the rage in the '80s), football writers sharpened their pens. Many reports were fulsome in their praise of the Multipart men. Stephen Bierley's *Guardian* article was headed 'Chorley Wolf their Chance'. He wrote: 'Edwards pounded through and Wolves of the Fourth Division (that fact still takes some believing) were gone. Chorley were chortling...' Others were merciless in their criticism of Wolves. In the *Express & Star*, David Instone's headline ran: 'Disgraced! Wolves sink to new low. Part-timers hand shot-shy Turner's men the final indignity.' The *Evening Mail* adopted a more ghoulish angle, leading with: 'Once proud Wolves buried by non-leaguers' and 'Proper Chorlies', and Leon Hickman's *Molineux Requiem* stated: 'The once great Wolves climbed unprotestingly into their coffin last night, fangs removed by the Multipart men from Chorley.'

Ironically, Chorley's lucky mascot was also distinctly macabre. The players acquired a model of Frankenstein's monster, complete with a bolt through his neck, stitching on his face and fake blood on his forehead. 'One of the directors unearthed it from a room at Victory Park,' explained Ken Wright. 'It became like a twelfth man during the cup run, and it even ended up in the team bath with the players.' Frankenstein's monster (which sadly went missing a few years back) travelled with the team to Ewood Park, for the second-round 'home' clash with a Preston North End team that gained promotion that season. In front of 11,219 supporters, the match ended in a 0–0 draw, but following just a single training session on Deepdale's artificial pitch, Chorley were powerless to prevent the hosts running out 5–0 winners in the replay. No matter – 'Singing in the Rain,' the song they'd adopted following the biblical downpours during the Molineux game, was blasted out at top volume in the team bath.

It took Graham Turner time to overcome his shellshock: 'I think most people reckoned the club was heading for oblivion.' Salvation lay within. Thanks in no small part to the performances of two bargain signings from neighbours West Bromwich Albion – defender Andy Thompson and crew-cut striker Steve Bull – Wolves rallied. Within eighteen months, they beat fellow former League Champions Burnley 2–0 in the final of the Sherpa Van Trophy at Wembley in front of over 80,000 fans. By the 89–90 season, Wolves were back in the Second Division. The modernisation of Molineux was by now also now in full swing.

The sickly state of Wolves in the mid '80s affords the tale of Chorley's 1986 FA Cup heroics a darker side, but Chorley's run is still talked about with pride in the town today, although as Ken Wright admits: 'The number of those that can remember it is dwindling.'

THE BEDE AND HIS BOYS

'We did it, Rainsy; we bloody well did it.'
NIGEL GOLLEY

The Recreation Ground, next to Gander Green Lane – January 1989, 10 a.m. Sutton United's training session is stinking the place out. Manager Barrie Williams wants his Vauxhall Conference League side to focus on set pieces, as the Surrey amateurs prepare for their FA Cup third-round clash with Coventry City, winners of the competition eighteen months previously. But with kick-off just a few hours away, his collection of brickies and bank clerks are worse than useless. After ten minutes of watching sliced clearances and shanked passes on a surface littered with canine mess (the players call it 'dog-shit park'), an unimpressed Williams calls time and blows his whistle. As the players trudge off, the mood is downcast. Dead-ball specialist Micky Stephens tries to lift spirits: 'Don't worry, it'll be alright on the night,' he laughs. Forward Matt Hanlan's mind flits back to the rather more productive floodlit training session at Gander Green Lane a couple of nights before. On that occasion, Hanlan had scorched a volley home from the edge of the box. 'You never know, Matt,' Williams told him afterwards, 'Saturday might just be your day.'

• • •

Promoted to the Conference in 1986, Sutton had packed a club-record 14,000 into Gander Green Lane in 1970 when they faced Don Revie's Leeds United in the FA Cup third round and received a 6–0 hiding. In the intervening years, upgrades to the ground took place, meaning the capacity was reduced to 8,000, but in essence, with its open, curved terracing at both ends and tea and burger shacks behind, the tree-framed Gander Green Lane was largely unchanged. Whenever the players arrived at training early, they headed straight to Rose's Cafe – a fixture for decades – where the tea was always on the house. Coinciding with the start of pipe-smoking Welshman Barrie Williams's time in charge, expectations rose. As well as securing two Isthmian League titles in the '80s, they finished runners-up in the Anglo-Italian Cup twice, after winning it in 1979 under Keith Blunt ('You won't find that in Arsenal, Liverpool or Manchester United's trophy cabinet,' Williams told me), but their FA Cup exploits in the late '80s put them firmly on the map. In the 1987–88 campaign, they defeated league sides Aldershot and Peterborough before being edged out in a replay by an emerging Middlesbrough side that would be promoted to Division One at the end of the season.

The 1987–88 run raised Barrie Williams's profile. An English literature teacher during the week, word got around that Williams would pepper his team talks with quotations from famous authors. A fanciful notion, apparently. 'Throwing in Shakespeare and Kipling would have made me look a bit of a pretentious fop, don't you think?' Williams smiled. That said, he did invoke the Venerable Bede's parable of the sparrow (which briefly enjoys fluttering around in a warm hallway before flying outside again into the harsh winter air), before the Middlesbrough tie, explaining to his players that they'd be like the sparrow if they lost. When Sutton fell to Paul Kerr's winner for 'Boro, the predictable sledgehammer response arrived, with one Sutton player remarking: 'I suppose that fucking sparrow is dead now then.' Did Williams really correct journalists on their grammar (both spoken and written), as has been rumoured? 'Only if they annoyed me,' Williams laughed.

One of the enduring stories about the Sutton v. Coventry tie is that the Sky Blues, perched in a healthy seventh place in the First Division, didn't approach it in the correct manner. It was an accusation that (then) manager John Sillett quickly refuted: 'Absolutely not. The boys were in a bit of a no-win situation. They were expected to hammer Sutton, and anything less would be a disappointment.'

The two sides seemed set to go in level at half-time, but Sutton skipper and left-back Tony Rains changed all that. From a Micky Stephens corner, he headed home past goalkeeper Steve Ogrizovic after a flick-on from forward Nigel Golley. Uppermost in Rains's mind was the advice he'd been given at a training session in his school gym: 'Always head the ball in the opposite direction it comes from.' The atmosphere was now cranked up several notches, and Coventry attacked down the slope in the second half. Welsh international David Phillips equalised after fifty-two minutes. 'Something in Dave's celebration annoyed me,' Barrie Williams said. 'When he kissed his hand and pointed to the sky, I think that he thought he'd got Coventry out of jail.' Just a couple of hours after that disastrous set-piece training session on 'dogshit park', it was time for Sutton to strike again. A Micky Stephens short corner found Phil Dawson, and his pass found Matt Hanlan, who volleyed home from close range. His celebration was memorable. Yelling and screaming, he ran, then strutted across to the main stand, where he knew his family – parents, nan, grandad and sister – were sitting. Lost in the moment, the self-employed bricklayer strayed rather too close to the Coventry dugout, where '87 hero Keith Houchen suggested none too politely that Hanlan might wish to celebrate elsewhere. What, I asked the still youthful looking Hanlan, was the furious arm waving all about after he scored?

It was partly the emotion of it all, but I'd heard rumours that Manchester United were sniffing around after me ['I think that Alex Ferguson wanted a wall built at Old Trafford,' scoffed Tony Rains]. I never did discover if the rumours were true or not, but as a young lad who dreamed of turning pro – and still does [he laughed], my head was a little bit all over the place.

Despite Coventry going close in the dying minutes, Sutton held on for a memorable 2–1 victory. At the final whistle, with a pitch invasion in full swing, the *Match of the Day* cameras panned to a girl sobbing with joy in the main stand. Unbeknown to the BBC, it just happened to be Hanlan's sister, Kelly. In the furore, Rains and Hanlan were buttonholed by Radio 2 on the pitch for so long that when they finally returned to the dressing room an hour later, it was deserted. 'They'd all gone up to the boardroom for a drink,' Tony Rains said. The publicity machine then clicked into gear. Barrie Williams reminded his team that they all needed to be fully focussed for their next Conference game. But it was nigh on impossible to stay grounded, for Williams as much as the players. Williams, as he put it, 'went into full thespian mode. In front of the TV cameras, I read out Rudyard Kipling's poem "If" – one of my favourites. Why not eh? This was a once in a lifetime moment.'

After the match, Hanlan was informed that he was wanted on *Match of the Day*, to appear with Des Lynam. The BBC sent a car for him and he didn't get home until about 12.30 a.m. He was ever so slightly miffed: 'Everyone else had been celebrating down at the club, but now I was stood at home.' An ITV team visited Tony Rains, along with fellow full-back Robyn Jones at Legal & General on the Monday, during which Rains mentioned that despite the glory of events on Saturday, it was 'good to have full-time work as security'. It was a disrupted week, with various newspapers phoning him for comments. The tabloids had fun with Rains's surname. 'TONY RAINS ON COVENTRY'S PARADE' and 'IT NEVER RAINS BUT IT POURS' were two such offerings. Along with Hanlan, Rains was whisked off to Shepherd's Bush to appear on Monday night's *Wogan*, with actress Billie Whitelaw, who played the mother of the infamous East End gangsters in *The Krays*. Their joint-appearance fees went straight into the players' pool. Hanlan was also invited to meet agent Eric Hall, who was starting to forge a reputation for himself in the game. 'He was all big cigars and loud shirts and "monster" references and all of that,' said Hanlan.

> He said that he reckoned he could make us another £20,000 in personal appearances. When we went back to Sutton and told them what he'd said, they weren't having any of it. We're a team, the directors said, and we can't have you going in another direction. Perhaps I should have challenged them, and pushed it a bit, but I didn't, and in any case, it wasn't all about the money.

At title-challengers Norwich City in the fourth round, Sutton were annihilated 8–0. 'Norwich's phenomenal speed and accuracy were too much for us,' Hanlan explains. The team also had a disrupted build-up to the game. Tony Rains explained: 'We were asked to come in morning, afternoon and evening by the press for interviews and rejigged training sessions. It was tricky for us to ask our employers to have the afternoon off.'

Despite harbouring some regrets that the chance of turning professional never presented itself, Hanlan says that he wouldn't swap a full-time career for the Coventry giant killing, a point reiterated by Tony Rains. 'It was the best of times,' says Rains, who earned £450 in bonuses for being ever-present during the cup run. Rains believes that Sutton's victory over Coventry was the last true non-league FA Cup giant killing because by the early '90s, many leading non-league clubs were turning professional.

The Sutton team from the late '80s still regularly catch up at home games, and the bond between them is as strong as ever. At the end of our 2002 interview, Williams, who later went on to manage the England Women's team, said: 'It was our Warhol moment in football. Wouldn't it be great if every footballer at non-league level could have just one of those?'

15

THE WEMBLEY HEROES

THE *GAUCHO*

'Instinct took over. I just headed towards goal.'
RICKY VILLA

Wembley – May 1981. Tottenham's Argentinian midfielder Ricardo Villa watches expectantly as fellow World Cup winner Ossie Ardiles expertly feints past two Manchester City defenders on the edge of the penalty area. His pass-cum-shot finds Steve Archibald, whose effort is well smothered by Manchester City keeper Joe Corrigan. But Corrigan can't hold onto the shot and the ball pings out to Villa. Four days earlier, the bearded Villa had cut a disconsolate figure, as he trudged away with head bowed after being subbed in Saturday's FA Cup final, which ended 1–1. Buoyed by manager Keith Burkinshaw's promise that he'd play in the replay five days later, Villa is transformed. Seizing on the loose ball, he slams it home from close range to put Spurs 1–0 up and tears across the pitch in triumph. He has fulfilled a childhood dream of scoring at Wembley, and in an FA Cup final too. As the Tottenham players prepare for City to kick-off, he asks himself: 'How can it get better than this?'

• • •

My 2010 interview with Villa, which coincided with the release of his autobiography, began well enough, but within a couple of minutes, Villa looked at me quizzically. It was slightly off-putting. Then a look of apparent concern spread across his face. 'All OK, Ricky?' I asked him. 'Yes,' he said, his easy smile quickly returning. 'I'm just wondering why you haven't yet asked me how Ossie is. Or where he is. That's how all my other interviews this week have started.' He then laughed, which he did a lot during our time together. Villa was staying with Ardiles in Hertfordshire in the midst of conducting signings and giving interviews. The pair remained joined at the hip. In broken English, Villa used humour in response to several of my questions. Given that he made just two substitute appearances for Argentina at the '78 World Cup, how come he'd cost Spurs £350,000 in 1978, compared with the £250,000 outlay on Ardiles, who played in every game? 'Because I am bigger than Ossie,' Villa said, puffing out his chest. 'He is a very small man.' We discussed Villa's weekly English lessons when he first arrived at Tottenham. 'My English wasn't much better after a year, but Matthew – our teacher – learnt a lot. He now spoke far better Spanish. He hadn't been fluent before.' And – out of interest, where *is* Ossie? 'He's talking to a man about a job. He's also very well, before you ask,' Villa grinned. Nicknames for his ex-Spurs teammates littered the interview. Ex-Tottenham skipper Steve Perryman is 'Stevie P', striker Garth Crooks is 'Crooksy' and stocky midfielder Garry Brooke, who replaced Villa in the first match against Manchester City, is 'Buddha'. He pulled scary faces when talking about the fried breakfasts served up at the training ground canteen and the warm English beer that teammates swigged on the bus after games. Villa always found it amusing when teammates expressed concern about their 'crown jewels', if a ball whacked them between the legs. A beaming smile spread across his face when he recounted seeing snow when he pulled back the curtains one winter morning. Villa clapped his hands together when he recalled seeing his garden covered in a white blanket. 'Wonderful memories; so much to enjoy,' he said.

Yet much of the time, Villa pined for his rural life back home in Argentina, in a remote farming community fifteen kilometres south of the nearest town Roque Pérez. Although the club gave Villa and Ardiles an allowance for phone calls home, Villa's family didn't have a phone, so his father had to travel to Roque Pérez on horseback at a prearranged time in order to speak to his son. Although he was now 6,000 miles away from his family, Villa always felt his father's pain as 'collection' day approached when a rent collector would appear, in a smart suit, demanding money from the peons [farm labourers]. 'He had no interest in whether it had been a difficult year, he just wanted his money,' Villa said. As soon as Villa was able, he bought the 350 hectares of land outright, and he's been back in Roque Pérez ever since his football career, which also saw him play in Colombia and the United States, ended. The harvested soya is sold each year. 'No more rent collectors,' Villa said proudly.

Homesick or not, Villa was keen to make his mark in England, but without Ardiles, who often acted as his translator, his stay in north London would have been a brief one. By his own admission, the intuitive Villa either played outstandingly well or faded out of the game completely. His inconsistencies drove him, and others, to distraction. 'I never could explain why sometimes, I just couldn't perform,' Villa shrugged. The more analytical Ardiles believed it was partly for tactical reasons. In Argentina, Villa was a thinking midfielder with a free role. '*Engache* – there's no direct translation into English,' Villa said. Forty-six years ago, English football was no place for free-thinking midfielders. Tottenham were a team in transition, after just being promoted from Division Two in 1978. Villa struggled to adapt. With the ball flying over his head during most matches, he was a lost soul. His sense of dislocation grew when he attended banquets and dinners where he couldn't understand much of what was being said. 'I went from being outgoing and chatty to being silent,' Villa recalled. The only things he could understand on English TV was *Match of the Day*, *Top of the Pops* and nature programmes.

But by the time the 1980–81 campaign began, Tottenham, who'd just invested around £1.5 million in strikers Garth Crooks and Steve Archibald, were becoming a force to be reckoned with. Villa's form improved. Keith Burkinshaw began slotting him in behind the front two, and with more freedom to roam, Villa began to demonstrate his skill at the *gambeta* – the art of dribbling. 'To leave an opponent for dead, wondering where you've gone, is regarded as highly artistic,' Villa said. As a young child, Villa practised the art of the *gambeta* for hours near his house, all by himself. He dribbled around the trees that provided shade from the burning sun. 'They were defenders. I went this way and that way' – Villa demonstrated, feinting left and darting right – 'and left dozens of them behind. It was good practice for what happened years later at Wembley.'

Tottenham eased past Queens Park Rangers, Hull City, Coventry City and Exeter City before drawing 2–2 with Wolverhampton Wanderers at Hillsborough. Ruled out for several months due to a knee injury, Villa convinced himself that, three years after putting pen to paper for the club, he was going to be sold in the summer. 'I was offered a contract with the same terms as those I was on back in '78. In other words, a pay cut.' Meanwhile, Villa got to hear that Ardiles's contract offer was far more generous. Brought back for the semi-final against Wolves, Villa was substituted at Hillsborough by Brooke. 'He was solid, determined, strong, dependable. Everything I wasn't,' Villa said.

Villa realised that the FA Cup had the power to turn players into club icons. A year earlier, he'd teed up Ossie Ardiles for his famous winner in a fourth-round replay at Old Trafford, the match where Glenn Hoddle spent most of the match in goal. 'The FA Cup was magic, and fans hadn't stopped talking about Ossie's goal since.' A similarly heroic cup intervention would do Villa's reputation no harm whatsoever. It was at Highbury, of all places, where Villa made his initial mark. Feeding off the energy of their supporters in the North Bank – usually home to Arsenal fans – Garth Crooks scored two fine opportunistic goals against Wolves. The first was a header looped over the stricken Paul Bradshaw; the second a fantastic shot, following Crooks' eviscerating run through the defence. But goal of the night was Villa's curling thirty-yard shot in front of Wolves' disconsolate hordes on the Clock End, which confirmed Tottenham were heading to Wembley for the first time in eight years. 'I never hit a better shot. Then things really went crazy,' Villa recalled.

The hoopla in the build-up to the final was deafening. There were visits to schools and local hospitals and multiple photo opportunities. Villa also noticed that the paps were obsessed with Ardiles, who'd landed himself a role in the Second World War film *Escape to Victory* alongside Sylvester Stallone and a host of other famous footballers including Pelé and Bobby Moore. 'Ossie first and Ricky second. Always,' Villa said. As if to illustrate the point, Tottenham's

FA Cup final song, written and performed by Cockney sparrow duo Chas & Dave, was entitled 'Ossie's Dream', with the narrative based on the fact that Ardiles had dreamed of playing on Wembley's hallowed turf since he was a child.

On *Top of the Pops*, the players sing along with gusto to the catchy number, especially winger Tony Galvin, whom Villa nicknamed 'the Russian' on account of the fact he'd studied it at university. The killer line is delivered by a smiling Ardiles, bobbing up and down at the front ('in de cup for Totting-ham'), despite the fact he was initially less than keen to deliver it. Villa is apparently there, somewhere. 'The words were delivered so fast, I never knew when to come in, so the cameras ignored me.' On the day of the final, the BBC arranged for a satellite link-up with Ardiles's and Villa's respective families back home. 'After speaking to my parents, I felt settled and confident that I would play well.' Villa's sister and her boyfriend flew across for the match. But Tottenham misfired, and Villa had, as he put it, 'one of those games'.

After being substituted , Villa opted to head straight to the dressing room, believing he'd let himself down badly and embarrassed his family. After getting changed, he later went out to the bench following Tommy Hutchinson's own goal that had gifted Spurs an equaliser. 'We got a replay. But I wasn't sure whether I'd be playing for Tottenham again.' Like many of the best sports stories, salvation lay just around the corner. There's no good reason why Villa played the game of his life in the replay. An improvised game of keepie-uppie with coach Peter Shreeve prior to kick-off, where the pair lofted the ball to one another over the heads of the marching band relaxed him, but as he said self-deprecatingly, 'I just got lucky that night'.

After slamming Tottenham into the lead, Villa then saw young midfielder Steve Mackenzie volley City ahead from twenty-five yards out. 'It was a superbly executed goal. Visually, it was amazing,' Villa said. Then after half-time, a Kevin Reeves penalty gave City the lead, before Garth Crooks levelled the score.

Six minutes after Crooks's goal, 'the Russian' – Galvin – galloped forward with the ball, stopped after being driven wide by a City defender and rolled it sideways to Villa. The Tottenham fans buzzed with expectation. 'Head to the penalty area and see what happens,' Villa thought to himself. He wasn't the quickest player on the pitch, but his mind immediately shot back to when he was a child in Roque Pérez, swerving and feinting past the trees near his house. The obstacles facing him at Wembley were mobile and sky blue. First up was Tommy Caton, the big blond defender, tipped to be an England regular in the near future. Villa darted to the left of him. Full-back Ray Ranson was next, and Villa moved the ball to his left also. Aware he was heading away from goal, Villa cut back past Caton once again in order to be more central. All that was stopping him now was the colossal figure of Joe Corrigan, England's perennial third-choice keeper behind Peter Shilton and Ray Clemence. As Corrigan prepared to throw himself at Villa's feet, the Argentinian executed the faintest of dummies and slipped the ball past 'big Joe', as everyone called him. 3–2. It was a breathtaking piece of skill, worthy of winning any football match. Made in Argentina and deployed to perfection at the home of English football. To celebrate, Villa sprinted past teammates Glenn Hoddle and Steve Archibald before coming to an exhausted halt near the halfway line. Tottenham held on. Just. A shot from City substitute Dennis Tueart skimmed the post. But for Villa, the '81 FA Cup final replay was redemption for his calamitous display five days earlier. A redrafted contract was couriered to Villa's house. 'The terms were much better this time,' he grinned.

• • •

For different reasons, neither Ardiles nor Villa played in the final or the replay as Tottenham retained the FA Cup in 1982, edging out Second Division Queens Park Rangers 1–0 thanks to Glenn Hoddle's penalty. The vibe wasn't quite the same as the year before. Another Chas & Dave ditty, 'Do It Again,' fared far less well in the charts. Perhaps it was because Ossie and Ricky were notable for their absence. After playing in the defeat of Leicester in the semi-final, Ardiles, following a prior agreement with Argentina, flew to South America to join the holders at their training camp for the forthcoming World Cup. Even if Ardiles hadn't been selected for the national team, it's doubtful whether he'd have played for Tottenham again that season, given the crescendo of booing that greeted him each time he touched the ball during the semi-final. In the previous week, the Argentine flag was raised over the capital of the Falkland Islands, Port Stanley. 'When politics and sport mixes, sport inevitably loses,' Ardiles reflected later. It wasn't just Stockport County, quickly ditching their plan to sport a white and blue away kit for the 1981–82 season, who displayed anti-Argentinian sentiments. Opposition fans turned nasty. 'Ossie and Ricky go home,' read one banner at the Villa Park semi-final.

Injured for the Leicester game, Villa did play league games in the lead-up to the final. 'I tried not to let the booing affect me, and the Spurs fans were great about the whole thing,' he said. But following discussions with Keith Burkinshaw, Villa didn't play in the final. According to former Sports Minister Neil Macfarlane, it would have been more than a little awkward for Princess Anne to have shaken the hand of, or handed a medal to, a player from a country with whom the UK was at war, a message that was conveyed to

Tottenham. Some thirty years after the conflict, Villa was tactful on the subject: 'At school, we were taught that the Malvinas were ours. Geographically, they were so much closer to Argentina. But there should always be diplomatic solutions to such conflicts.' Following his loan spell with Paris St Germain, Ardiles returned to White Hart Lane in January '83, where he and Villa were briefly reunited, before the latter departed to Colombia in the close season.

These days, on the vast rambling expanse of his farm, Villa lives the roving life of a *gaucho* – the romantic cowboy figure at the centre of so many Argentinian folk stories. Yet for someone who spent so much time pining for home when he plied his trade in north London, it's ironic that on most days, his mind flits back to the redemptive night at Wembley in '81, when he transformed himself into perhaps Tottenham's ultimate modern folk hero. 'It was a dream come true,' Villa smiled.

THE SHANKHILL ROAD SKINHEAD

'Norman Whiteside was built like Rambo by the time he was sixteen.'
ARNOLD MÜHREN

Wembley – May 1985. The cup final has been a drab affair, but in extra time, with both sides exhausted, Manchester United's Mark Hughes hits an expertly curled pass with the outside of his foot to twenty-year-old Norman Whiteside, loitering out on the right. Whiteside manoeuvres forwards, with Pat Van Den Hauwe tracking back and moving to close him down. Using the Toffees defender as a shield, Whiteside shimmies and does a little stepover with his left foot. With Van Den Hauwe now obstructing Whiteside's view of the far post – and therefore goalkeeper Neville Southall's view of it – the player from Belfast's Shankill Road expertly bends his shot around the defender, and the ball creeps past Southall, hitting the goalie's glove bag as it goes in. 1–0. The Toffees' treble dream is over. Today belongs to Stormin' Norman.

• • •

The subject of Whiteside's numerous nicknames appeared to be uppermost in many readers' minds as he signed copies and chatted to fans at the launch of his autobiography in 2007. The eyes were a little puffier and the face a little more jowly, but Norman Whiteside was still a big draw for United fans. More obvious monikers like 'Big Norm' and 'Rambo' were testimony to his imposing stature and his abrasive style of play. Some of the other nicknames help shed light on the Whiteside story. Several commentators referred to him as 'Roy of the Rovers' or 'Man-Boy' after he burst into the United first team in true comic-book hero fashion, aged just sixteen. Groups of United fans would light-heartedly shout 'Norm' at him if he ventured near the touchline, just as the *Cheers* studio audience did whenever the beer-swilling Norm Peterson wandered into the bar in the popular '80s US comedy series. 'Did anyone ever call you "Normski?"' (a rapper and DJ who fronted BBC's DEF II in the late '80s) one Whiteside fan asked him. 'Not that I recall,' Whiteside replied, looking slightly puzzled.

One inevitable nickname would prove to be both an honour and an albatross around his neck: 'the new George Best'. There were some clear similarities between the two Belfast boys. Both burst into the United first team very young, and United scout Bob Bishop un-earthed both starlets. 'Though in my case, I don't think he [Bishop] contacted United telling them: "I think I've found a genius,'" Whiteside laughed. 'George was in a class of his own.' However, there was no denying that when the kid from Shankhill Road burst onto the scene in the early '80s in a blaze of publicity, United clearly had a star on their hands. Growing up during the height of the Troubles in Belfast, Whiteside always had an easy-going, mature way of speaking to people. 'I was brought up to be myself and to try and get on with everyone,' he said. 'That helped me cope in a dressing room full of tough, older characters.'

No one appears to remember him playing in the United youth or reserve team. Ron Atkinson pitched Whiteside in as substitute against Brighton at the Goldstone Ground when he was just sixteen years and 352 days old, making him the youngest player in United's history. He was earning just £16 per week but pocketed an £800 win bonus when Ray Wilkins scored the winner. 'I felt like a millionaire,' Whiteside smiled.

Opportunities came thick and fast for Whiteside. He turned in some sterling performances for Northern Ireland at the 1982 World Cup. 'His performances were ridiculously good for someone so young,' said George Best about 'the new George Best'. Then in the 1983 Milk Cup final, he slithered free of Alan Hansen to give United the lead before Liverpool fought back to win. 'I always played well against Hansen and Lawrenson,' said Whiteside. 'Unlike many central defenders, they were good footballers. But I roughed them up a bit.' One problem though was Whiteside's relative lack of pace. 'Now there's a story,' Whiteside muttered.

When Whiteside was just fifteen, a groin injury saw him seek treatment from a renowned Glentoran physio, who apparently possessed faith healing powers. The massage given to his hips and groin, according to Whiteside, was brutally hard. 'At one point I could feel my pelvis moving,' Whiteside explained. 'It felt like I'd been beaten up.' From that point on, he was unable to rotate his hips properly, and his joints clicked and popped when he ran. The sorry episode accounts for his slightly robotic running style – clearly visible on footage of him playing and the fact that 'even Ron Atkinson could overtake me on training runs'.

Whiteside played in the first of his two FA Cup finals, or three, if one counts the replay against Brighton in 1983. It was Whiteside himself who had blasted United to Wembley, half-volleying a stupendous winner past Arsenal goalkeeper George Wood at Villa Park. Little wonder then that several of the banners made by United fans professed their love for 'Big Norm'. Slightly puzzlingly, one read: 'MAGGIE MAY BUT NORMAN CAN.' More straightforwardly another said: 'UNITED WALK ON THE WHITESIDE OF LIFE.' Remarkably, though, given United's enormous stature, it was Brighton and Hove Albion, freshly relegated from the First Division, who outdid them on the publicity side in the build-up to the final. With his beauty queen girlfriend Val Lloyd in tow and his love of boogying the night away in Brighton nightclubs, balding Albion coach Jimmy Melia, who'd played for Liverpool in the '60s, hogged the headlines. Thanks to a tie-up with British Airways, the cream-suited Brighton team flew to Wembley in a helicopter. As it passed overhead, Whiteside and his teammates mused about what might happen if it fell out of the sky. Thankfully, it made it. Inside Wembley, a United banner read: 'BRIGHTON FLEW HERE IN A CHOPPER BUT WHEN ROBSON SCORES THEY'LL COME A CROPPER.' The banner makers would have to wait for the replay for that prophecy to come true. Brighton's banner makers also gave it their best. There was a prominent 'BALD IS BEAUTIFUL' message (in homage to Melia) and the proclamation 'ALL THINGS

BRIGHTON BEAUTIFUL. On the pitch, an entertaining final ended 2–2 and is most famous for United keeper Gary Bailey's last ditch save from Gordon Smith. 'It wasn't a great save, but it's remembered more because of what would have happened had it gone in,' Whiteside said.

Brighton had been without their skipper, the bearded, headband-wearing Steve Foster, as he was suspended from the final, but he was available for the replay. Brighton were easily swatted aside. With United fans taunting: 'Stevie, Stevie Foster, what a difference you have made,' the eighteen-year-old Whiteside made history by becoming the youngest-ever goal scorer in an FA Cup final, heading in a corner to make it 2–0.

Whiteside and United were back at Wembley for the FA Cup final two years later. 'Even though he was only nineteen, it was as if he was a veteran,' Ron Atkinson said of Whiteside. But there were already concerns about the state of his right knee. He missed several games due to injury in early 1985, and by the time the FA Cup reached its business end, Atkinson had converted him into a midfielder, to allow the Mark Hughes–Frank Stapleton partnership to flourish up front. United had combative Irish international Kevin Moran in defence and Bryan Robson and Remi Moses in midfield. Now, with Whiteside in the middle of the park too, they were the most uncompromising of units. Atkinson's men were at their combative best in one-off knockout matches, and this was never better illustrated than during a truly toxic FA Cup semi-final at Goodison Park against the old enemy from down East Lancs Road.

By then, the rivalry was almost off the scale. Skirmishes between supporters on the streets were *de rigeur* before and after matches. In 1983, Ron Atkinson had ammonia thrown in his face before a match at Anfield, leading him to describe United–Liverpool clashes as being 'like Vietnam out there'. United fans were jealous of Liverpool's long run of domestic and European success and Liverpool supporters were annoyed at United's ability to hog column inches, despite not having won a league title since 1967. Whiteside loved the hurly-burly of United–Liverpool matches and later relished his moniker of the 'Scousebuster' later in the decade. 'Norman would have steam coming out of his ears before those matches. He was always hugely fired up,' recalled Bryan Robson. Liverpool midfielder Jan Mølby still shudders when he recalls a Whiteside challenge: 'When Norman tackled you, you stayed tackled.'

Even the ultra-combative Whiteside drew the line at the poisonous chants that rival fans were now trading. 'The songs went way too far,' he said. No themes or topics were deemed off limits. Liverpool supporters taunted their rivals about the 1958 Munich air disaster with 'Who's that dying on the runway, who's that dying in the snow? It's Matt Busby and his boys, there not making any noise and it's all because the plane wouldn't go.' Munich '58 banners were clearly visible at the Heysel Stadium in '85. United fans adapted the words to sing about Bill Shankly's death in 1981: 'Who's that lyin' on the carpet? Who's that lyin' on the floor? It's Bill Shankly on his back, and he's havin' a heart attack, and he won't be goin' to Wembley no more.' On the topic of the Shankly/Busby chants, Whiteside acknowledged: 'Fans seemed to be unaware that Busby played for Liverpool and was great friends with Shankly. But that was the prevailing atmosphere at our matches by then, sadly.'

As they prepared to run out for the match at Goodison, both sets of players were unaware that supporters from both sides were running amok in the streets around Goodison, using Stanley knives and hurling potatoes with nails sticking out at one another. On the pitch, the action was turbo charged, with the match ending 2–2 following Paul Walsh's late equaliser from point blank range after Gary Bailey's save from Ian Rush's header. The furious exchange in the United dressing room afterwards, where teammates suggested to Bailey in no uncertain terms that he might have done better with Rush's header leaked out to the press, reinforcing the view that United were A-grade tabloid fodder. 'We never did find out who the mole was,' Whiteside grimaced. United won the replay at Maine Road thanks to Mark Hughes's thunderous winner, but United remained underdogs against an Everton side that had won both the league title and European Cup Winners' Cup.

'It was an awful final,' Whiteside admitted. The game was enlivened by only two key incidents. Firstly, there was the dismissal of Kevin Moran in the seventy-eighth minute, sent off by referee Peter Willis in his last game as an official for bringing down Peter Reid. 'It was never a sending off, not in a million years,' Reid told me. The Everton midfielder pleaded with Willis to reverse his decision. 'They never change their mind, though, do they?' said Reid, speaking in the pre-VAR era. Then, with the contest drifting towards a seemingly inevitable replay, Whiteside curled home his precision goal. Van Den Hauwe blamed himself for not closing Whiteside down. Southall blamed himself for diving slightly too late. Neither Everton player blamed each other. Whiteside had got lucky, Everton players reasoned, using Southall's white keeper bag as a target. Some reckoned he'd intended it as a cross. 'If so, it was the worst cross in the world,' laughed Whiteside.

It was only when he joined Everton in 1989 that their players realised Whiteside's using a defender to screen his shot from the goalkeeper was his signature skill, something he'd practised since he was a kid on the Shankhill Road. After lifting the trophy for a second time, Whiteside joined his jubilant teammates in a melee of

'80s mullets and daft hats. Later, on *Match of the Day*, the thoroughly lubricated Whiteside, who'd indulged himself in copious amounts of free Guinness, received a clip round the earhole from his manager. On the programme, he'd responded cheekily to a question from Jimmy Hill. 'Mr Hill asked you a question,' Atkinson chided. 'Talk to him with respect.'

The incident said much about the persona of Atkinson, who'd always rise to the fore on the big occasion. 'He grew in stature on days like those. Ron wasn't massively into tactics. He rarely if ever spoke about the opposition. He always instilled the belief that we could win on the big occasion,' Whiteside said. But as the following season would show, he didn't have the attention to detail to instil the consistency in United to win the title. The chastising from Atkinson also demonstrated that although he seemed to have been around for ever, Whiteside was still little more than a kid. 'He wouldn't have clipped Robbo or Kevin Moran round the ear,' Whiteside pointed out. But nabbing the Wembley winner at least saw him get a hefty pay rise. As was the case at many clubs, the home-grown Belfast boy always felt a little peeved that he earned a good deal less than many of United's expensive signings.

The '85 FA Cup final was as good as it got for Whiteside. United, as fans from other clubs delighted in reminding them, somehow finished sixth in a two-horse title race during the following season, despite a phenomenal start, and although Northern Ireland qualified for the '86 World Cup, they crashed out at the group stage. Atkinson was dismissed after a disappointing start to the 1986–87 campaign, and as injuries began to take their toll, Alex Ferguson, who always had a beady eye on Whiteside's refuelling methods, sold him to Everton in 1988. Some of the fans, clad in their Norman

Whiteside 'Scousebuster T-shirts', were furious, given Whiteside's star turn in two successive Liverpool–United clashes. In October 1986, he drilled the winner at Anfield in a league game, and his appearance as a substitute inspired United to come back from 3–0 down to secure a draw at the end of the 1987–88 campaign. 'Scousebuster' he may have been, but ultimately the ends justified the means, as Ferguson's reshaped United team won the FA Cup in 1990, which lay the foundations of their domination of English football in the '90s.

Forced to retire aged twenty-six after a series of debilitating injuries, Whiteside admitted to having suffered from dozens of stomach upsets after 'decades of popping painkillers'. After retiring from the game, he pursued a career in podiatry. 'Having spent so much time on the treatment table, it seemed a logical career choice.' Instantly recognisable, Whiteside's patients often seemed more interested in talking football – and especially that goal in '85 – than discussing their own needs. 'I was always happy to oblige them,' Whiteside said. 'In fact, it was a privilege.'

THE SKY BLUES

'John, you nervous?'
'Just a little bit, David.'
'Well, just have this in mind: we've been here seven times and never lost.'
'Well, we've never been here and we've never lost either.'
CONVERSATION BETWEEN COVENTRY CITY MANAGER JOHN
SILLETT AND TOTTENHAM BOSS DAVID PLEAT BEFORE
THE 1987 FA CUP FINAL

Wembley – May 1987. In the cacophonous din, Coventry city striker Keith Houchen can't hear a thing, but his teammates are offering up advice anyway as he (very) briefly ruminates over whether to head or volley winger Dave Bennett's delicious cross. Defender Nick Pickering, standing a few yards away, urges him to try and win a penalty. 'Dive,' he yells. 'Dive.' Back on the halfway line, defender Trevor Peake screams 'Fly, just fly.' Peake's advice magically permeates the noise of the crowd. Houchen's spectacular diving header flies past Ray Clemence and brings Coventry City level at 2–2. It's the standout goal in a classic, no-holds-barred FA Cup final humdinger.

· · ·

In a decade dominated by trauma and tumult, the uplifting story of Coventry City's Class of '87 comes as a welcome tonic. Except, of course, for Tottenham fans. At Highfield Road, in the lead-up to the Sky Blues departing their home in 2005, nostalgia was very much in the air. Although their 34-year stay in the top flight had come to an end four years earlier, numerous fan events meant supporters could mingle freely and sup beer with the heroes of '87. They were possibly the most self-effacing collection of cup winners I ever met. Even joint manager George Curtis, nicknamed 'Godzilla' by TV pundit Jimmy Greaves, was an absolute teddy bear. So too was bearded 6ft 4in. skipper Brian Kilcline, only a horned helmet away from a one-man Viking invasion. 'I never tire of talking about '87,' 'Killer' beamed.

Up until that '87 cup run, Coventry City's main claim to fame was as English football's most prominent escapologists, avoiding the drop to Division Two by the skin of their teeth on several occasions.

Most famously, Don Mackay's team won their final three games of the 1984–85 campaign – including a 4–1 win over under-strength league champions Everton in the final match of the season – to relegate Milk Cup winners Norwich City and avoid the trapdoor by a single point. A year later, with City once again seemingly doomed, Mackay was sacked with just three matches left. Appointed chief coach along with George Curtis, John Sillett helped guide City to two victories to secure the club's top-flight status. It was a breeze this time. They stayed up by two points. But Sillett and Curtis reckoned Coventry's talented players were capable of more than just dicing with demotion every year.

I visited Sillett (or 'Snoz' as he was nicknamed, on account of his prominent nose) at his house in the early noughties for elevenses. Along with his lovely wife Joan, he couldn't have been more welcoming, and he treated me like I was a long-lost relative. 'Come in, son. Have you had a good journey up?' he beamed, before offering the warmest of handshakes. In advance, Sillett had asked me what cake I liked best, and I was treated to the biggest slice of fruitcake I'd ever seen with my cup of tea. 'It's a shame it's a bit early for anything stronger,' he laughed. Appointed as a coach at Highfield Road by chairman Jimmy Hill in 1979, Sillett had a two-year sabbatical from the game in 1984, after a row with manager Bobby Gould saw him leave his post. 'I had what you might call an existential crisis,' he said. 'I thought the style and systems in English football were primitive and I hated' – he looked around furtively to see if Joan was within earshot' – the fucking longball game.' Joan let John know that she'd 'heard that'. Sillett grinned, but not at the memory of football in that era. 'I vowed that if I went back in, I'd try to bring a smile to fans' faces, encourage my team to actually play some football.'

Not that Sillett was a utopianist. Although his former charges recalled that his eyes would brim with tears of joy when things were going well, he also possessed a volcanic temper. Cyrille Regis, signed from West Bromwich Albion in 1984, had struggled to replicate anything like his Hawthorns form at Highfield Road. 'John pulled me to one side after close season training in '86,' Regis told me. 'He bollocked me about the fact I looked like I couldn't be arsed. He was going right at me.' Sillett then threw an arm around Regis's shoulder and said softly: 'I don't want you to end up winning nothing in your career. You deserve so much better.' 'There were tears in his eyes,' Regis said. Normally, though, Sillett would leave the bollockings to George Curtis, who'd turned out 538 times for the Sky Blues, which at that point was a record.

'Most people expect me to come from oop North,' said the smiling Curtis, affecting a Northern accent when I spoke to him at one of those Highfield Road gatherings, 'and, with me minin' roots, I'm more like somethin' out of a *Monty Python* sketch.' In fact, Curtis was the second child of a Welsh miner who'd left Newport during the Great Depression in search of work. Curtis's father headed to Aylesham in Kent, where he found employment at the Snowdown Colliery. So did his brother and his mates. 'I'd done a year or so down there as a kid and I hated it,' he said, reverting to his southern accent. 'A career in football was a privilege in comparison. It's why I had no time for slackers. None at all.' Cyrille Regis discovered that Curtis had a particular loathing for players' lateness. Arriving two minutes late for the team bus on one occasion, Regis found the doors shut. 'It'll cost you £50 to get on,' barked Curtis through the glass. Regis paid up.

Steeped as Curtis and Sillett were in the city, they knew only too well the upheavals suffered by Coventry workers during the period of deindustrialisation in the early '80s. Unemployment reached 20 per cent as car plants including British Leyland folded entirely or downsized. 'The city was known as England's motor city, like Detroit in the US. But by the early '80s, that was all gone,' said George Curtis. Improbable though it may seem, John Sillett went to watch Coventry Ska band The Specials after hearing 'Ghost Town' on the radio. 'I wasn't really into pop music,' Sillett told me, 'but the lyrics of "Ghost Town" really struck me. I thought it was about the decline Coventry was going through, although [lead singer] Terry Hall always denied it, didn't he?'

The '87 FA Cup run galvanised the club, the city and several first-teamers, who Curtis and Sillett believed had underachieved in their careers. Goalkeeper Steve Ogrizovic was a nonplaying European Cup winner for Liverpool before joining Coventry in 1984. One of the last of the breed of cricketing footballers (he played several times for Shropshire), 'Oggy', as he was nicknamed, was often regarded as the best No. 1 never to win a full-England cap. David Bennett, a talented winger who'd played for Manchester City in the 1981 FA Cup final, then saw his career stall at Cardiff before moving to the Midlands in 1984. 'Inconsistency was my problem,' Bennett told me, 'but John and George cajoled me and encouraged me to produce my best form in 1986–87.' Brian Kilcline, once tipped for full-international honours as a youngster with Notts County, also felt that he had something to prove. 'It was time that I made the best of myself,' he said. Then there was Keith Houchen. The lanky striker whose penalty for Third Division York City had dumped Arsenal out of the FA Cup two years earlier hated life at bottom-tier Scunthorpe and suggested to his wife that he might even quit football for good. Much to his surprise, a £60,000 bid by Coventry saw him catapulted into the First Division overnight.

Coventry soon served notice that they would not be fighting

relegation in the 1986–87 campaign. From mid-September until mid-May, they remained in the top half of the First Division. After they won 3–0 in the third round at Highfield Road over Bolton Wanderers, the Sky Blues were drawn away in every round.

City chairman John Poynton had insisted that City's name was on the cup as soon as they beat Bolton, and at Old Trafford in the fourth round against Alex Ferguson's Manchester United, they really served notice of their intentions. The pitch was in a shocking state, due to the failed undersoil heating system. 'Half was mush, the other part was a frozen slab. Choosing the right studs was tricky,' said Cyrille Regis. Aptly, Coventry's winner was a spectacular mess. Latching onto a David Phillips flicked header, Keith Houchen (or 'Whochin', as many commentators still described him), wriggled past United defender Billy Garton, used his legs to block Mike Duxbury's clearance, toe-poked a shot that goalkeeper Chris Turner saved, inadvertently blocked the rebound with his face and then toe-poked the ball home to send Coventry's travelling hordes wild. City's victory ended any chance of new manager Alex Ferguson – who'd been appointed four months earlier – winning a trophy in his first season at Old Trafford. A Mickey Gynn goal saw off Stoke City at the Victoria Ground in the fifth round, before the Sky Blues brushed Sheffield Wednesday aside 3–1 at Hillsborough. Cyrille Regis surged forwards to thump in the opener, before Houchen sprang into action. On seventy-eight minutes, he hammered home a deflected effort before then charging down a weak clearance, striding into the box and slotting home. 'Whochin' was now officially Houchen.

Coventry returned to Hillsborough for the semi-final to face Billy Bremner's Leeds United. For Cyrille Regis, it would be his third FA Cup semi-final, and he was desperate to reach Wembley after two unsuccessful previous attempts with West Bromwich Albion.

Cyrille Regis had, by his own admission, 'a nightmare afternoon', missing three sitters. But fortunately goalkeeper Steve Ogrizovic played the game of his life, making point-blank saves to deny Leeds striker John Pearson and defender Brendan Ormsby. Then there was Dave Bennett, who was 'hyped up and ready to go', as he put it. With Leeds 1–0 up at the break thanks to David Rennie's header, Bennett kept the ball live in the second half after a scramble and nudged it across to Micky Gynn, who fired home. Houchen gave the Sky Blues a 2–1 lead, before a late equaliser from Keith Edwards sent the game into extra time. With the clock ticking down, Bennett scored from close range to take Coventry City to Wembley for the first time in their 104-year history. They'd face Tottenham, who'd hammered Watford 4–1 in the other semi-final at Villa Park. 'I felt that our moment had come,' Bennett said. 'In 1981, I'd played in the Manchester City team that lost to Tottenham after a replay. I was determined that history wouldn't repeat itself.'

Before the showdown with Tottenham, for whom midfielder Glenn Hoddle would be making his final appearance before departing to Monaco, the media machine whirred into action. First of all, there was the obligatory FA Cup final record, which the Coventry team performed on *Blue Peter*. Bobbing up and down and grinning at the camera, the Coventry players had a wail of a time blasting out 'Go for It' – which peaked at No. 61 in the charts. The mood was slightly teeth clenching. Mark Curry – he of the oversized '80s glasses and the mullet – observed: 'Doesn't Dave Bennett look like Michael Jackson, minus the glove?' Coventry's carefree ditty, with its 'Sky Blues, shooting to win', was in marked contrast with Tottenham's more triumphalist offering. A week earlier, they'd also appeared on *Blue Peter* with Chas & Dave to perform 'Hot Shot Tottenham!' David Pleat's team's confidence was buoyed by the fact that at the time, they were English football's most successful FA Cup team. This was borne out in the lyrics, which included the line: 'Seven times we've won the cup, and No. 8 is coming up, we're hot-shot Tottenham.'

TV crews zoned in on a buzzing Highfield Road, visiting the Sky Blues on the day they beat reigning champions Liverpool 1–0 thanks due to a Nick Pickering goal in front of their biggest crowd for six years, which generated record gate receipts of £101,000. The cameras also followed the team down to Bournemouth for their spa session. George Curtis – still looking every inch the 'tank of a man', as David Coleman described him in the '60s – ran straight into the freezing sea. 'I thought I'd set an example and get the old blood pumping. Most of them stayed on the beach, the soft bastards!' he smiled.

Seven matches unbeaten in the lead-up to the final Coventry may have been, but Tottenham, with their glittering array of international stars, were overwhelming favourites. 'Artisans v. Artists' was one unfavourable comparison in the tabloids between the two teams. But even though reliable full-back Brian Borrows was ruled out with injury, Sillett and Curtis headed down the motorway to their FA Cup hideaway, confident that in the contest between 'the pit pony and the derby favourite' – as the *Mirror* put it – Coventry would come out on top.

Footballers are a superstitious bunch, but by his own admission, John Sillett always took things to extremes. Fixated on lucky pants, suits, teacups, biscuits and meals in the lead-up to the final, Sillett had not only got it into his head that the players needed to be near a river on the day but that they also needed to see a wedding. 'The boys thought I was barmy', he told me, 'and George rolled his eyes at me.' Sillett's wishes were easily fulfilled. Coventry players enjoyed their brief residence at their plush hotel in Marlow, which sits on the Thames. After breakfast, Sillett discovered that a wedding was scheduled to take place at the church opposite the hotel. Immediately, a boat was dispatched to bring the newly betrothed couple back to meet the team, clad in their baby blue and burgundy striped Adidas tracksuits. Skipper Kilcline presented the bride (Mrs Mark Duffy) with a huge bouquet of flowers. 'Will Kilcline wear it for the match?' asked smooth operator Des Lynam on *Grandstand* after 'Killer' removed her garter. Attention now turned to the game.

En route to Wembley in their natty bus, the Coventry City card school – for once – downed their hands to soak up the experience. Sillett promptly told them to start dealing, partly for superstitious reasons but also because he wanted the players' routine to remain the same. Only when the bus began to crawl down Wembley Way did 'Snoz' tell them to put the cards away. 'I'll never forget the sight – there was sky blue everywhere,' said Brian Kilcline. Walking up the Wembley tunnel was similarly awe inspiring. 'You emerge into the sunshine and everything explodes like a firework. The cheers, the chants, the colour, the whole spectacle. Amazing sensory overload,' Cyrille Regis recalled. As well as instructing his players to fully immerse themselves in the Wembley experience, John Sillett warned his players NOT to concede an early goal. They didn't heed his advice. After just two minutes, Tottenham's Chris Waddle curled in a pinpoint cross for Clive Allen to notch his forty-ninth goal of the season. 'Some of us looked at each other with a "uh-oh" look, like it might be one of those days,' Regis said. The Sky Blues were level seven minutes later, when Dave Bennett rounded Ray Clemence and fired home an equaliser. For the second year in a row (Liverpool's Ian Rush had scuttled it in '86), the TV camera in the corner of the net was sent flying. After that, it was a fluid, tit-for-tat encounter, with both sides creating several chances. Tottenham went in at half-time 2–1 up, with Brian Kilcline inadvertently diverting the ball into his own net following a tangle with Gary Mabbutt.

On sixty-three minutes, Houchen's moment arrived. From an enormous downfield hoof by Steve Ogrizovic (who'd actually scored from a monstrous punt on a windy day against Sheffield Wednesday a year before), Regis flicked the ball onto Houchen, who nudged the ball wide. The jinking Dave Bennett curled in a pearler of a cross ('One of my very best', Bennett told me), at which point Houchen launched himself at the ball. His connection was faultless. On the photo, with his head brushing leather, he appears to be smiling, as if the outcome is preordained. After watching the ball nestle in the back of the net, Houchen admitted to feeling 'completely disoriented'. As he pogoed up and down behind the goal in front of the jubilant Coventry fans, he did so alone. 'It was a boiling hot day,' explained Brian Kilcline, 'and we were trying to conserve our energy. We left the celebration to Keith!' There was just time for Brian Kilcline to practically obliterate Gary Mabbutt with an awful tackle that saw the Coventry skipper tear a thigh muscle. 'The referee Neil Midgley asked me what I thought I was bloody doing,' Kilcline explained. 'He let me off without even a booking, and I was subbed soon after.'

When the referee blew for the end of normal time, John Sillett invoked the spirit of Alf Ramsey at the 1966 World Cup final when he instructed his tired players to look across to the exhausted Tottenham stars. 'They're out on their feet,' he yelled. 'Stand up you lot, and don't leave Wembley with any regrets.'

Coventry's winner wasn't a thing of beauty; Lloyd McGrath's cross was deflected over Ray Clemence by Gary Mabbutt's left knee, spawning the title of a popular Coventry fanzine in the late '80s. The Sky Blues had done it. The stricken Brian Kilcline hauled himself up the thirty-five steps to lift the cup, and on the pitch, John Sillett later held it aloft and blew kisses to the crowd. 'The feeling amongst so many of us was that finally – we'd actually won something. It was a mixture of relief and joy,' said David Bennett.

The mood in the opposition camp was anything but jubilant. Holsten officials were apoplectic that some Tottenham players – inexplicably – played without the Holsten logo adorning their chests. Sillett and Curtis had heard a rumour that Tottenham's post-final celebration plans had been drawn up well in advance of the game itself. Fans had, apparently, been invited to giant marquees at White Hart Lane before the parade down Tottenham High Road. 'We thought Spurs felt they had this one in the bag,' George Curtis told me, 'and we told our players all about it.' I asked Curtis whether he'd checked whether the rumours were actually true. 'Of course we bloody didn't,' Curtis grinned.

Back in Coventry, the party began in earnest. Police cars were clad in sky-blue balloons, the fountain in the city centre was dyed blue, and the cathedral's bells pealed for the first time in 100 years. In the weeks that followed Coventry's victory, bosses at the Peugeot factory noted an increase in productivity. 'Everybody was just blissfully… happy,' said John Sillett, with tears in his eyes. 'How often can you say that?'

THE CRAZY GANG

'Tony – do you expect us to come here just to please you, the media? Because we don't come here to please you. We come here to win.'
WIMBLEDON MANAGER BOBBY GOULD TO THE BBC'S TONY GUBBA AFTER THE 1988 FA CUP FINAL

Wembley – May 1988. It's the hottest day of the year so far. With the thermometer tipping ninety degrees pitch-side, Wimbledon goalkeeper Dave Beasant, wearing long sleeves and white gloves, appears a tad overdressed. Now, with his team 1–0 up in the FA Cup final, he's really got something to sweat about. Standing in front of him, with the ball placed on the penalty spot, is Liverpool striker John Aldridge, who's scored five out of five spot kicks for his team so far this season. The Republic of Ireland forward's penalties have been notable for his 'shuffle' before he takes them. It's a ruse to get the goalkeeper to commit to diving left or right, leaving him free to slot the ball the other way. Beasant reckons Aldridge looks nervous. Aldridge steps up and, after the faintest of dummies, places the ball firmly to Beasant's left. It's a good height for the man they call 'Lurch'. The Dons skipper guesses correctly and parries the ball away. As Beasant is congratulated by teammates, Aldridge sinks to his knees in frustration. Wimbledon, who were promoted from the Fourth Division five years earlier, are thirty minutes from achieving a fairy tale result against the best team in England. Albeit a fairy tale with a distinctly '80s flavour.

• • •

A decade or so after Wimbledon's crowning glory, fans at a nostalgia evening lapped up the stories told by their former skipper, who played in all four divisions for the club. The mop of curls may have gone, but David Beasant's hands are the size of shovels, his customary toothy grin as wide as the room, and when he stands up, he literally towers over everyone else there. He really is a giant of a man. No wonder John Aldridge looked worried. Beasant literally filled the goal.

Many of his stories about the Dons' scarcely credible rise to glory tended to revolve around Dave 'Harry' Bassett, who, as well as steering Wimbledon to two promotions, 'made me the man I am today', Beasant said. It was Bassett who introduced the long-ball game at Plough Lane. 'And anyone who doesn't like it can fuck off,' he told his Dons players. Most put up with it, although as midfielder Wally Downes said: 'It wasn't a popular decision at the time.' Under Bassett, Wimbledon mastered the dark arts. 'We'd do anything to get an edge,' he admitted. The opposition's changing room was tampered with; the heating turned up too high in warm weather or switched off in the winter. Salt in the sugar bowl for half-time cups of tea. And 'shithousing on the pitch', as one Dons fan put it. 'We always reckoned that we were at our most vulnerable when we'd just scored,' Beasant said. 'So someone would go down injured and kill time, annoy the opposition, or we'd put the ball to bed. Literally lamp it out of the ground. Anything to disrupt the flow of the game.'

In the 2015 BT Sport movie *The Crazy Gang*, the limelight is, perhaps unsurprisingly, hogged by the Dons' former big beasts – striker John Fashanu, who for reasons best known to himself is clad in a Swedish national team tracksuit, and midfielder Vinnie Jones, dressed as a country squire. In the Premier League era, Fashanu would find fame outside football as presenter of *Gladiators*, and Jones as an alpha male actor in gangster flicks like *Lock, Stock and Two Smoking Barrels*. Their tales are replete with stories of the Dons' combative approach. 'Fash the Bash' speaks of himself and Jones as 'warlords' and repeatedly slaps his hands together to emphasise the combative nature of the team's playing style. He tells wild stories of beating up an unnamed teammate in the dressing room. ('So what, Adam,' Fashanu says to his interviewer, 'No one died, Adam. It's part of the game, my man.') Vinnie Jones, who'd been working as a hod carrier and playing part time for Wealdstone until Bassett snapped him up at the start of the 1986–87 campaign, brags about squeezing Paul Gascoigne's cojones and telling him to 'stay there', whilst he took a throw-in. The infamous photograph, with a demonic-looking Jones, his hair shaved at the sides, his tattooed arm taut, applying pressure to Gascoigne's nether regions with the utmost relish appeared to sum up Wimbledon's approach to the game. As Wimbledon prepared to bombard their opponents aerially, Jones (still generally known as Vince until the 1987–88 season), would scream: 'Put it in the mixer.' Marshall arts expert Fashanu discusses his loathing of Lawrie Sanchez, and there is a plethora of tales about new Dons signings being forcibly starved for days, locked in car boots, and the 'hazing' meted out to new signings like the well-spoken John Scales.

After the documentary was released, the quieter members of the squad claimed that the image of the Wimbledon team as a collection of knuckle-scraping meatheads did them a huge disservice. Some of the original Crazy Gang (a moniker given to them not by John Motson, as is often stated, but by *Mirror* journalist Tony Stenson) who were present and correct as Bassett's side began their remarkable ascent up the leagues, like Steve Galliers and Bryan Gale, were simply airbrushed from history. As he watched the BT documentary on Boxing Day 2014, Dave Bassett's mobile phone lit up with irate former players complaining about how the club was portrayed. Bassett later said that Fashanu 'tucked us all up … He disrespected his former teammates.' Great television it may have been, but as one member of the squad told me: 'I wasn't party to any of what Fash said.'

The story of their path to Wembley glory is – for the most part – slightly more nuanced than communal thuggery winning the day. With a view to putting the record straight, Dave Bassett, along with Wally Downes, wrote a book, also called *The Crazy Gang*, that aimed to put the story straight, and give other former players their voice. Sometimes, though, Bassett couldn't help himself. At an event to publicise the book that I attended, he described the club as 'the borstal of football', 'raggedy-arsed Rovers' and 'the dirty dozen'. But he also discussed the parts that the BT documentary chose not to reach. Under Bassett, Dons players were instructed to complete their preliminary coaching qualification to 'think about the game in a more technical way', Bassett said. In the early '80s, statistics analyst Neil Lanham, a former acolyte of long-ball pioneer Charles Reep and one of the first to use home computers to analyse patterns of passing, contacted Dave Bassett. He outlined his conclusion that most goals either came from dead-ball situations or moves comprising four passes or less. It was, in effect, Charles Reep's philosophy. Bassett believed the long-ball game would give his side an edge. 'Dave asked me not to share these findings with any outside parties. It was all very much under the radar', Lanham told me. There was also Vince Craven's video analysis. The club paid out £10,000 (a major outlay back then) for Craven to install video editing equipment in his house. Wimbledon players embraced the cutting-edge, pre-Opta/Prozone approach. 'We were twenty years ahead of our time', Bassett told me, 'although the players grew a little tired of the video analysis. But adopting the long ball approach was based on the science and the analysis, and the thinking behind it, not just on a whim.'

When Bassett announced, after guiding the Dons to eighth place in their inaugural season in the top flight, that he was taking over at Watford in the summer of '87, Dave Beasant was one of the Dons players who pinned 'Harry' against the wall and informed him that he wasn't going anywhere. But, reasoned Bassett, he'd taken the club as far as he could. Things worked out rather better for Wimbledon than for Bassett, whose new club sank without trace in the 1987–88 campaign and were relegated. The Dons, on the other hand, were Wembley bound.

• • •

When Bobby Gould took over at Plough Lane from Bassett in the 1987 close season, he convinced former England and Arsenal coach Don Howe to join him, initially on a trial basis. Having heard all the stories about the Dons through the football grapevine though, Howe was unsure. 'I'd been spoilt with England and the Arsenal,' he told me. 'But the Wimbledon players really impressed me with their willingness to learn. They were better players than they were given credit for. And they knew how to get an edge.' Gould, Howe and the team got the measure of each other on a pre-season trip to Scandinavia. Unhappy with the stuffy motel they were staying in, the Dons' management duo told the tour manager to upgrade them to a four-star hotel. David Beasant explained: 'It showed that Bobby and Don had high standards. We were First Division now.' Using a whiteboard, Howe stood up and delivered his forensically prepared tactical notes. After letting him speak, and much to his surprise, the 'big cheeses' (as Howe described them), then stood up and delivered their piece. Fashanu, Jones, Beasant, Lawrie Sanchez and Alan Cork spoke of how they were willing to listen to Howe's approaches to closing down space, and set pieces, but that they wouldn't be changing their direct style as it had got them so far already. 'There was no point getting annoyed,' Howe told me. 'I actually thought it was quite an enlightened way of doing things, and they showed they'd got a good handle on tactics and leadership.' Howe visibly relaxed when reminiscing about the Dons, admitting to regularly checking his shoes to make sure 'nothing warm and brown had been dropped inside them'. He found it hilarious when, with the players training on a public park, the ball rolled into a pile of dog mess, and half of it ended up smeared on Dave Beasant's face when it was blasted in his direction. 'It wouldn't have happened at Arsenal, that's for sure,' Howe laughed, 'and I enjoyed it there [at Wimbledon] as it was so different.'

There were moments in the FA Cup run that were pure down-at-heel Wimbledon, like when Bobby Gould and Dave Beasant had to run the final half a mile to Mansfield's ground before the fourth-round clash to hand in their team sheet for the match. 'We'd got a fine pending for our disciplinary record, and we couldn't afford to pay another one for failing to hand in the team sheet in time,' Beasant said. Before the semi-final with Luton Town at White Hart Lane, with Gould driving the minibus, the car park attendant told him to 'disappear' as whichever footballers were in the bus clearly weren't a team one step from Wembley. For London matches, many Dons players made their own way to games to save the club from having to hire a full-size team bus. But other facets, like Beasant's penalty save at Mansfield when his team was struggling in the mud, and the backs-to-the-wall win at St James's Park against Newcastle in the fifth round, with the home crowd baying for Vinnie Jones's blood after 'cojones-gate', were a clear portent of what was to come in the final.

In the build-up to the showpiece match, the BBC sent a reporter to Wimbledon to ask locals what they made of the unfashionable Dons reaching Wembley. Most glanced uncomprehendingly at the camera and shrugged. One man had at least heard of 'Fanashu', as he kept calling him. But cup-final fever did not grip that part of London, although the players did shoot a *Clothes Show* segment with Jeff Banks, when they were measured for their suits. Nonetheless, the local environs played a big part in the day before and of the final. Wimbledon players agreed that rather than hold the post-match celebration in central London, they'd have their do, whatever the result, at Plough Lane. 'We only wanted family and friends there. Not hangers-on,' midfielder Lawrie Sanchez said. They'd also stay at the upmarket Cannizaro House hotel, situated near the common. On the subject of Wimbledon Common, the players had wanted to perform a rock 'n' roll version of the theme song from *The Wombles* for their FA Cup final song, but it never materialised. Instead, they trotted out a rather meek effort, entitled 'We Are Wimbledon', which failed to resonate with the general public. This was in marked contrast to the Anfield Rap, created by midfielder Craig Johnston. Clad in skew-wiff baseball caps and chain bling, it was a nod to the growth in popularity of rap in the UK and the mainstream success of acts like Run DMC and LL Cool J. 'Just the letter "C" missing before the second word "Saint"', harrumphed Jimmy Greaves on *Saint & Greavsie*. Execrable it may have been, but at least it shifted a good few thousand copies. Gould's men would not come off second best in the final.

On the morning of the game, Great Uncle Bulgaria was present and correct to wave off the Dons players as they left their hotel. So was Eric Hall, puffing away on his giant cigar like a real-life Del Boy and telling the players to product place for the cameras like their lives depended on it, lest the deals he'd struck for them were deemed null and void. The players were well rested. Many of them had been sent down to the village pub after dinner the night before by Bobby Gould because they were bored and misbehaving – lobbing bread rolls at their manager when he was being interviewed by the BBC's Bob Wilson. 'We never drunk as much as the press claimed,' Beasant told chortling Dons fans at the celebration evening. 'Just enough to settle us down a bit.'

Given 'special assignments' by Don Howe, the players were fully prepared and were to adopt their usual tactics of relentless harrying, but Howe pushed it further still. Terry Gibson, signed from Manchester United for a whopping £200,000, was given the job of closing down Alan Hansen. 'Don Howe said that Hansen was their first line of attack as he was so good on the ball, so I needed to shut him down,' Gibson told the audience. Dennis Wise was instructed to double-mark John Barnes, along with Clive Goodyear. Gibson played with a broken foot. 'I didn't want to say anything before the match because getting it X-rayed would blow my cover,' Gibson said. 'I even slept in my boot because I knew my foot would swell and otherwise I wouldn't be able to put it on next day.' Jones and Fashanu reckoned they had the game won in the tunnel, snarling, glaring and gurning at the league champions, but even the pair's former teammates didn't back up those claims. 'There were chants of "Yidaho!" which was our war cry,' Dave Beasant said. 'But that's about it.' Early on, in what must surely be the most '80s of challenges, Vinnie Jones put a marker down and sent Steve McMahon flying with a premeditated scythe. After landing heavily, McMahon smashed Jones in the face with his elbow, cutting his opponent's cheek. Honours even. The game was hardly a classic, but two key moments reflected Wimbledon's forensic preparation.

When they were awarded a free kick after thirty-seven minutes, Dons players knew what to do. At Don Howe's behest, they'd had a two-hour set-piece training session the day before. Dennis Wise swung in the free kick, and Lawrie Sanchez flicked home the ball with his head. 'I shouldn't have been there, to be honest. Alan Cork had forgotten where he should have been,' Sanchez said. 'And your celebration was crap,' Dave Beasant told him. 'It wasn't the best,' Sanchez admitted. Appearing shocked at what he'd done, the delighted Wise jumped into his arms. At half-time, Don Howe took over, instructing the players to place iced towels over their heads, the trick he'd picked up at the last two World Cups with England. Liverpool's penalty should never have been awarded. Clive Goodyear timed his sliding challenge to perfection, but John Aldridge tripped over his legs. Howe and Beasant had studied Aldridge's technique at length prior to the match, and Beasant vowed that he wouldn't commit until after the Liverpool striker had done his 'shuffle'. 'I had to see it through, to stand still and then I'd have half a chance.' Beasant did his homework to perfection, stood firm and became the first goalkeeper to save a penalty in an FA Cup final. Liverpool turned the screw in the final half hour, but the Dons held on to record a famous victory. As John Motson uttered his famous 'and the crazy gang have beaten the culture club' piece of commentary, and Wimbledon's players embraced on the pitch, a delighted Don Howe reflected on a job well done. 'For me, it wasn't a David v. Goliath encounter. We'd finished seventh in the league. We were a bloody good team that grafted our backsides off.'

After hoisting the trophy aloft, and Dennis Wise had yelled 'Oi oi, you bastards' a few yards away from a grinning Princess Diana, the team embarked on their lap of honour. By then the stadium, consisting mainly of Liverpool fans, had largely emptied. Each Wimbledon season ticket holder could apply for four tickets, a good deal of which had fallen into the hands of touts. Estimates suggested that there were no more than 12,000 Dons fans in the ground. The rest were Liverpool supporters. By Crazy Gang standards, the celebration on the Plough Lane pitch with their families that balmy evening was tame. 'But for us, it was perfect,' said Lawrie Sanchez, who ordered all the Sunday newspapers he could back at Cannizaro House, just so he could bask in the headlines next morning. The trophy parade, in front of an estimated 25,000 fans, ended with Dave Beasant clutching the trophy at the town hall and telling the ecstatic supporters: 'See you all at Plough Lane next season.' Except, things didn't quite work out that way.

For a start, Plough Lane couldn't have accommodated all of them, and in any case, crowds remained stuck around the 8,000 average. The cup final was Dave Beasant's final match for the Dons ('There are worse ways to finish,' he said) as he and defender Andy Thorn were sold to Newcastle for a combined £1.5 million to balance the books. Owner Sam Hammam made repeated noises about the need for the club to leave Plough Lane to generate more income and they departed in 1991 to groundshare with Crystal Palace. The club wouldn't return to Wimbledon for twenty-five years. The Football League opened the possibility for other Wimbledon-type fairy tales to happen in 1986 by scrapping the system of re-election at the end of each season. Instead, the winner of the fifth tier would gain automatic promotion and the team finishing bottom of the Fourth Division would go down. Scarborough were the first club to gain automatic promotion, but almost forty years later, only Luton Town have emulated Wimbledon's feat of going from fifth tier to top flight.

In some ways, Wimbledon's often loutish exploits were the very embodiment of English football in an era of hooliganism at home and abroad. Watching footage of Vinnie Jones's infamous sliding tackle on Tottenham's Gary Stevens in late '88, as Stevens tussled with John Fashanu, football writer Jim White described it as 'hod carrying filth.' Critics feared that their extreme style of play would, like Japanese knotweed, take root in and ultimately ruin English football. But aside from John Beck's Cambridge United in the early '90s that didn't happen. Yet the criticism still rained down. 'Wimbledon are killing the dreams that made football the world's greatest game,' argued Terry Venables.

Dave Beasant took a different view: 'We showed every small club what could be done without spending a fortune. We were role models for others.' And judging from the rapturous applause in the room after he'd said it, there wasn't anyone in the room who disagreed.

16

THE FANS, THE FANZINES AND THE INFLATABLES

THE INFLATABLES

'Football-wise, the banana craze happened in a different universe.'

IAN BRIGHTWELL

The Hawthorns – October 1988. Behind the goal, there's a murmur amongst Manchester City fans who have travelled to see their young team play West Bromwich Albion. Then it becomes a rumpus. Even the City players get distracted from the game and turn around to see what all the commotion is about. On one side of a gaggle of fans, an enormous blow-up Frankenstein's monster has just been hoisted aloft. On the other, a gigantic dinosaur appears. After edging slowly toward one another, Frankie and Dino have become embroiled in a full-on brawl, much to the delight of City fans, who are chanting 'Dino, Dino' or 'Frankie, Frankie' depending on which side they are standing. Goading them on, hordes of City fans jab both monsters with their inflatable bananas. Just as it seems things couldn't get any stranger, a blow-up dinghy and a giant fried egg are hurled into the mix too. The inflatables craze is in full swing.

• • •

Amidst the depressing backdrop of hooliganism and the imminent threat of ID cards, grounds during the 1988–89 campaign could be downbeat, grey and sometimes largely deserted. On the face of it, life could have been especially grim for Manchester City fans, given that this was now the second consecutive campaign they'd competed in the Second Division. But City still had the sixth-highest average attendance across the four divisions and, in their shiny sky-blue kit, had harvested a rich crop of English talent from their youth team, including lightning-quick winger David White, midfielder Paul Lake – tipped for an England call-up – and forward Paul Moulden, who'd plundered an absurdly high number of goals at youth-team level and was now scoring for the first team too. A year before, they put an eye-catching ten goals past Malcolm Macdonald's Huddersfield Town, with Paul Stewart (who was sold to Tottenham at season's end), Tony Adcock and David White each grabbing a hat-trick. But what also caught the eye was the fact that on the terraces, City fans really had gone bananas.

The inflatables craze was the most remarkable of the late-'80s football fads because, unlike the Mexican wave, hundreds of which now rippled around English stadia during quiet moments during matches, or strikers' penchant for aeroplane-styled celebrations, copied from Brazil striker Careca, it wasn't influenced by the 1986 World Cup in Mexico. Instead, it originated from a bet between Manchester City fan Frank Newton and his friend Allen Busby. During a visit to Busby's house, Newton spotted an inflatable banana and asked if he could 'borrow' it. Allen replied: 'Only if you take it to a City match.' 'That was exactly what I intended to do anyway, so the deal was sealed.' He recalled some amusement amongst the supporters around him at City's match against Plymouth Argyle. 'Being the type of person I am, if I start doing something, I'll continue doing it,' Newton told me, 'and it took on a life of its own after that.'

Another friend – Mike Clare – penned a face on the banana, adding a bobble hat and a City shirt for good measure. Then came the incident that made the whole fad literally go viral. With City fans chanting for the introduction of substitute striker Imre Varadi, Newton hoisted his banana aloft. The chant changed from 'Imre Varadi' to 'Imre Banana'. 'The whole thing was totally spontaneous,' Newton said. 'I never originally brought the inflatable along in homage to Imre, contrary to what's often been written.' Soon, there were bunches of inflatables proliferating across Maine Road and at their away matches.

Visually, the effect on the largely monochrome terraces and stands of the late '80s – an era before replica and retro kits were commonplace – was stunning. Novelty shops in the area quickly sold out of inflatable bananas. City's tiny club shop, with its battered front door, managed by Janice Monk, stocked a job lot of them but repeatedly ran out. The craze fitted perfectly with the fact that Manchester City were regarded as a little alternative. 'To support City back then, you had to go against the trend and have a mind of your own. There were rather easier options in the north-west when it came to supporting football clubs,' Frank Newton said. In contrast to the middle of the road dirge blared out by most stadium Tannoys in that era, the Maine Road sound system went all 'Madchester' – blaring out hits by local bands the Happy Mondays, the Stone

Roses and The Charlatans. Young City players, who sometimes also strutted their stuff at the country's most hip nightclub – the Hacienda – fully embraced the craze, tossing fully inflated bananas into the crowd on a couple of occasions. 'I thought it was brilliant,' explained former defender Ian Brightwell. 'It was about having fun and expressing yourself, which football should be all about.'

The inflatables craze quickly spread. West Ham fans started taking blow-up hammers to games; Bury fans, black puddings; Grimsby Town fans, haddocks; and even some Manchester United fans got in on the act, taking inflatable Red Devils into Old Trafford with them. City fanzines *King of the Kippax* and *Blueprint* were influential in whipping up the craze, and a *Daily Mirror* article suggested that in an era of fences and hooliganism, the inflatables craze was just the job. 'Bananas To You Maggie,' ran a *Mirror* headline. Newton – an assistant computer analyst – was labelled a 'banana boffin' who'd instigated the 'Bananarama craze'.

Satirical comic *Viz* got in on the act, with its cartoon strip about Tommy 'banana' Johnson. The titular character Tommy would unhelpfully offer his giant banana to people in order to solve their problems. Each strip ended with Tommy having the giant banana inserted into him by an irate policeman. I asked Frank Newton if City fans encountered similar opposition to the bananas at grounds. 'Crystal Palace objected on the grounds they thought it was racist,' Newton explained, 'which it most certainly wasn't.' Arsenal became the first club to ban the bananas, on the grounds they obstructed spectators' views. But after a last-day inflatables hurrah at Bradford City's Valley Parade on the afternoon City sealed promotion back to the top flight in 1989 ('We passed a pick-up truck on the M62, and there, in an inflated paddling pool at the back were some City fans, swigging cans of beer and saluting us,' recalled Ian Brightwell), the craze had petered out. 'It ran its course, like all fads do,' Frank Newton said. 'And suddenly, there were no inflatables at games.'

But City fans of that era will always remember with affection the beautiful and bizarre Boxing Day clash with Stoke City at the Victoria Ground in 1988. Some 12,000 supporters piled down the M6 in full fancy-dress mode, dressed as penguins, superheroes and Father Christmas, clutching bananas, paddling pools, giant golf clubs and crocodiles. 'It was,' reckoned City fan David Wright, 'the most glorious, eclectic sight I ever saw at a football match.' Tipped off that the Victoria Ground was about to be invaded, Stoke allocated both the Butler Street End and the Stoke End paddocks to the visiting fans. To the embarrassment of City's players, Stoke comprehensively beat them 3–1 despite the raucous atmosphere created by their fans. 'There were fellas dressed as clowns on the terraces,' recalled Paul Lake, 'but sadly there were eleven clowns on the pitch in sky-blue shirts. We let them down badly.' *Blue Print* founder Mike Kelly was at the game dressed as a Canadian Mountie and ended up standing in the middle of the street directing the traffic. One burly man wandered past Frank Newton outside the ground dressed in just a nappy. 'It was very surreal,' Newton said. 'But then, supporting City in those days often was.'

These days, Manchester City are all-conquering, and football, says Newton, 'is completely mainstream, with little scope to push the outer bounds of normality.' That said, the club have recently paid homage to the city's 'Madchester' past, incorporating Ben Kelly's black and yellow Hacienda pillar design into the sleeves of their 2018–19 away kit. In 2016, for a League Cup clash with Everton at the Etihad Stadium, the club announced it would be a banana-themed evening. Lads and lasses of a certain age dusted down their inflatables from nearly thirty years before and headed to the match. It was a reminder of an era when, with football fans vilified and the game's image seemingly tarnished beyond repair, the inflatables craze put a smile back on some fans' faces and showed that going to football matches could actually be fun.

And more than a little bizarre.

THE RED CARDS

'It's all about taking small steps.'

GED GREBBY, FOUNDER OF SHOW RACISM THE RED CARD

St James's Park – 1 January 1985. It's a distinctly bad day at the office for Sunderland. Winless over the busy Christmas period, a hat-trick from Newcastle's Peter Beardsley consigns them to a 3–1 defeat. To make matters worse, Len Ashurst's team also have two players – forward Howard Gayle and defender Gary Bennett – sent off in the second half. Although the brief television highlights edit out the white noise, the torrent of racist abuse that pours down from the terraces and stands as Sunderland's two black players trudge disconsolately off the pitch is ferocious even by the standards of the time. Appalled by what he hears and sees, Newcastle fan Ged Grebby, looking on from the stands, decides to do something about it. His actions, as well as those of Gary Bennett and Howard Gayle, will have long-term consequences in the fight against racism at football grounds.

• • •

Political currents swirled around St James's Park in the mid '80s. Former miner Jack Charlton, manager for the 1985–86 campaign, was a fervent supporter of the striking miners during their long-running campaign. On *Wogan*, World Cup winner Jack Charlton confirmed he would strike if he were in their position: 'Those lads, they're just trying to save jobs and their communities.' Charlton allowed striking miners to use his car during the dispute and donated generously to the fund to support the miners' families. Perhaps less well known was Charlton's stance against racism. In tandem with Brian Clough, 'Big Jack' was a sponsor and founding member of the Anti-Nazi League, signing the organisation's founding statement in 1977. Whilst at both Sheffield Wednesday and Newcastle, Charlton could sometimes be seen handing out leaflets outside the clubs' respective grounds, and Clough was often to be seen on the banks of the River Trent doing likewise.

Clough allowed the Anti-Nazi League to run adverts in the Nottingham Forest programme in the early '80s. As for Charlton, he said during our interview: 'I always told my players that they shouldn't be using racist language. If I heard something I didn't like I'd give them a bloody earful that they wouldn't forget.' But despite Charlton's best efforts, he was powerless to loosen the National Front's foothold at St James's Park. Kevin Keegan was the first Newcastle player to directly address the issue, ripping up a National Front leaflet at a press conference in 1984. 'It was a huge moment,' Ged Grebby told me. 'In those days, Keegan was such big news that if he sneezed it made front-page headlines, so him ripping up the leaflet sent out a real message.' Grebby, a Newcastle regular since the late '70s, recalls National Front literature being distributed outside the ground before most matches. 'The publication was called *The Flag*. One front page had a picture of a monkey on the front. The strapline read: "Do you want this man to take your job?" It was the norm outside many grounds in the '80s, unfortunately.'

A polytechnic student, Grebby was already active in the Youth Against Racism in Europe movement and was appalled at how racist language and gesturing was the norm at football matches in that era. On 1 January 1985, what was shocking wasn't so much what was shouted, because, as Gary Bennett said: 'I'd heard it all before. What was remarkable was the sheer volume and intensity of it. A local derby was always going to give it extra spice.' Howard Gayle spoke of how he'd 'long since normalised whatever came at me. It was part and parcel of my job.' When they arrived in the north-east, both men recalled how few visible black faces there were. It was a shock to them because Bennett and Gayle both hailed from multicultural communities in Manchester and Liverpool respectively. As he arrived at Roker Park, with a club official in tow, a pair of Sunderland fans asked the official who Bennett was. 'He's our new signing,' they were told. 'But he's black,' came the bewildered response. The two players formed a strong bond. It was Bennett who stopped Gayle from wading into the crowd after the latter was once struck by a banana thrown from the crowd. Both men glanced at one another when the verbal barbs flew. 'We'd nod or raise an eyebrow or whatever. It meant: "I've got your back,"' Gayle said. Three years earlier, he'd played on loan for Newcastle. 'Their fans were fine with me when I was there as a player,' he recalls. 'They'd sing: "He's black, he's broon, he plays for the Toon," which at least was meant to be friendly.' But now, with Gayle a full-time Mackem, the mood towards him had changed.

Describing the abuse that the Sunderland pair received as 'a lightning-bolt moment', Grebby, along with other politically active Newcastle fans, formed Geordies Are Black and White a year later. The group's logo – a black hand clutching a white hand – was eye-catching and effective. The technique the group used to get their message across, besides handing out flyers promoting multicultur-alism, was daring. 'Ten or twenty of us would encircle whoever was distributing National Front literature, to isolate them,' Grebby told me. 'We were all about getting our point across peacefully.' Word spread about Geordies Are Black and White through the medium of Newcastle fanzines and the Football Supporters' Association (FSA), formed by Liverpool fan Rogan Taylor in the wake of the Heysel disaster. In Yorkshire, some Leeds United fans, encouraged by the *Marching on Together* fanzine, formed Leeds United v Racism. 'We felt that football should be a unifying experience, not a divisive one,' Leeds fan Tim Ogilvie said. 'I'd seen Terry Connor [a Leeds striker] get bananas thrown at him and everything yelled at him, by our own fans, and I thought: "We've got to do better than this."' Dis-tributing anti-racist literature outside Elland Road in the late '80s didn't always meet with a friendly reception, especially when they also encircled National Front members. 'We had flyers snatched off us and ripped up, there were verbal threats, and I got punched once. But it didn't deter me from what we were doing. In fact, it had the opposite effect,' Ogilvie said. Copycat anti-racist groups also sprung up amongst Millwall, West Ham and Birmingham City fans.

Geordies Are Black and White still exists today, operating under the umbrella of the Tyne and Wear Anti-Fascist Association. Ged Grebby went on to form the Show Racism the Red Card organisa-tion in 1996, with the help of a £50 donation from Newcastle United goalkeeper Shaka Hislop. Grebby is now its chief executive. As the country's leading anti-racism charity, it works extensively across the UK and plays a role in tackling racism within professional and grassroots football. Two of its leading spokesmen across northern

England are Howard Gayle and Gary Bennett, who visit schools, universities and workplaces, educating people about race, appropriate language, and discrimination.

'Football allows you through the door and has the power to engage, to get youngsters to listen,' Gary Bennett says. The message he has delivered for the best part of thirty years is a clear one: 'It can be as simple as a nickname, which can turn into bullying, then into violence. People go along with it because they want to fit in. We want them to recognise racism and feel empowered to have a conversation and speak to a trusted adult.' Howard Gayle, who also advocates for Kick It Out, remembers how isolated black players were in the '80s. 'How do you play here, lad?' he asked Chelsea midfielder Paul Canoville during Sunderland's match with Chelsea in the mid '80s when Canoville was receiving racist abuse from his own supporters. 'I don't know, I really don't know,' Canoville shrugged. Canoville's teammate Pat Nevin, who spoke to the press at the time about his horror at the unpunished abuse Canoville received during matches, was in a minority of one. Gayle argues that although many English teams are now fully multicultural, that's not the case in the dugout or the boardroom. 'The number of black people in coaching and football administration is slim. Diversity and opportunity is lacking.' When Grebby rang Gayle in 2016 to inform him that he'd been nominated for an MBE, Gayle instantly turned down the offer: 'To accept a gong from a country that built an empire based on racist beliefs and made much of its wealth from the slave trade would have gone against everything I stand for.' Grebby didn't try to convince Gayle to change his mind. Gayle also remains unforgiving when it comes to the Conservative government of the '80s. 'They talked about "managing the decline" of Liverpool as a city and then supported the police in claiming that Hillsborough was the fans' fault. I still loathe them [the Tories] with a passion.'

Our conversation returned to Gayle's work with anti-racism charities. 'People are often wide-eyed with amazement when you tell them what it was like out there on the pitch back then in the '80s,' he said. 'Small steps have been made, and the situation is far better than when I played, but there are still many battles to win.'

The fight continues.

THE FANZINES

'The football fan is not an easily defined social stereotype, whatever the tabloid cartoonists may choose to believe.'
WHEN SATURDAY COMES EDITORIAL, MAY 1989

Warwick Road – December 1989. As they head towards Old Trafford, Manchester United fans look with curiosity at what fifteen-year-old Andy Mitten is holding in his hands. 'What's that, mate?' he's asked. The aspiring journalist is holding the first copy of United fanzine *United We Stand*. It has a distinctly homemade feel. 'Make it yourself, did you, mate?' they laugh. Mitten smiles. He's borrowed £20 off his mum to help him photocopy 100 copies and typed, cut and pasted everything himself. On the front cover, there's a slightly grainy photograph of Mitten's favourite player – Mark Hughes. Underneath, the strap line (not that the inexperienced editor knows what one of those is yet) reads: 'Away Ground Review – Team of the Eighties – Ralph Milne Story.' 'Can I flick through it, mate?' Mitten's asked. Prospective punters smile as they do so. Some laugh. 'Better

than the programme, mate. Better than what's on the pitch, actually.'
They hand over their 50p pieces. 'Cheers, mate. You here next time?'
they ask. Mitten nods excitedly. As a raft of fledgling editors discover in the late '80s, there's nothing that beats the adrenaline rush of
your first sales.

The heyday of the fanzine is here.

●   ●   ●

Fanzines gestated from the carnage of the mid '80s. The Birmingham-based *Off the Ball* and London-based *When Saturday Comes* were
the first national fanzines to emerge in 1986, and Bradford City's
City Gent, launched initially as a travel guide for away fans in 1984,
was the first club-themed fanzine. The largely DIY productions
proved that being a fan didn't necessarily mean that you were a
thug, and they were an antidote to frequently insipid official club
programmes. It quickly became a vibrant, left-leaning scene, driven
by a distinctly indie philosophy. In the pre-internet era, distribution
issues were often problematic, but the fanzine movement's gradual
coagulation was helped by the presence of Sportspages – the iconic
bookshop on Charing Cross Road – and the newly formed Football
Supporters' Association (FSA). Sportspages stocked dozens of fanzine titles, and as word got out, it quickly became a mecca on Saturdays for fans of different clubs, who often left the shop with armfuls
of publications. 'In those early days, word of mouth was all important,' explained Andy Mitten. 'We struck up good relationships with
fanzine editors from other clubs whom we initially met at Sportspages.' A large number of early fanzines publicised the FSA. Their
meetings became vital meeting points for supporters who wished to

improve football's terrible reputation and those groups of fans who attended slowly became more interconnected.

Cheaper printing technology and the launch of Amstrad home computers made it far easier for aspiring football writers to see their dreams of publication come to fruition. Fanzines provided a platform for opinions and were often small-scale publications that provided an alternative slant on the far from beautiful game. By 1989, there were an estimated 250 in existence, ranging in quality, production values and ultimately longevity. Some of the fanzine titles were distinctly off-beat and owed their inspiration to musical lyrics. The most memorable was arguably Gillingham's offering, which was a line from a Half Man Half Biscuit song: *Brian Moore's Head Looks Distinctly like London Planetarium*. A Gills fan, the ITV commentator told me: 'It was the greatest honour of my life, although I was quite mystified when I first heard about it.' Pushing *Brian Moore's Head* close for bizarreness was *4,000 Holes* – the Blackburn Rovers fanzine. In 1967, John Lennon read a *Mail* article on the dreadful state of the roads in Blackburn, Lancashire. He stuck it in 'A Day in the Life' on the *Sgt. Pepper's* album, and a quarter of a century later, Blackburn fans acknowledged the cultural reference. They never did answer the question of whether there were enough of them to fill the Albert Hall, though. To complete the hat-trick of off-beat musical themed titles, Les Chapman's unusual response to the classic 'How do you feel?' question after scoring the vital goal in Preston's 1986–87 promotion push (Chapman responded: 'fifty-three miles west of Venus') represented not only a welcome change from an 'over the moon' type response and inspired the name of Preston's fanzine, but it was also a reflection of his love for the B52s song.

345

Many of the zines were irreverent, sweary (in the case of the spectacularly foul-mouthed *Five to Three*) and satirical. Initially, many had a pub-speak tone, homing in on footballers' worst haircuts (there were plenty of '80s mullets to aim at), and the worst away-day experiences, invariably focussing on terrible beer, awful weather, crumbling terracing, dilapidated trains and rancid toilets. Yet the most successful and long-lasting fanzines went well beyond the quickly exhausted seams of tomfoolery and toilet humour and had clear mission statements from the beginning. Andy Mitten, who remains *UWS* editor some thirty-five years after its launch, explains: 'I had the belief that going to watch football should be, and could be, so much better than it was.' He went on to list the key issues that needed to be addressed back then – not just at United but in football as a whole.

> Facilities at matches were awful, there was the ID scheme, rising seat prices, ticket allocations for away fans… It was a chance to raise the issues that mattered to supporters. The other thing I wanted to say was that despite how football fans were portrayed by the media, 'I am NOT a hooligan.'

When 25-year-old Charlton fan Rick Everitt launched the *Voice of the Valley* fanzine in January 1988, his aim was simple: to help the campaign to end the club's exile at Selhurst Park and get the club back to The Valley. He timed the launch of the *VOTV* perfectly. Not only was local newspaper *The Mercury* supportive of the movement to get Charlton 'home', but Everitt told me: 'With Thatcher trying to bring in ID cards and the like, swathes of fans were way more politically conscious than they previously had been.' On selling those first copies to Nottingham (Forest), Everitt recalled: 'I moved my way around the carriage and explained what it was all about. Everyone bought a copy. Literally. There was a real clamour. It was fantastic, because I'd always wanted to start a fanzine, but I never lost sight of what its long-term aim was.' The original print run was just 500. It eventually sold 1,100, necessitating a hasty reprint. A year later, when the club confirmed its plan to return to The Valley, it sold 3,600 copies. 'Not bad, considering our gates at Selhurst Park were around the 6,000 mark,' Everitt said. When I asked Everitt why he felt it had resonated so well, he responded: 'Because there was more hard information about the situation with the ground in there than in the programme. I'm not great at writing about just the football. My passion is focussing on the politics that lie behind it.' By the end of the decade, the *VOTV* helped organise the Valley Party, which put up sixty candidates for sixty-two seats in the 1990 local council elections. After securing 15,000 votes, Greenwich Council finally approved the club's plans for the redevelopment of the Addicks' ramshackle stadium, and Charlton returned in 1992. 'It would be an exaggeration to claim that the fanzine was responsible for the club's return to The Valley, but it certainly brought pressure to bear,' Everitt said.

If one publication captured the mood amongst many supporters in the late '80s, it was *When Saturday Comes*. Founded by music shop employees Mike Ticher and Andy Lyons (who remains editor) in 1986, *WSC* 'was founded with a view to repairing the bad image in which football was held', explained Lyons. 'We wanted to provide a platform for the views of intelligent fans who felt passionate about the game.' Lyons cited the indie music zines of the mid '80s as the main inspiration behind founding the fanzine, rather than *Foul*, the short-lived publication from the '70s. By 1988, *WSC* had a healthy circulation of around 5,000 copies per month. From the outset, *WSC* was imbued with the true fanzine spirit. Its tagline – The People – plastered across the shirt of the running man on the front, reinforced the fact that it was written from a supporter's eye view. It always backed supporter campaigns and cast a beady eye on football hierarchies. In time, its caustic take provided an invigorating new template for football writing. But, as Mike Ticher alluded to in his opening editorial, much which passed for journalism in the late '80s was 'cliched, hackneyed and lazy' and tended to tar football supporters with the same broad brush.

WSC's famous front cover in the wake of the Hillsborough disaster and its incandescent editorial announced its presence as an alternative voice to a wider audience. Under the heading 'Hillsborough: Unanimous Verdict', the front page is divided into four photographs. FA chief executive Graham Kelly announces: 'It's not Our Fault.' The chief of South Yorkshire Police Peter Wright follows suit, as does Prime Minister Margaret Thatcher. In the bottom right box, a group of fans chorus: 'Oh well, it must be our fault again.' In the wake of the crushing at the Leppings Lane end of the ground, which killed ninety-seven supporters, the press was almost universal in its coverage that Liverpool fans were to blame for the deaths. *The Sun's* front page, which suggested that fans had picked the pockets of the dead, attacked the police, 'urinated on the brave cops' and caused the crush by arriving late in a drunken state and forced a gate open, fitted the narrative of the age. On the day after the disaster, government spin doctor Bernard Ingham claimed it was due to the work of 'a tanked-up mob'. The narrative was widely believed.

The accompanying *WSC* editorial represented a much-needed dissenting voice. The Hillsborough disaster, it argued, was the 'predictable consequence of the fact that the people who run English football have stumbled from one crisis to another', adding that there was 'no coherent, consistent policy to deal with any specific problem.' As for the supporters, they were 'herded, cajoled, pushed and corralled into cramped spaces'. And the toxic relationship between fans and police, *WSC* claimed, 'has served only to create barriers that are of as much significance as the perimeter fencing'.

The editorial then moved on to implicitly refer to the front cover and focus on the narrative surrounding fans in the wake of the disaster:

> It didn't take long for Hillsborough to become our fault. Indeed, initial reports pinned blame on supporters who were believed to have broken down a gate. Then the police's press department piped up, revealing that many were drunk and generally doing all the things fans are famous for. Had the television cameras not been present to record the disaster as it unfolded, many people would have unquestioningly accepted the garbage that has been pumped out by some of the tabloid hacks.

WSC made two predictions for the future. One – that 'teams will eventually be required to set up home on industrial estates in the middle of nowhere' in all-seater stadia was proved accurate in many cases. The other – that 'the ID Cards bill with provisions that almost guarantee that such a tragedy will be repeated is to be pushed through nonetheless,' was wide of the mark, but only because the forthcoming Taylor report, and not the Government, deemed ID cards unworkable.

Both independently of the *WSC* editorial and partly because of it, club-specific fanzines over the coming months ran stories about the long path to the Hillsborough disaster, albeit in an ad hoc manner. *A Load of Bull* (Wolves) and *Off the Shelf* (Tottenham) printed correspondence from supporters who'd witnessed the crushing at Leppings Lane in 1981 during the FA Cup semi-final between the two clubs. Several were injured that day, and some supporters climbed the perimeter fence to escape it. In their fanzines, Leeds United supporters recounted how tightly packed supporters had been at the same end during their semi-final clash with Coventry in 1987. The complaints that were made to authorities about spectator safety appeared to have fallen on deaf ears. Other letters also focussed on the non-football tragedies in the '80s, like the MS *Herald of Free Enterprise* ferry disaster, which killed 193 people, and the Kings Cross fire, which killed thirty-one. Was there, some letter writers asked – a general problem with public safety?

There was other correspondence about how, in football's 'heyday' in the '50s and '60s, the swaying, tightly packed terraces, filled to the brim so clubs could maximise profits, were downright dangerous, leading some supporters to actually leave matches before the match began as they feared for their safety. Being squashed and squeezed in and around matches, and being swept off one's feet wasn't, in hindsight, actually very much fun. The Hillsborough disaster encouraged supporters to begin sharing their experiences. Andy Lyons told me how, at the time of Hillsborough, politicians were 'striking poses about the game'. Fanned by the (largely) Conservative-sympathetic press, much was said about 'football needing to get its house in order' and, amongst leading ministers about the state of football being a consequence of 'falling standards in society'. Fanzines started to provide an independent view on the terrible events of 15 April 1989, hinting at the (largely) uncoagulated truth that would take decades to be recognised in the law courts. The Hillsborough disaster wasn't the fault of drunken, ticketless football fans. It was the result of long-standing, unresolved public safety issues at football grounds.

THE BANNER MAKER

'It was like being in the sea with a strong current. I had no control
over my movement. There was no sign of it abating.'
PETER CARNEY, LIVERPOOL SUPPORTER

I travelled to Hillsborough looking forward to a classic match, between two proper football teams – Nottingham Forest and Liverpool. It was a lovely sunny day. A fella outside was walking around selling shades. 'A pound a pair to keep out the glare,' he was saying. It was busy outside. We went in the Leppings Lane turnstiles the year before, but sat in the north stand, when we played Forest in the '88 FA Cup semi-final. As we went down the middle tunnel at around 2.55, my mate, Mick, said: 'At least we know the way out.' We shuffled our way down the tunnel. Dark, claustrophobic. The players were already out. People were anxious to get in. I lost my footing, caused by the dramatic incline of the walkway. I was swept onto the terrace, and I tried to right myself, swaying about. I settled facing the way I'd come in. This wasn't good. Something was seriously wrong. It was like being in the sea with a strong current. I could see people passed out where they stood, or lay. I tried to take control of my movement, to get to a safe place. I shuffled left, trying to get in front of a barrier. People were screaming. Some were going blue. Time passed. Now I was close to the front. I yelled at a copper just in front of the fence to help us. He looked me in the eye for a second or two, then he looked through me. I was trying to control my breathing and was moving from one foot to another. I was hemmed in. Squeezed. I thought I was head and shoulders above those around me. Gasping for air like a goldfish in a bowl. I tried to focus on looking at

Garry Parker – the Forest midfielder – running in a straight line. Focus. Focus. I lost him. I changed my focus. I looked at the other stands, then the hills beyond the ground, then the sky and the clouds above their Kop.

I had visions that I was travelling down a tube or a tunnel, with walls of cotton wool or clouds. I looked back at myself on the terrace, surrounded by a perfect circle of people, all head and shoulders above me. My last conscious thought was: 'What about Tina.' 'Tina and the baby.' Tina, my wife, was six weeks pregnant. I blacked out.

I like to think I fell into a pocket of air, between the legs of a barrier, that saved me. The first sensation I had was of being beaten on the torso, maybe receiving CPR. I remember feeling my body stretched, my vision dark, and echoing sound. I think I was being carried back down the tunnel. My first thought was: 'I'm here, I'm here.' The subsequent subconscious sentence was: 'I'm here, on this earth.' My thinking wasn't coagulated. I could hear sirens. I saw a fella against the wall with a shirt over his head. He was dead.

•   •   •

Peter Carney, a youth worker at the time of the Hillsborough Disaster, is a busy man. As well as running local sightseeing tours in the city, he's best known for his iconic banners, which are a focal point of Liverpool matches. He's also a Hillsborough survivor, whose life in the intervening thirty-five years has been shaped by what he experienced on that fateful afternoon. After being checked out at a Sheffield hospital, he returned home, with his head, as he put it, 'totally cabbaged'. The next morning, he went to Anfield with Albie, another mate whom he'd gone to the match with the day before. They laid flowers at the Shankly Gates then went to see Peter's friend, Fred Brown, who lived seven doors from the gates, for a cup of tea. Carney thought about the banner that he was working on for Liverpool's forthcoming centenary in 1992 and suggested to Fred they should make a banner about the disaster. Taking one of three pieces of cloth he had intended to use for the centenary banner, he created a memorial to those who had lost their lives at Hillsborough. Unlike the floral tributes, Peter always planned to bring it home. 'I survived, so the banner survived. In a different way. Its purpose is to keep alive the names and memories of the people who were killed,' he told me.

Along the top it says: 'To the Victims of Hillsborough.' At the bottom is written: 'You'll Never Walk Alone.' In the middle is a Liver Bird, surrounded by black shadows of the League titles and European Cups the club had won. Made over three days, with Fred, John Fay (a survivor) and Tracy Ryan, in the week following the disaster and measuring 10ft by 24ft, it was displayed at Anfield. The victims are named on the trophies. 'They are the people the message is to – you'll never walk alone, and we'll always be thinking of you. That's something people connected to immediately.' Carney told me.

It's faded now. In 2011, representatives from the People's History Museum put together an estimate for its conservation, a testament to its cultural significance. They described it as 'unique and irreplaceable'. Peter felt the banner could/should be improved but struggled to summon the energy or the will. He deliberately left the banner to have its own time and vowed to come back to design changes a generation later.

His second Hillsborough memorial banner was made two decades into the killed victims' families fight for justice and legal recognition that their loved ones had not been responsible for causing their own deaths. The Spirit of Shankly supporters' group has described the creations as 'the Scouse Bayeux Tapestry'. Friendly and open, Carney tells me that he'll 'gab about anything'. He talks me through the textures of his second banner, which he designed with the purpose of 'triggering all the senses'. Senses he had come to recognise more acutely since making the original banner. Different materials were used to try to carry the message through the sense of touch. The Christian names of the killed victims are embroidered on black blazer cloth, to get closer to the person and to add clarity. There's piping around each trophy, so one gets a sense of how its surface might feel. Flames are in silk, so they shine. The changed text on the top, 'We Never Walk Alone', is also in silk, so it's smooth, emphasising the communal experience. The Liver bird is padded out and has a smaller head to make it look young. The 'Hillsborough' wording at the bottom is written in a material that has knots. It feels rough. Deliberately so. 'April 15th 1989' and 'Sheffield' have been put on. 'It amazes me that some people don't know the date, or even where Hillsborough is,' he told me. The banner also has two pockets for flowers to sense smell and represent people who went to the ground in the week following the disaster.

Whilst his banners don't appear overtly political, Carney told me that Hillsborough became a 'focal point for the anger and the view that the establishment had abandoned the city'. The banners symbolise community, togetherness and a deeply caring side, which is something that 'the Thatcher government most certainly did not', Carney says. Also fluttering at Anfield on match days is the 'Iron Lady' banner, a tribute to Hillsborough campaigner Anne Williams, whose son Kevin was killed at Hillsborough in April 1989. At the initial inquest in 1992, Coroner Stefan Popper ruled that nobody could have survived beyond 3.15 p.m. Anne Williams fought the ruling and was vindicated in 2012 when the Hillsborough Independent

Panel swept Popper's judgement aside and determined that as many as fifty-eight victims might have been saved, had the police and ambulance services responded appropriately. The 'Iron Lady' banner was not Carney's creation (it was made by an Indonesian fan called Sam Irooth), but he describes it as 'a brilliantly subtle dig at Thatcher, whilst celebrating the life and work of one of our own, Anne Williams.'

In the days, weeks, months and years that followed the Hillsborough disaster, Peter, like so many survivors, struggled to process his thoughts:

As the car that took me home left the hospital, it said on the radio that ninety-three had died. In my mind, ninety-three and thirty-nine spun round and round, I kept thinking of Heysel. Was it divine retribution for what happened there? It was nonsense to ask myself that, but I know others did the same.

Some survivors were offered counselling and social workers. Though they were entirely well meaning, it 'didn't really match up to our hopes', he said. More helpful to the survivors was sharing their experiences. 'It was a case of "you tell me your story, and I'll tell you mine".' In contrast to the negative tabloid headlines, which were portraying Liverpool fans as instigators of their own misfortune, survivors exchanged recollections of the bravery that many showed administering emergency CPR and hoisting those who were struggling up to the stand above the Leppings Lane terrace. The police, they said, had opened Gate C; it wasn't forced open by fans, as some newspaper outlets claimed. There was no robbing of corpses either. 'People would have opened up if that had happened,' Carney said. And, on the subject of the police, there were numerous references to their callousness and obstreperousness on the day. Of their failure to open the small gate at the front of Leppings Lane, of telling fans scaling the fences to escape the crush to 'fucking get back in there' and of staring emotionlessly at those who were dead or dying at the front. 'A core question that echoed through the '90s and beyond was: 'Who exactly polices the police?' he said. 'A groundswell of personal experience and opinion was stirring. We knew what really happened that day, and many of those whom I spoke to all that time ago went on to play a key role in the long fight for justice.'

'I discovered, through another survivor, Peter Rankin, I'd been through a near-death experience – the senses fading away, the cloudy tunnel vision, watching myself being crushed.' Some in-depth research since has helped him clarify the nature of his experience at Hillsborough. The study of near-death experience straddles the space between the sensible and the spiritual self and is a serious sphere of interest in the margins of medical practice.

It wasn't until 2016, twenty-seven years later, that a jury ruled that all ninety-seven victims of the Hillsborough disaster died unlawfully and that their deaths were in no way caused by their actions, or the actions of survivors. The near thirty-year truth fight was officially over, but through Peter Carney's wonderful creations, the names of the victims and of those who fought for truth and justice will never fade from the collective memory.

17

THE SHOWDOWN

These days, Sky or TNT Sports would bite off your hands and your legs and pay you a king's ransom to televise a match of that magnitude.'

Jim Rosenthal, former TV presenter

Anfield – May 1989. The top two are locked in a stalemate in the final match of the season. With fifty-two minutes gone in the title decider, second-place Arsenal are awarded a free kick just outside the area. They need to win by two clear goals to win the title after eighteen years, otherwise it'll be Liverpool's again. No team has achieved that at Anfield since Everton three years earlier. It's a seemingly impossible job. Bruce Grobbelaar bellows instructions to his defensive wall, but he can't make himself heard over the din. Gunners full-back Nigel Winterburn curls in an indirect free kick, and forward Alan Smith glides in to guide the ball into the bottom corner of the Liverpool net. Kenny Dalglish's players harangue the referee, insisting that he talk to his linesman because they are convinced that Smith hasn't made contact with the ball. Years later, Smith recalled: 'We just stared at them and hoped and hoped, because at Anfield, 50–50 decisions tended to go their way.' The goal stands.

Liverpool players look uneasily at manager Kenny Dalglish on the bench. Settling for a 1–0 defeat isn't their style. But pushing forward means they risk losing it all. For Arsenal on the other hand, it's a Hollywood ending or bust.

• • •

On the face of it, the signature of Steve Bould, a prematurely balding defender from Stoke City, didn't suggest that George Graham's team was about to launch a title assault, particularly given the fact that, in the previous two seasons, Arsenal's title challenges petered out disappointingly after Christmas. At least Gunners skipper Tony Adams was confident, betting ITV football presenter Jim Rosenthal £100 in the close season that Arsenal would win the league in 88–89. 'No chance,' Rosenthal reckoned. Adams seemed to be in a minority of one. *Shoot!*'s verdict? 'A top-six finish is the best Arsenal can hope for.' In stark contrast to the Gunners' less-than-eyecatching summer signing, north London rivals Tottenham splashed out £2.2 million on the country's brightest talent, Paul Gascoigne. In the previous summer, despite registering an interest in Watford's John Barnes, the winger signed for Liverpool, who'd romped to the title during the 1987–88 campaign.

One of the club's earliest fanzines, the *Arsenal Echo Echo* [sic], lampooned Graham's perceived parsimony in the transfer market. 'SHOCK: GEORGE GRAHAM CAUGHT SPENDING A FIVER. INTERPOL ALERTED,' ran one front-page lead. The editor, Guy Havord, selling copies on the North Bank, was promptly carted off to the club office and informed that Graham would find such humour offensive. Given the Scot's opening salvos in the transfer market, that seems highly unlikely. With Arsenal reputedly around £1.5 million in debt when he arrived at Highbury in June 1986, Graham was informed that the era of signing big-ticket internationals was over and that it was time to harvest the rich crop of youngsters emerging from the youth team. Fortunately, this chimed with Graham's vision of building a 'one-for-all' ethos at Highbury. He had a distinctly dim view of 'star' players. 'The word "star" is overused in the modern game,' Graham said. 'For me, stars are players who win trophies and medals, not players who hang around nightclubs and get their photos in the papers.'

Graham, in his immaculate white shirt and club tie, spoke passionately about how he aimed to rejuvenate a club that had finished sixth the season before and had seen its attendances plummet – in some cases, to below the 18,000 mark. As manager at cash-strapped, hooligan-beset Millwall between 1982 and 1986, he'd understood all too well the need to balance the books when he sold striker John Fashanu to Wimbledon. At The Den, Graham took time out of his busy schedule to learn about accounts and balance sheets from regular fact-finding visits to Companies House. Hardly a glamorous pursuit but perhaps a necessary one for a coach about to join an institution as stagnant and financially ailing as Arsenal. Some found Graham's new persona mystifying. Nicknamed 'The Stroller' during his playing days at Highbury in the late '60s and early '70s, Graham was an elegant playmaker, lacking in pace but possessing a delicate first touch. Often with best friend Terry Venables in tow, Graham loved London's social scene. 'I could see George managing a nightclub, but not a football club,' his former coach Don Howe said. When asked about his miraculous morphing from 'The Stroller' to a disciplinarian boss, Graham responded: 'It's simple. George

Graham the manager would not pick George Graham the player in one of his sides.'

With scalpel in hand, Arsenal's former Double winner set about his squad in those early months. England forwards Tony Woodcock and Paul Mariner were given free transfers to FC Köln and Portsmouth respectively. Forthright twenty-year-old defender Martin Keown, who had the temerity to ask for a pay rise of £50 a week, was sold to Aston Villa for £200,000. Once touted as a future England captain, injury-prone midfielder Stewart Robson went to West Ham United for a hefty £700,000. Within six months, Graham had slashed the wage bill and recouped nearly £1 million. It was the red-headed Colchester United winger Groves who proved to be Graham's only signing in that first summer, for a none-too-princely £75,000.

His arrival may have been low-key, but Groves made waves with teammates when he parked his decrepit old Volkswagen Beetle alongside assorted models of gleaming German engineering. 'They took one look at my shitty car and thought: "Who the fuck is this?"' Groves told me. 'Here's your contract. Sign it,' Graham told his new signing. Groves complied. Just in case the player doubted Graham's authority, the Scot raised his office chair to a higher level, in order that he could peer down at his new signing.

Gunners players discovered that Graham was a zealot, both on and off the training pitch. 'There was George with his clipboard, timing us on shuttle runs, urging us on. He'd strut around the training pitch,' recalled elegant midfielder Paul Davis. Charlie Nicholas was reminded that on match day, the earring was to be left at home. England full-back Kenny Sansom, who'd been coached by Graham as a youngster at Crystal Palace, made the mistake of calling the new manager by his first name. 'It's "Boss" or "Mr Graham" from now on,' Sansom was told. The old guard was wary of Graham from the start. In the mid '80s, Graham often joined the players at the Orange Tree pub in Totteridge for a post-match beer, and he'd once informed Nicholas that he wasn't a typical Arsenal player. 'Then he turns up as manager, and I thought: "Oh Christ, here he we go,"' Nicholas said.

From the off, Graham urged the defence to act as a unit. Full-backs Kenny Sansom and Viv Anderson were told to 'work' on their linesmen during games. 'Linesmen go to sleep. Urge them to get their flag up if you think an attacker is offside,' he'd tell them. The England duo complied. An urban myth circulated that Graham tied the back four together with rope to ensure they acted as a unit. In fact, Graham told his back four to 'imagine you're connected by rope', but the message was abundantly clear: Graham's Arsenal would defend as one, and to the last man. Conceding goals was simply unacceptable. In the 3–1 victory over Queens Park Rangers in November 1986, the Gunners conceded late on. After letting the rest of the team go home, Graham locked the dressing room door and held a forty-five minute inquest with the defenders into what had happened. 'George was fuming,' Kenny Sansom recalled. 'It set the tone: no matter who the opposition was, if we let one in, we hadn't done our jobs properly.'

But in the early weeks of Graham's reign, there appeared to be little improvement. Arsenal beat Manchester United in the first game of the Graham era courtesy of an uncharacteristic poacher's goal from Charlie Nicholas, but they then won just one game in six. Some of the football was dire. 'Arsenal are big and growing smaller – certainly in the minds of their fans. It's time George Graham listened… and spent some money,' wrote Stuart Simons in the *Daily Mail*. Following this inauspicious start, a spate of injuries to Nicholas, Stewart Robson and Graham Rix inadvertently steered Arsenal in a different direction and saw youngsters Martin Hayes and Perry Groves slotted into the first team. They gave Arsenal pace up front. The Gunners went on a long unbeaten run and surged to the top of the league. Essentially, Arsenal played the high-press game. 'We squeezed opponents to death and then hit them on the break,' Perry Groves recalled. In the league at least, the wheels came off after Christmas, but opportunity came knocking in the Littlewoods Cup and a two-legged semi-final against local rivals Tottenham.

So often a barometer of Arsenal's fluctuating fortunes on the pitch during the '70 and '80s, Tottenham appeared to have eased ahead of their north London rivals when it came to innovation and commercial acumen by the time Graham arrived in N5. With Tottenham mired in £5 million worth of debt due to the rebuilding of White Hart Lane's west stand, the Tottenham board, at Irving Scholar's behest, floated the club on the stock exchange in 1983, with the intention of raising £3.8 million. Spurs were the first English club to 'go public'. The target was reached, and by 1987, Spurs fans who invested in the 3.8 million shares available – the minimum investment was £200 – saw the shares double in value before the economic crash of 1987. It was a classic example of football mirroring societal change, as the Thatcher government rolled out its privatisation campaign throughout the '80s.

Innovations flowed. White Hart Lane had played host to the first of ITV's live league matches in October '83, as Tottenham took on Nottingham Forest and in October '87 hosted the UK heavyweight clash between Joe Bugner and Frank Bruno. After hiring advertising agency Saatchi & Saatchi, the club also released a TV and radio advert, featuring celebrity fan Peter Cook and a gaggle

of supporters running out behind the players, to encourage supporters, and especially families to come to White Hart Lane during
the 83–84 campaign. The advert's selling idea: 'This Saturday, Spurs
will be fielding 38,000 against Coventry City. Make sure you're
one of the team,' was effective, with home crowds buoyant in the
early stages of the campaign. The new commercialisation wasn't to
everyone's taste. Manager Keith Burkinshaw had resigned after Tottenham won the 1984 UEFA Cup. 'There used to be a football club
over there,' Burkinshaw may or may not have said. Irving Scholar
was adamant though: 'Football clubs need to wise up and attract
commercial investment from a variety of areas.'

Off the pitch, Arsenal would catch up fast on their north London
neighbours in the late '80s, and on the pitch, they were about to
nose in front too. Alex Fynn, who knew David Dein and Irving
Scholar well, spoke of the differences between the pair:

Scholar was hands-on, often to his manager's irritation. Dein
willingly accepted a supporting role to George Graham, who was
master of all he surveyed at Highbury. Scholar appointed Terry
Venables manager in '87, because he was impressed with how he'd
won La Liga with Barcelona and personally masterminded the
transfer that saw Steve Archibald move to the Nou Camp from
Tottenham. What Scholar found out to his cost was that whilst
Venables could raise the game on the big occasion and was ideal
for Spurs' FA Cup jaunts, he was the polar opposite of his good
friend George Graham, who loved slogging through a 38-game
season.

In the semi-final, Arsenal twice fought back; once when they were
2–0 down on aggregate in the second leg and ended up drawing

2–2 at White Hart Lane, and then in the replay. One nil down at half-time to Clive Allen's goal – he'd score forty-nine that season – Tottenham's stadium announcer relayed instructions to the supporters about how to buy their tickets for the final after the final whistle. 'George looked at us, and then we looked at him and one another,' recalled Paul Davis. 'No further instructions were needed.' Graham's team fought back to secure a famous 2–1 win, with David Rocastle making himself a hero by bursting through and bundling the winner under goalkeeper Ray Clemence. With Tottenham now vanquished, Liverpool lay in wait in the final.

In the '80s, Arsenal had been swept away with almost monotonous regularity by their Littlewoods Cup final opponents. For the first thirty minutes at Wembley, Kenny Dalglish's team threatened to run riot, and Ian Rush gave them an early lead. There was a hoary old Ian Rush statistic: he'd scored in 144 Liverpool matches and his team had never lost when the Welshman had found the back of the net. Yet Charlie Nicholas poked the Gunners level before half-time, and his deflected effort won the match for Arsenal late on. 'Charlie the prince for one glorious day,' ran *The Times* headline. 'George still wasn't convinced about me though,' Nicholas said. The less-heralded star of the show was Perry Groves, brought on in the seventieth minute and instructed to run hard and fast at Gary Gillespie. The compliant Groves did as he was told. His scampering run past the tiring Scottish defender set up Nicholas's winner. Not bad for a young player mistakenly called 'Terry Grouse' a year earlier in an Essex newspaper. For the first time in a generation, Arsenal had got under Liverpool's skin.

The Littlewoods Cup run gave Graham the kudos, leverage and funds to sculpt his squad. Arsenal had made a £2 million profit in his first season as Highbury attendances rocketed. Over the next eighteen months, all of the club's big-money signings from the early to mid '80s were jettisoned: Kenny Sansom, Viv Anderson, Steve Williams and Bonnie Prince Charlie himself – sold to Aberdeen for £400,000. Arsenal's mid-'80s cavaliers had been purged by their roundhead manager. Their replacements, which included striker Alan Smith from Leicester City (£800,000) and defenders Lee Dixon from Stoke City (£400,000) and Nigel Winterburn from Wimbledon (£400,000) were young, blue collar and malleable.

Liverpool eased to the title in 1987–88, not losing a single match until March. Arsenal failed to retain the Littlewoods Cup, stumbling to a 3–2 defeat by Luton. But piece by piece, Graham completed his jigsaw. By the end of the campaign, both Lee Dixon and Nigel Winterburn were in place as first-choice full-backs. Tony Adams, though shredded by Marco Van Basten in the clash between England and Holland at the 1988 European Championships, was Graham's choice as captain. In front of the back four was the triumvirate of home-grown midfielders: Paul Davis, David Rocastle and converted full-back Michael Thomas. 'George told the three of us to shield and protect the back four with our lives. "You'll play until you're thirty, and they'll play until they're forty," he'd say. That's pretty much how it turned out,' Thomas explained. Up front, the partnership between Alan Smith and youth-team product Paul Merson blossomed. Although not blessed with great pace, Brian Marwood, a winger signed from Sheffield Wednesday, possessed a canny ability to drift wide of his man and deliver a pinpoint cross onto the head of Smith.

Come the start of the 1988–89 campaign, Graham reckoned his side possessed the tactical nous to start making life difficult for the champions. It came through the relentless drilling of each and every one of the Arsenal players. Graham schooled them in the art of squeezing the life out of the opposition. The back four protected goalkeeper John Lukic, the midfielders protected the back four, and the strikers – Smith and Merson – operated between the right/left-back and the right/left centre-half. There was hell to pay if either striker allowed the central defender to ghost in between them. When it came to the pace and incision of John Barnes, Arsenal's pack mentality kicked in. Perry Groves explained:

> On no account were we to allow Barnes to go down the outside, as he'd skip past you and run riot. Jockey him inside, so if he got past Lee Dixon, who was always excellent at closing Barnes down, Rocky or Tony Adams would deal with him. You knew that on most occasions, someone would be waiting for him.

There was no deviation from Graham's method of running things. The new signings got the message loud and clear. Lee Dixon always felt that it was he who was singled out by his manager. 'He'd be waiting in the dressing room at half-time with a bit of paper. I'd look over his shoulder for a peak. My name was always on it. Sometimes I'd try sneak off to the toilet to avoid George. "Hurry up and sit down, Lee," came the response.' When Perry Groves pranked Graham by sneaking up behind him and placing a condom on his shoulder, Graham was incandescent. 'Gadaffi,' as the players called him (never to his face, of course), had no time for such fripperies.

Remarkably, Liverpool and Arsenal clashed on six occasions in the 1988–89 season – and five of the meetings came before Christmas. In September, Arsenal defeated Liverpool 1–0 in the generally unloved Mercantile Credit Centenary Trophy semi-final at Highbury. The tournament was arranged to celebrate the 100th year of the Football League and in an era when English clubs were banned from Europe, it was meant to be a coffer filler. Injuries disrupted Liverpool's flow. Bruce Grobbelaar was in hospital suffering from meningitis and skipper Alan Hansen had been out injured since the beginning of the campaign. Up front, the returning Ian Rush – who had been re-signed after a difficult season with Juventus – had been suffering from a virus since August. Dalglish had attempted to play Rush alongside lookalike John Aldridge, but Rush wouldn't score in the league until late October and Liverpool didn't win a game in which the pair started together until the middle of that month.

The two clubs then met in the Rumbelows Cup third round at Anfield in November. Liverpool took the lead, but Arsenal were level within minutes. On the edge of the box, Rocastle evaded Barnes to rifle in a thunderous shot from just inside the area. Crisp, clean and clinical, the 1–1 draw encapsulated the growing maturity of the team.

'That game took away a lot of our fear of playing Liverpool,' recalled Brian Marwood. In the Highbury replay, Arsenal tangled Liverpool up in a spider's web of defensive play, springing the primed offside trap with mind-boggling regularity to force a 0–0 draw. Arsenal's second replay performance, however, was insipid and they lost 2–1. It was a remarkably open title race by the time Arsenal took on Liverpool at Highbury in the league on 4 December. Norwich led the table with Arsenal three points adrift whilst Liverpool, level on points with newly promoted Millwall, lay fourth. Derby and Coventry were just a single point further back.

The game was broadcast live on *The Match*. ITV had acquired the rights to broadcast twenty-five live matches throughout the season via a roundabout route. In May 1988, a new player emerged to challenge the BBC/ITV cartel. British Satellite Broadcasting (BSB) offered the Football League a ten-year deal to broadcast live games, with a guaranteed payment of £9 million per year, rising to around £25 million a year further down the line. But ITV's Greg Dyke acted quickly to undermine the new rival. In a London meeting with the chairmen of the big five, Irving Scholar asked Dyke outright whether the BBC and ITV had previously operated as a cartel. Despite ITV's controller of sport John Bromley reminding Dyke that he didn't have to answer Scholar's question, Dyke admitted that a cartel had indeed been in place. His honesty impressed Scholar and David Dein. He then proposed a tailor-made deal guaranteeing £1 million to each of the big five per season. Dyke realised that other clubs needed to join the party for the deal to work, so Aston Villa, Newcastle, Nottingham Forest, Sheffield Wednesday and West Ham were added but at a far lower remunerated rate. With Dein and Everton's Philip Carter on the league management committee, the proposed deal was effectively rubber stamped. When the other members of the committee and rival chairmen found out, both Carter and Dein were immediately thrown off. Before the ITV and BSB proposals were put to the vote, however, BSB withdrew from the race and the Football League was left with a fait accompli. ITV had won an emphatic victory (for now), and the cartel was finally broken. 'Maybe the initial presence of BSB had forced the hand of the cartel as theoretically, it would provide more competition, which is what Margaret Thatcher had always championed, and convinced ITV that they would have to pay more for the rights to broadcast matches,' Alex Fynn told me.

At Highbury, a disappointing 31,000 crowd turned out, doing little to change the prevailing view that live football would have a detrimental effect on attendances. The game ended 1–1, with Alan Smith salvaging a point for the hosts. Arsenal finally hit top spot after winning at Charlton on Boxing Day. Liverpool continued to nag away at Graham. 'The fewer points Kenny collects before he gets his injured players again, the better. Liverpool will be neck and neck with us when we play them towards the end of the season at Anfield,' he told the *Mail*'s Jeff Powell.

•   •   •

Arsenal encapsulated the tradition of English football's past, with their direct and uncompromising approach. 'Fast, fit and pragmatic,' was how *The Guardian*'s David Lacey described the late-'80s Gunners. Earning an average of £400 per week, it was a team patently lacking box-office talent. The state of their mud-swamped Highbury pitch added a primitive feel to many of the home games that season. Narrow victories against Luton and West Ham were notable for the fact that most players' kit was completely soiled within about twenty minutes of kick-off. Brian Marwood described it as being a 'winkle-picker's paradise,' which didn't resonate well with Highbury's ground staff. 'It made it difficult for us to string too many passes together,' recalled Perry Groves. 'You'd get teams coming to camp out in the mud.' The defence was vulnerable at home against nippy forwards like Aston Villa's Tony Daley and Nottingham Forest's Franz Carr. Their home record was unexceptional. The goal celebrations are also of their time. There are no showboating sliding celebrations amongst George Graham's men; they celebrate as a unit, hug one another and shake hands. 'Nothing was choreographed for cameras back then,' recalled Alan Smith, whose twenty-three goals that season won him the Golden Boot.

Yet Arsenal's two public-relations own goals that season did demonstrate the growing omnipotence of TV. In October '88, a rogue ITV camera caught Paul Davis aiming a left hook punch at

Glenn Cockerill, which broke the Southampton player's jaw. Davis insisted Cockerill had 'provoked me throughout the match, with late and high tackles.' Davis was banned for nine matches and fined £3,000. Four months later, ITV broadcast a *World in Action* special entitled *Offside*. Unbeknown to the Arsenal players, referee David Elleray was miked up for a fiery London derby between Millwall – a top-flight club for the first time in their history – and Arsenal at the Lions' Den. Arsenal players David O'Leary, Kevin Richardson and David Rocastle questioned the referee after decisions were awarded against them. Regular use of the F-word was bleeped out. In the second half, when Tony Adams squeezed the ball over the line and Elleray deemed that the ball hadn't gone in, Merson and Richardson harangued the beleaguered Harrow schoolmaster. Screaming at top volume, skipper Tony Adams yelled: 'It's our goal, it's our goal. That is over the line.' Adams was then booked for shouting: 'Fucking cheat' at Elleray. Arsenal players later laughed at Adams' comically high-pitched voice as he vented, and the fact that when told to 'stand up straight' by Elleray, he did so without question. Graham's opinion on 'Ref-gate'? 'We won 2–1.'

That footballers used the F-word was hardly revelatory, and Elleray later claimed the Gunners were unfairly criticised in the aftermath. But, against The Den's foreboding backdrop of metal cages topped by barbed wire, Arsenal's aggression illustrated what a hard-bitten crew they were. Off the pitch, many Arsenal players drank a great deal. The 'Tuesday club' hit the north London bars after training if there was no midweek match. The family men disappeared by early evening, leaving the boozers to carry on the 'bonding' session, with Arsenal fans often round and about. 'We'd bump into players from Charlton, QPR, Tottenham. Everyone did it. It was the culture of the '80s,' Perry Groves explained. It wasn't until several years later that Paul Merson's and Tony Adams's revelations about their respective addictions that such a boorish lifestyle was proved to be so debilitating.

Away from the Highbury mudflats, Arsenal were a formidable unit, with a defence that could absorb seemingly endless punishment before moving the ball forward rapidly, either through long passes or via powerful runs from Thomas and Rocastle. In Alan Smith, the Gunners had perhaps the most in-form target man in the country. In the opening game of the season at Plough Lane, Smith's hat-trick helped Arsenal claim a 5–1 win against FA Cup winners Wimbledon. The Gunners plundered three or more goals away from home on seven occasions in the league.

Off the pitch, Arsenal were certainly a club on the move. Against Tottenham over the Christmas period, George Graham unveiled their new Clock End stand, which incorporated sixty-four executive boxes towering above the old terrace. The official programme was abuzz with commercial ventures. At £14 a pop, fans could buy videos of games, and a hefty £100 outlay via cheque or postal order would buy you a George Graham-signature Aquascutum coat. Rooms at Highbury could be rented for parties, quizzes and company dinners. Then there was the hefty slice of income the club received from ClubCall, which was the closest thing to a pre-internet, non-interactive website for '80s football fans. Calls cost 48p per minute at peak times and 25p on a weekend. If Gunners supporters dialled 0898121170, the comforting voice of former goalkeeper Bob Wilson would provide them with a list of options, including team news, recorded interviews with players and, for an eye-watering £35, live commentary of matches. Given that the club received up to 2,500 calls a day and pocketed around 80 per cent of the money garnered, David Dein reckoned the annual income from Club-Call was equivalent to that received from Division One sponsors Barclaycard.

Via the medium of its programme, the club actively encouraged Arsenal fans to write to local MPs – who included Margaret Thatcher (Finchley) and Jeremy Corbyn (Islington North) – to protest about the government's proposed national identity card scheme. The Football Spectators Bill, deemed unworkable by those in the game because of the inconvenience that would be caused to law-abiding supporters, and it's reliance on computer technology, had already suffered a partial defeat in the House of Lords, which ruled that the four divisions could introduce ID cards year by year, rather than all at once. Jimmy Greaves had recently shoved a mocked-up ID card up the backside of Sports Minister Colin Moynihan's latex *Spitting Image* puppet on *Saint & Greavsie*. With an almost-hysterical Ian St John pleading with him not to do it, Greaves did what he felt needed to be done. 'It was my finest moment in broadcasting,' he told me, 'despite Saint saying we'd be taken off air permanently.'

• • •

On 15 April, as Arsenal laboured to a 1–0 win over relegation-bound Newcastle, which kept them top of the league, news began filtering through about the Hillsborough tragedy. In a scenario mirrored at multiple grounds across the country that afternoon, many fans with transistor radios clapped to their ears listened to Radio 2's Peter Jones's account of the unfolding horror of events. On the terraces and in the stands there was talk of 'trouble' at Hillsborough before the game, and then the match being halted due to a pitch invasion.

There was eye rolling and a degree of resignation. This was all par for the course in '80s football. Fans had long since normalised that kind of news. It wasn't until later, as Jones described the wailing ambulance sirens, advertising hoardings being used as makeshift stretchers and the deployment of oxygen cylinders that the full enormity of what was happening began to sink in. 'The atmosphere was really subdued by the end,' recalls Brian Marwood, who grabbed Arsenal's winner that day. 'We'd already got wind at half-time that it was a serious situation.'

That information came courtesy of Alan Smith, ruled out for four matches due to a cheekbone injury, who'd watched the running commentary of the unfolding disaster provided by John Motson on BBC1. 'There was no training for that kind of afternoon in the commentary box,' Motson told me, quietly. 'You had to process what you saw and do the best you could when the scene in front of you is so unspeakably awful.' The Arsenal players were numbed as the news filtered through, with the normally lively dressing room plunged into almost total silence. Heading to the Tube stations, Arsenal and Newcastle fans processed the news, speaking in hushed tones. Those with transistors heard Peter Jones's moving report from a now almost-deserted Hillsborough, which began and ended with the phrase: 'And the sun shines now.'

It was clear that there would be a break in league matches. When, after a few days, some of the players tentatively asked George Graham when he thought football might resume, they were informed: 'We'll follow Liverpool's lead and go from there.' Many of the players felt guilty even asking the question. There was talk of the FA Cup being suspended and even rumours that the season would be ditched. Perhaps it should have been. But in the back of their minds, with training sessions every inch as competitive as normal and Graham's beady eye checking that standards remained high, the Arsenal players knew that league matches would resume sooner rather than later.

They did so over the May Bank Holiday weekend. Victories over Norwich and Middlesbrough gave Arsenal an eight-point cushion over Liverpool, who had two matches in hand. Then the roof fell in. In the penultimate Highbury league game against Derby, Alan Smith's late goal couldn't stop Arsenal plunging to a 2–1 defeat. For the final home game of the campaign against Wimbledon, Graham announced that he'd jettison his unorthodox 5–3–2 sweeper system, which had seen a back three of O'Leary, Bould and Adams deployed for the previous four games, and revert to a 4–4–2 formation. It didn't work. An agonising 2–2 draw with football's ultimate party poopers – Wimbledon – appeared to leave Arsenal with no hope. The lap of honour was distinctly muted. Many fans slunk away disconsolately. 'We were kind of saying: "Sorry we messed it up, we'll try hard again next year,"' Alan Smith recalled. Liverpool, who'd won the FA Cup the previous Saturday in an all-Merseyside encounter with Everton, crushed West Ham 5–1 to send the Hammers down. They'd gone almost twenty matches unbeaten. The Gunners were now three points behind Kenny Dalglish's side and needed to win the final game of the season on Friday 26 May at Anfield by two clear goals to lift the title.

The English media gave Arsenal precious little chance of shocking their hosts. Newspaper headlines in the lead-up later became almost as famous as the match itself. The *Evening Standard* conceded: 'Barring a miracle, Liverpool now look certain to end this harrowing season with a record eighteenth league title as a memorial to those who died at Hillsborough.' The *Daily Mirror* screamed: 'You Don't Have a Prayer, Arsenal.' The *Sun*'s heading, 'MEN AGAINST

BOYS', became the most infamous of all the tabloid assessments of Arsenal's chances. Former Liverpool star Graeme Souness added:

> The November night I watched Liverpool beat Arsenal in the Littlewoods Cup at Villa Park also told me who would be champions. It was a case of men against boys and my old Anfield team were the gaffers for the whole ninety minutes. For me they are the *best* – mainly because they have the *best* players.

The 3,000 supporters who travelled north on the late morning of 26 May boarded the coaches and trains more in hope than expectation. Even the normally optimistic London newspapers appeared to have given up the ghost on Arsenal's title challenge. Gunners photographer Doug Poole was one of only two London-based photographers to venture to Anfield. 'At least I didn't have to jostle for position with the others,' laughed Poole, whose shots of the match would soon be seen around the world. Liverpool had gained in strength over the passing months. Their injured cohort was now restored to full fitness. Jan Mølby explained to me: 'After what had happened, it would've been a fitting end to the season if we'd completed the double. But football doesn't work like that, and Arsenal owed it to themselves and their fans to do a job.'

Graham informed his players that he would revert to the sweeper system for the Liverpool match. They were a little surprised, but he justified the decision by explaining that Arsenal simply had to prevent Liverpool from scoring otherwise the visitors would need to score three or even four goals. And that, reasoned the Scot, would be 'a bit tricky'.

Taking his inspiration from the Desmond Morris book *The Naked Ape*, Graham decided that his Arsenal team would travel there and back to Liverpool on the same day, thus increasing the possibility of a 'smash and grab' on hostile turf. Following a pre-match meal at their team hotel, Graham asked the dining room staff to vacate the room, where he proceeded to deliver arguably the most prophetic speech in English football history. After referring directly to the 'Men Against Boys' article (the players claim this was the only time he referred to a specific article in front of them), he set out his grand vision for the game.

> Be patient, we don't want the game won in the first five minutes. If it's 0–0 at half-time I won't mind. Score early in the second half and Liverpool won't know whether to go forward or defend and then the next goal will come. You've got nothing to lose. Go out and play and don't be frightened.

When the Arsenal players – average age twenty-one – ran onto the pitch, each of them carried sprays of red roses and laid them in front of the Kop in memorial for the Hillsborough victims. The match was shown live on ITV, some of whose staff had the hump because it impinged upon their time off. Hosted by Elton Welsby, there was a fifteen-minute build-up, with Bobby Robson ushered in as late studio guest. 'In that era, it was often five minutes and onto the match,' said Jim Rosenthal, who was pitch-side for ITV that night. 'We drafted in Bobby because we knew he could talk a bit and would fill the time.' On a calm summer evening, the early stages of the match were a phoney war, with both sides probing one another for weaknesses. When Liverpool ventured deep into Arsenal territory, it was John Barnes whose powerful runs caused most problems for O'Leary and Adams, and Ian Rush had the best chance to score when he cracked in a shot from outside the box that flew over Lukic's crossbar. Steve Bould's early header was destined for the net until Ronnie Whelan nodded over the bar. Liverpool looked assured, with no pressure on them to go for broke and score. Arsenal trudged in at half-time defiant. Alan Smith recalled the atmosphere in the dressing room: 'Confident. Relaxed. Tony Adams urging everyone on. George reminding us not to panic. He was confident we would score early in the second half.'

When Smith guided the ball into the bottom corner of the Liverpool net from an indirect free kick after fifty-two minutes, the Arsenal players' reaction was to gallop to the goal scorer, whilst the Liverpool players surrounded referee David Hutchinson, insisting that he talk to his linesman because they were convinced that Smith hadn't made contact. Hutchinson gave the goal, although afterwards he made a beeline for Jim Rosenthal, asking him: 'I did get it right, didn't I?' Rosenthal confirmed that Smith had indeed applied the faintest of touches. On the bench, Perry Groves looked on. 'They looked to Dalglish on the bench, and he didn't seem clear on what to do. I thought at that stage we had them.'

A wave of confidence swept through the Arsenal players. Liverpool tried again to score. A blistering Ray Houghton effort whistled inches over the bar before they dropped deeper into their own half to defend a 1–0 defeat. Mickey Thomas – so long in the doldrums in the New Year and described by Brian Glanville in the *Sunday Times* in January as 'exactly what he is, a muscular, adventurous full-back converted to midfield' – probed for weaknesses in Liverpool's backline. The combative Kevin Richardson delivered the coolest of through-balls to Thomas in the eighty-sixth minute, but the midfielder hurried his weak shot, and Grobbelaar smothered it easily. 'It was there and gone in a flash,' recalled Thomas. 'I'm glad that miss is largely forgotten. It wasn't my best moment on a football pitch.' Three minutes later, time was officially up. Unlike at Highbury, there was no visible clock at Anfield. Yet the combative Steve McMahon gave his teammates the 'one minute' sign and, perhaps symbolically, Gunners midfielder Kevin Richardson slumped to the turf, writhing in agony from cramp. For all of Arsenal's gallant efforts, it wouldn't be enough.

But there was to be one last chance.

As Barnes slalomed his way into the right-hand side of Arsenal's penalty area, Richardson rose from the turf to dispossess the Liverpool winger and tapped the ball back to Lukic. In a scene that – thanks to the film adaptation of Nick Hornby's novel – is now part of cinematic history, Lukic threw the ball out to Dixon, and his measured pass found Alan Smith. Chesting the ball down, he knocked it onto the galloping Thomas, who moments earlier told Richardson that he was 'going upfield to see if I can grab us a goal'. Despite being surrounded by a pack of Liverpool defenders, a lucky break off Steve Nicol's legs put him clean through against Grobbelaar. Thomas waited for the Liverpool keeper to commit himself. Everything stopped. The Anfield crowd, whistling for the end, fell into silence. Grobbelaar moved low to his right, and Thomas, dropping his shoulder, flicked the ball to the goalkeeper's left.

As Thomas performed his somersault on the pitch, and the Arsenal fans ('a mad sea of blue and yellow bobbing up and down in the far corner,' recalled Alan Smith) celebrated, the camera panned to Kenny Dalglish, slumped against the dugout and scarcely able to take on board what he'd just witnessed. Thomas explained: 'I waited for Bruce to make the first move and he took such a long time making up his mind whether to come out or not. I knew that Liverpool couldn't come back.'

The tabloid headlines: 'KING GEORGE!' (*The Sun*) and: 'MIRA-CLE MEN' (the *Daily Mirror*) were simple and predictable enough, but what was lost in the immediate aftermath was the fact that Graham's predictions about the match had come startlingly true. 'I was sat with Steve Bould afterwards,' explained substitute Perry Groves, 'and I said to him: "Everything turned out the way George said it would."' ITV rounded off their coverage with Jim Rosenthal interviewing Arsenal captain Tony Adams on the pitch. 'Tony reminded me that I owed him £100 from our bet a year earlier. I didn't actually have it on me, though I did get the money to him later,' Rosenthal said. 'I then had to remind Tony to go and pick up the trophy. It was all quite ad hoc. Five minutes later, it was time for *News at Ten*. Football had to fight for every second and every minute back then.' News bulletins mentioned Arsenal's title triumph, but Sandy Gall's piece lasted only two minutes. Then it was done. 'We all operated within the parameters of the time,' Jim Rosenthal said. The year 1989 had a resoundingly *fin d'epoque* feel about it. The Berlin Wall fell and the Soviet Union began to disintegrate as Mikail Gorbachev's policy of glasnost and perestroika released the forces of nationalism, religious bigotry and anarchy in the Red Empire. In the UK, Margaret Thatcher was already meeting fierce resistance from within her Cabinet about the controversial poll tax, which would ultimately hasten her departure as Prime Minister. And now, Liverpool had been deposed as champions in their own back yard.

There is a lingering feeling amongst Arsenal players that they never received the credit they deserved. Perhaps it's because, for all his side's doggedness, Graham's team will always be regarded as the 'spoilers' who capitalised on Liverpool's numbness following the Hillsborough disaster. Or perhaps – as the graininess of the action from that night proves – it's because it happened in the pre-Sky era and therefore isn't afforded the same gravitas as it would have been post '92.

The sheer drama of the Friday night Liverpool v. Arsenal clash in May 1989, with its converging themes of tragedy, salvation, crushing disappointment and, juxtaposingly, youthful joy and victory against the odds, made for stomach-churningly riveting viewing. It was *Monday Night Football* and *Super Sunday* all rolled into one. And then some. It simply couldn't have been scripted better. Mickey Thomas remains the most understated of footballers. 'I was never comfortable with all the attention that the goal brought with it,' he admitted. 'At the time, I didn't think about what rested on that shot.'

A great deal, as it turned out. In television terms at least, Thomas had catapulted the sport into a new era. After the match, David Dein asked Greg Dyke if he was now happy with the deal he'd struck with the Football League a year earlier for the rights to broadcast live matches. The ITV chief's beaming smile said it all. 'I got flak for the money we paid. That seems funny now,' Dyke later said. It may have been more by accident than design perhaps, but the drama at Anfield was a timely reminder that football at its best was pure box office, and that here was a product that was very much worth investing in.

AFTERWORD

Champions Arsenal, who'd pocketed £50,000 from Barclaycard for winning the league and the same amount from Makita for winning the pre-season tournament at Wembley, travelled to Old Trafford in August to begin the defence of their title. There was, of course, no European route open for George Graham's side due to the ban. 'For now, our wings were clipped,' Graham said. The Gunners were obliterated 4–1 by Alex Ferguson's Manchester United. The game was, to a large extent, overshadowed by the appearance of Michael Knighton, whose offer to purchase chairman Martin Edwards's 50.2 per cent stake in the club and invest £10 million into revamping Old Trafford had been accepted a few days before the new season began. Knighton, a former teacher and property developer, ran onto the Old Trafford pitch, juggling the ball, before blasting it into the net in front of the Stratford End. 'Fergie, Fergie sign him up,' chanted the United fans. Aware that footage of Knighton's brassy 'hello' would be broadcast around the world, the United directors shifted uncomfortably in their seats. Within a matter of months, the proposed deal had collapsed, not because Knighton couldn't raise the funds, but because the supporters and the board turned against him. Despite the ridicule he faced, the much-derided Knighton's proposals were a clear indication of where not only United but English football was heading in the '90s.

His plans, which recognised, as he put it, 'the boundless limits of football', focussed on expanding the United brand. This included developing a United superstore, club TV channel and stadium tours. Knighton also spoke of how the growth of satellite TV could be worth billions for football. Within a decade, everything that Knighton, a beneficiary of the '80s enterprise culture outlined, came to pass. His claim that United would be worth £150 million as a business within fifteen years was also scoffed at, yet by 1998, with United now dominating English football, Rupert Murdoch had offered £625 million for the club.

The interim findings of the Taylor report, also released in August, challenged the lazy narratives that had been held towards the Hillsborough disaster. Taylor said that the fundamental cause of the tragedy was the failure to prevent fans entering the central pens at the Leppings Lane end once Gate C had been opened. Taylor also swatted aside police allegations that copious numbers of Liverpool fans had turned up late with forged tickets or no tickets. As he said, fans weren't expected to turn up until fifteen minutes before kick-off. He dismissed claims that large numbers of fans were drunk and later uncooperative. 'In that crush most people had no control over their movements at all,' he said.

There were strong rumours – which were proved correct – that in his final report in January 1990, Taylor would recommend that top-flight stadia were turned all-seater. This was football's Year Zero. As historic stands like Old Trafford's Stretford End, and indeed entire stadia, were redeveloped or razed and completely rebuilt, the game entered a new era. The very notion that football culture – so often seen as a blight on the nation – would soon be popularised seemed absurd in the '80s. Yet thanks to the already germinating forces of TV exposure, commercialisation and the free market, that's precisely what happened.

A whole new ball game was about to be played.

ACKNOWLEDGEMENTS

This book wouldn't have been possible without the co-operation, kindness and good humour of so many people over the past twenty-eight years. Firstly, I'd like to thank Mike Ingham, for so long the evocative and stirring voice of 5 Live, who wrote the foreword to this book.

Secondly, my huge thanks to the players, managers and directors who spoke to me, some many moons ago, some briefly, some at great length. Several have sadly passed away during the intervening period. Gentlemen, it was a pleasure to speak to you either face to face or via the various miracles of modern technology more recently. I've done my best to ensure that your distinctive voices ring loud and clear throughout the book: Raddy Antić, Gary Bailey, David Beasant, David Bennett, Gary Bennett, George Best, Luther Blissett, Ian Brightwell, Terry Butcher, Nigel Callaghan, Kevin Charlton, George Curtis, Paul Davis, Alan Hudson, Ray Clemence, Tony Cottee, Gordon Cowans, Steve Daley, Martin Edwards, Doug Ellis, David Evans, Terry Fenwick, Trevor Francis, Howard Gayle, Ivan Golac, Andy Gray, Matthew Hanlan, Adrian Heath, Ricky Hill, David Hodgson, Ray Houghton, Don Howe, Emlyn Hughes,

Howard Kendall, Ray Kennedy, Brian Kilcline, Mark Lawrenson, John McGovern, Paul Mariner, Frank McAvennie, Terry McDermott, Sir Neil Macfarlane, Mirandinha, Jan Mølby, Tony Morley, Derek Mountfield, Charlie Nicholas, Vladimir Petrović, David Pleat, Mark Proctor, Tony Rains, Kevin Reeves, Cyrille Regis, Nicky Reid, Peter Reid, George Reilly, John Robertson, Michael Robinson, Bobby Robson, Lawrie Sanchez, Kenny Sansom, Graeme Sharp, Gary Shaw, John Sillett, Allan Simonsen, Alan Smith, Jim Smith, Graham Taylor, Michael Thomas, Dennis Tueart, Ricky Villa, Paul Walsh, Peter Ward, Norman Whiteside, Ray Wilkins, Nigel Winterburn, Peter Withe.

Thanks also to the commentators and journalists, whose voices and pens illuminated football during such turbulent times: Charlie Burgess, Barry Davies, Rick Everitt, Alex Fynn, Brian Glanville, Harry Harris, Guy Havord, Jimmy Hill, Simon Inglis, Hugh Johns, John Keith, Andy Lyons, Andy Mitten, John Motson, Bert Patrick, Jim Rosenthal, Roger Wash.

And finally, to the supporters and entrepreneurs who were so candid about their memories of watching matches, many of whom altered the course of English football: Peter Carney, Ged Grebby, John Harmer, Chris Hawkins, George Kendall, Brian Kendrick, Chris Maudsley, Frank Newton and Bert Patrick.

I'm also grateful to the following for opening their contact books both virtual and real and helping me gain access to some of my interviewees: Ryan Baldi, John Devlin, Jo Glanville, Leo Moynihan, Anton Rippon and Adrian Tempany.

Also to my schoolmates Phil and Barry, for their ongoing friendship and support for the past forty-three years, and to Seb and Brummie for all those hours watching football videos at Keele. We always knew it was time well spent. And to William and Sharn for being such excellent sounding boards on football-related stuff and every other topic under the sun too.

I'm hugely grateful to James Stephens and Olivia Beattie at Biteback for commissioning the book and to Ryan Norman for his encouragement, fact checking and diligent editing of the manuscript. Thanks to all of you for your boundless patience with my consistent failure to meet deadlines.

And finally, to my wife Helen and my lovely girls Phoebe and Lacie. xx

BIBLIOGRAPHY

Ardiles, Ossie, *Ossie's Dream: My Autobiography* (London: Corgi Books, 2010)

Barrett, Norman, *The Daily Telegraph Football Chronicle* (London: Hutchinson, 1993)

Bassett, Dave and Downes, Wally, *The Crazy Gang: The True Inside Story of Football's Greatest Miracle* (London: Bantam, 2016)

Bidmead, Steve, *Stan Bowles* (London: Virgin, 2002)

Bowles, Stan, *Stan Bowles: The Autobiography* (London: Orion, 2005)

Clough, Brian, *The Autobiography* (London: Corgi Books, 1996)

Crooks, Richard, *What Was Football Like in the 1980s?* (Sussex: Pitch Publishing, 2020)

Domeneghetti, Roger, *Everybody Wants to Rule the World: Britian, Sport and the 1980s* (London: Yellow Jersey, 2023)

Duffy, Phil, *They Played for David Pleat at Luton Town* (Stafford: Curtis Sport, 2022)

Evans, Tony, *I Don't Know What It Is But I Love It: Liverpool's Unforgettable 1983–84 Season* (London: Penguin, 2014)

Evans, Tony, *Two Tribes: Liverpool, Everton and a City on the Brink* (London: Bantam Press, 2018)

Everitt, Rick, *Battle for the Valley* (London: Voice of the Valley, 2014)

Foot, John, *Calcio: A History of Italian Football* (London: Fourth Estate, 2006)

Francis, Tony, *Clough: A Biography* (London: Stanley Paul, 1989)

Francis, Trevor, *One in a Million* (Sussex: Pitch Publishing, 2019)

Hart, Simon, *Here We Go: Everton in the 1980s: The Players' Stories* (Liverpool: deCourbertin Books, 2016)

Hateley, Mark, *Hitting the Mark: My Story* (Liverpool: Reach Sport, 2021)

Hayward, Paul, *England Football: The Biography: 1872–2022* (London: Simon & Schuster, 2022)

Herbert, Ian, *Quiet Genius: Bob Paisley, British football's greatest manager* (London: Bloomsbury, 2017)

Hern, Bill and Gleave, David, *Football's Black Pioneers: The Stories of the First Black Players To Represent The 92 League Clubs* (London: Conker Publishing, 2020)

Inglis, Simon, *The Football Grounds of England and Wales* (London: Willow, 1983)

Jordan, Gary, *When Dave Went Up: The Inside Story of Wimbledon's FA Cup Win* (London: Pitch, 2023)

Kelly, Stephen F., *Back Page Football: A Century of Newspaper Coverage* (London: Queen Anne, 1988)

Kendall, Howard, *Love Affairs & Marriage: My Life in Football* (Liverpool: deCourbetin Books, 2013)

Ley, John, *Rags to Riches: The Rise and Rise of Oxford United* (London: TBS The Book Service Ltd, 1985)

Lovejoy, Joe, *Bestie: A Portrait of a Legend* (London: Pan, 1999)

McSmith, Andy, *No Such Thing as Society: A History of Britain in the 1980s* (London: Constable, 2011)

Mariner, Paul, *My Rock and Roll Football Story* (London: Reach Sport, 2021)

Morris, Desmond, *The Soccer Tribe* (London: Cape, 1981)

Plenderleith, Ian, *Rock 'n' Roll Soccer: The Short Life and Fast Times of the North American Soccer League* (London: Icon Books, 2014)

Preston, John with John, Elton, *Watford Forever: How Graham Taylor and Elton John Saved a Football Club, a Town and Each Other* (London: Viking, 2023)

Rippon, Anton, *Soccer: The Road to Crisis* (Derby: Moorland Publishing, 1983)

Ronay, Barney, *The Manager: The absurd ascent of the most important man in football* (London: Sphere, 2010)

Sandbrook, Dominic, *Who Dares Wins: Britain, 1979–1982* (London: Allen Lane, 2019)

Sharp, Graeme, *Sharpy: My Story* (Edinburgh: Mainstream Publishing, 2007)

Smith, Jim, *It's only a game* (London: Andre Deutsch, 2000)

Spurling, Jon, *Rebels for the Cause: The Alternative History of Arsenal Football Club* (Edinburgh: Mainstream, 2003)

Taylor, Graham, *In His Own Words* (Hemel Hempstead: Peloton Publishing, 2017)

Taylor, Rogan and Ward, Andrew, *Kicking & Screaming: An Oral History of Football in England* (London: Robson Books, 1998)

Tossell, David, *Big Mal: The High life and Hard Times of Malcolm Allison, Football Legend* (Edinburgh: Mainstream, 2009)

Tossell, David, *Playing for Uncle Sam: The Brits' Story of the North American Soccer League* (Edinburgh: Mainstream, 2003)

Tossell, David, *Hero in the Shadows: The Story of Don Howe, English Football's Greatest Coach* (London: Pitch, 2022)

Villa, Ricky, *And Still Ricky Villa: My Autobiography* (London: Vision Sports Publishing, 2010)

Wagner, Malcolm and Page, Tom, *George Best & Me: Waggy's Tale* (Manchester: Empire Publications, 2010)

Wash, Roger, *Luton Town at Kenilworth Road: A Century of Memories* (Essex: Desert Island Books, 2020)

Wilson, Jeremy, *Southampton's Cult Heroes* (London: Know the Score Books Ltd, 2006)

Wilson, Jonathan, *The Anatomy of England: A History in Ten Matches* (London: Orion, 2010)

Wilson, Jonathan and Murray, Scott, *The Anatomy of Liverpool: A History in Ten Matches* (London: Orion, 2013)

INDEX